S0-FCW-638

A Pioneer in Northwest America

A Pioneer in
Northwest America

1841-1858

The Memoirs of Gustaf Unonius

TRANSLATED FROM THE SWEDISH BY JONAS OSCAR BACKLUND

EDITED BY NILS WILLIAM OLSSON

WITH AN INTRODUCTION BY GEORGE M. STEPHENSON

VOLUME I

*Published for the Swedish Pioneer Historical Society by
The University of Minnesota Press, Minneapolis*

Foreword

EVEN before the last notes of the Centennial of Swedish Immigration in 1948 died down, the same association which had planned this nation-wide celebration, in which also the Royal House and Royal Government of Sweden took part, organized itself into an Historical Society dedicated to the preservation and publication of the literary memorials of the immigrants and their deeds.

The translation of Gustaf Unonius' *Memoirs* is the first fruit of the Swedish Pioneer Historical Society. In presenting Volume I acknowledgment is hereby gratefully made of the work of the translator, Jonas Oscar Backlund, of Chicago; of E. Gustav Johnson and Karl A. Olsson, both of North Park College, Chicago, and of Nils G. Sahlin, of the American Swedish Institute of Minneapolis, in reading and revising the translation; of Nils William Olsson, of the University of Chicago, in providing extensive notes; and of George M. Stephenson, of the University of Minnesota, in writing the Introduction. The following people, all grandchildren of Gustaf Unonius, have submitted helpful original documents and photographs, for which we wish to thank them: Mrs. Gunhild Hermelin, of Torsvi, Sweden; Mrs. Anna Tamm, of Fånöö, Sweden; and Mr. E. Tamm, of Björsäter, Sweden. Even this list indicates the widespread interest in the publication of a translation of Unonius; it is through an unusual spirit of cooperativeness that the task has been accomplished. The Society is honored that the University of Minnesota Press has undertaken the printing of the volume.

The program of the Society calls for the early publication of Volume II, and of a series of books and monographs which will preserve for coming generations of Americans a record of the achievements of the sons and daughters of Sweden who, through their own and their children's careers, have enriched the life and affected the destiny of America.

On behalf of the Swedish Pioneer Historical Society,

Vilas Johnson, PRESIDENT
Conrad Bergendoff, EDITOR

Chicago

Introduction

George M. Stephenson

PROFESSOR OF HISTORY, UNIVERSITY OF MINNESOTA

GUSTAF UNONIUS, after an eventful residence of seventeen years in the United States, in 1858 returned a disappointed man to his native Sweden. Moreover, he had no sooner set his hand to the writing of his *Memoirs* than the country he had learned to admire hastened to the crisis that culminated in four years of civil war. The two volumes were published at Uppsala in 1861 and 1862, respectively, before the wager of battle clearly foreshadowed the preservation of the Union.

It had been Unonius' original intention to write a detailed narrative of his own experiences, together with an account of the life of the Swedish immigrants and a history of their early settlements. To this end he prepared, during the first weeks of 1858, a questionnaire and sent it to Norwegian and Swedish clergymen, but the responses were few. Much of the material he had collected was eliminated; and a confluence of events, personal and otherwise, made him change his point of view and revise his conclusions.

It is somewhat of a mystery why the Unonius volumes remained untranslated for nearly a century. Unonius was the leader of a handful of emigrants who were among the first subjects of the King of Sweden to avail themselves of the recently granted privilege of leaving the realm without special permission. Moreover, Unonius' prominence among the early emigrants won many readers for the letters of his that in January, May, and June, 1842, were published in the influential Stockholm daily *Aftonbladet* and were striking examples of the "America letters" that infected parish after parish with "America fever."

Unonius was not a "typical" immigrant; his experiences were more spectacular than were those of thousands of his countrymen who were attracted to the "common man's utopia," where farms could be had almost for the asking, where tradition counted for less than in Europe, and where the "cake of custom" had not formed.

In his native land Unonius was essentially a student and saw at first hand the glamor of the society in which the privileged classes moved. His first letters written in the primitive cabin of a pioneer farmer in Wisconsin Territory reveal the idealist who had found his dream of a republican government and of a democratic society realized. "The soil that gives me sustenance has become my home; and the land that has opened opportunities and has given me a home and feeling of security has become my new fatherland," he wrote.

In writing his *Memoirs* Unonius profited by a wealth of experiences which had accumulated during the score of years that had elapsed since he recorded his first impressions of America. He retained his critical faculty and his sense of obligation to posterity; but he was more conscious of the limitations and shortcomings of the Americans and their country. He gave vent to caustic comments about Swedish Lutheran clergymen who regarded him as a traitor to Lutheranism, which they had transplanted from Sweden to America. With this rankling religious controversy in mind, Unonius wrote his "Apology" for his decision to take orders in the Protestant Episcopal Church. He was convinced in his own mind that he could officiate in that church and remain loyal to the Augsburg Confession. On his visits to Swedish settlements he argued that the Protestant Episcopal Church and the Church of Sweden were cut from the same pattern. In his effort to recruit members, however, he was no match for the pietistic Lutheran ministers, who contended that liturgy, gowns, vestments, and bishops were incidental to the great mission of the Christian Church. Upon his return to Sweden he found sectarians infecting many parishes. Proselyters in the livery of various faiths, many of them returned emigrants who had been infected with the virus of the American free-church system, worked in collaboration with political and social radicals to assault the outer works of the Church of Sweden.

The vicissitudes of history and a long chain of personal experiences on both sides of the Atlantic changed the idealistic Uppsala student into a "constitutional" conservative. He cited the transformation of the Calvinistic churches of the Puritan founding fathers into Unitarian and Universalist societies as one of the lamentable consequences of the free-church system and the absence of the liturgy. He warned that the separation of church and state in Sweden would reduce the fat livings of ecclesiastics to something resembling the poverty-ridden mission congregations in the United States.

Before his emigration from Sweden, Unonius had acquired something of a reputation as a reformer, notably in the temperance cause; but in his book he was a bit caustic in dealing with an avalanche of reform movements and their noisy and persistent crusaders in America. It was difficult for him to adjust himself to the preferred position accorded American women. Not only did he shy at the ordination of women into the ministry, but he lamented that his distinguished countrywoman Fredrika Bremer was so taken in by America that she was moved to write words of praise for Women's Rights Associations and Amelia Bloomer's costume. Unonius was happy to report that the overwhelming majority of women disapproved of their sisters who joined peace societies and anti-hanging organizations and who took up with phrenology and other movements that grazed the lunatic fringe.

Unonius could not endorse the methods of the Abolitionists. In his opinion the evils of slavery and of the slave trade were exaggerated, and he believed that the circulation in the South of abolitionist tracts and *Uncle Tom's Cabin* had done more injury to the slaves than the lash. On his own admission, he did not write from first-hand knowledge of conditions in the South. His observations were confined to Maryland, Delaware, and the District of Columbia.

Unonius is at his best when he discourses on those aspects of American life with which he had close contact. His location of a land claim in Wisconsin Territory, his experiences as a pioneer farmer, and his career as a minister of the gospel give to his story a unique quality. His description of the practical working of pioneer democracy in a meeting of a claim association is a classic.

New Uppsala — the nucleus of what was intended to be a "colony" — is today but a memory; it lives in the pages of history chiefly because it is associated with the founder, who wrote a book to alleviate poverty until such time as he could make better provision. Nostalgia and the smarting wounds of religious controversy inspired his concluding remark that he could not rid himself of the self-reproach of two major mistakes in his life. The first was that he migrated to America; the second was that he ever left it.

Table of Contents

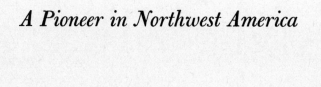

A Pioneer in Northwest America

FAIR and happy time, when one is only nineteen!" In this fashion one of our distinguished writers begins a little story in which his nimble fancy portrays all of India's flower beauty and summer warmth.

The words have in themselves nothing unusual. On the contrary, they are an everyday sigh in human life, a cry one is likely to find rather hackneyed, for there are few who when older have not frequently uttered it. Almost involuntarily I too gave vent to my feelings in this way, in thinking, not exactly upon my nineteenth year, but upon what happened nineteen years ago. In a way, I, too, then saw before me a charm-filled India with its riches, perhaps not in gold and precious pearls, but in realized dreams and hopes of a happy life, of freedom and independence. To be sure, I had then long since passed my nineteenth year, but it was still with the enthusiasm of a nineteen-year-old that I not only felt within me but stood ready to fulfill a youthful desire to attempt to build for myself a new world, with God and the faithful beloved at my side.

And now when I begin to describe from scattered letters and notes what I experienced during those nineteen years, I am unable, as I recall the period at which my story begins, to hold back the

cry, "Fair and happy time, when one is only nineteen!" — or, as
more applicable to me, "Fair and happy time, when one thinks and
feels as if only nineteen!" But in this exclamation lies no complaint or
dissatisfaction arising from comparison between the present and the
past. At this moment I cannot withhold a sigh of thankfulness to
God, who has granted me these nineteen years and who in their
course has so guided my fortunes that even though I have had many
of life's worries, troubles, and sorrows, even though much of a
happy past is now only a happy vision, I still possess, both within
and without, many causes for joy tending to quench every vain and
sad complaint that in my youth I was happier than now.

At that time I rejoiced, perhaps with rather too much youthful
daring, at the thought of a future that seemed to smile at me an assurance of almost fabulous adventures. Now I find, after my life
has taken many an unexpected turn, a real joy in returning for a
few moments to the circumstances and the frame of mind in which
I went to face the varied events that serve as material for these
pages.

In my imagination I return to a meagerly appointed chamber of
the sort that was occupied by university students in Uppsala.[1] It was
so poor and bare that according to the demands of our day it
hardly justified the name of student-room. There was the traditional piece of furniture the bookcase, with its small collection
in a somewhat unkept — or rather kept — state, though this or that
spider, "immersed in research," had spun its fine web between the
wall and the books. This circumstance created the impression of
something stable, which, however, was hardly a characteristic
of the owner himself. Over by the window stood a large writing
table, occupying a considerable part of the floor. On both sides of
a gigantic inkstand had been placed several big bundles of manu-
scripts that might have created in the mind of one not too well acquainted with the conditions an impression that the small student
chamber housed a writer with the productivity of a Goethe or a
Voltaire. But far from it! To be sure, the inkstand might at some
time or other have been taxed for some poetic outpourings, but
the judgment of the reviewers, at least in this case, had had the excellent result of making the author's own not much more lenient.
By this time the poetic efforts, instead of gracing the table, had

been placed underneath it, enclosed in a seldom opened wrapper marked "My Youthful Follies." The bulky packets now on the table contained no material for the printing press and not very much for public enlightenment, but still they had the high destiny, not granted to many poetic and scientific creations, of being carefully preserved as long as it might please the Lord to keep them from crumbling to dust. These bore testimony to my occupation at that time in the service of the provincial accountant's office.[2] That the greater part of this work consisted not in producing original documents but in making all kinds of copies indicated that the job was that of an assistant, a sad chapter in many a young man's life history.

That, too, was the way it appeared to me, as I gave earnest thought to the work I had for a time been mechanically doing. The prospect of future advancement did not appear very promising. I had already had my little experiences in applying for better positions. A few more years, I reflected, and the purse would be empty and the debts increased. "What shall I eat and drink, and wherewith shall I clothe myself?" are questions not easily answered. A glance at the plain gold ring on my finger made the sigh produced by the questions still deeper. Within me was that feeling of bitter dissatisfaction, so unjustified, that often in our youth comes to the fore when we reflect on the station and condition in which our lot has been cast and when the desires that appear to us quite reasonable are not fulfilled so quickly as we feel they should be. Then a youth becomes unfair with himself and others, with everything that seems to stand in the way of his demands for advancement. Government, social order, and economic conditions are judged harshly. In all of it something seems to be rotten; one longs for a change, one longs for — one hardly knows what. But in that very longing there is a certain vivacity, a joy of life, yes, a kind of ambition that prevents our dissatisfaction, complaining, and faultfinding because of so-called misfortunes and adversities from making us truly unhappy. Liberty, self-reliance, independence, war on old prejudices beckon in the distance. Then, if possible, we take a decisive step to realize these and other ideals which we ourselves have conjured up.

Is it possible for me, I thought, to take such a step? I had heard about America. Its rich soil and industrial advancement right now offered a home, a means of livelihood, and an independent life to thousands of Europeans who in one way or another had found their hopes dashed in their own homelands. Labor, no matter in what sphere, if only honest, was no disgrace. There, every faithful worker had in his civic reputation his certificate of nobility. Conventional prejudices, class interests, petty public opinion, and the harlequin-wraiths of changing fashions did not cling to one's coat tails or dog one's heels. America—what was there to prevent me also from going to that country, which like a new El Dorado appears before every venturesome youth? Her fabulous birth and history had excited our wonder from our earliest school years, when we learned to point out its position on the map; she had realized (possibly also deceived, but to that possibility I gave no thought then) millions of hopes, had become a tomb for age-old prejudices, a cradle of true civil liberty, equality, and of such new social ideals as are destined to bring happiness to mankind. America, yes, there I should find what I was seeking and what perhaps I should still have to wait years for here—a home and a hearth of my own. I was able to work; I was still young. The springtime of my life "spread still its golden wings." A faithful, loving *heart* was mine already; the *cottage*, in which the youth and the poet find their dream of happiness fulfilled, was already growing in the primeval forests and only awaited my hands to be built.

Thus my argument, and though many obstacles were thrown in the way of carrying out my decision, the result was that after due permission had been granted by all concerned, the banns were read the proper number of Sundays in the cathedral of Uppsala, and I was married.[3] These events, not to mention our prospective emigration to America, became a general subject of conversation in the university town, where both of us had numerous friends and relatives who sought in vain to dissuade us from the venturesome undertaking. Emigration to America, later quite a common occurrence, had not yet begun. As far as I know, we were the first to avail ourselves of the right that had recently been granted citizens of Sweden, namely to leave the country without special royal permission.[4] At that time very little was known of conditions in western America, although emigration from other European countries, especially from Germany, had been going on for some time. In general, our undertaking was considered something extremely strange. To be sure, I cannot deny that even to me, with our limited resources and our scant knowledge of the country to which we were going to establish a home, the venture, when I gave it more serious consideration, seemed exceedingly risky. I was no longer alone with my hopes, whose failure now would change my life's course into one of bitter regret and make me pay for my youthful rashness with the peace and happiness of my entire future. A young and devoted woman had now united her life and future with my own in a holy, indissoluble bond. In her all-sacrificing love she thought she heard a higher voice say to her, "Get thee out of thy country, and from thy kindred, and from thy father's house, unto a land that I will shew thee." For my sake she was willing to leave everything which life in her earlier years had made dear and precious. To be sure, I loved her with all the ardor of my heart. But was my love alone enough to insure her happiness amid the toils and self-denials she was certain to face with me? Delicate and weak as she was, would she be able to endure all the privations of pioneer life? Should I be able to offer her a home from which want and pressing cares were barred, even if it would not be possible to secure for her wealth and a carefree life? Would our fortunes never bring tears of sorrow and regret to her eyes that were now looking up to God and to me with courage and faith? So far my life had been that of a light-hearted and spirited youth, but I still recall how these thoughts and questions which I tremblingly asked myself awakened within me, not the first, but the often forgotten prayers to Him from whom all help comes. As I realized this I experienced already the blessings of a union into which we had entered in His name, and drew from it a calmer and more confident hope that this blessing would not be wanting in the future. Thus I committed into God's hands my task and my path.

It was the eleventh of May, 1841. The preparations for our journey had already been made.[5] Two weeks of honeymoon had ended, each day filled with invitations from one or another of the numerous families in Uppsala with whom for years I had enjoyed social intercourse and who were now vying with each other to show us the warm sympathy that accompanied their good wishes. At the farewells that precede a long journey we learn as never before rightly to value and appreciate the bonds of fellowship that have bound us together, the kindness we have had, and the happiness we have enjoyed in one another's company.

We had decided to sail to New York with a ship soon leaving from the port of Gävle.[6] A good deal of our baggage, including a large supply of heavy clothing and many other articles we considered suited to pioneer life, had already been shipped to that town. Now we ourselves were ready to follow. The hour was at hand when the daughter was to be torn from the arms of her fond mother, by whom she was never again to be embraced; when the sister was to leave the family circle, where the spring of her life had been spent in joy and peace. The time had come when I myself was to say a final farewell to the town where I had enjoyed so many happy, unforgettable hours; to older friends and teachers I had learned to love and revere; to younger friends and people of my own age with whom in my happy student days I had sung and jested. I was to retain always the memory of their fraternal friendship and affection as one of the most precious of my life, long after necessity had given us its stern *concilium abeundi*[7] from the university.

The hastily written, brief notes in my diary[8] tell of my farewell to Uppsala. They read as follows: "It is as if I said farewell to Sweden at the same time, and that does not prove as easy as I anticipated. Say what you will, our native soil is dear to our hearts. If nothing else could persuade me of that, these last few days and the experiences that have gone with them are evidence enough. I have now spent ten years in Uppsala, and I have a keen realization that it is a home I am leaving; for since I left my parental abode I have known no other home. One of my last undertakings in this town has been to write a briefly outlined description of its memories and sights. But the memories I carry in my heart are more precious than any others. When cathedral and castle, Carolina Rediviva,[9] and the rest are reduced to faded pictures in my mind, then I shall no doubt still carry vivid memories of many a plain student chamber and the friends who lived there; then I shall still recall, as if it were yesterday, *Valborgsmässoafton* [Walpurgis

Night];[10] the festivities of Östgöta Nation;[11] and the popular student song, *Friskt slår vårt hjerta och lifsådern svallar* [Our heartbeat is strong and our life spirit surges].

"Were I a man of wealth I should like to follow Molbech's[12] example in Denmark. I should like to remain a student as long as I live. I believe it is Hufeland[13] who says in his book *The Art of Living Long* that the breath of young people is able to refresh and prolong the life of older folk, and that constant association with youth is a sure means of attaining a ripe old age. This is evidenced by schoolmasters, who as a rule die old men. I believe in the truth of that observation, and I wish I could live forever among these young men with their initial, holy striving for truth and knowledge and retain the lyre on my collar as in my hand until death shall put a finale to all our stringed music."

But getting started from Uppsala is slow business, and the reader may grow weary even before we have a chance to land in the new world. And yet it is not easy to dispel the thought of that day. I am inclined to flatter myself with the belief that there may still be one or another who recalls with a certain interest the memories of our last days at home, for there were many hands that pressed our own in farewell, many hearts that, like our own, were deeply touched by the approaching separation. How often have I recalled them and those hours that now seem almost like a dream!

My brother-in-law O[ldberg][14] had seen to it that the bitterness of our departure should be felt as little as possible. To the last we busied ourselves with packing and all sorts of activities that were designed to postpone as long as it could be the word "good-by" and restrain the tears that still kept coming to our eyes. Finally, however, nothing except a farewell breakfast remained at his home, where we enjoyed love and hospitality until the very last — and where he himself had recently added the blessings of the church to his own upon our marriage. For the occasion many friends had been invited. As far as possible we sought to keep up our courage. Once again we were to hear the old student songs and the ringing of glasses as in former days. But there was something of a funereal air about the party. No toasts were drunk, no speeches delivered, no words of farewell uttered, but it was all in the air, and we felt it within ourselves.

A retinue of no less than twenty carriages was in readiness to depart for Högsta Inn,[15] to which our near kinfolk and others had decided to accompany us, in order to prolong to the last our association. Our departure had brought out almost half the town. From sidewalks and windows the good friends so well known to us waved their last farewells. Across the door of the carriage we pressed many a hand that we were never in this life to press again. Many a heart paid its tribute to the young wife whose courage did not flinch and whose love did not waver in one of the hardest tests. What precious memories were to follow us on our journey! With a deep and genuine feeling of gratitude we still recall those moments. They were often the subject of our conversation later on in that faraway corner of the world where many a time we "scrutinized by-gone days," viewing in recollection well-known scenes from the beloved homeland and images of the friends we were now leaving.

The singers had seated themselves in the first carriage, from which were heard inspiriting songs urging us "with strength and courage to journey down life's long river." At Högsta we were given additional refreshments, until finally evening was approaching and we realized that one of the happy, gala days of life, perhaps the very happiest, was drawing to its close. Another period was to begin; we were to face entirely new conditions; youth with its diversions and joys had come to an end; the sun of its day was setting. But still there was a glow which gave promise of the light and summer warmth of a new day. Was that day to be as free from clouds as the one now ending? I shall not seek to describe further the last moments with mother, brothers, sisters, and friends. Such a moment can be described indeed, but hardly realized by one who has not himself experienced all that it involves.

I had not engaged a carriage to Gävle. Whether it was from forgetfulness amid the multitudinous activities and invitations that had occupied our last days in Uppsala, or on purpose to inure us to the hardships and privations we were to face, or from the need to economize our limited traveling funds, I cannot now remember; but we proposed to continue our journey in a farm wagon from Högsta. However, my friend Carl S.[16] would not permit this, for the sake of my wife, but placed at our disposal the carriage in which he and his wife had accompanied us from Uppsala. Favors like this, insignificant as they may seem in themselves, speak in such moments more than words of kindness and friendship. Such things are not forgotten; they are farewell cards, on which the names are never erased. There was still a brief delay while horses and wagon were made ready. Still a few tears and a farewell cup; yet a song, the last one to be sung in our honor by selected voices from "the knightly guards of light" [17] from the city of youth. I still remember it. It was the beautiful idyll of Valerius:

> I hail thee, thou peaceful streamer!
> Come, flag-adorned ship for the dreamer
> Rock safely the lovers to sleep! [18]

Amid the chords of this song the carriage was set in motion; a soft "God be with you!" sounded from the lips of the bystanders. Soon we were unable to recognize the hands of our loved ones that still from the distance continued to wave us their farewells. The tones of the song died away, and we were left to ourselves to continue in each other's company "our journey to the port at the end of the world."

However, we were not quite alone. From our past, three good friends still remained with us. One of them, Ivar Hagberg,[19] a student from Uppsala, twenty-one years of age, had thought for some time with two of his brothers of emigrating to America. When our undertaking was first broached, many had announced their desire to join our company, in order to found a Swedish colony in some section in the western territory of the New World. But when the plan was finally to be realized, they had all, with the exception of Ivar, changed their minds and withdrawn from the undertaking. To our great joy he was determined to see the venture through. He, too, had taken farewell of mother, home circle, and friends at Högsta. Now he had taken his place on the driver's seat, with trained hands driving the rather spirited steeds.

At his side sat Carl Groth,[20] a near relative of ours, of about the same age as Ivar. Strong, seasoned, and not unaccustomed to manual labor, he was perhaps the only one of us really suited to pioneer life in the virgin forests of the American West. He had not had much time to decide upon and prepare himself for the journey. At our wedding, while he was drinking our toast and wishing us a successful journey, we had said to him, half in jest, "Carl, you ought to come along with us." He emptied his glass, thought for a moment, and looked us in the eye, whereupon he gave a hearty handclasp, saying, "Yes, I will." Those were purposeful words, and a voice within assured us that here was the hand of a faithful brother extended to us. That voice did not deceive us. He really proved a brother throughout all the years we shared of thick and thin, and though Providence once separated us for a time, the bond of brotherhood has ever remained unchanged.

Facing my wife and me, as we were seated in the carriage, was the third and not the least esteemed of our fellow travelers. It was Christine,[21] for years a faithful servant in the home of my parents-in-law. She will appear often in this story and deserves some mention here. She was at this time about thirty years of age, brisk, lively, enterprising, and from her earliest youth accustomed to the hard work that often falls to the lot of a woman in the rural districts. Her fresh and frank looks reflected honesty and trustworthiness. She was born in Livonia[22] and had grown up as a bond-woman on one of the Stackelberg[23] estates. Wretched in their thralldom, she and eight of her fellow serfs had determined, at the risk of their lives, to obtain their liberty. We often enjoyed listening to her simple tale of her quest for freedom. Embarking in an open boat, they set out one evening from the coast of Livonia to row across the Baltic Sea to Sweden. Sails they had none. Men and women spelled each other at the oars. Before they had traveled far they found themselves pursued by two boats. Once the pursuers were so close to them that they were able to distinguish their voices. Plying their oars in deep silence, they were determined rather to plunge into the sea than to permit themselves to be brought back into bondage, where they well knew the grimmest treatment awaited them. However, Providence protected them and favored their flight. The darkness of the night and a heavy fog at sea prevented their discovery. Their pursuers departed, and with the strength of despair the fugitives rowed in the opposite direction. However, they had not calculated correctly either the distance to the Swedish coast or the course they had to steer to reach it. The wind began to rise, and it taxed all their strength to guide their little craft through the waves. After a couple of days they spied land; convinced that it was the coast of Sweden, they felt greatly. cheered. They caught sight of a fort, beyond which they were planning to land. Finally they approached so close to it that they were able to distinguish the soldiers on the ramparts. Not till then did they realize their mistake: the uniforms were Russian, and the fort was Kronstadt.[24] The frail fishing smack, which had excited no suspicion, set out to sea again. Once more tired hands were compelled to battle foam-flecked waves. After a few days the exhausted and starved Livonian fugitives reached the skerries of Roslagen,[25] where kindhearted people took them into their employ. At that time Christine was seventeen years. Together with one of her companions she was received into the household of my father-in-law, where she cared for my wife from her early childhood and became especially attached to her. When my father-in-law died, she did not wish to be separated from the family but followed them to Uppsala. When the question of her departure to America arose, she voluntarily offered to accompany my wife. And in truth she was not the least precious of what we brought with us from my wife's parental home. The former bondwoman from Livonia was now to become a citizen of free America. As she sat beside us she was more a friend than a servant. In preparation for democratic equality, we had already erased certain class distinctions, as seemed right and proper in view of her orderly, proper behavior and her good native qualities.

The company in the carriage thus consisted of five persons, but there was still another member of the company that we must not overlook. Running by the side of the carriage was the dog Fille, a good hunting dog that Carl had obtained, but he was still unused to his new master and did not seem eager to emigrate. He had to be kept on a leash in order to reach the land of liberty, where we planned for him extensive activities amid the game of the forests.

Another wagon was loaded with our trunks and various things we had considered necessary for the journey and for setting up housekeeping in the new world. Our equipment was really far more complete than was necessary, as we had occasion to realize after our arrival in America, where we were compelled to pay considerable sums for overweight. Furthermore, we could have bought some of these things much cheaper in America. Others proved to be entirely useless. A dozen guns, single- and double-barreled, of various sizes and calibers, pistols, sabers, etc. protruded here and there between bags and trunks. Hence it was not surprising that on our arrival in Gävle we were mistaken for a traveling theater troupe, especially as Carl and I were dressed in new dusters, red neckerchiefs, and rather wide-brimmed straw hats.

On our arrival in Gävle we were sorry to learn it would be some time before our ship was ready to sail. Thus we had several days, perhaps weeks, which we might have spent with our relatives and friends. However, we decided against returning to Uppsala since that would have involved new farewells, which under such conditions always prove more trying than the first. Hence we decided to exercise patience and await our embarkation in Gävle. We attempted to get lodgings that would be less expensive than the City Hotel. But that did not prove an easy matter. In applying for rooms we had to submit to the most bothersome and prying questioning. It was impossible to get a definite response to our request for lodging in any house we tried until we had stated where we came from, what kind of people we were, where we were going, why we did not stay at the public inn, and why we wanted to stop in a city that really had nothing to offer in the way of special attractions. We did not take time to reply fully to all these questions, without which the good householders of Gävle, though otherwise accustomed to let rooms to travelers, were unwilling to receive us into their homes. Wagons and luggage were still standing in the street and would probably have had to remain there all night, had not a kindly widow taken pity on us. She permitted the examination to wait at least until our bag and baggage had been brought into the house. She was surprised to learn that we belonged neither to Torslow's [26] or Berggren's [27] theater troupes, that neither Mademoiselle [Jenny] Lind nor Mr. Günther [28] nor Professor Prume [29] were members of our company, that we were planning neither to travel to Torneå [30] with the steamer *Norrland* nor to proceed to Dalarne [31] with our own carriage — but that we were emigrants sailing with Captain Bohlin on his ship *Minnet* to New York. It required but a few hours for this news to become the subject of general conversation throughout the good city. As a result, during our stay in her home, our hostess enjoyed a dozen more daily visits than ordinarily.

Soon I was visited by Lector E[manuelsson],[32] an honest and tried friend from my early university days. He and his lovely wife succeeded in consoling us during our unexpectedly prolonged stay in Gävle, a city where time otherwise would have hung rather heavy on us. Their kindness and hospitality was the last dear and precious memory we carried with us from our native land.

With E[manuelsson] I paid a visit on board the good ship *Minnet*, where we met its commanding officer, Captain C. J. Bohlin, a genial, middle-aged man, generally acknowledged to be an able and skillful sailor, who had recently become known for a fine and noble deed. A French family in New Orleans, harassed by illness and without means, had long sought in vain to secure from European captains, some of them their own countrymen, passage to France, where the husband, formerly a soldier in Napoleon's army, was to receive a small pension. He finally appealed to Captain Bohlin, who was about to sail from New Orleans to Marseilles. Although he could expect no payment for the passage of this family or for their maintenance during the journey, he took them on board, in addition to meeting some of their necessary expenses ashore out of his own pocket. On their arrival in Marseilles he advanced more money to defray their expenses in reaching their final destination in the interior of France. This kindly and unselfish act toward a simple soldier and his poor wife and children came by chance to the knowledge of the King of France, who did not fail to reward him. Captain Bohlin was reimbursed for his outlay on their behalf, and in addition got a letter of thanks signed by King Louis Philippe, accompanied by a large, beautiful gold medal.

The vessel[33] which had been entrusted to this man was one of the biggest and, I dare say, one of the best launched in Gävle. With what interest we examined this bit of space that was to serve as our home and our little world during a lengthy sea journey! The cabin was really inviting, as it generally is on large vessels, where the cleanliness, characteristic elegance, and miniature comfort often inspire delighted surprise on the part of those unaccustomed to life within the railings. In this case the cabin was freshly painted, and the doors had been polished to a shiny finish. Small cabinets had been built into every nook and corner, which the experienced captain had known how to utilize in the most attractive and practical manner. Thus the whole had taken on a certain homelike appearance. The sun sent its rays through the open skylight set in polished brass and shed from above a far more pleasing light upon all objects than that coming through the windows of an ordinary dwelling. Instead of a chandelier, the ceiling carried the mystical compass which surely and constantly pointed out the course to be followed over the wide waters and which served as a reminder that on our journey through the storms of life we should lift our eyes toward heaven, there to receive unfailing guidance on the way to our final haven.

As far as we were concerned, we were quite happy to be installed in this mezzanine apartment, which somehow reminded us of a summer pavilion. We suspected that our first home in America would offer far scantier comforts. In addition to adequate space aft for our provisions and heavy baggage, we had at our disposal all of the rather roomy outer cabin, of which Carl and Ivar took possession. Beyond the cabin was a pleasant saloon with an upholstered sofa, mirror, bureau, and other furniture. At night this room was to serve as sleeping quarters for our good Christine, and in the daytime it was to be used by all the members of "the colonial society" as dining and sitting room. In addition to this saloon there was still a third room, a comfortable bedroom, the furnishings of which left the newly married couple little to be desired.

We made our arrangements with the captain, who agreed to carry us to New York at the very reasonable cost of 500 *Riksdaler Rmt*,[34] but we were to supply our own provisions. As the only passengers we were to have the rooms already mentioned at our sole disposal. The captain himself had his quarters on deck in a cabin constructed aft and furnished somewhat like a neat summer pavilion. This he was to occupy unless rough weather made it necessary for him to share the outer cabin with Carl and Ivar.

However, it was a considerable time before we were permitted to occupy our new quarters. Unforeseen conditions caused a delay in the loading and not till May 22 did the ship move out into the roadstead. In spite of the kindness shown us by our friend E[manuelsson], the stay in Gävle proved rather tedious and though it by no means caused me to change my decision, it gave me abundant time for serious reflection.

From my diary I read as follows: "People have found fault with my undertaking, which they term a rash venture. But I know best what has prompted me to do this, and I leave the outcome to Him who is with us wherever we are. I do not go to America to 'get rich quick.' Many labors, many difficulties, many privations await me. I shall have to do without the comforts to which I have been accustomed. In a literal sense I shall have to eat my bread in the sweat of my brow. My hand, unaccustomed to hard labor, will perhaps often grow weary of the axe, spade, and plow. For all of that I am prepared. But I hope for freedom and independence. I expect to secure a home of my own, simple though it may be, and enjoy domestic happiness, untroubled by the needless cares and worries that a perverted mode of living has made almost inseparable from the life of a poor official. Furthermore, I look at this journey from another and more serious point of view. My position in the homeland — and I am willing to admit that the fault may really be my own — does not inspire me with any special hope of becoming actively useful either to myself or to others. It is possible that in me as in many another there is a passing radicalism that makes me see in the present institutions and social conditions of Sweden many things that are patched up, shrunken, and pitiful, and I have little inclination to become a cog in the worn-out machine. It is possible that all this is just a temporary daze from which I shall awaken some day to find that I was wrong, but that is the way it is now. Many share my views and feelings, and the time will no doubt come — may not be far away — when many will also share my decision and emigrate to America. I venture to prophesy that in Sweden as in other countries thousands of individuals and families of the commonalty, from the artisan as well as from other classes, will shortly, for one cause or another, become dissatisfied with their present condition and seek to improve their lot in another country where, it is said, people will find their needs, spiritual and material, supplied in a better fashion. In that country simplicity of life and social policy, the fertility and excellence of the soil, and gigantic industrial progress make it possible for one and all, as it is said, to forge their own future. If such be the case it may be a good thing if someone undertakes to examine conditions over there in greater detail, conditions which we in Sweden are still rather unfamiliar with. My own example and the experience I am likely to gain ought to make it possible to supply information, warning, and guidance to many. As for me, I may succeed or fail, my lot may prove to be wealth or poverty; the vicissitudes I shall face may establish or change my opinions; the conditions I am about to encounter may realize or ruin my hopes of the greatness, beauty, and wonder that the new Atlantis seems to promise from afar: at all events I shall tell the truth to those who are planning to seek its shores in the future."

Deep in these meditations, with my thoughts on the future, I made my way along the river bank and the shore of the harbor, the fairest spot that Gävle has to offer and the only place where this prosperous business town is likely to engender some poetic exaltation. Here is life, movement, and activity. The merchant fleet of the city was just being enlarged with several big and excellent vessels, a couple of them ready to be launched.

I have often felt that ship building ought to be classed among the fine arts. A well-planned and well-constructed design of a ship certainly demands as much taste and sense of beauty as any other branch of the building arts. An esthete has called architecture "frozen music." If indeed it is, we may well think of ship building as that department of architecture in which the ice is melting, redissolving into living tones. It almost appears as if there were life, as if a spirit lived and moved in a ship speeding through the waves.

Finally the time for our departure seemed to approach. The captain had enlisted his crew and sent us word to come on board. Still we had an evening ashore, and we spent it with our friend E[manuelsson] and some acquaintances from our student days. Among them was a Mr. H.,[35] generally known for his extraordinary talent as a singer of Bellman's songs,[36] and Brother H[ollander],[37] even better known in Uppsala as "the Skipper," and vividly remembered from the time when "Turkish music"[38] was all the rage. In such company it was unavoidable that we should enjoy to the utmost the last evening ashore before our departure. It was the last happy echo of the dithyramb of our student life. Once again my ear was

charmed by the old, well-known songs and ditties with which
the Skipper used to regale us at our social evenings in Uppsala and
which he knew how to execute in his own masterly fashion. Once
again I had the pleasure of hearing some of Bellman's glorious songs
sung by H. in a fashion I shall probably never hear again. No wonder that on an evening like that I was able to discern more clearly
than ever "the lines of melancholy 'round the brow' of the greatest
poet of the North." Was this evening to serve as a new farewell
to youth and song? No, it must not be that. As long as man has
something in life to love, he is still young. The ancients were right
in depicting love in the likeness of a youth. As long as love dwells
in the heart life's vernal flowers will blossom also, and even the
flowers of song cannot altogether fade.

May 29. Went over to say my last good-by to E[manuelsson]
and his family. He was not at home, but we met later in town,
where, touched and grateful for the kindness he had shown us and
remembering our friendship of many years, I gave him my hand
in farewell. He promised to come and see me on board before we
sailed, but the look and handclasp that accompanied his words
made me suspect that I could not be sure his promise would be
kept, but that it was a subterfuge to make the farewell brief and
not too wordy, thus saving us both some of the bitterness of parting. Nor did we see each other again. In parting from him I broke
the last bond that joined me to those in the homeland with whom
I had been in intimate contact.

And so at last we are on board. With a smile I see Carl and Ivar
install themselves in the outer cabin assuring me they are going to
be very comfortable. Having a little more experience with the
water than they, I know unfortunately how the rolling seas often
put an end to comfort. While we are still engaged in getting
adjusted to our floating home, we are surprised to see another passenger, who has made special arrangements directly with the shipping company for passage to New York. A few years ago I
became acquainted in Uppsala with Wilhelm Polman,[39] a former
student belonging to the Västmanland and Dala Nation,[40] and now
I am happy to renew our acquaintance. After taking his medico-
philosophical examination[41] he got his practical medical training

at the Army Hospital in Stockholm. Eventualities during a voyage across the ocean may make it desirable to have a man with medical training on board.

Everywhere on the ship there is life and movement. The seamen are busy with the sails and a number of other chores that claim their attention before setting sail. Now and then they stop to stare at the newly arrived passengers, wondering, no doubt, if they may not share in the contents of the kegs and jugs they have helped to bring across the railing. Knowing the custom on such occasions and realizing furthermore how wise it is for passengers, especially on a long sea journey, to be on good terms with the crew, who can add materially to the comfort on board through many a little service and attention, we open a couple of bottles. The men do not hesitate to come aft, where they introduce each other in rather humorous terms characteristic of the sea. They empty their glasses after wishing us a happy journey and hurry back to their work, while we keep walking back and forth on the spacious deck seeking to familiarize ourselves with our new surroundings. The old cook, or alderman as he is called, introduces Christine to the mysteries of the galley and shows her the various arrangements made there. A member of the crew, a weather-beaten seaman, is relating in genuine sailor fashion various tales of shipwrecks and other strange marine adventures to an attentive apprentice sailor about to make his first voyage and now assisting the older man in his work, moving about unfamiliarly in his still spotless sailor's breeches. There we see the thirteen-year-old cabin boy, who has already made two trips to America, coming to feed the chickens, one of his special duties. Over there the ship's dog is leaping about to express his delight at having got Fille as his companion. From the cabin the captain's canary is sending forth his encouraging trills to all of us.

The deck is cleared at an earlier hour than usual. A certain sabbath stillness sets in, for tomorrow is Pentecost [Whitsunday], and it seems uncertain whether or not the skipper's shore hours are to end with that day.

Day of Pentecost, May 30. In a happy mood we greet each other good morning after our first night on board, and a good morning it really appears to be. All nature is in its holiday dress, like a pretty country girl waiting outside the church door, hymnbook in hand. At some distance, to the right and left of us, lie small skerries, like blossoming lilies around the baptismal font in a rural church. Ahead of us is the open sea, rippled by a gentle breeze, gilded by the rising summer sun, a picture of the Eternal, where faith seeks and finds what the eye cannot perceive — a harbor.

What little wind there is, if in this deep calm it may be called a wind, is landward. It is not likely that the captain will come on board or that we shall set sail this forenoon. Church bells are ringing in the distance, calling to divine service, but we are rather far from the town and dare not leave the ship in case the wind should turn more favorable and the captain come back. Instead we meet in the saloon for common devotion and read a sermon from a collection that we have brought along. This was our first service together. When two or three are thus gathered together in His name, Who promised even then to be in the midst of them, it seems that their hearts open not only to God but also to one another. On such occasions they learn to understand one another better, move closer to one another. That is how it appeared to me, in spite of the fact that I had often heedlessly failed to engage in private devotions and also, at least since the years of my childhood, seldom taken part in home worship. If such acts of devotion can result in genuine blessings under ordinary conditions, how much more will that be the case in circumstances like these? Our small group is all that remains of our happy fellowship in the home community we have now left, but we are united in a common undertaking — that of seeking our fortunes and new experiences in a foreign land. It seemed that our common devotional service taught us better to understand how much we needed one another's aid and support on the hard road that we had elected to walk together. At the same time we realized more fully that we could not be sufficient unto one another but must seek a stronger support than any or all of us could offer, and that it was necessary often to unite in prayer and supplication in order that our labors might not prove too arduous and that the end of our earthly striving might not become a fragile, easily bursting bubble.

Heretofore I have often thoughtlessly permitted weeks or even months to pass without seeking out the house of the Lord. But now that that privilege is denied me, I feel, in spite of the really solemn service which we have just concluded, how gladly I should attend the beautiful high mass of our Swedish Church. Now it appears to me that I have really never attended it, and I should like to carry with me a clearer impression of it, of the hymns and prayers that the memories from my home and childhood have made most precious to me. Within me is a voice that assures me they shall never be forgotten; that however familiar I may become with the customs, manners, and language of a foreign land, my prayers, whether expressed in thought or word, must rise to the throne of the Almighty in the tongue of my mother, as I learned them in my earliest childhood.

I have been told that many who have left their homeland have forgotten their mother tongue after living for many years in a foreign land. I shall not dispute the possibility, but I ask in all sincerity how it can be forgotten, if one has been accustomed, at least now and then, to pray to God with real devotion. If this habit is never permitted to die and this duty is never neglected, then one's mother tongue can surely never be forgotten. The prayers that loving lips taught us to lisp forth must also always remain the most natural expression of our devotion. And if any sacred memories cling to us from the morning of our life, if our thoughts love to dwell sometimes on things dear and precious in our parental home, and if our childhood faith has not been quenched, then it seems to me impossible ever to forget entirely our mother tongue. The very term in itself surely has a sacred meaning.

June 3. For days the wind had been against us, and after a vain effort to start to sea we had been compelled to cast anchor somewhat farther out in the roadstead. However, the captain had come on board during the night, and as the first friendly rays of the morning sun shone through the window of our small cabin, I was awakened by an unaccustomed noise on deck, above which I was able to distinguish the somewhat monotonous but still gay chant the sailors are accustomed to sing while hauling or raising sails, in order that the work may be done more easily and according to a certain rhythm: "Cheerily men, oh cheerily!" This chanting, in addition to the movement of the vessel, made me realize that we were finally under sail. When I went up on deck I was surprised to find that we were already a good way out at sea. My own sleep as well as that of my fellow travelers must have been so sound that none of us had awakened when the anchor was weighed. Now a brisk wind filled our sails, and soon we were able to see nothing but sky and water. By noon we passed the small town of Öregrund,[42] and farther on, at not a very great distance, the archipelago of Roslagen.

In spite of my longing, after I had decided to leave my homeland, to leave the coast of Sweden behind me as soon as possible, it was a still precious experience once again to rest my eyes on "the skerries and islands that I knew so well." One after another, the beautiful birch-draped islands disappeared behind us. Soon we were outside a wide bay where neither cliffs nor islands hid the shore of the mainland. Only a single rocky islet with a lonely pine on the otherwise naked rock rose from the waves. The twilight did not prevent me from distinguishing the well-known landmarks. On those shores I spent my childhood years in play; the waves on which I was now riding bathed my boyish feet before they were wounded by the thorns on unaccustomed paths; by the sound of these waves I slept at the end of the day's play; among those mountains I climbed, and from their summits I watched the sea gilded by the dawn and listened to the tales of faraway lands told by the wind; in those pine woods I picked my first flowers, and there I heard for the first time the heartbeat of nature. On that hill beyond I sang my first song; in that home close by the sea, surrounded by a little garden whose lilac hedge was sometimes washed by its spray, I was embraced for the last time by the arms of a loved father. Not far from that spot is the grave that contains his mortal remains. I see the window where my mother used to sit, watching her boy playing among the pebbles on the shore. The sun is setting over what was once my world. And now, home of my childhood, land of my youth, farewell. Forgive me for what I have done amiss. Accept my thanks for what you have given me, my thanks for this moment. The last thing you granted me was yet one more glimpse of places vividly recalling my dearest and

most sacred memories and bidding me as I passed never to forget
them.

Perhaps I have dwelt too long on my departure from Sweden
and have been too lengthy in the quotations from my diary. For
the reader the excuse is not valid, I know, that I have found
pleasure in reliving the conditions under which I left my fatherland. But perhaps one or another of those whose friendly sympathy
for me was so unmistakably revealed those last days and hours we
were permitted to be together, will like myself have no objection
to letting their thoughts dwell for a moment on this sketch of an
event two decades old. To others these pages may serve as a preface
to what is to follow, to introduce the author and give them a closer
acquaintance with his personality, before they accompany him on
his further adventures and experiences. Perhaps he has begun his
story too much in the form of a novel, but his life and much of
what he is about to relate from it seem indeed to belong to fiction
rather than to reality.

Do not expect, my reader, a complete travel narrative from the
country to which I now invite you. I left Sweden not to take a trip
to America, but to build a home and live there, and it is rather a
record of my own life that I have given here than a story of cities,
buildings, institutions, political events, and social conditions. Those
things have been described by others who have more insight and
ability than I. Only insofar as I myself have come into personal
contact with general conditions peculiarly characteristic of America, only insofar as I myself have experienced them and gathered
impressions of them — only to that extent will they be touched
upon. Hence I am passing by much that might deserve to be more
carefully described. There are many things that do not escape the
travel writer's attention that entirely elude the pioneer settler's,
or on which he cannot comment for lack of adequate information.
For many years my *home* was in America. What happened to me
happens to thousands of people who live in a locality for years,
or perhaps are born there. The town is rich in history or other
notable features, but they think, "Some other time I'll always have
an opportunity to see those things," until one day they go the way
of all flesh, largely unacquainted with the very things in the

midst of which their life was spent. A passing traveler, on the other hand, informs himself about them fully and immediately. I must confess that in many respects this has been my case. I regret having to admit that there are many things in America to which I ought to have given more earnest attention and which I might be expected to have studied, but I am able to make only passing mention of them in these pages. It is principally through what I myself experienced, through the account of my own fortunes and of the circumstances that more noticeably affected my individual life, that the reader will gain some knowledge of the country *in* which, rather than *about* which, I have written these notes.

Chapter 2

SEPTEMBER 9. Only a person who has spent three months or more within railings without being in any real sense a sailor, and who meanwhile has struggled with seasickness and contrary winds, can realize the feeling of being drunk with joy that one has when finally approaching the desired destination. True, we had set foot on solid ground for a few hours at Helsingör,[1] and in Portsmouth we had landed for a few days to repair some minor damages suffered by the ship during a heavy storm on the North Sea. But after leaving that port on July 17, and catching a glimpse of the beautiful island of Wight, we had seen nothing but sky and water.

The trip has had its fair share of trouble, and our patience has sometimes been taxed, though our good captain has done everything in his power to make our trip as pleasant as possible. But with all his good intentions he has not succeeded in ruling over the winds and the waves. The latter have often been riotous; the former, except for a few days, always contrary. Indeed, we have been compelled to tack the entire distance between the British coast and Sandy Hook, and to that spot we still have some fifty miles of sailing. But a more favorable wind is now filling our sails. To be sure, we are still unable to see land, but the very thought that we are not far from it and that we are now making good headway toward the goal of our journey makes us feel something of a shore wind both within and without us.

In the distance we detect an American pilot boat. It is coming our way with good speed. With interest we watch the fast vessel as it speeds over the waves. A few persons moving about on deck represent something strange and wonderful. They come from the shores we have been longing for. It seems to us that they must absolutely bring us news from well-known regions and from those we already feel we have been separated from for a long time, and who have often during our journey on the sea been the subject of our thoughts and conversations. We forget for the moment that they are coming from a country where everything is new to us and where we have no one — almost nothing — to inquire after.

The pilot boat is one of those small, decked, well-built yachts on which pilots, sometimes numbering only three or four, set out to the middle of the stormy sea. There are instances of these boats sailing all the way to Europe. A few years ago three Americans made the bold decision to sail in such a boat to England to take part in a regatta, certain that they would carry off the prize. After a few days at sea one of them died, but the two survivors were determined to carry on. A Yankee does not easily give up an undertaking from which he hopes to gain profit and glory. "Go ahead" is his motto, whether ashore or afloat. If a thousand obstacles rise up against him, if a railroad train crashes, if one steamboat after another explodes, if there is a crisis that overturns his financial world — in spite of everything, his motto is, "Go ahead!" And he does move ahead both in private and public undertakings. But to return to the story. The two brave men reached Liverpool in their small craft. The race came off, and old, staid John Bull this time even had to award the prize to his young brother Jonathan.

However, the small pilot boat had come alongside our ship. With some curiosity we looked at the brisk, middle-aged man who leaped across the railing. Could this be a pilot? I wondered. Accustomed to our Swedish pilots, whose dress and appearance bear the stamp of poverty and want, I was surprised at this man, whose bearing and dress both, in no small degree, suggested the gentleman. In many travel stories about America I had read descriptions of the rudeness and impertinence of the pilots — a hint from the very beginning of the lack of polish characteristic of the American nation. Hence I was particularly glad that my first sight of an American tended to disprove what I had right along suspected to be an unreliable description — a description called forth by ill will or prejudice, or perhaps by disappointment with a country where exaggerated expectations of personal success had built up demands for perfection in everything else.

Even I could not prevent myself from imagining in the manner and way of the first American to bid us welcome to the new world something representative of the people among whom I was now going to live and make my home. I must confess that the impression of that representative was far from unpleasant. In his personality there was something decisive and earnest, but also a trace of good nature. When he took command of the ship, it was with a spirit of calm self-confidence in which there seemed to us a trace of consciousness of his own superiority. A thing of which I specially made note was his well-groomed appearance. For more than two weeks he had been sailing to and fro: the small cabin on the pilot boat could surely not offer opportunity for a very careful toilet, and yet he was carefully shaved, his blue coat was free from dust and spots, and his open vest revealed a fine, white, and well-laundered shirt.

At four o'clock in the afternoon we caught sight of land, but it was still lying like a cloud on the horizon, and night came before we were able to discern any of the contours of the shore. Our joy, however, at being so close to the goal of our journey was beyond description. At once we began to prepare to leave the wooden walls within which we had so long been confined. We packed away our traveling clothes and brought out other garments to be ready for the following morning. Our own provisions had given out a couple of weeks ago, and if the ship had been as poorly equipped as we in this respect, and if our good captain had not shown us hospitality, for which we can never be too grateful, we should have had a bad time of it. Nevertheless, our stomachs were beginning to yearn for something besides pork and peas, and we were longing for a meal without the musty odors of food cabinets surrounding us and without the risk of having the whole mess spilled over us. The joy of being soon to set foot on *terra firma* had in it no little element of hope for a good roast beef, a good glass of milk, and in addition some of the glorious and rare fruits which our imaginations had made to grow in the new world.

That night we could not make ourselves go to bed. It was not only the hope of satisfying our appetite that kept us awake and made us walk the deck all that night. Serious thoughts engaged us, and it was not without some anxiety that we were looking forward to an unknown future in a country also quite unknown to us, where we were now about to land. During our journey over the stormy sea such thoughts had been put in the background by that soul-numbing seasickness that makes one insensible to everything but present misery. Now we were at the portals of the Eden of our dreams, fearful lest we find it only a beautiful mirage.

September 10. Day is finally breaking. We see land — we see America! I seem to understand the feeling of Columbus when he saw before him the hoped-for western land. Soon we pass between high shore banks, where hundreds of ships crowd their way into the metropolis of the new world. All of a sudden a vista opens that would appear one of the most beautiful in all the world even if one had not spent three months on a sailing vessel and in that time often resigned oneself to deep weariness. Everywhere our eyes meet smiling, verdant shores, adorned with the most pleasing dwellings and other structures. Over there is a small island on which has been constructed a fort, which seems far from adequate, however, to protect the entrance to this rich city in case of war. But the United States needs no great forts; the entire country is a great citadel, strong in its freedom, incapable of being invaded, protected by its national strength and a motive power stirring and developing everything within it.

On one side of us is the New Jersey shore, on the other Long Island, both surrounding this harbor, which is twenty-five miles in circumference, sufficient in size to contain all the fleets and navies of the world. From a mercantile standpoint it is perhaps the world's greatest harbor. From that of scenic beauty, the world has hardly its equal. Now the city of New York meets our eyes, on one side bordered by the mighty Hudson River rolling past, which here more resembles a bay, on the other by the East River, or Long Island Sound. We hardly know where to turn our eyes: to the city with its magnificent buildings and hundreds of church spires glimmering in the morning sun, or to the moving city of ships, which in part are swimming in the harbor and in the river, in part moored at the vast quay, the length of which cannot be contained within our range of vision. As we sail along to find anchorage near the pier where the captain hopes to unload his Swedish iron, in every direction there is a constantly moving and changing panorama from which one cannot readily choose the view most worthy of admiration. In its totality it presents a sight that once seen leaves an impression never to be eradicated, especially when as now it appears in the glory of the early morning sunlight. Finally the ship turns its bow into the wind. The anchor drops. The rattling of the heavy iron chain is music to our ears. And I am sure passengers have rarely been more deeply grateful for the greeting customary on board on such occasions, "Welcome to anchorage!" To be sure, we have not yet reached our final destination, but the long and trying journey across the ocean is over. Having appreciated the works of the Lord and His wonders of the deep, glad are we that they be quieted, that He hath brought us to our desired haven.

We do not fail to take the first boat that leaves the ship to go ashore. Perhaps there is some truth in the impression that other travelers have given of their first landing in New York: the filth of the piers and of the streets adjoining; the herds of swine and armies of rats through which one must make one's way by wading through foot-deep filth; the unattractive and shabby houses lining the streets near the harbor — all these things may be true to a degree, but today I do not notice them. Almost before I realize it, we reach Broadway, and like a person waking up after a spree, I have but a dim idea of what has just taken place. Our captain is our faithful guide, and a few Swedes [2] who have come to the pier to meet us are walking along at his side, reminding us that one of them has promised to take us to a boardinghouse where we can stay for a few days at a moderate cost. He pauses but a moment to find an opportunity to cross the street, crowded with omnibuses, carriages, wagons of all kinds, and a surging throng of people. But this moment is sufficient to give me at least a vague notion of this street, eighty feet wide and more than three miles long, said to be not only the greatest but also the most beautiful in the world. It seems that the two eyes with which Providence has supplied men and which generally are quite enough for their needs, are altogether insufficient when it is a question of passing from one side of Broadway to the other. One is really inclined to agree with the schoolmaster in "The Altar of Freya"³ and consider oneself ill supplied in this respect. One feels the need of a pair of eyes in the back of the neck and of an eye at each ear, in order to escape being run over or trampled down.

We managed, however, to get across with the aid of the two eyes allotted to us, and after being conducted through a labyrinth of narrower streets, we stopped finally at the house where it was thought we might get lodging. The door was locked, but after a couple of jerks at a brass knob by its side, it was opened by a young woman, and we were invited into a clean, carpeted hall, and then into a sitting room, likewise carpeted, where our Swedish companion told the hostess what we wanted. Since we were unable either to speak or understand English, he made arrangements for our room and board at a dollar a day per person.⁴ The captain was now compelled to leave us to look for the commissioner of his shipping company, and our new acquaintances also departed with him. He promised, however, to return in the early afternoon in order to help us get our things in order, help that was really needed since we were quite unable to understand or make ourselves understood by our fellow boarders.

We were left in the parlor or common reception room to converse with one another and take a closer view of the furnishings of this, the first house in America we had entered. On the whole it was not very unlike any middle-class house in Sweden. A neat and well-upholstered drawing-room sofa made of mahogany, and a couple of comfortable easy chairs placed by the side of a center-table in the middle of the room made up its principal furnishings. On the table were a few books in rather showy bindings along with a couple of volumes of illustrations containing some engravings of good quality. I pictured to myself in advance how several of the male boarders would after dinner seat themselves comfortably in those chairs and, according to the description by Trollope,⁵ pick their teeth and put their feet on the center-table.

For the additional comfort of Americans, who, according to all reports, in a sitting position like the greatest ease, the room had also been supplied with a kind of rocking chair, in which a man could certainly enjoy a siesta. The longish room had two windows to the street, which, however, did not offer a very attractive view. The wall opposite the windows was occupied by two gigantic doors of the same height as the room. These could be pushed aside to make a single room out of the outer and inner parlor. The latter room we did not as yet have the opportunity to give more than a cursory glance at, but it is sometimes, as in this house, used as the dining room. A good deal of the wall facing the door to the hall was occupied by a colossal fireplace with a marble mantel, on which were arranged a few seashells and china ornaments. Everything was neat and clean, although it was clear enough that we had not landed in one of New York's more elegant boardinghouses, but rather in one of the middle-class kind, where artisans and moderately paid bookkeepers have unpretentious but decent living quarters. The room was well kept: walls and ceilings were calcimined, with a glossy white polish such as I do not recall ever having seen before. There were no spider webs clinging to the ceiling cornice, and it would have been hard to discover a trace of dust on the table and chairs.

Here we were really like lost sheep. We did not dare to take a walk lest we lose ourselves in the crowd, unable as we were to ask our way; nor did we know whom or what house to ask for if with the aid of a phrase book we should be able to stammer forth a few English words. There seemed really to be nothing we could do except to submit to house arrest until our captain returned.

Presently, however, we seemed to hear the rattling of platters and plates in the next room. The company in the parlor was augmented by a few ladies and gentlemen. The hostess entered and contrived a sort of introduction. "Mrs. and Mr. ——." I suspect she had forgotten our name and was asking to be reminded of it again. I gave it, and she tried to repeat it, but never in my life have I heard my name so badly mispronounced. But it must pass: "Mr. and Mrs. —— from Switzerland, and ——." Here followed the names of the persons to whom we had the honor of being introduced, but I was consoled by the fact that their names to me were as incomprehensible as my own to them. A kind of conversation began which on our part consisted of head shakings and now and then a stammering "I don't understand." "Ah," interrupted a young man in broken and hardly understandable German, "You are from Switzerland — Germany — speak German — me too."

Well, that was encouraging. I made an effort to use my limited knowledge of German, and though not offended at being taken for a Swiss, I still found it right and proper to give my new acquaintance a lesson in geography and inform him that Sweden is an entirely different country from Switzerland. I had some difficulty, however, in convincing him of that fact. "Sweden, Switzerland, Deutschland, alles the same; nicht England, nicht Holland, nicht Frankreich."

I realized here that, as someone in Sweden had once said, "Before the Lord we are all Smålänningar." [6] So all Europeans who do not speak English must be French, Dutch, or German to such Americans as do not have a wide knowledge of the world at large. The entire company seemed to be of the same opinion, as far as I was able to gather from the young man's explanation after I had succeeded in correcting his mistake and enriching his geographical knowledge. But the table in the meanwhile was set, and the hostess gave us a sign to take our places. We paused a moment behind our chairs with folded hands for table prayer, as had been our custom in Sweden. Every eye was directed our way. Some of our table companions looked somewhat surprised; the rest of them viewed the matter with complete indifference, as something they had seen before though they did not care to follow our example.

The table conversation was not very lively. The men in particular seemed to be in a great hurry; luncheon to them was apparently a bit of business that had to be attended to as speedily as possible. We, too, ate in silence. Rarely has a meal tasted so good. Each diner helped himself and his table neighbor to the dishes that were before him. If we were unable to make ourselves understood in English, we could still make it perfectly clear that we had excellent appetites and that we were enjoying not only the excellent roast beef with all its trimmings, such as fried and boiled potatoes, sweet potatoes, lettuce, cabbage, and beans, but also the tart with its filling of some kind of fruit preserve,[7] entirely unfamiliar to me. I do not wish to tire the reader with a detailed description of the luncheon; let it suffice that we all ate and were satisfied. Some of the gentlemen left the table with no formalities as soon as they had satisfied their needs, without waiting for the rest of the guests and without saying good-by. Others, who may have had more time at their disposal or perhaps, filled with curiosity, wanted to give the Swedes, or "the Swiss," closer scrutiny, kept us company until we too arose and — let me confess it — wishing to avoid the remarks of our companions and deciding to adjust ourselves to the customs of the place, left the table without thanks to Him who is the Giver of our daily bread. So easily are we led, out of consideration for the opinion of our fellowmen, to ignore Him whom we have been commanded to confess before men.

Early in the afternoon our captain came to take us to the ship, which in the meantime had been moored at one of the piers and from which we were now to remove our luggage. Our possessions were not examined by the customs officers. As a rule little attention is paid to the luggage of immigrants unless for some reason or other they are suspected of bringing with them contraband goods. Furthermore, those who are about to settle in the country are permitted to bring with them household equipment and tools and agricultural implements, unless what is included in their luggage is clearly meant to be offered for sale. Moving our goods entailed considerable expense, and it would have been still greater had not members of the crew assisted us.

Immigrants with heavy luggage ought to engage some transfer company to take care of it immediately upon their arrival and have it sent to their destination, or rather, they ought to continue their trip at once rather than wait in New York. But in our case the trouble was that we did not really know where we were going, and we thought it best to stay in New York a few days in order to get information about some place in the sparsely populated western states where we might find the conditions we were looking for.

We spent the evening with Captain Bohlin and a Captain Bräcke, also from Gävle, who had arrived in New York an hour after us. With this event a strange coincidence is connected that is well worth recounting. Captain Bräcke had left Gävle when we did. He had followed almost in our wake all the way to Öregrund, after which the two ships had been separated by a severe storm in the Baltic, only to arrive in Helsingör the same day and hour. From there we had sailed in each other's company, but had lost sight of each other the following day. Finally, after we had been tacking almost a month in the North Sea and the English Channel and still another four weeks on the Atlantic Ocean, one day we saw a ship to the leeward of us. Since there had been no opportunity to feast our eyes on another sailing vessel, it was with great interest that we watched the white sails, which reminded us that we were not, after all, alone in the world. An experienced sailor has a wonderful capacity for distinguishing vessels of one nation from those of another and to recognize a ship's identity even at a great distance, just as a person on shore will recognize another by his dress and appearance. It was not long before our captain exclaimed, "It is a Swedish ship, and I believe it is the *Victoria*." The Swedish flag was hoisted, and our greeting was responded to with the yellow and blue colors. The captain hoisted the company's flag to the top of the mainmast, and soon we saw the same signal from the other ship. We approached each other, and since the wind was moderate we paid Captain Bräcke a visit in the captain's gig in the middle of the Atlantic Ocean. It was really an unusual and happy meeting. The *Victoria* had sailed north of England whereas we had taken the route through the British [8] Channel and had in addition spent several days in Portsmouth; hence it was all the more striking that the two ships should meet in this fashion. The two veteran sailors could not recall that anything like it had ever happened in the course of their long life at sea.

That same night we were separated once more by a storm. The *Minnet* was a far better sailor than the *Victoria*; yet we had hardly arrived in New York before the *Victoria*, aided by a favorable wind, rounded Sandy Hook.

It was natural that we should give each other a hearty greeting, and our first evening ashore was spent in a most agreeable way. We drank good wines, we consumed a few oysters, oranges, bananas, pineapples, and other delicacies; but the aftermath of the feast was terrible. Never before in my life have I suffered such pain. Seasickness was a paradisiacal experience in comparison.

The entire boardinghouse was in a state of complete upheaval during the night. Carl believed he was going to die, Ivar believed he was going to die, and I believed I was going to die. But, praise God, we survived, all three of us, to warn other newcomers who do not have the superior stomach of the sailor, which can tolerate anything, not to overload themselves with all kinds of food and fruits after a long season of fasting, and after they have been for a long time reduced to only salty foods.

Chapter 3

A FEW MORE DAYS IN NEW YORK · FOREIGN IMMIGRANTS · SO-
CIAL LIFE · A CLOSER DESCRIPTION OF OUR BOARDINGHOUSE
REMARKS IN GENERAL ON JUDGING AMERICANS · FIRES

W E SPENT a few more days in New York, seeking to
get further information about the West, in order to determine upon our future location. We were surprised
to learn, however, that the people there, as a general rule, knew as
little about it as we did ourselves; as a matter of fact, we knew far
more about conditions both in Iowa and Illinois than did the native Americans with whom we conversed through an interpreter.
However, a Swedish businessman by the name of Brodell, a resident of New York and a man of wide information and culture,
assisted us with advice which proved really helpful. Furthermore,
we had the good fortune to meet a countryman of ours who had
been living in Illinois for many years and who having acquired a
little wealth was now on his way back to Sweden. He advised us
to make our home in that state, which he described as one of the
most beautiful regions in the world—a region of wide, fertile,
and easily tilled plains where any man who wanted to devote himself to farming had an abundance of land to select from, and where
many other opportunities to make a living were to be found. So
we decided to go to Illinois.

But it was hard to leave New York without learning any more
about it than was possible within the four walls of a boardinghouse
and from a few walks between that house and the ship *Minnet*,
to which we returned again and again, like carrier pigeons to their
well-known dovecote.

New York, which at the beginning of this century had only
50,000 inhabitants, now has a population of half a million, more
than one-half of which consists of immigrants from Europe. Of
these it has been estimated that about 56,000 are Germans, 23,600

English, 133,800 Irish, and about 5,000 French.[a] As far as I was able to ascertain, these strangers who have made their homes in New York are generally making a good living. To be sure, there are many compelled to earn a scant livelihood through sweat and toil, and some of them may even be in want of the necessities of life, but I believe I can state definitely that the tales that have come across the Atlantic of the misery among the immigrants in America, and especially among those who have settled in New York, are largely exaggerated. The descriptions of social life in America written by Hauswolff[1] and translated into Swedish have a coloring that is untrue, at least as far as my observations go. I cannot refrain from quoting certain passages from this book, which I had brought along with me to determine whether sober reality agreed with its frightening description of conditions in America, and from adding certain remarks of my own.

After describing his first landing in New York and the city's sewer-like wharf-region,[b] the author mentions the "hundreds of strangers lying about in the streets where the city has granted them the privilege of camping. Their pale and wan faces have been browned by the burning sun, rags are fluttering about their bones which are no longer padded by flesh; their eyes are staring toward the ocean; their thoughts turn eastward where they left their old homes; homesickness and regret are grinning dismally from their visages." An awful description! But during the eight days I spent in New York, visiting the wharves every day, my eyes fell upon none of the poor wretches the author describes with such gusto. They must have disappeared in the course of the years, or, which is far more likely in a country where more is done than anywhere else for those who really need assistance, they have either been cared for in public institutions of mercy or have finally managed to get work to earn their food and clothing. In New York I found strangers from every nation. They pour into the country in numbers that increase year by year. It is estimated that last year 83,000 European immigrants arrived in America, and no doubt the number this year is greater. It may be surmised that half of this number lands in New York.

During my stay in the city I had the opportunity to mingle with various crowds of these newcomers, but instead of pale and thin faces, I saw as a rule wholesome and powerful-looking men, prepared to face whatever fate they might meet in the Far West, eager to work, animated in spirit, and firm in the hope that in some way they should be able to make a living for themselves in their new homeland. That among so many people are to be discovered some poor wretches European countries are glad to be rid of may certainly be supposed, but if in America these do not show up in a better light than they did in their homelands, America should not be blamed. Many of them lack the means to continue their journey. In such cases they are frequently helped by the city or by private parties, who often pay to the transportation companies the fare of poor people;ᶜ or if they remain in New York and have the ability and will to work, they rarely lack the opportunity to make a living. European artisans and laborers who had taken up residence in New York and with whom I chanced to get into conversation told me almost without exception that they were doing well financially, in spite of the fact that many of them had big families to support.

During my stay in New York I saw very little of its social life. Hence on that subject I can say very little. In the boardinghouse where we lived, which, as I have already suggested, was not of the highest class, I ought to have had occasion to note the coarseness of manners and the lack of good behavior frequently charged against the American people. But I must confess I found no reasonable cause for complaint. From what I saw there, as well as from what I was able to gather during my long trip westward, I do not believe Americans are more wanting in culture and social sense than any other people. Our situation hitherto has, by necessity, brought us in touch only with what we might call the lower classes, but it is just among them that national characteristics are likely to show up most clearly. I cannot deny that there are many things that grate on the sensibilities of those who in Europe have been accustomed to other conditions and another social environment. But should we be less inconvenienced if we were placed, for instance, in Sweden, in close touch with the common laboring class, and compelled to adopt their living standards? Americans whose behavior shocks the sensibilities of European travelers accustomed to a more refined mode of living are as a rule of that class. Outwardly they

39

differ very little from representatives of other social classes. The lower tradesman or the laborer often appears dressed in a way we are accustomed to see only among the gentry. In his manners he is generally characterized by a certain freedom. He expresses himself without constraint. He is at ease in any company, and he feels he has just as good a right to express himself as any other man, no matter what his social or economic status may be. Equality equalizes all, he reasons, and it does that in the eyes of Europeans too, but in a way that leads them to incorrect conclusions. We are apt to expect too much from an uncultured person who many times — we must admit — claims with a kind of challenge that he is just as good as a cultivated one. We sometimes forget that this class in America should be compared with the lower classes in Europe rather than with the upper or, as they sometimes are, even with the highest classes at home.

From such a comparison they must of course suffer, while if they were placed side by side with the comparable classes in Europe they would undoubtedly appear to advantage. The half-educated people are the group in this as in other countries most likely by their behavior to grate on the sensibilities of those who demand a more complete decorum. That class perhaps constitutes the majority in America, while only a small fraction can be classed as really uneducated. The line of demarcation between them is, especially for a European, hard to distinguish. Those whom we in Europe should account the lower, uneducated class are often here the half-educated, and instead of doing them justice because of the higher plane they have attained to, we are inclined to speak of their rudeness and offensive manners as if they were representatives of the higher or educated classes, which is entirely erroneous.

It seems to me that in spite of equality in outward and public life, there is a distinction of class in America just as sharply drawn as among us. It would be well, in judging the manners and social habits of the American people, to recognize this fact more fully, instead of placing all on one plane because of the political equality existing there. Furthermore, as to the offensiveness of manners and social customs that European travelers have so often satirized and have adduced as evidence of lack of breeding, it may be true that American unconventionality sometimes hurts one's finer sensibilities and one's sense of propriety, but it never wounds the moral sense; it may be crude, but it is never indecent; it may be laughable, but it is never boorish; it may cause a refined lady to wrinkle her nose, but it never compels her to run off in disgust.[d]

Nevertheless, it may be too early to put down in writing reflections on these and similar subjects. I may not have seen enough at close range. But after living for a week in one of New York's boardinghouses, where each day some twenty guests, certainly not of the highest social class, met for their meals and in between times often kept us company in the parlor; after traveling fifteen hundred miles inland, part of the time on a canalboat, where the passengers were certainly not of the most select type and where an equality existed sometimes a little embarrassing; after covering part of the distance on a steamboat, in the steerage, or forward lower-deck saloon, where I had the opportunity to become acquainted with the attitude and manners of the lower, or less well-to-do, class — after all this I have considered myself competent to express my opinions to this extent. At our boardinghouse I never noticed anyone using his fork to pick his teeth after the meal. Sometimes, it is true, it seemed to me that the men assumed too careless a position on the sofa or in the rocking chair, but I never discovered them with their feet on the table or the window sills.

Once when I attended the theater in Niblo's Garden [2] I looked in vain for heels resting on the railing separating the boxes. Many such things, in themselves of minor importance but mentioned by travelers as characteristic of American manners and customs, must either have been described with some measure of exaggeration or must, in the course of time, have given place to more polished behavior. In barrooms and in hotel reading rooms, visited only by men, however, I have sometimes seen men sitting or lounging in chairs with their feet on the arm rest of another and their legs extended at an angle of twenty degrees. But that position is rather comfortable, and I do not know why there should be anything offensive in it when only men are present and when no one is inconvenienced by it.

Something I have considered rather offensive, however, is the tendency among men to appear with covered heads in places where among us custom demands that hats be removed. In the saloons of the canal- and steamboats they do not hesitate to keep their hats on, even when ladies are present. Even in private homes and at social gatherings it sometimes happens that the hat remains too long on the head or is donned too soon before leaving. But that does not happen among cultivated people and can never happen at a visit or a party, where hats and overcoats are left in the hall and men do not, as is strangely enough done among us, keep hat in hand in greeting the host or in taking leave.

A characteristic of Americans that I must not miss mentioning is their cleanliness. I have not had opportunity to notice conditions in the homes of socially prominent and well-to-do people, but I am able to draw my conclusions from what I have seen in less pretentious dwellings.

In this country people do not occupy apartments but houses. With the exception of the larger ones on Broadway and on Fifth and Sixth Avenues, where many are veritable palaces, most houses have a narrow front toward the street and extend a considerable distance toward an alley, which divides the block into two sections. From this alley houses have their rear entrance and driveway into the yard. The only entrance to the street is the one leading into the front hall. Even in houses occupied by people of moderate means, this is carpeted, as are also the stairs. Through this door or on these stairs wash buckets and anything else of the kind are never carried. The kitchen has its own exit to the yard, and the entire house has general access to it through a rear stairway. On the ground floor of a house of two or three stories, the family parlor and dining room are located. The upper floors are used for sleeping rooms, which are rather small and furnished with little if anything but the bed. Even in many wealthy homes these sleeping rooms are hardly bigger than fairly roomy steamship cabins. For those of us who have been accustomed to using our sleeping rooms as reception rooms, they seem rather inadequate. They are quite big enough, however, for purposes of resting and dressing. Beyond that they are not occupied. Not to have to spend night and day in the same room is no doubt beneficial from a sanitary point of view. A family occupies a house with a sufficient number of small bedrooms for its requirements. No strangers are admitted to them. When the rooms are tidied up in the morning, the beds are made up for the evening, and servants have seldom very much to do after tea has been served.

In our boardinghouse, as well as in ordinary homes, I found that the sleeping rooms, with their comfortable, well-made beds and fine, white sheets, always gave evidence of the utmost neatness and cleanliness. Several families of limited means were living there. In addition to a bedroom they also occupied a room that was somewhat larger and served as their private living room. The parlor on the ground floor was common to all, and was available to the private families accommodated in this way as well as to the other guests.

In addition to Carl and Ivar, there were about a dozen unmarried young men in the house. Some of them had their own small rooms, but several, among them my fellow travelers, had to share not only the room but also the bed with others. That is an inconvenience that even in big cities often falls to the lot of those who have to travel economically and that in the West nearly everyone has to undergo. Frequently in traveling by steamboat or stopping at a hotel, one is obliged to share his bed with a total stranger. Of course that does not happen in the better and more expensive hotels in the eastern states, but as a rule the host in such hotels has supplied the rooms with double beds, and if a person wishes to occupy one of them alone, it is well to make arrangements in advance.

In spite of the inconvenience of several persons sleeping in the same room, Carl and Ivar declared they were quite comfortable. In theirs as well as in the other bedrooms there was running water. By turning a tap above the washbowl one could get all the water needed for drinking and washing, and by removing a plug in the bottom could drain it out. The annoyance of having to use a common washbowl was thus lessened by the ease with which it could be rinsed out. But the necessity of using a common towel was eliminated only by supplying one's own. In spite of everything, however, Carl and Ivar bore favorable testimony to the decency and cleanliness of the other guests. Some of them belonged to the better sort of the laboring class, but we never saw them at the table except with shirts as clean and well kept as their own hands. The worst habit of this class of Americans is no doubt the excessive tobacco chewing common to them and the spitting connected with the habit. It would be hard on boardinghouse carpets if a sufficient number of spittoons were not placed in strategic spots. If the men's sleeping rooms — as they were not here — are not covered with carpets, the floors in time take on a curious marbled effect not very pleasing. In more pretentious houses, summer and winter, the floors are carpeted.

The kitchen, which my wife and Christine were permitted to examine, was described by them as more like an ordinary living room than a kitchen. Here there was no gigantic brick fireplace surrounded by water barrels, pails, etc., but a neat, movable iron stove, always kept well polished and a real ornament. In this workroom the women could move about and lift off pots and pans, yet in the next moment appear in the parlor without a speck on their dresses. No kitchen utensils were visible except those in use and standing on the stove. When not in use they were put away in a cupboard in a corner of the room, and not, as among us, arranged on walls and shelves. The stove was covered with flat pans or plates, and there was hardly anything to indicate that the room was a kitchen. Nor was there anything in its furnishings to suggest it. There stood a table where one could easily sit down and write a letter without risking a grease spot on the paper. Around the walls, in addition to a couple of cupboards, there were a few painted wooden chairs (known as Windsor chairs) on which one could safely sit down without coming into contact with any dishcloths. A part of one of the walls was occupied by a settee. This is not our sofa couch, a piece of furniture that I believe is completely unknown in America. Unknown also is the settle-bed so common in Swedish kitchens, where its proximity to the food and the equipment used in preparing it is not an ideal arrangement.

Here the kitchen was not the sleeping room, but the parlor, of the servants. They had their bedroom or bedrooms on the second floor, with which the kitchen was connected by a back stairway, enclosed by one of the walls of the room and separated by a door. The space under the stairway provided a closet for kitchen utensils or for the day's coal or wood supply. In one corner stood a table, the upper part of which, instead of being a flat surface, was made into a zinc-lined receptacle some two inches deep; its lower part was covered with a calico curtain that hid the dishwashing equipment. Above the zinc receptacle, which was two or three feet long, were two faucets, through which a supply of water could be drawn as needed for the kitchen. In houses that have a furnace, through which ordinarily one of the water pipes is conducted, it is possible at any time, day or night, to obtain from one of these faucets warm, sometimes even boiling hot, water; at times this makes it unnecessary to build a fire in the kitchen stove. In another corner of the room was another piece of furniture, in appearance a small cabinet, but in reality an icebox, or refrigerator, in which a supply of ice for the day was kept. Every morning at sunrise the wagons of the ice company would make their rounds and deliver ice at the gate. An icebox has double walls and a double bottom and is lined with zinc. The space between the double walls and bottom is tightly packed with crushed coal. The box is well made, and if the doors are not left open it is possible to keep ice from one day to another. In this way butter, cream, prepared dishes, and other food stuffs needed daily in the house can be conserved. Lotten and Christine could not praise too highly the pleasant kitchen, the convenience of its equipment, and the easy way, free from fuss and fury, in which meals were prepared, so unlike the rattling and ado customary in a Swedish kitchen where food is to be provided for thirty daily guests.

Having described the kitchen so minutely, I ought perhaps to say a few words also about the dishes served daily at our table. But I understand better how to eat and enjoy the good things supplied than to describe them. Besides, I may later have the opportunity to say something about housekeeping in a plain American home, which seems to be very much the same wherever one goes. Here I merely want to say that all my experience hitherto with American ways and customs has shown a cleanliness and order I cannot forego commenting upon and which is very different from the descriptions given by Hauswolff and others. Ours was one of the plain boardinghouses in New York, but from the tablecloth to the dishes on it, the cleanliness was fully comparable to that in the better inns in Sweden. Napkins, however, were not used, and I have heard it said that even in more pretentious places they are regarded as a needless luxury. The table service in all hotels and boardinghouses, as well as on board canalboats and steamboats, is performed exclusively by young men. These are usually dressed in fine white jackets made of cambric or some other cotton cloth. Even in this plain house, where the proprietor's son waited on table and also served as carver at a side table, he appeared every day in a clean, white, newly laundered jacket and vest and in an apron with which a young lady might very well have covered her finest ball dress.

This description, however, must be taken as my response to conditions in this country only insofar as I came in contact with them. These are my personal impressions rather than a full account of things; about some things I naturally could not as yet have complete information. That this description may be countered by one showing conditions distinctly in contrast I know very well. In such a large city as New York it is natural that there should also be poverty, filth, and misery. The wealthy city offers in this respect the most appalling sights. The question, however, is whether these sights are to be taken as typical or whether they should not rather be put in the background in favor of more prevalent and striking ones. From what I have seen and heard I am inclined to believe the latter. If one wishes to collect material for a description of New York, one comes closer to the truth by spending more time on Broadway than in the region of *Five Points*. To depict American manners and customs and the fundamental characteristics of the American people a man will fare better if he borrows the well-prepared paints of an artist than if he is satisfied, as many have been, to use the brush and pigments of a dauber and make a mess of it all. There are shadows in the total picture, that is true, and I shall not hesitate, when it is required, to employ to the best of my ability, the dark colors that are necessary faithfully to render them.

For the rest, I confess that in the long run I do not believe I should be happy in a big city like New York. The mercenary spirit ascribed to Americans in general is perhaps more in evidence here than elsewhere. Yet is this really such an outstanding and predominant trait in their character? We are living in an industrial age, and Americans are perhaps to a greater degree than other peoples the representatives of their generation. They want to make money; but so do the Swedes and Europeans in general. The only difference is that Americans seem to know better how to do it. Perhaps the American businessman does not always use the best means to gain his end; but would others not do likewise if they were as clever as the American and knew, as he does, how to devise ways and means to attain their ends? The American is a speculator rather than a servant of Mammon in the real sense of the word. He is rich, and with his wealth we well know what it is that is harder for him to do than for a camel to pass through a needle eye. But what is hard is not impossible. With his wealth he often supports liberally undertakings for the welfare of his country. As he plans his own future, he often has in mind also the advancement and improvement of his community. He does not hover greedily over the gold he has accumulated; he does not keep his wealth in idleness. As a rule he is not a good economizer. He is avid for money, but he is not mean and avaricious. Most of the universities and other institutions of learning, homes for the care of the poor, and hundreds of other institutions established and maintained for the good of society are supported by voluntary contributions from individuals, and to these undertakings the American businessman is the biggest contributor. Canals, railroads, and other enterprises are begun by men combined into companies from which there is little prospect of gaining more than a meager profit; and thus their accumulated fortunes serve to promote the common welfare of the community and the nation as a whole. In view of such purposes, one is inclined to forgive an eagerness to accumulate profits that sometimes goes a bit too far.

In addition to his eager striving for the almighty dollar, the American has been accused, and perhaps not without reason, of a tendency toward boasting and overweening pride. He loves his country with passionate affection, and he cannot close his eyes to the advantages it has been blessed with above every other country in the world. He realizes that through its immeasurable resources and its growing prosperity, it is destined to become a great and powerful nation that, in not too far distant a future, will have a determining voice in the international affairs of the world. There are the Atlantic states with a coast line of some eight thousand miles, including islands, bays and promontories, an area of a million square miles, watered by countless rivers, with a fertile soil that yields all manner of agricultural products. Then, in the West, a mighty empire has sprung up as if by magic, extending clear to the shores of the Pacific Ocean, with a coast line of forty-five hundred miles, an area of about two million square miles, with more than fifty thousand miles of navigable rivers and lakes, the so-called Mississippi Valley and the vast stretches beyond the Rocky Mountains — a realm far exceeding the eastern states in fertility of soil and in boundless metal and mineral wealth. All of this vast territory, known as the United States of America, consists, all told, of an area of 3,260,000 [3] square miles and is inhabited by a people as free as the air it breathes, an industrious, strong, and enterprising people, brave, and possessed of all the qualities that constitute greatness and wealth in a nation. From these there have been developed political and social institutions that, unique in the history of mankind, have attracted the admiration of the entire world. When we take all this into consideration, we should not be too critical of a young nation awakening to its strength and power if its young blood boils over at times. Nor should we be too hard on individuals who sometimes reveal a truculent self-love, accompanied by an intolerant patriotism and, if I may say so, an unbearable national pride. This last exhibits itself especially among the half-educated, who, possessed of an absolute conviction of the excellence of their own country, will hardly admit that other countries have anything comparable, not to speak of their having anything that is preferable in any way whatsoever. Instead of the jealousy common among other nations, this failing, if one is willing to call it that, has fallen to the lot of Americans. In the midst of the storms that shake and set in turmoil the nations of the old world, they see within their own country, through the freedom and untrammeled development of its industrial life, such results as seem impossible to achieve under any other conditions. And if I do not want to dispute this last point with them, neither can I deny that they are inclined sometimes in their self-satisfaction to express themselves on matters of small importance with an almost ludicrous assurance. In these matters I have found some piquant examples supporting the characterizations given by Hauswolff and Trollope. Yet even so, I think I can prove that these characterizations are exaggerated and give a false impression of conditions in the North American republic.

It is time for me to end these reflections, provoked to a great extent by the reading matter I brought along for my journey, and by a definite wish at the very beginning of my story to disprove such statements, for instance, as those Herr von Hauswolff has given his Swedish readers. I hope I shall not be forced to change my opinion as I get more information about these matters. If such be the case I would rather be guilty of a self-contradiction than violation of the truth.

One of the things that appear quite terrible in New York is the frequency, not to say regularity, of conflagrations. Almost every day there is a fire somewhere, and no night passes but that there are fire signals, often announcing that fires have broken out simultaneously in two or three places in the city. But unless it is the house next door that is burning or unless something threatens one's own residence, the fire is disregarded and no one pays much attention, leaving the fire brigade to take care of what concerns it and nobody else. I hardly know which to admire the more, the phlegmatic unconcern displayed by the American people on such occasions or their excellent fire-fighting equipment.

"When the fire breaks out tonight," Carl said to me one day, "we'll go out and take a look at it." It was like deciding to go to the theater to see a play that had been announced and that could be counted on with certainty to come off. And sure enough, we did not have long to wait for the spectacle. When we went out into the street, we saw a fire only a few blocks from our boardinghouse It was a four-story brick building, and the fire had started on the ground floor, occupied by several stores with their stocks, among which must have been some very combustible material, for the flames spread to the upper floors with fearful rapidity. Their curling tongues were shooting out from the windows, beautifully lighting up the entire neighborhood. The houses here have seldom, as in Sweden, solid double floors, but only thin wooden boards separating one story from another. Even in brick buildings which do not boast of very thick walls, narrow slats of a certain kind are nailed to the inside of the walls, about three feet apart, and to these are fastened thin laths, an inch in width, on which the plastering is applied. When fire once breaks out in such a building it is not long before both walls and floors separating the stories are bright with flames. And if the roof, as it is frequently, is made of wooden

49

shingles, the fire engines must be on hand very quickly if the house is to be saved from complete destruction.

The house now on fire must have been of a very combustible kind. Nor did the fire brigade seem to exert itself to save it. Only a couple of fire hoses were directed on the flames while the main effort was expended upon saving the adjoining buildings. The fire company worked with a calm orderliness that, in spite of the misfortune involved, was a joy to see. Those who handled the hose showed an almost unbelievable boldness. As long as possible they kept their position on the ladders that had been placed against the walls of the burning building, estimating from long experience how soon the walls were likely to fall. That happened finally, accompanied by a frightening crash. A flood of water was poured on the smoke-covered ruins, and the fire was over.

In the meantime we had had the opportunity to watch the fire fighting equipment, which was unusually trim and ornate. Every part of it was smart and well polished, and its gilded ornaments, oil-paint designs and shining brass standards were intended more to please the eye than to be of real use.[f] Even in the outfitting and equipment of fire fighters in America, strangely blended with democratic simplicity is a general tendency toward pomp and display. They have their special uniforms, less used, however, in fighting fires than at parades, dances, and on other festive occasions.

These voluntary fire brigades are sometimes quite powerful corporations and wield considerable influence in the community. In a sense they may even be regarded as garrison troops, and they are called out in case of disturbances other than those caused by fires. It is only to be regretted that they themselves are sometimes the cause of these disturbances, sometimes even of real riots, for which reason in many localities the idea of disbanding them has been seriously considered. In many cities the most honored and prominent men of the community belong to these volunteer fire companies, but in other places they are made up largely of prize fighters and groups of young men who in spite of their promptness and enterprise, often prove between their calls to duty to be rowdies and inclined to cause much trouble.

Every piece of fire-fighting equipment has its commander and other officers elected by the members themselves for a given period. All are under the general direction of the city mayor and the chief engineer, who has at his side one or more assistants, the whole group elected at the annual elections for public officials. Often one sees the persons in charge calling out their orders through big, artistically constructed silver megaphones which have been donated to them or their brigade because of some extraordinary exploit they have performed.

The only kind of work at which outside assistance is sometimes needed is at the pumps. Any bystander is by law required to assist if called upon to do so by the commanding officer or engineer. We too were made to pay for our curiosity with a good bit of hard exercise at the pumps.

Next day in the forenoon we had the opportunity of watching a new conflagration and a new fire-fighting action. It was a real pleasure to see the orderliness with which everything was done and to watch the ornate but practical fire equipment. On this occasion there was a terrible tumult and noise, and a greater crowd of spectators had gathered than on the previous evening, but on the whole everything went its calm and even way. Passers-by stopped perhaps for a moment or two to watch the flames, and to speculate about how far the fire was likely to spread, but they soon went about their business as unconcerned as if nothing had happened. On the street, which was rather wide, the fire hose had been laid out, but that did not prevent carriages and buses from passing back and forth. From lowered carriage windows a head would sometimes look out and its owner say with perfect unconcern, "I guess here is a fire."

This time the fire had started in one of the upper floors of a brick building several stories high. The building must have been built more solidly than the one we had watched the previous night, for in spite of the fact that the fire had spread extensively in the upper part, we saw in the house next door a businessman and a couple of his clerks sitting quite calmly at their desks, taking care of their work as usual, without showing any sign of moving out. But perhaps it would have been possible, if necessary, to transport both office and strong box in their pockets.

Notes

[a] Here, as well as in other places, I have departed from the earlier statistical notes in my diary and have followed the census of 1850.

[b] It is possible that the wharves visited by the author in 1834 resembled a sewer. Now, to be sure, I did not find them in the condition one might expect in a city with the population and resources of New York, but still they were far from being what they were pictured by the author. Moreover, part of this wharf structure is only three years old. In the years intervening since 1834 two streets of the quay have been widened by being filled in beyond their former location along the Hudson River. The leveling is still going on, and the pavement has not yet been completed everywhere. For this reason it still happens in rainy and wet seasons that the wharf in spots is such as described by the author. Large and substantial buildings have now been erected on the site of the old wharf, and I have no doubt that the new harbor buildings are destined in a few years to compare well in neatness and elegance with similar places in any European city.

[c] Laborers without means should nevertheless not make their emigration plans with such assistance in view. There may not be enough for everybody. And even if an indigent immigrant manages to beg transportation to the Far West for himself and his family, he must not imagine that his troubles are over. With all the opportunities America offers, one must not expect the country immediately to supply food and shelter for masses of people who thoughtlessly and without personal means rush across the Atlantic expecting "roasted sparrows to fly into their mouths."

[d] After a few years my social life in America became entirely different from what it was in the beginning. I do not know whether I shall have the opportunity to describe it, but to the earlier impressions that living conditions made on me, I cannot fail to add that there is no truer and better description of American life than Fredrika Bremer's in her book *Hemmen i den nya verlden.*[1] Whatever one may say about some of the details in that author's letters from America, and however little I personally sympathize with her in many of her reflections, I must confess that regarding social activities in this country, and its very life, she has given a beautiful and true picture. With far more limited capacity than she for comprehension and description, but with a richer experience enabling me correctly to evaluate and appreciate whatever is great, noble, good, and truly cultured in a people often subjected to the erroneous judgment of capricious travel narrators, I refer to her book describing public and private life in America as more faithful to conditions here than any other book I have read on the subject.

[e] A district in New York so called because of five narrow, filthy streets meeting at a small square not far from the extensive East River quay. It was formerly, and is probably yet to some degree, a haunt of thieves and murderers and the abode of all kinds of vice in their most brazen and shocking forms. Some years ago there was a large building known as the Brewery, which was a den of crime and vice. In this region no one was sure of his life or purse if he passed through it by day; and unlucky the wayfarer that strayed there after dark. Since 1856 the place has passed through a great change. Part of the Brewery has been torn down, and part of it rebuilt and made over into a school and a workshop. A charitable society, which counts among its members many good and noble women, has not only through contributions of money but also through personal effort sought to improve conditions in these habitations of human misery, relieve poverty, and save the unfortunate victims of vice. These efforts have already borne a greater fruit than it was possible to hope for. "Five Points" is now a mission; a sanctuary to the Lord has been erected on the ruins of the temple of vice, and though crime and immorality still ply their trade by night in its shadow, numerous prayer

hours in the sanctuary testify to the longings of many a Magdalene and the cry of many a repentant thief for divine mercy and peace.

A comparison between this place when I first visited New York and what it is now offers one of the most convincing proofs that the fruit of God's kingdom may grow in the soil of a community full of tares but in spite of them still capable of yielding a harvest for time and eternity as good as if not better than those brought about in Europe by regular church activities and social efforts. And yet this growth has been achieved almost without the cooperation of civic authorities; only through a spirit that manifests itself in individual lives and the labors that proceed from it.

ᶠ Today fire engines driven by steam power are in use. I have seen such an engine, from which, if necessary, six hoses can be operated and directed upon various spots in the fire, each of them delivering a stream of water equal in force and volume to that supplied by one of the engines used in our bigger cities. If necessary, all the hoses may be combined into a single hose which is capable of delivering floods of water almost powerful enough to overturn such poorly constructed houses as one usually finds in the new western cities. These engines are always supplied with a sufficient quantity of water, coal, and kindling. At the very first fire signal the watchman of the fire company lights a fire under the boiler, and while the engine is speedily transported to the scene of the fire, a sufficient head of steam is developed to enable the company to start immediately its fire-fighting operations.

Chapter 4

TRANSPORTATION COMPANIES · FAREWELL TO THE SHIP *Minnet*

LEAVING NEW YORK · A NIGHT ON THE HUDSON RIVER · CANAL-

BOATS · ALBANY · A SPECULATION THAT FAILED · THE FIRST

NIGHT ON A CANALBOAT · SCHENECTADY · A DISTURBANCE ON

BOARD

HAVING observed New York as far as we cared to, at least outwardly, we began to feel rather keenly the fact that our journey was not yet finished. To be sure, there were still many things about which I should have liked to know more, but to learn it I should first of all need a better acquaintance with the English language than I now had, and besides that a better-filled purse. Furthermore, the object of our trip was not to take in New York and its sights, but to make a home for ourselves out West.

To get started we had to bargain with a certain class of men that in general do not give new arrivals the best conception of the American people. I refer to the transportation companies and their agents. Hardly has a ship with immigrants on board had a chance to enter New York harbor before a flock of these persons, known as runners, put in their appearance. With an obliging air and holding out the most attractive prospects for comfortable traveling conditions and other conveniences, they seek to persuade immigrants to use their lines, each one presented as the best and most inexpensive. In their service these lines generally have Germans and other foreigners; these are really the ones that seek to deceive unwary immigrants. Many are the frauds to which travelers are exposed, and in a thousand ways the agents know how to enrich themselves at the poor immigrants' expense. These agents are often self-appointed ones, and the companies they represent exist not infrequently only on paper. It happens sometimes, unless the immigrant exercises the greatest care, that he is compelled to pay twice for his trip to the West. Agents surround him on every side. If one of them notices that his intended victim is cautious and draws away at his approach, he assumes an air of not being particularly interested in what the immigrant is planning to do, or to whom he is planning to give his business. In the meantime, he will enter into conversation with him and seek to learn his plans. Then he suggests, as if by chance, that the person to whom he is speaking is really the one with whom he ought to do business. Sometimes the conversation will be turned to matter-of-fact subjects that do not seem to have anything to do with the business in which he is concerned, but just then is the time to be on guard. Americans generally avoid wasting time, and these persons would not squander precious minutes in talk unless they had one plan or another by which to gain advantage.

No matter how much I wish to place Americans in a more favorable light than that in which most of our travel writers have pictured them, I cannot do so at the expense of truth and justice. Transportation companies, land jobbers — for there are such men also at the New York wharves, who offer for sale parcels of ground that may not be easy to locate after a deal has been made — and their agents are, it must be confessed, a type with whom it is better not to do business. An immigrant, however, who is on his way to the West, can hardly avoid doing business with one of the first. But he will do well to take care lest he be duped by the ridiculously low price quoted for the transportation of himself and his belongings. No doubt the agent will find some way of indemnifying himself. Either the ticket he sells does not take the passenger beyond Albany or Buffalo, even if the agreement calls for the entire distance to Milwaukee or Chicago, or else somewhere along the way, at some change of canal- or steamboat, some mistake will be discovered through which the immigrant will be compelled to make additional payments, as for excess luggage weight or something of the kind. These demands he will be obliged to meet or be detained at some completely strange place where he would be subjected to still greater expense.[a]

We finally contracted with a transportation company to take us to Chicago for twelve dollars a person. This seemed like a real bargain. To travel 250 Swedish miles at a cost of forty-eight riks-

daler in Swedish money! The agent brought us on board the
steamer that in a couple of days was to take us to Albany. He
showed us the tastefully furnished saloon in which we were to
travel that part of the trip, without mentioning, however, that
beyond Albany we were to have entirely different accommodations. But at this low price we could not expect to get first-class
cabin conveniences on the Great Lakes, where such accommodations include free meals on board. However, it amused us to let him
point out, as bait for us, the paintings, mirrors, gildings, sofas, and
easy chairs adorning the spacious saloon of a steamer on which we
well knew we were to spend not more than ten to twelve hours.
A short time indeed to enjoy these glories! For our baggage, we
were told, we should not have to pay any overweight. Mr. Brodell,
however, advised us not to rely on this. He was quite certain that
the Erie Canal Company and the lake steamers would stand on
their rights. Later our experience was to bear this out. But our
friend Brodell thought the price very reasonable — so reasonable,
in fact, that he suspected the transportation company in question
would never be able to live up to its agreement with us. He foresaw
that with the tickets we had bought we should be prevented at
some point or other from continuing our journey, and to insure if
possible our reimbursement in this event, he made the agent enter
on his books the amount he had got from us in return for the agreement to transport us to Chicago. This precaution proved later to
be quite necessary.

Once again we paid a visit to the good ship *Minnet*, which, in
spite of the long and wearisome trip, had really become a happy
memory to us,[1] because of the constant kindness shown us by the
captain and the helpfulness and attentiveness of the crew. In a
foreign port one harbors a friendly feeling for the vessel that has
carried one away from the shores of the homeland; it is like a
bridge spanning the distance between that land and the foreign
country. Especially after a long sea voyage one feels a family at-
tachment to the entire crew. During our stay in New York we paid
daily visits on board without having any real reason for doing so.
Now with some emotion we said a last farewell to the members
of the crew — that is, the few who were still on board; for most of
them had already, as happens frequently in American ports, de-

serted to get better wages and food in the American Merchant
Marine. We learned later that of the entire crew only one member
finally remained. To seek to reclaim the deserters was no use. In
such circumstances the captain could do nothing but scrape together a new crew composed of all kinds of nationalities and
tongues.

In the evening of September 17 we went aboard the steamer
Rochester, one of the ships specially built for traffic on the big
rivers. About these ships Arfwedson [2] writes in his factual description of America — a description completely unprejudiced — that
nothing can excel them in magnificence and that those we have in
Europe are as inferior to them in size and elegance as a Roslags-
smack is to a Gävle-vessel. [3]

Now, however, I could not devote much time or attention to
either the gigantic machinery or to the tasteful and expensive furnishings of the cabins. As long as I live I shall never forget that night
on the Hudson River. Darkness and fog made it quite impossible to
catch a glimpse of the beautiful shores. Furthermore, a pouring rain
compelled us to stay below deck. An autumn storm was raging and
whining around the great smokestacks, from which there rose great
whirling masses of smoke that to my eyes had something dreadful
and menacing in them. Our numerous chests and trunks had been
thrown aboard and stowed away here and there, and it seemed
only by a miracle that we should ever find our own goods among
these mountains of piled-up freight and baggage. In this chaos we
sought to catch a glimpse of at least some of our belongings, so as
to know where to look for them in the morning at the point of
debarkation; but in vain. It was like looking for a needle in a haystack.

The steamer was packed full of people of various classes and
nationalities. To me everything on board seemed a disorderly mess.
Everybody was crowding and pushing as if his life depended on it.
A strange fear took possession of me. I was afraid — I did not know
why. It was as if these surroundings awakened in my fancy scenes
from stories I had sometimes read depicting the shadier sides of
American life.

In a melancholy frame of mind I managed to push my way to
the ladies' saloon, where my wife and Christine had found refuge

and where, after some search, I finally found them crouched in a corner, timid and dispirited. With trembling heart I pressed the hand of her who now had no earthly support but mine. We understood each other. We had said a painful farewell to our homeland and to those near and dear to us, but never had we felt so lonely and lost as now. Our kind and friendly Captain Bohlin had hitherto served as a bond with the friends beyond the ocean. During our stay in New York he had served as our interpreter in whatever affairs we had to attend to in a language that was as yet to us almost entirely strange. Now this last link had been broken. Now we and our fellow travelers were alone in a strange land, among people that were total strangers, whose language we did not understand and to whom our own was still more strange; on our way to settle down in a far country about which we had only vague notions. I realized the venturesome character of our undertaking. With tender concern my eye rested on the youthful and lovely being sitting by my side, who on my account had forsaken mother, brothers and sisters, and home, trustfully joining her fate and future to my own.

Finally we went to bed, but I was unable to sleep. Early the next morning I was on deck to get a glimpse if possible of the beautiful shores of the Hudson River. But no, everything was covered by a heavy fog.

On our arrival in Albany we found proof of the unreliable nature of the agreements of the transportation company. "One dollar," "two dollars," "three dollars" were the words repeated again and again as our trunks were brought to the gangplank, across which we were not permitted to carry them until we had paid to the ship's clerk a fee that seemed entirely arbitrary. The transportation of our goods, we had hoped, according to the agreement with the agent of the company, was to have been made without extra charge — at least for this part of our trip; for the agent had insisted that he had made special arrangement with the commanding officer of the steamer to that effect. Our protests, registered in broken English, were all in vain. The fees were exacted, though the officer in charge did not even take the trouble to weigh our luggage. No mercy was shown. For every piece of luggage that was brought ashore we had to open our purse, and with the calmest air in the world, but also with a trace of malice, the ship's clerk pocketed one dollar after another. Thus far we had traveled only 149 miles, and we reasoned that if this were to happen at every stopping place, there would not be much left for purchasing cattle and farming equipment.

From Albany we were to continue our journey on the Erie Canal to Buffalo. We went at once to the office of the Erie Canal Company and showed our tickets. We were immediately brought on board one of those queer-looking Noah's ark boats on which freight and passengers are pulled along through the country from one end of the state to the other. Once again we had to pay overweight on our goods, but this time they had at least the grace to weigh our luggage with great care before it was brought on board. We learned that it weighed more than 2,500 pounds, and since travelers are not allowed more than 50 pounds apiece on their tickets we now had to pay $20 for overweight.

These canalboats are of various kinds. Some of them, both decked and open, are used only for freight shipments; others are furnished both for passenger service and freight; while still a third kind, somewhat better looking than the rest, is used exclusively for passenger traffic. The last are known as packets and are drawn by three horses, which are frequently changed, so that in them one can sometimes make as much as six miles an hour. They are completely decked, with a narrow stairway aft leading to the saloon. Another leads to the kitchen, which is so small that no one but the cook can find room to move in it. The saloon takes up the entire length of the boat, probably eighty or ninety feet. It is generally divided into two parts, of which one is used at night as sleeping quarters for women, the other for men. In the daytime it is used by all passengers as a lounge and dining room. In the wall are low windows, through which passengers sitting on the sofas arranged about the walls can watch the landscape as the boat moves along. The room is high enough to permit a man to stand upright unless he is too tall or insists on keeping his hat on. In the daytime this floating retreat did not appear to me so very uncomfortable, but how all these people were to pass the night was a complete puzzle. No sign of bed or bedstead could I see.

I was not permitted to spend very much time examining the

packet boat, for I was soon informed that it did not fall to our lot this time to get any closer acquaintance with its conveniences or lack of them. All of us, along with our baggage, were stowed in one of the second-class boats — one of those provided for immigrants or for people who like ourselves had elected to travel cheaply, if not much to our own convenience, yet greatly to that of the canalboat captain and the transportation company.

The boat on which we and all our possessions were stowed had a saloon only half as big as that of the packet boat. Even so, this boat seemed clean and neat, with tiny red curtains in front of the windows, a long wood-stained table in the middle of the floor, and on either side of it a rather comfortable sofa covered with red damask, on which, when the table was pulled out, it was necessary to practice in earnest the old game "I Sit Where I Sit." So we had not, after all, thanks to our transportation company, been relegated to one of the real immigration boats, which are nothing but freight scows with a big, dark room below deck and with walls, floors, and furnishings like the empty hold of a coastal freighter.

On the packet boats meals are always included in the price of the ticket, and on the kind of boat we were traveling on it was also possible at an additional price to enjoy this privilege. This was not included in our bargain, however. We thought we might save a little by providing our own meals, knowing as we did that there were cities, villages, and inns all along the canal line where we could augment our food supply at any time. In great haste we supplied ourselves with some bread and other provisions, for the captain informed us that the boat was ready to leave at any time. Since we were the only passengers on board we rejoiced in the hope that we might possibly have all the small cabin at our disposal. It really did not seem to have accommodations for many more. Little did we know about the traffic on the Erie Canal, or about the length of time the skipper might decide to delay the departure!

These boats do not leave at certain hours like the packet boats, but wait like omnibuses until enough places have been engaged to pay to make the run. They keep stopping incessantly, now here, now there, to take on and unload freight and passengers, and everywhere they take their time. From the snail-like movement of the boat through the muddy canal passage down to the smallest details in connection with this means of transportation, everything betrays a tardiness exceedingly trying to the patience of the passengers, and quite unlike the usual American hurry and speed. After walking to and fro on deck for a couple of hours without seeing any signs of an early departure, we asked the captain if we might take time to go into the city for a little while. "I guess so," was his laconic reply. "Do you think we'll leave before evening?" "I guess not," he said. On the strength of this guessing of his, which we imagined to be based on good reason, we started off to learn for ourselves, at least to some small degree, what the city of Albany was like.

The city is excellently situated on the Hudson River. It was founded in the beginning of the seventeenth century by Dutch colonists, being an important and strategic spot for their trade with the Indians. Now it is the capital of the state of New York, and through the Erie Canal and its railway communications with other parts of the union, it has become one of the state's wealthiest and most important cities. It is true, its population has not increased so fast as that of some other American cities; but in its manner of increasing and through its beauty and splendor, it will stand comparison with any other city. The population, which at the beginning of this century was about 5,000, has now reached over 50,700.[b] Here one finds not only general prosperity, but wealth such as is rare even in this country. Everything about the city testifies to that fact. It is located on a hill that rises gradually from the low, muddy, and narrow river bank, till it reaches a height of 220 feet above the water. Then the terrain becomes even again. The streets are especially broad and straight, particularly the one leading up to the Capitol, a rather attractive building surrounded by a park with shady trees and well kept hedges and walks — one of the principal attractions of the city. A short distance from the Capitol is another park surrounding the city's stateliest and most beautiful building, the City Hall, which is constructed of marble. In addition, Albany has many other public and private buildings, which, both for beauty and size, compare favorably with the best that New York City can offer.

While we were walking about, admiring all these glories, which bore eloquent testimony to the wonderful advance of this country in industrial and mercantile matters, it occurred to us to try out a little business venture of our own.

A professor in Uppsala,[4] who knew a little of everything and wanted to have his fingers in a number of pies, gave us a good deal of advice when we were about to leave for America. Among other things he advised us to get as many so-called "Dala rings"[5] as possible. He had learned that a Swedish officer in New York, who had chanced to have a number of these rings, had offered them for sale and had got as much as twenty-five cents each, which meant a profit of eight hundred per cent. He encouraged us to do likewise. On his advice I wrote to a friend in Dalarna, who set the peasant women of Mora[6] to making horsehair rings in such quantities that they were probably never before so busy at that industry nor ever are likely to be again. There they were working at high pressure in every house and hovel to manufacture the gayest, many-colored rings with English inscriptions like "I love you" and "Remember Me." If I remember correctly, the quantity of these articles we had brought with us had cost us some eighty riksdaler. In New York we had not felt like offering our wares for sale. To tell the truth, we were somewhat embarrassed before our countrymen with whom we associated daily, and could not persuade ourselves to stand on street corners to offer our wares. Here, however, we felt we could afford to lay aside our genteel fashions without embarrassment. All the world about us was doing business, bargaining and making money. Why, then, should not we try our luck? To do business in horsehair rings was surely better than doing nothing.

Supplied with a dozen rings displayed on colored silk ribbons, Carl, Ivar, Polman and I — Polman had joined our company in New York to go West with us to seek his fortune — went each his own way to offer our rings for sale in the streets. It may have been our lack of experience and our shyness at engaging in this kind of activity, or it may have been that the gentlemen did not care to take time to look at our goods or the fine Albany ladies deign to trouble themselves with such simple things as horsehair rings, but in any event we did not have much success at our business. I was the first to give up, and with an oath at poor Professor W., who, by his well-intentioned meddling had induced us to engage in this poor venture, I was tempted to throw our entire stock into the river. Polman was the only one who had succeeded in selling any at all — a few at twelve cents each. But then he was also the one best gifted to speak for his wares. It was my wife who later, during our canal trip, sold the greatest number of rings, to women passengers who in their search among "Tom, Dick, and Harry," generally managed to find a ring with the right name.[c]

The sun, however, set on our day in Albany, and our canalboat was still moored to the same spot. That it was soon to start we gathered from the two horses waiting on the shore, by the mass of freight that almost filled the hold, and by the number of passengers that had crowded themselves into the small cabin. A curtain now cut off one end of the cabin, making a separate room for the women; through further scene shifting, the entire room had been changed into the strangest and most compendious sleeping quarters for no less than twenty-four persons, not to speak of the number that might be accommodated on chairs and tables. On both sides of the walls half a dozen shelves, bunks, or whatever they may be called, were hung. The steward, as if by magic, extracted these from the aforesaid sofas. As they were hung up, each of them was supplied with a thin mattress, or pad, on which sheet, pillow, and blanket were spread — everything as smooth and pressed as if it had been tacked to the shelf, which proved wide enough to serve as a bed for an ordinary man not accustomed to sleeping on his back. As already said, these bed-shelves were now hooked on the wall, in two rows, one above the other, with the sofas serving as the third and lowest row. On one side they were attached by hooks to the wall, on the other by ropes to the ceiling. The contraption really looked very fragile and altogether risky, especially for those who were to occupy the lower beds. The places were given out by lots, and I was unfortunate enough to draw mine in the second tier, where I was unable to lift my head more than a few inches above the pillow without pushing the person above me. During the night the crowded condition also made me frequently aware of the stirring of my neighbor on the sofa beneath.

Of canal trips and canalboats Gosselman's *Journey* [7] gives a complete and extensive description, although this author paints these experiences in colors that are far from disagreeable and are even pleasant. In Hauswolff's description, on the other hand, this part of the journey is depicted as a veritable torture. Undoubtedly in this case the latter author comes closer to the truth.

We spent our first night in a small room, not a full twenty feet in length and eight feet wide at the floor. In all, we were sixteen stowed away on our shelves. In the women's compartment, on the other side of the curtain, in size about a third of our own, there were six full-grown women, and if I may judge from the shadow pictures that fell on the red curtain, two of them were not at all of the slender and willowy type. In addition, there were in the women's compartment three small children, who along with the repeated bumps of the boat against other boats, or against the walls of the canal locks, served to keep the entire company awake most of the night. I managed to fall asleep for a while, but my bed was very short, and since I lay with my feet toward the curtain which separated us from the room occupied by the other sex, they must, unknown to me, have strayed into forbidden regions and perhaps come in contact with some small nightcap on the other side, for I was awakened by a gentle tickling at the soles of my feet, which made me immediately withdraw them into my own territory.

With joy I saw through the small window at my head that day was beginning to dawn, and I hurried up on deck, where I was rewarded for my early rising by being the first to use the common towel, six feet long and half a yard wide, its ends sewed together, and placed like a skein of yarn on a roller close to the cabin stairs. This washing arrangement has been well described by Dickens in his *American Notes for General Circulation.* [8] But he goes too far in his English humor at the expense of Brother Jonathan when he says that passengers on the big steamships are just as badly off in that respect as those on the canalboats, and when he insists that whatever the mode of travel, American habits as far as arranging for the traveler's neatness and cleanliness is concerned are extremely careless and filthy. This may be true of the canalboats, but it is far from true of the steamboats. Just as clean and comfortable as the common saloon and just as comfortably furnished are the hundreds of bedrooms located on either side of it, each of them supplied with individual and complete washing equipment and a sufficient number of towels. Hence, if the European traveler cannot keep himself clean, the fault certainly does not rest with customs in America. This custom of a common towel on the canalboats, however, which I have also found in some inns and hotels in the Far West, is really horrible; and on our continued trip through the Erie Canal we considered ourselves fortunate not to have soiled all of our towels on board the *Minnet*. We now found them clean and well ironed, ready for our personal use.

In the meantime we had not advanced very far. At the very beginning of our trip we had lost a good deal of time because the entire boat with its freight and passengers had to be weighed in order that a fee corresponding to its weight — and I imagine also to its draft — might be paid to the Canal Company toward the maintenance of the canal. Furthermore, we met with long delays at the locks as well as at small communities along the way.

Not until two o'clock in the afternoon did we arrive at Schenectady, only thirty miles from Albany, on the shores of the Mohawk River. With a population of about seven thousand it has a number of plainly built churches and is on the whole neat and pleasing to the eye, though we might have been fully satisfied with spending less time looking it over. For some reason or other, we remained there until nine o'clock in the evening. In the meantime the number of passengers had increased, so that we were now a sufficient number to occupy all eighteen bed shelves in the men's sleeping quarters. However, through a special arrangement with the steward, I managed to get a bed on a few chairs where I was not in danger of kicking the women beyond the curtain in the head and of being tickled on the bottom of my feet. Nor did I run the risk of having some of the rest of the sleeping passengers tumble down on me.

We remained on deck as long as possible, but the low bridges we had to pass under which compelled us to throw ourselves down on the wet deck, together with the raw and unwholesome night air and the most disharmonious chirp of the crickets along the shore, made walking on deck unpleasant. We had therefore no choice but to go to bed and take our rest, if rest is really ever to be achieved on board an American canalboat except when it stops at the landing stage of some embryonic city during the day and remains stationary for four or five hours. At such a time it may be possible, without paying any attention to the rest of the company, to stretch out full length on one of the sofas in the cabin.

During the night several other passengers came on board, and now tables, floors, and chairs were occupied. One of these new passengers was placed next to me. He was one of those persons who if they had asked for lodging in Sweden, would undoubtedly have been sent to the stable room. My close proximity to him was far from agreeable. Being compelled to move my whole bed and myself to one side, and not too well pleased at having my slumber disturbed, I was unable to restrain my temper. A verbal exchange resulted between me and my neighbor, an exchange that fortunately proved just as hard for the one to understand as the other. I thought the man came too close to the chairs I considered to be at my sole disposition. This occasioned a certain amount of pushing and jostling that no doubt were more easily understood than my English. I am not sure but that we might have started a scene resembling one in the House of Representatives had not our canalboat bumped against another boat with such violence that I feared it was being crushed like an egg shell. The result was that chairs, beds, and those resting on them were thrown about in a heap. The lamp hanging from the ceiling fell down and spattered its supply of oil over us. This was truly oil on the fire, but did not have the usual effect. In spite of all my misery I couldn't help laughing, and it seemed to affect my antagonist in the same way, whereupon for the rest of the night we sought to realize the old saying, "When you live at peace with your neighbor, there is no lack of room."

But I wish to spend no more time recalling these nocturnal adventures. It is enough to have experienced them. In passing I merely wish to say, in order that the reader may get a real idea of conditions on the canalboats, that for several nights the women's territory had to be extended an extra four feet, while the men's domain was correspondingly decreased. The reason for this change was that no less than nineteen feminine souls were writhing within the little closed room back of the red curtains, suffering the very woes of purgatory.

This mode of traveling, however, is not now nearly so general as in the early forties, owing to the more common use of railroads. Immigrants from Europe are now entirely relieved of the tribulations incident to this kind of locomotion.

The discomforts of the nights, however, were compensated for by the beautiful, fertile, and glorious regions that delighted our eyes during the day. No doubt this was the best season of the year for such a trip. The cool nights had already destroyed the hosts of mosquitoes that in the summertime, added to the burning heat of the sun, make this mode of traveling almost unendurable, night as well as day. Only a few of these American pests, of which we had heard so much, found their way into our oven-hot cabin at night. They are not of any unusual size, no larger than the common gnat in Sweden. I doubt that their sting is any more poisonous. The reason why almost every traveler in his stories speaks of them and describes the suffering they cause is that they are so numerous and ubiquitous. In addition, we learned the strange fact that they seem to be more attracted to newcomers from Europe. It is as though European blood were a special delicacy to them. When one has spent some years in America and has become acclimated there, one does not suffer nearly so much from these pests as at the beginning. "There is a kind of mosquitoes," said an Irishman, "that bite all day long, and when they leave in the evening they are followed by another kind that feast on European blood at night."

Notes

[a] National and local authorities have now taken measures to protect immigrants against tricks and frauds, so that if they permit themselves to be hoodwinked at the present time the fault is really their own. In the first place, transportation companies are under stricter control. They are made responsible for every fraudulent act and are made to repay anything that the immigrant can justly demand from them. Their runners or agents are now in reality a kind of public official under a bureau specially established to supervise everything that concerns immigration — to take note of the needs and plans of immigrants, to aid where aid is needed, and in general to assist them in carrying out their plans for the future.

All of this is under strict control so that the immigrant no longer needs to suffer even if he has no friend or acquaintance to advise him. Upon the arrival of immigrant steamers, no one is admitted on board except these responsible agents under the control of the State Immigration Commission; all others are by law prohibited from entering. Commissioners of Immigration appear personally on board to inquire into the health of the immigrants. Those who are sick are brought to hospitals where every care is given them until they are able to continue their journey. The rest of them may, if they wish, get quarters at Castle Garden, a former fort, which has now been converted into a spacious meeting place used for various kinds of entertainment and other gatherings and as a place of refreshment, with opportunities for walking about in the beautiful park surrounding the building. This entire place is used for the entertainment of the immigrants, who are assured of good treatment and are protected from any kind of extortion.

Generally, however, they take lodgings in some immigrant hotel or common boardinghouse in the city. The owners of these places are not permitted to embargo the luggage of any guest who has been unfortunate enough to live beyond

his means. This provision is a means of protecting immigrants who may sometimes in their joy at having reached harbor, spend too much money treating their
friends and themselves, enjoying entertainment they later find themselves unable
to pay for. These are steps taken by the public authorities to protect them
and to be of assistance to them in the difficulties they sometimes fall into on their
arrival in a foreign land, the language of which they are frequently unable to
speak or understand. But not in every single case can the authorities relieve their
sufferings and aid them in the difficulties they may have got into because of
their own inexperience or lack of foresight. In this connection we need only
think of the vast number of those that have left their European homeland for
America during the last few years, of whom many have but little if any financial
means on their arrival in America. For example, the number of immigrants in 1852
was 398,470, and of that number 304,879 landed in New York.

[b] As previously stated, these statistics follow the census of 1850.

[c] Several years later when I visited Niagara, I found at the side of the heavily
traveled road, close to the falls, an Irishman seated at a small table making horsehair rings, which he sold to passers-by at a price of fifty cents each. In a nearby
store, among other curios, rings of this kind were sold at the same price, and I
was told there was a good demand for them. So it would seem that Professor W's
idea was not so very bad after all, if we only had had more patience. Now it was
too late.

Chapter 5

WE TRAVELED now past one little city or market town after another, all of them betokening prosperity and a spirit of enterprise. Between towns we saw comfortable-looking country houses, some of them located at a distance from the canal, some of them close to its shores, but all surrounded by fertile fields, fruit trees, and gardens. "The entire country appears not like a young but rather like a dying country," one reads in Hauswolff's description. To pass such a judgment a man must carry desolation in his own heart, he must be dead to every impression of life. This country instead is a land whose varied wealth, movement, active enterprise, and beauty, presenting ever changing panoramas, make the beholder feel that new life is ever streaming into view.

Of special beauty is the valley of the Mohawk River, one of the tributaries of the Hudson; its waters run through 135 miles of the fertile regions of the state of New York. It is really worth suffering a little on board a canalboat to travel through this valley, which presents views with which few regions in the old world are able to compete.

Little Falls, a small city located on both banks of the Mohawk River, offers perhaps the most beautiful view between Albany and Buffalo. At this point the river forms a fall, 42 feet in height, and to that height the river is elevated by means of five locks. While the boat is being raised from one lock to another, there is plenty of time to walk ashore and contemplate the wonderfully beautiful valley in the distance as well as the strange rock formations which serve as a setting for the foaming river as it makes its way through the narrow gorge and takes its roaring leap from the steep rocks into the abyss below.

But it is not only nature that awakens the admiration of the stranger. The gigantic achievements wrought by man's hands are also abundant cause for awe and wonder. The high stone wall erected from the very edge of the river, or, so to speak, from its bottom, along which the canal has been conducted; the long aqueduct made out of hewn stones; the perpendicular rocky wall on both sides of the locks — everything testifies to the wonderful power and immense resources possessed by a people whose energy when any great national undertaking is to be carried out, will allow nothing to bar its progress.

Above Herkimer, a small city, or rather village, also located on the Mohawk, at a distance of 95 miles from Albany, the level land expands into a wide and most charming plain known as German Flats. Its name suggests the birthplace of its early settlers. In this region there are still a great many German families, among whom the German language is used as the mother tongue.

The Germans, more than immigrants from other countries, retain the customs, usages, and language of their homeland. Where they have settled in great numbers, they usually make up a community of their own, with their own schools, in which their children are often taught entirely in German. Thus one finds among them at times even persons, now elderly, who came to America when young but who are still completely ignorant of the English language. Indeed, there are said to be old men, born in America, who are total strangers to the language of their own country. In this neighborhood there are a number of cities and localities that show how the colonists have, along with their own persons, sought to transfer even *das grosse Vaterland* to America. Here we find Minden, Oppenheim, Manheim, Vienna, Danube, Frankfort, etc.,[1] and on the signs in the village shops, along with the names of the tradesmen, often the German words for tailor, shoemaker, watchmaker, etc.

In one of these places we received as fellow traveler for a couple of days a German minister, with whom I found it a pleasure to converse. He had spent several years in America and was very well satisfied with his position as pastor in a small church composed of his own countrymen living in the neighborhood. In religious matters he gave me no special admonition, but all the more on economic subjects, on which he advised us concerning our intercourse with Americans, whom he was inclined to judge with a bit of asperity. This gave me occasion to ask him about the condition of his countrymen who had immigrated to America. It happened that some printed notices had recently been thrown aboard, stating that hundreds of laborers were wanted for the construction of a new canal at a wage of a dollar a day. I asked the minister whether these laborers could be sure of getting their daily wages as promised, and if it did not happen sometimes that, after they had been hired, their wages were reduced to one-fourth, a reduction which the poor European immigrants were compelled to accept rather than starve to death. I translated to him the awful picture painted by Hauswolff in connection with this subject. He declared, however, that that description was grossly exaggerated. He admitted it sometimes happens that a subcontractor who has contracted for a certain piece of work and has hired a number of laborers to do it, after collecting for the work has run off without paying his workmen. Therefore the laborers ought never to leave too much of their wages unpaid but insist on collecting them every week. If the arrangement is such that part of the wages are left unpaid, as they sometimes are to induce laborers to serve out their time according to agreement and not leave the subcontractor without workmen, it is important to have the company guarantee payment of the outstanding amount.

Furthermore, he said, there was such a shortage of workmen that they need never fear a cut in wages, which necessarily would cause a stoppage of the work. For in such a case the workers would rather lose a few dollars and go elsewhere to look for a job, which they could always be certain of getting. He declared, however, that in all such matters it was necessary to be very careful and not depend too much on the honesty of the individual subcontractor. As for the work itself, he was of the opinion that it was no harder than comparable work in Europe. On the contrary, the workmen had far more time for rest and recreation here than in the old country. Only a very few Germans accepted employment at canal and railroad constructions. The Irish were as a rule used for digging and leveling. They came to America in greater numbers and in poorer circumstances than other nationalities, and they were also those who had to carry the heaviest burdens. But they did not work without getting well paid and they understood, as a rule, how to look out for themselves.

The Germans were more inclined to settle down on the land or enter trades immediately on their arrival. If they lacked funds to start a shop or buy land they generally hired out to someone of their own craft. The German minister said that while he did not care to encourage emigration, he must confess that as far as his experience went, his countrymen in this country generally were doing well, and most of them were making a good living. "Instead of the human bones that, according to your countryman's description," he said, "protrude from the marshy ground, marking the graves of the unfortunate laborers, or rather the battlefield of their toil, and which in their grisly way ought to warn European people to remember the ghosts of hunger and want that were created here,[a] you find, to be sure no great and magnificent estates, but rather pleasant, homelike farms which German industry has created and under whose roofs you will find few who are not well satisfied with their lot."

Among the numerous lovely cities and villages we passed during our trip along the canal, I must not fail to mention Utica, 110 miles from Albany, located on a hillside on the southern shore of the Mohawk River, and in the midst of a broad valley, in appearance like a great lake. This city, like many other communities, may thank the canal for its present flourishing condition. At the beginning of this century this community had only three or four buildings, but now it is one of the foremost cities in the western part of New York State, with a population of 17,700. Here several large wool and cotton factories have been established. The usual delay of the canalboat at every place of any importance gave us the opportunity to take a walk on shore. Like all other American cities, Utica is built very regularly, with broad, straight streets crossing each other at right angles, thus dividing the city into blocks which are perfect rectangles or squares. From the higher part of the city there is a beautiful view of the river and the valley, which is crossed by railroads and canals. Here as in four other places canals were being constructed to connect the Erie Canal with other watercourses which crisscross the state of New York in every direction. All these undertakings have since then been completed, and at this time there are scarcely two cities in that extensive state which have not been linked together by this means of communication.

In addition to the branches which connect the Erie Canal with Lakes Ontario and Champlain to the north, and with the inland lakes Oneida, Canandaigua, Geneva, Seneca,[2] and other watercourses in the central part of the state, and with Pennsylvania to the south, the big navigable rivers Hudson and Delaware are connected through a canal that extends clear into the heart of the almost inexhaustible coal fields of Pennsylvania.

In addition to Utica we got acquainted with numerous other communities named for classical and famed cities of the old world. For instance, there is Rome, which probably has nothing in common with the city on the seven hills except the name; though a patriotic Yankee, who is inclined to pride himself on the advantages his own country has above all other lands in the world, would no doubt insist that his Rome is every bit as good as the papal capital of the Church State. We passed this Rome by night and hence failed to catch a glimpse of its well-furnished stores and warehouses, and above all things of its banks (for no city is so unimportant that it does not possess at least one institution of this kind), which are the curiae and the basilicas of the American cities of Rome.

The next day, however, at one o'clock in the afternoon, we had the pleasure of visiting Syracuse, a city located 171 miles from Albany, at that time boasting a population of 6,500, now increased to something more than 22,000. The city is not, like ancient Syracuse, famous for its vineyards, but is notable instead for its abundance of salt, manufactured in great quantities here as well as in the neighborhood of Lake Onondaga, not far from Syracuse. The salt thus manufactured is shipped to every part of the country.

The entire region hereabout is riddled by wells, some of them drilled to a depth of 300 or 350 feet, yielding water which in salinity far exceeds that of the sea. In general, 80 gallons of this well water produce as much salt as 700 gallons of sea water, or 15 to 18 pounds of salt from 100 pounds of water. Spring and fall, at which seasons most of the salt is manufactured, two million gallons of water are pumped up every day, yielding about 35,000 bushels of salt, each bushel weighing 56 pounds. In 1848 the salt production amounted to 4,700,000 bushels, an amount equal to half of the salt imported into the United States for its own consumption from other countries.

These wells are the property of the state of New York and, according to an article in its constitution, neither the wells nor the ground needed for the manufacture of salt may be sold. The wells are drilled and the water pumped by the state into vast reservoirs, from which it is later piped to privately owned factories at a price of one cent a bushel of salt. The salt is produced by allowing the water to evaporate either in wooden troughs, twelve inches deep, or in iron pans of lesser depth; or else by boiling it in vast iron kettles. The latter is the more common method, although the salt produced in that manner is not so pure as that produced by slow evaporation. In this neighborhood there are almost 400 acres of land completely covered by rows of troughs, vats, and kettles.

Our attention was attracted to a number of exceptionally beautiful country homes, laid out on a grand scale, some of them located within the city. For the rest of the picture, here, as in most other places, such a constant building and hammering was going on that in spite of the many neat wooden houses with their ornamental piazzas and trellises, one could not help agreeing with Gosselman when in describing the speedy growth of American cities he suggests that a person gets tired of the eternal smell of lumber mills and planers.

At this point the canal is crossed by the New York and Erie Railroad, which after running side by side with it in a number of places here dips underneath it through a tunnel. Two new locks, of hewn granite, were under construction, and here, too, they were advertising for laborers to help complete the new canal to Oswego on Lake Ontario.

As a result of the previous dry summer and possibly some fault also in the construction, the water in the canal at this time was unusually low, so that in several places the horses were hardly able to drag the boat, which almost scraped the bottom of the channel.

Here and there passengers were forced to walk to lighten the load. As we arrived in Syracuse it seemed all of a sudden to be entirely impossible to proceed. Our heavily loaded craft stuck here as though it were glued fast in the mud. Even when two more horses were hitched to the towline and all the passengers pushed and pulled to the best of their ability, it would not budge. We were very much afraid that we were to be marooned there until the good Lord should give us a heavy rain or the canal board tap some source of water we knew nothing of. More than thirty other boats were in the same predicament. There was no end of toil and noise. On the shore people from the queue of stranded boats were milling around — most of them immigrants, of many nationalities and tongues. It was a strange experience to walk about in this motley crowd, which had drifted together from almost every part of the world, all yearning to reach their destinations. Perhaps the goal was a peaceful hut beyond the Great Lakes, a place where they might rest after their long and toilsome journey and look forward to a secure future. Now their hopes, like the canalboats, had foundered and stuck tight in a muddy ditch, out of which they didn't know how they were going to get them again. Here children of all ages were running around. They seemed to be the only ones glad on this occasion of freedom, after days and days of limitation to the narrow space on the boat deck and the still more circumscribed area in the cabin below. The canine species, like the human family, had representatives from Holland, Germany, France, and other countries. Their bold familiarity stirred the Swedish temper of our Fille, who otherwise was in the habit of displaying the greatest calm. He went beserk, and a general European war broke out, in no small measure adding to the general disorder and confusion.

It was far into the night before it became possible in some way to tap a feeder, get a little more water into the canal, and so enable the collected flotilla to move again. The Erie Canal, which undoubtedly, even after numerous railroads have been built, will continue to be one of the most useful American enterprises, just as it will remain throughout time one of its greatest national undertakings, might nevertheless well have been dug a little deeper. At least so it seemed to us during the long hours when we feared that our journey was to be materially delayed — an eventuality that might have caused us and hundreds of other immigrants detained there much inconvenience and expense. Ordinarily the depth of the canal is only 4 feet, while its width at the surface is 30 feet and at the bottom 28 feet. The margin is therefore very small, and if an accident happens or if the water supply grows scant, canal-boats, which often draw 2 feet of water, may easily either be grounded or find it difficult to pass.

At twilight on September 22, after another two days of slow motion, we finally arrived at Rochester, a city even in America known as a marvel for the rapidity with which it has grown up. Whereas in 1812 there were only eight or ten insignificant houses, 26,000 enterprising people have here now built their homes. Arf-wedson in his journey of 1834 gives the population as 13,000. When we went through the city seven years later it had doubled, and according to the census of 1850 its population at this time is no less than 36,400. No wonder this city, only a few years earlier little more than a wilderness, now seemed to have come into being by magic. Its manufacturing plants, wool and cotton textile factories, paper mills, carpet mills, and, above all, its great foundries and shops for the production of all kinds of machinery, threshers and other farm implements, have cooperated to place it on the map. However, in later years, as will appear from my notes, greater things than these have been done elsewhere, and Rochester is not now reckoned anything remarkable.

The city is located in the Genesee Valley, famed for its fertility and its wheat. It is beautifully situated on the banks of the river from which the valley has derived its name, and which at this point forms three perpendicular waterfalls, the highest about 100 feet. The canal passes through the city and crosses the Genesee River through an aqueduct 800 feet in length, the longest of the eighteen aqueducts between Albany and Buffalo. The approaching night — not lack of time, for as usual we spent between three and four hours in this place — prevented us from getting a good view of the city and the falls. To our regret we had to satisfy ourselves with auditory evidence of the magnificence of the nature that surrounded us. Had we not known we were in America, we might have imagined ourselves in some romantic spot in the Rhine or Danube Valley. Big, tall buildings, partly located at the falls themselves, partly below them, towered above us in the twilight like old forts or medieval castles, casting their dark, sinister shadows upon the foam-flecked waters. However, they were merely gigantic flour mills, of which there were many. These mills have probably done more than all manufacturing and machine shops to make Rochester the enterprising and prosperous city that it is. In some of them up to 2,000 bushels of wheat are ground daily. The flour produced from the grain grown in the Genesee Valley is regarded as the best and finest in the country. It is transported via canals and railroads to the eastern and western states, and not a small part of it goes to Canada.

Here, as in all the new cities we passed through, we were surprised to notice the great number of churches and banks — evidence perhaps, in spite of the failures that occur in both these institutions, of the greater intensity of both spiritual and material activity here than in older communities. While in the smaller European cities only one or possibly two church buildings may be found, and very seldom a bank, it is impossible to walk very far along these newly planned streets, where the mortar and paint have hardly had time to dry on the new houses, without almost in every block coming across some temple erected for the worship of either God or Mammon. The city of Rochester has no less than twenty or more of the former and seven or eight of the latter kind.

This time the asssurance we had counted on that the canalboat would be getting a late start came near to giving us a costly lesson. After taking a walk downtown, the women went back on board, while the rest of us waited awhile to drain a farewell glass in honor of one of our countrymen, Ahlmark,[3] who had been in our company from New York and was now about to leave us. He had arrived in America about the same time as we, and though his funds were low, hardly enough to pay his fare out West, he still wanted to get some employment there. Throughout our trip he had offered his services to one American after another, but in vain. Coming from an upper-class home in Sweden and frail in body, he was unused to hard labor and knew no trade. Such a person is always likely to find it more difficult to make his way in this country, especially when he is ignorant of the English language. The only position in which he is likely to fit is in business, but his ignorance of the language would naturally be an obstacle to him. During the canal trip our friend Ahlmark had finally come in contact with a shoemaker living in Rochester, who had promised to take him in hand and teach him his trade. Therefore he was now about to leave us and try his fortune at the last and awl, instruments he had never, during the twenty odd years of his life, had occasion to use.

While we were drinking, the canalboat had been set in motion. We knew of course that it would not be hard to catch it, but in the darkness and among thirty or forty other craft it was not easy to find the right boat. On the narrow canal bank we were constantly meeting horses pulling other boats and so were delayed in our race. Irritated at the captain who, just this time, had decided to leave earlier than usual, we finally managed to hail a boat, which by chance proved to be one of those we had been traveling in company with the last few days. We had managed to strike up an acquaintance with some of its passengers. Among them were several German immigrants who advanced the opinion that our boat had probably not left Rochester, for they had seen it towed further into the city where it had stopped to take on additional freight and passengers.

Could we depend on this information? Was it not possible that the Germans had made a mistake about the boat since, in the dark, one boat was very much like another? In such an uncertain situation was it advisable to go back? If our boat was not behind but ahead of us, it might be that the loss of time would prevent our catching up with it till the next day, and then by means of some packet leaving Rochester. I thought of Lotten's anxiety and the unpleasant situation in which she would find herself, alone with Christine, in a constantly changing and not always very agreeable company. As usual when one has dallied too long at the cup, regrets began to assail us, this time not accompanied by headache or loss of balance, but with all the greater trouble of mind. We decided, however, to follow the advice of the good Germans and turn back, calling to all of the dozens of canalboats we met, moving past us with their colored lanterns at the bow and their small lighted windows like veritable will-o'-the-wisps. Angered by the malicious laughter which frequently was the reply to our questions, and enraged because we found ourselves an object of derision to certain Yankees who had their fun at "the poor Dutchmen's" expense, we returned finally, out of breath and dead tired, to Rochester, where we found our craft lying peacefully just a few yards from the place where we had left it. Here we were greeted by the captain's "What the d——l have you been running about for?" He really had had the courtesy to wait for us. When we had set out to reach our boat we had sought for it among the moving craft; we had not thought to look for it among those that were stationary.

The next day we had the misfortune of reaching Lockport at night. This was a place which, according to what we had been told, was well worth giving a closer view. Here is a double row of five locks, one after another, through which the water from Lake Erie drops 60 feet. Taking warning from our adventure of the previous evening we did not dare, in spite of the long delay in ascending the locks, to take a walk in the dark to the small city located on a nearby hill. Like the canal, which for some distance passes through a mountain, it had to all appearances been blasted out of the solid rock.

We had been assured that this would be our last night on board, and our joy at the prospect increased in proportion to all the unpleasant things possible on a trip by canalboat, which now in concentrated form combined to make the last twelve hours worse than any of their predecessors. The closer we came to Buffalo, the denser grew the crowd of passengers. The packed condition of the rooms occupied by both ladies and gentlemen was worse than ever before. I said "ladies and gentlemen" to adopt an expression used in this country, though the Lord knows that so far as most of the individuals in the present company were concerned, "women and men" would have been titles of extreme courtesy. On this last leg of the trip we were unfortunate enough to add to our company a few Irish people. These are unpleasant enough as neighbors ashore, but having them on board made us wish they might depart for *Blåkulla*,[4] a more suitable destination for them and one I suspect most of them will eventually, willy-nilly, reach. A genuine Paddy had seated himself at the table with us. In his entire person he reflected something of that rag-bag bully which generally characterizes the Irishman, especially after he has come to America and been enfranchised as an American citizen. One can readily see by looking at him that he feels his citizenship entitles him to any public office just as his membership in the "only true Church" entitles him to a place in heaven by the side of St. Patrick and St. Columcille. With a clay pipe in his vest pocket and a whiskey bottle in his coat, he is fully prepared for a fist fight with anybody who dares dispute his right in either of these respects. By his side is his better half, whose dress is somewhat better than her husband's. This suggests that they have been in America for some time and have managed to get a fair start in life. In her arms she carries a child, some two or three years of age, a dirty and squalling brat. The Irishman pulls out his whiskey bottle, and his wife a small teacup from her handbag, where along with some bits of toast it has been wrapped up in a linen article used to complete the toilet of a child. The husband first takes a drink and wishes to treat all around, both ladies and gentlemen, but we, at least, are unable to avail ourselves of his well-intentioned courtesy. Finally he fills the cup for his wife. After she has drunk part of it she dips some pieces of toast in the remainder and gives them to her little boy, who swallows them greedily, accustomed already to the diet.

This little scene serves to indicate the kind of company we were enjoying. As for Lotten, who had been compelled during this part of the journey to undergo many hardships she was entirely unaccustomed to, she had the satisfaction this forenoon as on previous days of associating with some rather agreeable women. Foremost among them was a talkative little woman from Canada, who had been in our company all the way from Albany and who had given my wife much motherly care and attention. She did not seem to be much of a friend of the Yankees, but attached herself instead to Lotten, to whom she was determined to teach as much English as possible in the course of a week.

That night it was impossible to keep my place in my bed on the chairs. The man at the wheel must have felt that we had had too little experience of what we might call his canal punches — shocks of greater power than any electric battery could ever have delivered. The boat seemed to be a plaything in the hands of some giant who, as long as we were passing through the channel blasted through the mountain, took pleasure in bumping us from one side to the other of the mountain wall.

Finally, September 26, early in the morning, we arrived at the Niagara River, along whose shores the canalboats are pulled for the last three miles to Buffalo. It was a cold, raw morning, and we found good use for the sheepskin coats we had got in Helsingör. The wind blew sharp from Lake Erie, which we saw in the distance, and it didn't have to blow any stronger to make us realize that a canalboat can better stand hard buffeting against mountain walls than the rolling waves of the Niagara River. Between nine and ten o'clock in the morning, however, we arrived in Buffalo.

For eight days, through eighty-three locks, we had now traveled the long New York–Erie Canal, that boldly conceived undertaking so energetically carried out and at such a great cost. For it America may well thank Governor Clinton,[5] whom Gosselman, very aptly, has named the Platen [6] of the United States. Like Platen, he met much opposition in bringing to reality his country's great undertaking. Those who were in charge of the finances of the state raised many objections and made his task most difficult before he finally succeeded. The indebtedness of more than ten million dollars which the state of New York had to assume to accomplish the great undertaking has been fully paid off; the canal is now a source of considerable annual income, and in other ways, indirectly, of incalculable value to the state. Before there were any railroads between Albany and Buffalo, the canal was the one artery through which business and communication were carried on between the western territories, via the Great Lakes, and the Atlantic states. It also became the means of developing within an incredibly short time the rich natural resources of New York State. Commerce and industry have been lifted to a height which they might not have attained to for centuries without this easy, extensive, and economical system of communication.

The entire length of this canal, which connects the navigable Hudson River with Lake Erie, is 360 miles. But together with the canals that branch out from it to Lake Ontario and the above-mentioned lakes, as well as those that connect the Hudson with Lake Champlain and with the Delaware River, there is in New York State alone a navigable system of canals amounting to not less than 804 miles. I have seen it stated that even now, after railroad communications have considerably decreased traffic on the New York and Erie Canal, there have been years when the value of goods transported through it has been 145 million dollars, from which the state, after paying its repair and maintenance bills, has reaped a profit of $3,250,000, or a net gain of 2⅓ million dollars.

Note

^a Carl Ulrik von Hauswolff, *Teckningar utur sällskapslifvet i Nordamerikas Förenta Stater* (Norrköping, 1835), II, 13.

Chapter 6

IMMEDIATELY upon our arrival in Buffalo we went to the office which was to handle the next part of our journey and to which we had been directed by the agent of the transportation company in New York. The name of the office was separately printed on our tickets besides. We hoped not to have to remain there very long. But it was Sunday, and the office was closed. Those whom we managed to speak with for a minute said that nothing could be done that day. We could not stay on the canalboat. Not even our luggage could remain there till the following day. Our heavy trunks and boxes were thrown ashore, and there we were, surrounded by our worldly possessions, not knowing which way to turn for shelter. While Carl and I went up into the city to see about lodging, Lotten and the rest of our company remained to look after the luggage. Finally we succeeded in finding a German boardinghouse. Its exterior and interior were very different from our pleasant boardinghouse in New York, but the price was moderate, and we had come to realize that it was necessary to exercise the strictest economy. When we returned to the shore, we found our company, but our baggage was nowhere to be seen. In spite of the energetic protests of Lotten and Ivar, it had been transferred to a big warehouse. No doubt a service had been rendered us in this, but we were uneasy at the thought that our things might not be properly taken care of. They might either get lost or mixed up with all the rest of the immigrants' goods, all stowed in a disorderly pile. There was nothing to do, however, but set out for our German boardinghouse, carrying a couple of bags and the box containing our diminishing cash funds, cared for by our faithful Christine, who never, day or night, let it out of her hands. In our lodging place we spent a dreary Sunday, and a number of unpleasant incidents made the night scarcely quieter or more peaceful than the preceding one on board the canalboat.

The next day we called at the office to which we had been directed. When we showed our tickets, however, we were told that they neither knew about nor had any connection with the transportation company with which we had been dealing. But they asked us to leave our tickets, and assured us that in a day or two they would "make it all right" so that we might continue our journey to Chicago without further trouble. This was really cold consolation. We did not understand all the reasons they gave for the delay, but we understood that it would be connected with additional and perhaps considerable extra expense.

Our embarrassment at not knowing what steps to take to defend our rights was augmented by our inability to deal directly with those who seemed to have our fate in their hands. We decided to use our German host as an interpreter. But there must have been some mutual understanding between him and the agent. Apparently they had agreed to assist each other to their individual gain. It is possible that our landlord had agreed to send as many of his countrymen as possible to the agent and that he in his turn was to help increase the earnings of the boardinghouse by detaining passengers as long as possible. I was strengthened in this belief when I called on the landlord again in the afternoon and was told that the matter now had been arranged and the tickets approved, but that we could not leave (be *shipped* would perhaps be the more suitable word) till the following Wednesday inasmuch as there was no steamer leaving for Chicago before that date. This, we learned, was an absolute untruth, for at that moment there were three ships in the harbor leaving for Chicago, one the same evening and two others the following forenoon.

No doubt we should have had more trouble still had not our good fortune brought us into contact with a Swede who was living in Buffalo and who helped get things straightened out. This Swede, whose name was Morrell,[1] had lived in America many years and had married in this country. At first he found it difficult to carry on a conversation in Swedish. After a few hours, however, he managed it with greater ease. In Sweden he had been a harness maker's journeyman, but now he was a jeweler; that is, not one practicing the trade, but a vender of jewelry. He had one of the most elegant stores in Buffalo with a valuable stock of all kinds of watches and clocks, as well as of gold, silver, and other jeweler's goods. According to his own statement he had come to Buffalo with twenty-five cents in his pocket. At first he had hired out as a farm laborer, but he soon realized he had not been born to hard labor. He thought, though, he would make a success as a businessman. In some way or other he managed to obtain a small stock of lace, needles, rings, stickpins, and other trinkets — what is known as "Yankee notions," the sale of which brings an immense profit. Most of it consisted of imitation gold and silver ornaments, purchased in quantities at low prices and sold as genuine to farmer lasses with a weakness for gewgaws and bits of finery. With a box on his back, he walked from house to house. Where he was unable to make a sale, he managed at any rate, as is customary among peddlers, to get his meals and lodging in exchange for a brass ring or a few glass beads. In the course of time he extended his business and established his credit. Now he had a large establishment from which he furnished a dozen peddlers, who sold his wares on highways and byways, at good profit to themselves as well as to him.

We were now only twenty-one miles from Niagara, and we might have had time to look at the famed Falls, but had to forego the pleasure. All the delays along the way had made our purse lighter and lighter.

In Helsingör we had bought ourselves several sheepskin coats, which Captain Bohlin had insisted we could sell at a good profit in America. The season, however, was too mild to make the sale of furs very profitable. On our way we had offered to sell these coats at a very moderate price, but in vain. We had begun to fear that this venture was to be as much of a failure as the one with the horsehair rings till we met with the German minister on the canal-boat whom I have already mentioned. After he had bought one of our coats at a reasonable figure, he advised us not to sell the rest of them for less than twice what he had paid. "Say that they are made of Siberian lamb," he urged. "The American people can never tell the difference." This advice seemed to us more German than ministerial, but when we recalled that others had not hesitated to cheat us, we considered ourselves justified in engaging in reprisals. With the coats on our arms we walked along the streets of Buffalo and actually succeeded in disposing of a few of them at three times the cost to us. Following Morrell's advice, we decided not to sell the rest of them till next winter, when we could surely expect to get at least four times as much as we had paid for them.

Buffalo was without doubt one of the most beautiful cities we had seen in America. It is built on a slope, the top of which presents a glorious view of Lake Erie, the Niagara River, and of Canada beyond. The city was founded in 1801 by the Dutch Land Company and had in 1813 a population of only 1,500, when in the war with England the British and their Indian allies completely destroyed it by fire.

It might be interesting to compare the accounts that two Swedish travelers have given us of this city, now one of the most flourishing in the country. In Hauswolff's description, published in Norrköping in 1835, partly translated and adapted from the works of a German authoress who had traveled in America a few years earlier, we read: "Buffalo is the real center of the bartering and fur trade of the American hinterland, and here American life begins to show its other side. Here one notes the impossibility of disposing of farm products for money, since cash no longer is to be found. The city is a mass of houses and huts without arrangement. The streets are unpaved, and one drags onself along in the mire. The first room one enters in a house is the kitchen, which also serves as the living room. Sticking out the door there will be a long log, one end of which is burning in the fireplace, being moved up as required. In this way the trouble of chopping wood is saved. Only cold, smoked, or salted food is served, and the drink is tea. The residents of the city are without the least moral or intellectual culture, but nevertheless develop a good deal of commercial enterprise. Such are conditions everywhere." [2]

Arfwedson, on the other hand, in the story of his travels in the United States and Canada from 1832 to 1834, hence contemporaneously with the publication of the description cited above, writes: "Buffalo is an attractive and growing city, no doubt destined in time to become one of the great cities in the interior of the country. The immigrant feels that he is bidding farewell to civilization" — now he must cross the Mississippi before he has a good reason for saying such farewell — "and here he rests up before giving himself to the vast forest lands of the West. Here goods are loaded and unloaded that are destined to be shipped hundreds of miles away. Buildings spring out of the ground faster than can be imagined. The streets are laid out with a breadth that suggests the wise city planners foresee great future growth. The stores are filled with goods from Paris, Cincinnati, London, and Rochester. Style magazines are read as avidly as in the capitals of Europe, and tailors and modistes are personages as important as with us."

As an addition to the latter description and in confutation of the former, may I be permitted to state that Buffalo now has a population of more than 50,000 and more than twenty churches. Some of these, built out of carefully hewn stone in Gothic style, compare well in architectural beauty with most of the newer churches in Europe. There are several banks where both gold coin and bills are exchanged daily and circulated in the lively business activity which the city engages in both locally and with faraway places. Its comfortable five-story hotels, furnished with luxury and elegance, surpass in some cases the best hotels in the capitals of the old world. Its gas and water systems, its fine buildings, private as well as public, its numerous charitable institutions, its literary organizations, printing offices, bookstores, and well-stocked public libraries — all these things in Buffalo are among the indisputable proofs that the North American republic in a greater measure than any other country possesses the physical, intellectual, and moral elements that make for national greatness and prosperity.

We were reminded, however, in a disturbing way, that many of these elements of greatness require organization or, rather, need to be placed under proper control. The thriving navigation on the Great Lakes and the rivers is still undeniably fraught with perils, which greater superintendence and foresight on the part of those concerned might, as least to some extent, forestall. The absence of good harbors in these waters is why many ships annually founder in the terrible storms that rage here. The lack of caution among responsible parties results from time to time in the most heartrending accidents, as when steamships with hundreds of passengers on board explode or are destroyed by fire.

A few hours before we left Buffalo we heard a rumor, which later proved to be well founded, that the steamer that had sailed the day after our arrival, carrying a number of immigrants to the cities on the coast of Lake Michigan, had been lost in a storm. Our request for permission to leave on that ship had been refused by the transportation company—for what reason we never knew. Of several hundred passengers and members of the large crew, only three were saved.[3] Among those who went to their unexpected graves were no doubt many whom we had known on our trip through the canal. Undoubtedly some of them had shared our cabin, and we had often heard them speak with happy anticipation of their future home in the rich land of the West, and of their plans for earthly pleasure and comfort. They had now found another home, of all pilgrims the final goal, alas too often overshadowed by dreams of lasting habitations built on this side of the grave. Here was in truth a reminder of the warning words: "There shall be two men in one bed; the one shall be taken and the other left."

It was therefore not without a certain trepidation that we finally, on September 29, boarded the great steamship *Illinois*,[4] on which our transportation company had finally consented to give us passage through the Great Lakes. Our accommodations here were very different from those on the Hudson River. Instead of a place in a well-appointed, richly furnished cabin on an upper deck running the entire length of the large steamer, we had to be content with crawling downstairs into the so-called steerage, or second class. Fortunately we came early enough to select the best and most comfortable bunks, constructed in triple rows around the walls of the rather roomy cabin and all furnished with green curtains. But it needed to be big and roomy to accommodate all the men, women, and children packed together there. Most of the beds were designed for two persons, and it was of no use to register any objection to a bedfellow, of the same sex of course, who chose to take the vacant place at one's side. We were fortunate enough to find under the double berth my wife and I occupied a single bed for our good Christine, while Carl and Polman made arrangements to take the bunk just above our own. Ivar, on the other hand, who had arranged to leave the ship at Cleveland, let fate decide which one of the milling throng was to share his bed for the night. This room was located far forward. Since its passengers did not have access to the afterdeck, we could not console ourselves with the thought that if an explosion occurred, as it sometimes does, we should be as far aft as possible, which is the safest place in such eventualities. Such reflections, occasioned by the recent shipwreck, were none too pleasant as we busied ourselves arranging our luggage and placing our bedclothes in the empty berths.

It was three o'clock in the afternoon when we embarked, and in an hour, we were told, the engine would start. Nevertheless it was not until late in the evening that we got going, and the light from the brightly polished metal mirror on the beacon at the end of the pier had been throwing its rays over Lake Erie for some time when the gangplank was raised. We had sailed, we had used the canalboat, and we were now to try a third mode of travel over the water before reaching the goal of our long journey.

According to schedule, we were to arrive in Cleveland the next morning, where Ivar was to leave us. His plan was to get a job until spring in the neighborhood of Cincinnati, where a few Swedes had settled, and then, if his luck held and he had succeeded in earning a few dollars, to join us again. Since he was the only passenger bound for Cleveland, however, the captain did not think it worth while to put in at this city just on his account; so Ivar, in spite of all his protests, had to continue to the next port of call, Detroit, where he was to get free passage to his destination the next day. This was most arbitrary on the captain's part and contrary to his agreement; for Ivar had already while in New York purchased his ticket to Cleveland and not, like the rest of us, to Chicago. Although he did not lose anything on his transportation, he was given nothing for the extra expense for board made necessary by the additional time spent on the way.

The trip on Lake Erie, during which we enjoyed calm weather and a bright sky, would have been a real pleasure excursion had it not been for the inconvenience of traveling in steerage. On the afterdeck there was plenty of room both to sit and to walk, but from this part of the ship we were barred. I blamed myself for not having bought first-class passage, at least for Lotten, and it seemed hard that she should be kept from the circle to which she really belonged. I felt this all the more as I saw among the elegant "ladies and gentlemen" many who, to judge from the exterior, ought to have been relegated to steerage rather than we. But here no favors were shown to anyone except those able to pay for them. My self-sacrificing wife nevertheless accepted her lot without a trace of jealousy or grumbling, just as happy at my side on the foredeck, among German and Irish laborers, as she would have been seated on the afterdeck among the grand ladies, who in their expensive silk dresses and got up in a somewhat flashy way, seemed rather to be decked out for a dance than for a steamboat trip to the wilds of the West.

How often in later years when we have traveled together on the Great Lakes and mingled in first class with some of the socially highest, have we looked down into the steerage room, and upon the so-called lower folk, remembering our first trip on Lake Erie. Such lessons in life ought to have their usefulness for many others in the same way that they had them for us.

But though we did not have admittance to everything, we were still able to get a general view of the variegated and in many respects interesting life on board the big steamer.

Here we saw proof of a statement for which we later had still more evidence, that Americans are undoubtedly the most mobile and roving people on earth. Even when they are very well off, living in the northern, central, or southern states, they will pull up stakes, sell their possessions, and move west with a resolute courage one would expect only from those pressed by extreme want. Passengers in first class are for the most part either people that have lived for some time in the West, and having acquired wealth are now returning from a business or pleasure trip to the eastern states, or they are capitalists or speculators who are going out to reconnoiter. Probably there is also in the company some bankrupt business man who is now retiring to a new territory with a nest egg kept from his creditors, ready to try his luck again and after a few years become as rich as a nabob in the new neighborhood. Some are planning to purchase a piece of fertile soil and become farmers.[a] They are not yet inured to the hardships of pioneer life, look down with an air of superiority on the rough and patched working clothes of their fellow mortals, and as long as they can, they lead a gentleman's life, keep the silk lining in their coats, the panama hats on their heads, and a chief place in the cabin.

Among the second-class passengers we find all kinds of folk. We ourselves are the only representatives of the Scandinavian peninsula, but the foredeck and lower decks are crowded with Yankees, English, Irish, Germans, etc. They all have their heads full of plans for the future and how to establish themselves in a region of which they have only the slight knowledge to be derived from rather unreliable newspaper propaganda and guidebooks or the even less reliable and highly colored descriptions given by fly-by-night land agents.

We do not spend any more time than necessary in steerage, where it is difficult to make one's way through luggage and children, whose mothers crowd close to the stove or in front of the coal fire to make the necessary toilet changes from time to time. About the fire is a shifting array of washbasins, small frying pans, tin cups, bundles of food, etc. It is quite impossible to detail everything. On the lower deck, outside steerage, the immigrants' luggage is piled in high rows, between which the second-class passengers have a kind of Broadway to promenade in. As we walk a little farther aft, which at this point is permitted, we come to a place that is still more open, just beyond the wheelhouse. Here we have a better opportunity to watch different groups and scenes that in a strange way reveal the national distinctions among those who take part in these modern migrations.

Here is the Yankee with his light equipment — hardly more than the clothes he wears, a small trunk, a blanket, a few pieces of linen, an axe, a saw, and a few small tools. These will be the core of his personal effects in the log house soon to be erected, where his handiness and inventiveness presently will supply him with everything he needs for his first home. There, on the other hand, sit several Englishmen surrounded by their far more substantial equipment; for when John Bull migrates, apparently he not only wishes, like the Trojans, to take all his possessions to the new country, but would take even his well-anchored island if he could only get it loose from its anchorage. Therefore, wherever one sees an old and worn-out bureau, an old-fashioned mirror, or some carefully cherished relics of an old china set, one may be sure that they belong to some honorable Englishman who has crept away to a corner of his own and who concerning all that is taking place around him seems to be saying, "This is no affair of mine." But a person who thinks that everything concerns him and who concerns himself with everything is the Irishman. He, too, has brought with him from the island of his birth a number of things; but instead of being stowed in bureaus and trunks they are generally packed in big bundles that serve as places for his wife and children to lie down on. Somewhere in these bundles one can be certain of finding a spade of the Irish type, its handle three yards in length, and in addition one or two bottles of whiskey.

Strangest of all, however, are the Germans and the equipment they have brought with them from Hamburg. For before they have succeeded in getting this equipment to their cottage in the forest, it will no doubt have cost in transportation five times its value. Here is a wagon that seems better suited to a museum of antiquities than to the modest new settlement and that if it finally reaches its destination is quite likely to end up as a pigsty or chicken coop. Now it is packed full with all sorts of things, evidence of German industry and genius for saving. Plows, horseshoes, spades, harnesses, wooden tubs, chairs, old clocks, candlesticks, old engravings, and broken tobacco pipes — everything lies where it may, but closely guarded by its owner, a small, good-natured, well-built man, dressed in a blue jacket, with a hunting bag over his shoulders. He has probably not the faintest idea of the country where he is going. The American passengers look at him as though he were a recent arrival from another planet. Yet visit him six or eight years later on his well-cultivated farm, and unless he has made his home in one of the settlements where his own countrymen predominate (in which case the remarks already made concerning German immigrants hold good), you will find him completely at home with his new neighbors. He will be an active and useful citizen, whereas the Englishman over there in the corner never will be anything but a stranger in a strange land.

I have often since that day had these impressions of the immigrants who settled in the West confirmed. The German, wise, calculating, and speculative, will accommodate himself to all sorts of conditions, while the Englishman will always, come what may, swear over the Yankees and their Yankee tricks, and feel that the clear, pure air of America never can compare with the coal smoke of England.

Among the passengers I also noticed three Indians, the first of the aboriginal inhabitants of this country I had seen. The romantic notions I had formed about this people from reading Cooper's novels [5] and other descriptions, tumbled down completely before the reality as I now saw it. These belonged to the Chippewa tribe, once very powerful but now reduced to a few hundred families. There was something melancholy and depressed about their entire being, but in their eyes burned a banked fire. They reminded me of a caged eagle dragging its wings, by means of which nevertheless it knows it is capable of rising above the clouds. Their faces, half-wrapped in dirty blankets, were a sealed riddle of what was passing through their minds. But could they without experiencing a depth of agitated feeling move among white men, of whom they saw one band after another coming to take possession of their old hunting grounds and forcing them farther and farther from the graves of their fathers? One cannot without deep sadness meet for the first time the remnants of this people, whose entire known history is one long war of extermination, whose whole past is a wandering in the wilderness, and whose only future is early and complete extinction.

Note

[a] Apropos of farmers, I have heard that word used exclusively of country people and tillers of the soil, no matter what their kind or character — owners of bigger or smaller pieces of land. On the other hand, I have never heard the word peasant used. This word, according to my limited understanding of the language, I had imagined to be the correct one for *bonde*, or the lower class, one might say, of tillers of the soil. To learn the difference between these words I turned to my daily guide and support — my dictionary. I found that *farmer* means sharecropper, tenant, rustic; a *skyfarmer*, on the other hand, is a cheat — one who has his estate in the skies; that is to say, nowhere. A *peasant*, on the other hand, is a rustic, lower than a farmer. I cannot deny that according to these definitions there were no peasants in my environment, many farmers, but still more skyfarmers. Either one or the other of these last terms undoubtedly fitted at least half of the passengers, who declared that they were planning to settle in the new land as farmers.

Chapter 7

DETROIT · TAKING LEAVE OF IVAR · UP THE ST. CLAIR RIVER AND

ACROSS LAKE HURON · THE STATE OF MICHIGAN · NEWPORT

BANKER · PRESQUE ISLE · CARRYING WOOD · AT MACKINAC · A

STORY FROM THE INDIAN WARS · THE INDIANS AND THEIR WORK-

MANSHIP · A BROTHER AT THE FORT · VIEW OF THE LAKE

MEMORIES OF THE MISSIONARY LABORS OF THE JESUITS · LAKE

MICHIGAN · THE GREAT LAKES, THEIR LENGTH, ETC. · BEAVER

ISLAND · A FEMALE ROBINSON · WORSHIP ON BOARD · ALTERED

PLANS · ARRIVAL IN MILWAUKEE · LANDING IN THAT CITY

EARLY in the afternoon of October 1 [1] we arrived in Detroit. As the steamship remained till the next morning, we had plenty of opportunity to survey the well-located and well-built capital of Michigan.

The city is of French origin and was founded at the close of the seventeenth century. From the very beginning it was an important trading post for the Indians and became historically important later through the war of 1812, when the city was captured by the British. The population, which in 1810 was only 700, is now 21,000. Here we saw several attractive church buildings and other structures. We were particularly impressed by the wide streets and avenues, some of them up to 200 feet wide. The city is located on an elevation along the shore of the sound that connects Lakes St. Clair and Erie and that serves as a boundary between the British possessions and the United States. Communication between Detroit and Canada is very lively, and steam ferries constantly pass from one shore to the other. Now that the great Canadian railroad has been completed, most of the travelers between the northwestern and the Atlantic states pass through Detroit, and from there through Canada to Niagara.

Here we took leave of our friend Hagberg, who immediately upon our arrival in Detroit had the opportunity to leave for Cleveland on another steamship. We had not expected that our association of pioneers was to be dissolved so soon. On the sea and in foreign lands friendships are formed that under other conditions would require years to develop. It was with deep emotion that we separated from each other, well knowing that we should, each in his own place, experience many difficulties and hardships before we met again.

The next day [2] we continued our journey from Detroit, up the river bearing the same name, into Lake St. Clair, and from there through the St. Clair River into Lake Huron.

This section of our journey seemed to me the most pleasant of the entire passage from Buffalo. The river, or rather the sound between the United States and Canada, is here so narrow that it is possible to distinguish even small objects on either shore. Neat and pleasant cottages line the shores, surrounded by fruit orchards in the French manner. Small, green islets, with a few little white buildings, lie like bouquets of water lilies floating on the waves. On the Canadian side we see numerous windmills turning their wings over the fertile landscape. Herds of small horses, hardly bigger than our own *Öland* variety,[3] caper about on the meadows. Here and there are small redoubts or military posts. A company of soldiers is just training. A cavalcade of women in neat, trim riding habits canter on swift English horses over the country road following the shore. One can clearly see that on yonder side is the territory of Her Royal British Majesty. There is something of Europe over there, a touch of the gentry and the manor. The neat, varnished picture is complete as it is. On the other side, it is still in process of completion, but gives promise, once done, of being just as artistic, though belonging to different genre, as the former, if not more so. No forts or military outposts suggest that one is at the border of another sovereign power. The industrious frontiersman is busily hammering on an addition to his small home, plowing his soil, and clearing his woodland, quite undisturbed by the redcoats across the sound, while a troop of small citizens scamper off to the newly built schoolhouse to learn to spell the words of the Declaration of Independence.

The state of Michigan is now to the left of us. It consists of two big peninsulas surrounded by five inland lakes, the greatest mass of fresh water on earth. The northern peninsula, bounded to the north by Lake Superior and to the south by Lake Huron, is still sparsely settled, but it contains inexhaustible mineral deposits, especially copper and iron. The southern peninsula, or the real Michigan, around which we now have to travel some 700 miles to reach our destination, is bounded to the east by Lakes Erie, St. Clair, and Huron, as well as by the sounds and rivers connecting these lakes; to the north by the Michilimackinac Sound,[4] and to the west by the 360 miles of Lake Michigan.[a] As soon as we had passed St. Clair Sound and had reached Lake Huron, the Michigan country seemed to be an entirely unpopulated wilderness. The interior northern part of the peninsula is in reality largely unpopulated and consists of impenetrable forests, swamps, and sandy ridges. Only near the shores are there occasional fishing huts and mill structures at the mouths of the rivers, from which timber, lumber, and shingles are transported to the Atlantic states and to the new territories on the other side of Lake Michigan. The greatest part of the land along the shoreline, rich in timber, is unsold, and here timber stealing is carried on on a grand scale, something the authorities now seek to prevent by stern legal measures. Both the eastern and western shores in their natural wild state present many highly picturesque and beautiful scenes. Here a wild, foaming river is bursting forth from the forest; there the eye is attracted to a small level meadow, grazed only by the wild animals of the forest. At this point the coast rises in steep, wavy sand banks, some of which, overgrown with trees and brush, form an even slope down to the shore, while others present a steep, almost perpendicular wall of sand 300 feet above the water. At that point the restless waves, aided by rain-fed rills that have made their way through a dip in the sheer bank, have hollowed out a veritable abyss into which the overhanging mass of earth along with century-old pines and cedars have finally crashed in chaotic upheaval.

In the afternoon we landed at a small city called Newport, the appearance of which suggested that we had finally reached the great West. The city was very big on paper, but in reality consisted of only four wooden houses, on one of which had been painted in gigantic letters the word *Bank*. In the same building were an inn of sorts and the only store in town. A little distance away stood the schoolhouse, which also served as church whenever an itinerant missionary came to visit the place. This was a truly embryonic town. Trees and stumps had been left undisturbed where the streets and squares had been outlined. Here and there a piece of board had been attached to some tree, giving the name of a street which as yet was impassable not only to vehicles but even to pedestrians. There was really no danger of getting lost among the houses, but all the more among the trees and bushes. Yet for all this, who knows but that the town would in a few months have its own print shop, from which the *Newport News* or something similar would be published? Judging by the large city plat they showed us at the inn, the glowing account given us of the town's excellent location, and the assurance that lots were much in demand and that one family after another was settling down there, an early transformation of the community seemed not entirely impossible. The entire city area was owned by the landlord of the inn and the banker. I suspected that the two were one and the same person. The publican volubly demonstrated that it was really no use to go any farther. Here, he maintained, was just the place for us. If we bought lots, which still could be had very cheap, and established a business here or some similar enterprise, we were certain to be rolling in wealth in a few years and should be able, if we wanted to, to "go back to Germany" with abundant capital. These glowing prospects, however, did not attract us, and we decided not to become pioneer citizens of Newport.

To me the idea of establishing a bank in the middle of what one might call a wilderness was something incomprehensible, even though a village or town might grow up in time. It seemed like buying the cradle before the child is born. Yet I have heard of several banking establishments of this kind in towns where the law gives too much freedom and where there is insufficient control to safeguard the public. These are private banks in the original and most comprehensive sense of the word. The prestige and imagined wealth of a single person is the only guarantee of the security of the notes issued, which in reality are nothing but the banker's personal notes with his pledge to redeem them for currency on demand. Under such conditions it is a good plan to locate the bank in distant parts, if possible in the middle of a wilderness, so that the holders of the notes cannot come to exchange their paper money (popularly known as shin plasters) too easily. Of this money they may in the course of a day's business have obtained a small amount, which they never keep on hand but pay out again as soon as they can. Thus it is possible for a person living in Illinois or Wisconsin, where the new bank laws safeguard the notes of banks chartered in these states, to establish a bank in some morass, say in Georgia, print the bills in New York, and circulate them in Illinois. There he may have some kind of office, but if one puts in an appearance to get his bills redeemed, he will be referred to the bank in Georgia. The trip down there would cost a hundred times as much as the amount of the notes in his possession, and the place might not even have a postal address. Thus matters go on for some time. The notes are circulated in good faith, passing from one to another, until finally somebody takes the trouble to collect a bigger amount and make the journey to Georgia, where he has much trouble finding the bank, and still greater reaching its money vault. Very probably the bank in Newport was this type of institution, and its money vault limited to the bar in the taproom of the inn.[b]

The steamship did not stop very long at this place, but continued up Lake Huron along the Michigan coast, which presented the same wild, lonely aspect I have already described.

On October 3,[5] the fifth day after leaving Buffalo, we touched at a small point, Presque Isle, far up on the northern part of the lower peninsula. All the names of islands, rivers, and places are either Indian in origin or mementos of French colonial history. Now they are pronounced entirely according to English rules of pronunciation. Presque Isle is no exception. The place, like the surrounding region, was an almost uninhabited sand bank. On the lonely shore we saw only a couple of small, low huts. The purpose of the stop at this place was to take on wood, which the lonely shore dwellers had cut and piled up in long, high piles along the shore. This constitutes almost the only industry of these people, who are almost completely isolated from the rest of the world. I was unable to see the least attempt at agriculture, and the soil is probably too sandy and dry to produce any crops, at least along the shore. For all that, we were told that these wood choppers, whose product is always in good demand, are soon able to accumulate a small capital. The ground on which they live costs them nothing, nor the trees they chop down, and after a couple of years they are likely to exchange the lonely hut on Lake Huron for a tract of fruitful soil in Wisconsin or Iowa, where, if they invest their money wisely, they may look forward to economic independence for themselves and their children.

I shall always remember Presque Isle as the place where I dedicated my hitherto untrained muscles to hard manual labor. We learned that it was the duty of the steerage passengers to help the members of the crew carry wood on board. A small fee would purchase ransom from this duty. Carl and I felt, however, that we might as well now as later, become used to earning our bread by the sweat of our brow. After we had been asked if we wanted to pay the usual fee to be relieved of the duty of carrying wood for the rest of the trip, we peeled off our coats and attacked the job like the rest of the laborers. We went along, with our wood billets, one on each shoulder, just as steadily as the rest of them, across the long gangplank. After an hour of fine exercise the captain told us to discontinue for this time, and the steamer was off once more.

In the evening we reached Fort Mackinac, a fortress on an island in the sound between the upper and lower peninsulas of Michigan. The fort, on one side enclosed by a tall wooden stockade instead of a parapet, was as insignificant as the small town lying below it at the harbor. This town, the home of a few hundred inhabitants, had been founded by the French about two hundred years ago. Everything, with the exception of some buildings erected recently, appeared antiquated and in bad repair. The houses were small and the streets narrow. The location, however, was altogether attractive and romantic. After doing our duty once again carrying wood, we had the opportunity to make a brief visit to the fort. It was certainly one of the simplest products of the art of fortification, but with its eight cannon it was entirely adequate to its present purpose as a border fortress. It was in reality a fort for defense against the numerous Indian tribes still existing in this region should they ever decide to go on the warpath. Located on a rocky eminence, from which at sundown we had one of the most glorious views I can remember ever seeing, it was one of those places which, as someone has said, seem to breathe religion. As one looks from the crest of this rock over the clear, ocean-like inland lakes which surround it on every side, with their bays and islets, the land looming in the distance, it is impossible not to cry out with a full heart,

How good is God, and how beautiful is his world!

Yet everything was a reminder that we were standing at the edge of civilization, or rather that already we had passed it. A group of Indians were encamped on the slope near the shore, while others could be seen between the islets beyond paddling their canoes made from hollowed-out tree trunks. Over there, according to their traditions, dwelt their mighty Manitous, and there perhaps yet at times the red men gather together in the lonely forests to light as of old their sacred fires while they sing praises to the sun as the symbol of the Great Spirit. That time, however, is now almost past. Near their former sacrificial groves Christian temples have been erected, and the message of atonement is now sounded forth in the regions that once echoed to wild war cries, with which the Indian tribes encouraged each other to inflict the most frightful cruelties upon the white invaders of their tribal land.

The old fort at Mackinac, as well as Presque Isle, which we just mentioned, where also a small fortification had been built in earlier times, was captured by the Indians in 1763, a short time after the French had ceded their American possessions to England. The great Ottawa chief Pontiac, famous in Indian war history, had been able to unite the powerful western Indian tribes in alliance against the English. He declared that their great father, the King of France, had appealed to him to drive the English out of the land, and he strengthened his case by what purported to be a revelation from the Great Spirit, who to the chiefs of some of the Delaware tribes had said: "Why do you permit these dogs in red coats to invade the land that I gave into your possession forever? Drive them away, and I will help you." Frightful raids followed wherever the English had taken possession of the former French border forts.

At that time Mackinac had a garrison of only ninety-five men and, enclosed within its palisades, thirty small houses occupied by as many families. At the time set by Pontiac for the attack, scattered groups of apparently friendly Indians gathered around the fort. Pretending that they were celebrating the birthday of the King of England, they engaged in a great *baggatiwa*, an Indian ball game, in which one team seeks to drive the other to the opposite side of the field. About four hundred Indians were taking part in the game, and many members of the garrison had gone out to watch it. Just when the game was at its height and there seemed to be a fine spirit of happy merriment, the ball, as if by chance, was thrown inside the palisades. A number of Indians representing both sides of the game rushed in, as if vying with each other to get the ball. The unsuspecting garrison did not seek to keep them out. Scarcely had they entered the fort when each Indian bared his tomahawk, till then kept hidden. A terrible massacre followed among the English thus taken by surprise. Most of them were scalped while still alive. Amid a wild dance the Indians continued to slash at their victims. With blood-dripping tomahawks they opened one fresh wound after another, filling their hands with blood as it streamed forth, drinking it with wild cries of triumph. The Frenchmen in the fort were left alive. Not a hair of their heads was touched. Several Canadian colonists watched the massacre without trying to prevent it, or without seeming to be at all affected by it.

Such scenes need not be feared now. The red men may possibly, during their wanderings, attack white colonists here and there, but a general conspiracy against the people that now rule the country need hardly be feared. The Indian tribes that built their wigwams here from time to time, even after the old French possession came under the British throne, in spite of their early enmity toward the English have since become their faithful allies. The independence won by the United States did not change their attitude, and the republican government has not been able either to earn or purchase their friendship. England has sacrificed much to keep it. Till recent times the Chippewas, Ottawas, Potawatamis, and even chiefs of tribes living at a greater distance, have made annual pilgrimages to upper Canada from their own camping grounds within the United States to receive gifts and rewards from the great chief across the ocean. The English are astute in thus keeping them in their pay. This was proved in their war with America when their Indian allies performed deeds in which scenes such as we have described here were not uncommon.

Mackinac was until recently the center of the Indian trade, and even now hundreds of Indians come to this place for the purpose of offering their stock for sale to travelers and to what is left of the former fur companies. This stock consists of all kinds of furs, such as beaver, otter, marten, mink, wildcat, and civet cat; of large quantities of maple sugar and wild rice; and of articles made by the squaws, such as moccasins, small bags, baskets, and various kinds of toys devised from birch bark, everything fashioned very neatly and sometimes quite tastefully ornamented with beads and fine porcupine quills.

Indian women have acquired great skill in producing such articles. Their embroideries are made without patterns, and judging by samples that we examined they can stand comparison, both in choice of color and skill in construction, with many fine tapestries in European gift shops. I really had to exercise much self-restraint to keep from buying some of these articles, to me so unfamiliar. To the passing stranger their greatest value lies in their having been made by members of this strange and lamentable people, of whom perhaps the last remnants were here now walking about, like pale, restless ghosts around the scenes recalling the blood-guilt of their fathers.

These objects attracted our attention more than the insignificant fortifications and cannons in which our American fellow travelers seemed to be especially interested. It appeared to me that they eyed the soldiers and their warlike display with the wonder and admiration of a child watching its first military parade. And understandably enough, for everything pertaining to military life has been so much overshadowed by peaceful works and industrial enterprises in this country that most American citizens are completely unfamiliar with even the most elementary matters related to the art of war.

Both my wife and I would no doubt have paid less attention to the attractive views and to the Indians and more to the soldiers' barracks had we suspected that so close to us, within the walls we passed by with perfect indifference, was a brother whom we had not seen for many years and for whom, in addition to a hearty embrace from ourselves, we had loving greetings from mother, brothers, sisters and friends.[6] My brother-in-law had left for America some years earlier and there enlisted in the army. According to our information before leaving Sweden, we had reason to believe that he had been ordered to Fort Snelling, in Minnesota Territory. From there, however, he had recently been transferred to Fort Mackinac. We were indescribably sorry when we learned of this transfer a few months later, and realized that we had missed an opportunity, not likely to be repeated very soon, of catching a glimpse of a near relative, the only one we had in this far country. Had we shared the curiosity of some of our fellow passengers to view the interior of the fort, it is very likely that we should have found him and at least for a few moments have had the pleasure of a meeting that would have been the greatest joy that could have come to us during our long journey to the West.

The sun had gone down when we set out from shore, but a full moon lighted up the night and revealed even small details in the panorama which opened up before us as we moved out from land: on the shore variegated figures in European and Indian garments; behind them on the hillside the city built in terraces, its small, white, irregular buildings mirrored in fantastic forms in the calm, crystal clear water; on the height, which dominated the entire landscape, the fort illuminated by the bright moonlight; and last the whole shape of the island, in contour a perfect replica of what had given it its original Indian name, Mich-i-li-mack-i-nack — the great turtle.

Farther to the west we saw a point of land known as the Point of St. Ignace, historically notable as the location of one of the earliest colonies of white men in America. On this point Jesuit missionaries as early as 1607 had erected a church and started a school. The only thing that remains of that pious undertaking, which no doubt cost those consecrated men much devoted labor, is the memory of their sacrificial toil, perpetuated only by the name of the place where they sought to plant the cross and establish the Church.

Strange that the history of the Jesuit missions should be the same everywhere! After two or three generations very little is left of them. There is hardly a single example of their real permanence or of their success in taking root. Here as elsewhere the early missionaries displayed an admirable persistance and zeal in their cause — a zeal with which the history of Christendom since the days of the Apostles can present nothing to compare. They were in the real sense of the words "in peril of waters, in peril by the heathen, in peril in the wilderness." They had to make their way through wild, immeasurable forests. They had to cross big, stormy lakes in frail birch canoes, endure hunger and thirst, cold and nakedness — yes, and many of them finally suffered a bloody martyrdom. But even here the results are the same as in China, Japan, and other countries.

Everything is just a beautiful legend, more inspiring to our esthetic than our religious nature. In the course of the centuries the incredible toil of the Jesuits has been like the struggle of one flailing the air. Yet why? If the blood of the martyrs is the seed of the Church, how is it that the saying has not been realized in their case? Is it not perhaps a sign their entire system is wrong? Does not their scant progress, compared to their really powerful and earnest efforts, perhaps prove that the doctrines they preach are too much admixed with fundamental errors operating against the growth and advancement of the kingdom of God?

We now entered Lake Michigan, next to Lake Superior the greatest of these vast inland lakes, connected with each other by navigable rivers and sounds. Few persons who have never traveled on them can rightly imagine their size and expanse. They are truly inland seas, and navigation on these waters is accompanied by as many dangers and unexpected changes as on the Baltic, the Black Sea, or the Mediterranean. Of all the great bounties a good Providence has showered on the American continent there is perhaps none greater than this extensive navigable mass of water in the midst of the country, providing as it does, even for the most remote regions, direct communication with the Atlantic Ocean, and thereby also with Europe and South America. In the innermost heart of the country, where astounding new life streams are flowing forth, the real springs of the mercantile importance of the

United States have their source. To this source also is owing the influence which this country is exerting, and increasingly will exert on the commerce of the world.

Perhaps the following tabulation of the length, width, area, etc. of the Great Lakes may be of some interest:

	Length (in Mi.)	Width (in Mi.)	Area (in Sq. Mi.)	Depth (in Ft.)	Feet above Sea Level
Superior	400	80	32,000	900	596
Michigan	320	70	22,400	1000	578
Huron	240	80	20,400	1000	578
Green Bay	100	20	2,000	1000	578
Erie	240	40	9,600	84	565
Ontario	180	35	6,300	500	232
St. Clair	20	14	360	20	570

Thus we have in this connected chain of lakes an area of not less than 93,060 square miles. It has been estimated that they contain 1,400 cubic miles of water — that is, more than five-sevenths of all the fresh water on the entire globe.

The comparative depth and extensive area of the Great Lakes have occasioned a variety of theories. The bottom of Lake Ontario lies as low as that of St. Lawrence Bay; on the same geological level lies the bottom of Lakes Superior, Michigan, and Huron, notwithstanding the higher level of their surface. From these facts as well as from the fact that the volume of water which runs through the Detroit River plus what is lost through estimated evaporation is incomparably less than the quantity of water which the three upper lakes are estimated to absorb, some scientists have concluded that an underground river must connect Lake Superior with Lake Huron, and Lake Huron with Ontario.c This theory, however, is disputed by others, who are of the opinion that in the evaporation of the water, both in the cold and warm seasons, together with the natural outflow, they can find a natural explanation, without reckoning in an underground river, for the strange fact that the lake bottoms lie at the same level.

Of the origin of the Great Lakes there is an Indian legend to the effect that when the Great Spirit had created the earth and was busy filling it with all kinds of vegetation and animals, he also created gigantic bears. These would not obey the Great Spirit, but longed for the unlimited liberty and free life of the wilderness.

They tore themselves loose from him and ran with a few mighty bounds over to America, where the earth had not yet settled. As they landed they made vast hollows with their feet, and these soon filled with water. The surrounding land became solid and fertile, and the Great Lakes still carry the marks of their origin, in shape resembling great bear tracks.

On our way down Lake Michigan we passed, to the left of us, a group of islands known as Beaver Islands, the greatest of which later became a refuge for a group of Mormons who under the leadership of one of their prophets here sought to create an independent dominion. For a time they constituted a real pirate band, against which the United States government found it necessary to send a couple of warships.[7]

Some years ago one of these islands became the scene of an adventure offering material for a new Robinsoniad, all the more interesting because the leading person in it was a female Crusoe. A young girl living in Detroit or somewhere on the eastern shore of Michigan, one summer paid a visit to a relative in Green Bay, Wisconsin. When she was to return in the fall she got passage on a schooner on which her brother was the commanding officer. She was the only passenger, and consequently the only woman on board. The ship was loaded with hides and lumber. Hardly had they left the harbor before one of the violent storms which sometimes rage across these waters broke loose. The ship was wrecked and tossed on one of those islands. The captain and the entire crew were drowned; only the young woman was miraculously saved. A huge wave tossed her up on the rocky shore. Her strength almost spent, she sought to make her way to some human habitation, but soon learned to her terror that the place was an island, entirely uninhabited, in area only a few acres.

It was already late autumn, and traffic on the lakes had stopped for the year. One day after another passed, but no sail appeared to catch sight of the distress signals she had attached to the branches of the gaunt trees. One of her first sad duties was to dig a grave in the sand and bury two members of the crew whose corpses the waves had tossed up on the rocks and beside whom she thought she herself would soon find her final resting place. She did not, however, give up. The storm abated after a couple of days, and with tremendous effort she managed to save from the wreck some food and, what was to be of just as great value, several bales of buffalo hides. Out of these she made a tent to shelter her from the wintry winds, which at this latitude are exceedingly cold. The small island was densely covered with trees; hence she was not in want of fuel. Among the things she had salvaged from the ship were a few boxes of matches, an axe, and a few other tools. Displaying the courage and inventiveness which characterize the American woman, she labored to shelter and feed herself until Providence should send her aid.

In this way she passed three years on that uninhabited island. Again and again, with dashed hopes, she saw sailing vessels and steamships in the distance, pursuing their course far from the shore of her island, which no boat ever sought out, and from which her cries were drowned out by the roaring waves. Finally, there was an unusually cold winter. The lake froze between her island and the mainland, but since she was uncertain about where her island was located she hesitated to venture out on the ice, which might soon break up. Moreover, the land which she saw in the distance might be just another island where, deprived of everything to sustain her life, she might perish from cold and hunger. While uncertain what to do, she saw one day a few Menominee Indians walking on the ice, seemingly directly toward her island. Without awaiting their arrival she ran out on the ice to meet them. The keen eyes of the Indians soon discovered her. They took her in hand and conducted her to the mainland, through the uninhabited regions of northern Michigan, through vast and desolate forests in which it was possible only for the red man to find his way, and to Fort Mackinac. The following spring she was returned to her loved ones, who had long mourned her as dead.

To the same romantic story belongs also the fact that the young woman was engaged to be married. But alas, it is seldom the masculine, but more frequently the feminine loving heart, that in such times of testing can sing with the maiden in the old Swedish ballad:

> Three long years will I wait for thee,
>   But if thou comest not to me,
>   Then I still shall waiting be
>   'Mid the roses.

The young lover had married another. Three long years, with his picture in her heart, she had fought bravely against toil and privations. Now she was saved from the shipwreck only to suffer another tragedy, "deceived in her dream of life."

October 4, Sunday.[8] A number of written notices put up in various places on board, informed the passengers that divine service was to be conducted in the big saloon on the afterdeck. On such occasions even the steerage passengers were admitted. Despite the fact that we had not acquired enough knowledge of the language to expect much edification from a sermon in English, we did not hesitate to take our places in the room, which was filled to overflowing.

As to the minister, I do not know of what denomination he was. There was nothing in his dress to suggest his profession, unless it might have been his white necktie, which, I have been informed, is used exclusively by clergymen. The service began with a hymn, which was taken up by a woman. Most of the members of the congregation must have known it by heart, since only two or three persons had books in their hands. Everybody stood up during the singing and remained in that position while the minister, at the conclusion of the song, gave a long extemporaneous prayer. Afterwards he read a chapter from the Bible, taking a part of it as the text for his sermon, of which, of course, we understood very little. However, we realized that it was a testimony of Him, whom all tongues shall confess. Little though we were able to understand of this service, our first in America, it was still a season of devotion for our hearts. He to whom no language is foreign undoubtedly listened to our prayers for relatives, distant from us in space, but at that very moment close to us in their Sabbath meditations.

Many are inclined to criticize religious practices in America, and especially what is regarded as the extreme stiffness and formalism of the American Sunday. This has been held to be, like so many other things, an evidence of national hypocrisy. God alone knows and is able to judge the inward man; we can judge only from externals. Perhaps Sunday in this country is generally kept too strictly and with a severity which in some respects may go too far. But the American Sunday really bears the stamp of what it is meant to be, the Lord's Day, and not a day dedicated to amusements and worldly pleasures. One can hardly pronounce judgment on the way the day is observed without at the same time rejecting it as a day of rest and as a divine institution. Reject the observance of Sunday and you reject both the day of rest and its sacred significance. That simple service on board the American steamship made me consider whether we in Sweden should not profit by becoming a little more puritanical than we usually are in the matter of keeping the Lord's Day. If I were to compare that service with the customary observance of Sunday on our Swedish steamboats on their Sunday-forenoon pleasure jaunts, I must confess that the manner and the spirit prevailing in this country, where a religious service always has a part in Sabbath plans, are far better than the habits, customs, and attitudes that sanctify Sunday only as a day of pleasure.

It is customary on all longer steamship journeys in America, when there is a minister on board, to have him conduct services even if he has not been requested by the passengers to do so. It happens also rather frequently that he conducts evening devotions in one of the saloons before the passengers go to bed. Even if some of the passengers find this an unwelcome interruption of the pastimes for which such trips present an opportunity, they submit to it without objection. Even if many take part in the service only as a matter of form, the impression cannot be anything but wholesome. Even those who are inclined to scoff at sacred things make at least a show of reverence, which they can hardly withhold without placing their good breeding in question. As a rule no disrespect is shown religion in America even though many may not in their hearts feel inclined to make much of sacred things. And ministers are treated in the same way. As a rule they meet with respect and consideration even from those who regularly pay little attention to the church or the doctrines for which it stands. It is generally the minister's own fault if proper respect is not shown him or if someone in his presence is guilty of an action or speaks a word of which he because of his profession must disapprove.

Sometimes, though seldom, there are exceptions to this rule. Then public opinion is quick to react, and frequently in a way one would hardly expect in this free country which has been so harshly judged for its flagrant self-indulgence. I recall an occurrence a few years later on a Mississippi River steamer.

The old and venerable Bishop C[hase],[9] who was making visitations in his diocese, was for a couple of days a passenger on one of those floating palaces which ply between the shores where yesterday were only scattered settlements and here and there the wigwams of the red men. A few hundred passengers were on board with him. One evening the bishop wanted to conduct a devotional hour in one of the cabins and invited the passengers to take part in it. By some mischance it was darker than usual in the cabin, which normally was brightly lighted. The old man had taken a place at the end of a table and asked that a lamp standing at the other end be moved a little closer to him. One of the passengers complied with his request, thereby depriving some card players sitting far off in the end of the saloon of the light by which they had been carrying on their play. The rest of the passengers took for granted that the card game would now cease. The players, however, were not pleased. Hardly had the bishop begun to read a chapter from the Bible, which, by the way, is found in all steamboat cabins, than one of the card players came over and moved the lamp back to its former place. The simple service was finished amid complete silence.

The bishop went to bed without a word of criticism of this discourteous behavior. Nor for the moment did it bring any expostulation from any of the rest of the passengers or cause any disturbance, though a feeling of protest was general. But it was decided to inform the captain, who had been unable, because of his duties, to take part in the evening devotions. A little while later the steamboat stopped at a lonely, sparsely settled river village where it did not generally make a stop and where there were neither passengers nor freight to unload or take on. The captain sought out the gamblers and informed them that the honor of the American flag made it his unpleasant duty to escort them across the gangplank. He refunded them the money they had paid for their fare and asked them on behalf of himself and the rest of the passengers to be kind enough to hie themselves off. Their protests were of no avail. His word was law and had to be obeyed. Had the captain acted otherwise it is certain that his boat would have got a bad name — even worse than if one after another of its boilers had exploded. The opinion which expresses itself on such occasions as this and in such a way, testifies at least to an external regard for religion and morality in a country which many have unjustly sought to disparage in this as in many other respects.

It was reported that we were about to arrive in Milwaukee, a city in Wisconsin, one of the new territories of the United States. In New York we had heard of neither one nor the other. But during our trip through the canal we had met several, both Americans and Europeans, who had spoken of Wisconsin as one of the most attractive and fertile districts in the great West, and under present conditions the most favorable to immigrants. On the lake steamer we had heard similar reports, and most of the other immigrants were preparing to disembark in Milwaukee that evening. We really had no good reason for continuing to Illinois, where most of the land, according to reports, already had got into the hands of individual speculators. Besides, we were tired of traveling and were anxious as soon as possible to exchange our place in steerage for a plain log house. One state, we felt, was probably as good as another. We really knew as much or as little of Illinois as of Wisconsin. Perhaps it might be just as well for us to look around in this region since everybody seemed to be going there and since, besides, it was right on our way. So after some consultation with each other we made our decision and notified the captain that we too wanted to leave the ship in Milwaukee.

Thus in a single moment, or by what men unjustly call fate, may our entire future life be determined. It is quite likely that had we followed our original plan and gone on to Chicago, my future course would have been entirely different from the one toward which Providence in a remarkable way was now directing me.

At ten o'clock in the evening we cast anchor in the roadstead off Milwaukee, where the captain planned to remain no longer than was necessary to disembark passengers. A small steamer came out from the city to pick up them and their luggage. We were prepared once more to pay a heavy charge for overweight, but there was such a hurry that no one took any notice whether one chest more or less was transferred to the freight boat lying by. In order that no one might determine how much we carried with us, we moved our own boxes and trunks. To be sure, the ship's clerk called to us for his dollars, but we were in more of a hurry with our baggage than with paying. We thought ourselves perfectly justified in seeking to escape this extra fee since we had already paid much more than we were supposed to by our agreement with the transportation company.

With much labor we had just managed to get our baggage from the steamboat when the captain, who in the meantime had weighed anchor, called out, "All leave that are leaving!" At the same moment the engine was started. But where was Lotten? She had remained on deck as long as possible to see that nothing was overlooked. The gangplank between the two boats had already been pulled in, the wheels had begun to turn, and I had thought I had everything on board the freight boat when a well-known voice called me by name and I found that the most precious thing I possessed was still on the high deck of the other steamboat. If all my trunks and boxes had been filled with gold, this price would still have been too dear a one for the overweight I'd gained. Was I to be punished for not being too scrupulously honest in paying these new charges by having to leave her, alone and forsaken, to continue her journey to Chicago? But there was little time to consider the matter. In my despair I called out in Swedish, English, German, and God knows what else, whereupon a merciful member of the crew put his arms around her waist and practically threw her from one rocking boat into my arms on the other. Another moment and it had been too late.

The waves were rolling high, and we were happy not to be far from shore. The water splashed over the deck of the unpleasant little freight boat, which had no railings. There was no way of sitting down or holding on to anything. The passengers stood tightly packed together, balancing themselves, as the small boat kept rolling from one side to the other. This passage seemed to me to be the most adventurous part of the entire journey. It was a miracle that neither passengers nor luggage tumbled overboard. Finally, wet and weary, we came to the mouth of the Milwaukee River, and in an hour we were ashore. It was now two o'clock in the morning, but by good luck we managed to get our possessions stored in a warehouse. We ourselves went to a hotel.[10] It was at that time the best in Milwaukee, a four-story wooden building, in which we got a couple of pleasant rooms with clean, comfortable beds, where we enjoyed a rest such as our tired bodies had not had since we had left New York more than two weeks before.

Notes

[a] Now that several railroads have been completed, connecting the western and the eastern states, the traveler does not have to take the roundabout way we were compelled to travel.

[b] It may be added that the city as well as its bank probably now belongs to the things that have been, or perhaps rather, that never came into being. I have not again visited the place or ever thought of asking about it. Possibly the town to which such bright hopes were attached changed its name, or it may, along with its former bank building, be only an unnoticed monument to an unsuccessful speculation. In the latest list of cities in Michigan the name Newport is missing, and in the commercial life its bank has, as far as I have been able to ascertain, been completely forgotten.[11]

[c] John MacGregor, *British America* (2 vols., Edinburgh and London, 1832); cited by Samuel Strickland in his *Twenty-seven Years in Canada West; or The Experience of an Early Settler* (ed. Agnes Strickland, London, 1853).

THE FIRST MORNING IN MILWAUKEE · MEETING A SWEDE · A MILWAUKEE HOTEL · VISITING THE LAND OFFICE · LAUNDRY WORK IN AMERICA · PUBLIC SAFETY PROTECTED BY THE LYNCH LAW · BRIEF DESCRIPTION OF WISCONSIN TERRITORY · ITS LOCATION, RESOURCES, ETC. · ANTIQUITIES · THE HISTORY OF THE COUNTRY

W E HOPED now that we were close to the goal of our journey and that we should at least have no further need of either canal- or steamboats. Gladly we greeted the day when, following our plan, Carl and I were at last to go out reconnoitering to find a suitable location in this sparsely settled region for our future home. We were just conferring with each other about this matter when a young, good-looking waitress in the hotel, listening to our conversation, which we did not imagine she could understand a word of, cried out to our unspeakable joy and surprise: "De ere da saa Gud svenske folk!" [Well, I declare, if you are not Swedes!] Never has the Norwegian language sounded sweeter to my ears, never so much like a message from home. She informed us that several Norwegian families had already settled in the neighborhood and that one of our own compatriots, a Mr. Lange,[1] was just then staying at the same hotel as we were.

If meeting with one of our countrymen ever was welcome, it was now when we were so much in need of advice and guidance. Fortunately Lange was in a position to give us the help we needed. Having lived several years in America, he was fully familiar not only with the language of the country but also with its customs and conditions. For several years he had not encountered any of his countrymen, and our happiness at meeting was mutual. He verified the information we had picked up about Wisconsin during our journey and did not believe we should have to go far to find extensive tracts of both good and beautiful land to choose from.

Our conversation was interrupted by a din in the corridor loud enough to wake the dead. We thought the wild hunt in *Friskytten* [2] was taking place at our door. It was the same terrific alarm that an hour earlier had waked us from our sweet slumber and now was being repeated — a highly disharmonious music as from a hundred drums and copper kettles. Lange explained to us that it was a gong, a copper instrument somewhat like a tambourine, beaten with a club to wake up the guests — I should like to see the guest that it would not awaken! — and to announce that meals were being served. This time it was the call to breakfast.

In the big dining room we found three long tables set for more than a hundred persons. Nor did it take long for all the places to be filled, the ladies, as is customary in this country, occupying the places of honor, with their gentlemen partners if they had any. Here as in all other American hotels, the meals were served table d'hôte. Except for the coffee, which seldom, either in hotels or in private homes, is prepared as in Sweden, the meal was excellent. There was certainly nothing here to suggest that I had arrived in the wilds of western America. I had imagined something entirely different. Milwaukee, I had thought, was now to western America what Buffalo used to be at the time when the Hauswolff descriptions were written: a city just a few years old, built up in the wilderness, a community of some 2,000 inhabitants, farther separated from the civilized world than were those who lived in Buffalo in those days. I had imagined "houses and huts without arrangement"; an inn "with a big log in the middle, one end sticking out the door, and the other burning in the fireplace." For breakfast I had believed nothing would be served except "cold, smoked, or salted food," with which I should personally have been completely satisfied. Instead we were now in a hotel which, though not elegant, was roomy and well kept. We had rested in a couple of well-furnished bedrooms, and now were sitting at a breakfast table where in addition to the smoked ham with eggs and the cold salted meat, we were also served very tender and well-done beefsteaks, not to mention exceptionally good butter and fresh white bread. I was also to find out very soon how the little city of Milwaukee in almost every other respect too refuted the exaggerated descriptions which ill will toward America and its institutions had given us concerning life and manners in this country.

After breakfast Lange conducted us into a large reception room where he introduced my wife to several women, explaining that she was the first Swedish woman to set foot on the western shores of the Great Lakes. In the room was a pianoforte, on which lay a number of musical compositions by some of the modern masters of music, and on the center-table were the works of Byron, Thomas Moore, Longfellow, and other authors, as well as a copy of Cervantes translated into English.

The usual American curiosity, quite the regular thing in the West, was not lacking here. This curiosity, natural in a country so sparsely populated, makes people interested in the lineage and whole life history of every newly arrived family or individual. We were made the center of a number of questions, most of which we left to our new friend Lange to answer as he thought best. Most of those present had probably never before seen a Swede in his natural state, if I may use that expression, since Lange was completely Americanized. They regarded us therefore as real curiosities, examined our clothes with extreme care, and listened to our conversation as to the most wonderful sounds that had ever reached their ears. A few of them had already seen some of the Norwegian country folk that had settled in that section and whose strange clothing and customs had naturally enough attracted their attention. They had imagined that all of us Scandinavians must be Saeterdalians [3] or Vossingers, [4] and they could not understand why Lotten came dressed differently from a Norwegian saeter-maid. [5] According to what we heard later, the women came to the conclusion that my wife's hat and dress must have been bought in New York, of which they tried further to assure themselves by subjecting our Norwegian hotel maid to a close questioning. We soon learned, however, that they were not all equally ignorant of life and conditions in our beloved Sweden. Many of them had read Longfellow's translation of Tegnér's *Nattvardsbarnen*, [6] and, something that caused a still greater stir in certain circles, Mary Howitt's recent translation of some of Fredrika Bremer's *Teckningar ur vardagslifvet.*[7] The latter was one of the standing subjects of conversation when and wherever one of us had the pleasure of being presented to some of the better-educated ladies and gentlemen of Milwaukee.

We soon realized, however, that some of us, at least, should have to remain several days in Milwaukee, and a continued stay at the hotel would mean living according rather to our class than to our cash. We therefore rented from a German a couple of rooms where we could prepare our own food, and moved immediately into our temporary home. To this place we also transported our chests and trunks, whose contents really needed both airing and washing, a task which Lotten and Christine immediately prepared to undertake.

Accompanied by Lange, Carl and I went to the Land Office to get information about which way to go on our exploratory expedition. We were asked what kind of land we wanted: prairie, timberland, or so-called oak openings.[8] They pulled out maps of counties and sections, exclaimed over the excellent soil in this place or that, and the result of it all was that one of the clerks gave me a letter of introduction to a settler living some thirty miles west of the city. In that neighborhood there was much attractive land still unoccupied, and he was certain the man in question would be glad to serve as our guide.

We could not start off on our expedition at once, however. We had left Uppsala the eleventh of May, and since that time had been traveling constantly. We certainly needed a general unpacking and, as already remarked, a complete clothes washing, for which Carl and I were needed to carry water, chop wood, and otherwise make ourselves useful.

The laundering process here is quite different from that in vogue in Sweden. Here the washing is not done at the lake or river but always in the house, where it is generally a Monday chore. The great linen supplies of Swedish households are entirely unknown here. Even well-to-do families have hardly more than is needed for their daily use, and every Monday they wash what has been used the preceding week. When a piece of linen is worn out, it is replaced by a new piece. Many have been astounded when we described to them the immense linen closets considered necessary in so-called well-equipped houses in our homeland. They really cannot understand why such a considerable capital should be tied up lying idle; and still less can they see any practical or sanitary excuse for hiding away soiled clothes for six or even twelve months.

The woman-killing work on the laundry-piers in Sweden, where the poor women even in the cold season are as good as prostrate over the water, is here something unheard of. All such things are done in the kitchen, unless a special room has been provided for the purpose. Instead of the rubbing and pounding in Sweden, in this country a small washboard is used, made either out of wood or zinc, with horizontal grooves or corrugations against which the clothes are rubbed. At the same time the clothes are rinsed in the tub, on the bottom of which stands one end of the washboard while the woman doing the washing leans against the other. My wife and Christine, the latter of whom because of her years of experience ought to be a good authority on such matters, declared that the method is much better than ours and less hard on the clothes. Furthermore, the work is easier and the clothes get just as clean and white, this being the only point on which I can regard myself as competent to testify. The only thing we found it hard to accustom ourselves to, at least at first, was the absence of a mangle. Everything, sheets and towels as well as collars and handkerchiefs, had to be ironed. Where the washing is a weekly event, the ironing can no doubt be done without much trouble, but in our situation just now the women would have been glad to order Carl and me to man either side of a Swedish mangle.

These household affairs really created quite a stir in the neighborhood, where it came to be generally believed that we had brought with us from Sweden a linen supply sufficient for coming generations in the new settlement. I cannot forbear mentioning at the same time that the clothes were hung out for drying in an open yard close to the street, where they remained both night and day without a thread being missing. I do not say this as evidence that property rights are always respected in America. Indeed it is not my purpose to depict this country as if it were any more than any other a land peopled by angels. The fact is but an indication that in new and embryonic communities, where one might expect a great deal of lawlessness to prevail, truly there is greater security of both person and property than in the so-called better ordered and more civilized. Thefts and robberies are rare, and if they do occur every member of the new community becomes a self-constituted secret police officer. To say that the criminal will be caught is generally quite safe, and Judge Lynch [9] is a relentless and stern dispenser of the law.

In this connection, I recall the story of the man shipwrecked on a strange coast who, when he saw a criminal dangling on the gallows, cried out, "Thank God, I have come to a civilized country!" In these new settlements and cities founded yesterday, there will certainly be much to remind the observer that the country he has come to is not a place pre-empted by intellectual refinement and the civilized arts. But he can also count upon the absence of such criteria of civilization as this anecdote might suggest. A person may say what he will about the lynch law — I am far from inclined to recommend it in our ordered and lawfully established societies — but certain it is that in these new communities it has often proved both practical and just, and that under the conditions obtaining there, it is better adapted than any other law to maintain order and prevent crime.

Lange promised that if we waited a couple of days he would accompany Carl and me on our excursion into the country. That proved another good reason for postponing our trip. We busied ourselves in the meantime in various ways. First, we helped the women with the laundering already mentioned; then we undertook to clean our guns, which had got very rusty during our long sea journey. We found time to begin also, at least on paper, to familiarize ourselves with the land in which we were now going to settle down.

As is well known, the extensive territory which constitutes the northern and western part of the North American continent is made up of two vast basins, named for two great rivers, the St. Lawrence and the Mississippi. The St. Lawrence basin embraces the five great western lakes, which together with a part of the St. Lawrence River constitute a big part of the northern boundary of the United States. The Mississippi Valley, on the other hand, comprises that part of the United States located between the Alleghenies and the Chippewa, or Rocky, Mountains, all the rivers of which join the Mississippi and empty into the Gulf of Mexico. Part of this immense territory is Wisconsin, which is located north of Illinois. It is bounded on the east by Lake Michigan; on the northeast by the Montreal and Menominee rivers, which serve as a boundary between this territory and the northern peninsula of Michigan; on the north by Lake Superior, where it abuts on the British possessions; and on the west by that part of the St. Croix and Mississippi rivers forming the eastern boundaries of Minnesota and Iowa. Thus Wisconsin is located between 42°30' and 47°10' N. Lat. and 87° and 92°25' W. Long. The greatest length of the territory from north to south is 285 miles; from east to west 250 miles. It has been estimated that it comprises an area of 53,924 square miles,[10] or 34,511,360 acres.[a] The population, which ten years ago scarcely exceeded 3,000 white persons, is now estimated at 45,000, which does not seem an unlikely figure inasmuch as immigration to these parts has been very steady, especially during the last two years, although a great many immigrants also go to Iowa and neighboring states, where vast tracts of land are still unoccupied and untilled.

Like all the rest of the western states and territories, Wisconsin is constantly increasing in importance. It is growing more and more interesting not only to European immigrants and native Americans, who are constantly moving in with their heads full of extensive speculations and industrial undertakings, but also to communities of the old world, on which these new commonwealths, both for historical and mercantile reasons, will necessarily soon come to exert a wide influence. The natural resources of the country are being developed with astounding speed. Here as elsewhere cities are springing up as by magic; agriculture, business, even manufacturing are beginning to flourish. As for literature, science, and the fine arts — well, what can one expect from a country which only a few years ago was populated exclusively by wild Indian tribes? The newly cultivated or uncultivated land is more in need of a man accustomed to axe and plow than to one whose entire life has been spent in moving between the desk and the lecture platform. And yet, almost simultaneously with the new settlements, lower and higher institutions of learning are being established. Hardly has a city got a couple of thousand inhabitants before it has its academy, its literary societies, its historical and scientific organizations. Before the streets have been leveled, printing shops are established, and periodicals, religious, political, commercial, agricultural, and literary in content, are scattered in all directions throughout the new territory. Hardly a backwoodsman does not subscribe to a paper and so, at least to some degree, keep abreast of his time and inform himself of the most important questions and events of the day.

Wisconsin is mostly level country. There are no real mountains, although the great, wide plains are broken in some places by high, though generally arable, hills. These, especially in the prairie sections, give to the country a wavelike appearance, sometimes extending for miles. The altitude of this region varies from 600 to 1,500 feet above sea level. The country is most rugged near Lake Superior and north of the Wisconsin River, one of the tributaries of the Mississippi. From there in a northerly direction there is a range of hills that makes the terrain very uneven and rough. But it also forms a number of dells watered by tumbling, foaming rivers. These with their rapids and falls give the country an appearance that, though it is somewhat wild, is romantic in the highest degree.

In addition to the great world-renowned lakes to the north and east, Wisconsin has a multitude of smaller lakes which drain the interior of the territory. Some of these are twenty to thirty miles in length. They are often rather deep, and generally dotted with bigger or smaller islands which in varying groups point their wooded promontories toward the shores of the mainland. The water in these lakes is of a crystalline clarity and purity and except during the hot summer season is excellent drinking water. They abound in fish. Where the shores are not muddy the water's edge is marked by layers of all kinds of pebbles, many of them strange in shape and coloration, among which may often be found agates, carnelians, jasper, and other rarer stones. In the bays, where the water is shallow and is not too much disturbed by the wind, there is an abundance of wild rice (*Zizania aquatica*), which constitutes one of the staple foods of the Indian tribes that still roam these forests.[b] In taste and other characteristics this rice has some resemblance to oatmeal.

Besides the Mississippi, Father of Waters, which, as has already been said, serves along with its tributary the St. Croix as the western border of Wisconsin, the country is crossed by numerous rivers, larger or smaller, so that there is no part of the territory not enriched by some watercourse. The Mississippi is navigable all the way up to St. Anthony Falls, 1,944 miles from its mouth. Of other rivers only a couple are navigable, but all are very useful to the country, offering excellent opportunities for establishing mills and manufacturing plants.

Like the rest of the western states, Wisconsin retains many souvenirs of a time when North America was populated by a people entirely different from the Indians of the present day. Of this people, however, nothing is known except what little can be learned from these relics of antiquity. In several places in these regions walls as of ancient buildings have been discovered, sometimes entirely hidden in the ground, but in some instances also above ground, made from irregular bricks, in which one can find traces that straw was mixed with the clay. From this the conclusion has been drawn that these people must have belonged to a race possessing a higher degree of culture than the modern Indian. These relics have been found especially in the Rock River Valley, where, it is even thought, can be discovered vestiges of an old city. This once gave rise to the suggestion that the old Mexican Indians originally lived in this region. To this place and a small town that has been built near the old ruins, the name of Aztalan has been given, in the belief that it is the same mentioned in the old traditions of the Aztecs which hint that their forefathers came from a country far to the north, a land near some great lakes.

Later investigations, however, do not support this view. Instead, research into the language, customs, and psychological peculiarities of the natives who inhabited Wisconsin when the land was first taken up by the whites, points to the conclusion that these Indian tribes, who still range this part of the country and who differ in many notable ways from those in nearby regions, have their origin in what is now New Mexico. This view is supported by the fact that among all the many antiquities in which this territory is so rich, the old walls of Aztalan are the only remnants hitherto found having circular brick walls, such as the aboriginal inhabitants of the country were accustomed to build about their altars and other sacred spots. Such circular walls are frequently found in other western states. Here the one just named is unique of its kind, though in several other places one comes upon other stone constructions from a past age and a vanished people — probably in some cases fortifications, in others walls surrounding their burial grounds.

In addition, we find in Wisconsin a number of mounds consisting either of earthen walls, frequently of strange shape, or of round, cone-shaped hills resembling our old sepulchral mounds. These also are of several kinds. Some of them have undoubtedly served as fortifications, others as a kind of fence around old places of sacrifice and temple groves. The cone-shaped mounds frequently, though not always, are, like our own sepulchral mounds, memorials erected over the bodies of dead warriors. Excavations have revealed that some of these contain only a single skeleton while others are composed almost entirely of human bones. The mounds within the earthen walls that were enclosures around holy places have been found to contain sacrificial altar relics. Others, also within such earthworks, have contained a variety of potteries, adorned with figures; weapons, also ornamented, made from both stone and metals; and in addition, according to some statements, a sort of coin — all suggesting a people of Asiatic origin. Generally these earthen walls and mounds are found on the shores of some river or lake, and diminish as a rule in size with the distance from such watercourses. Some of them are overgrown with trees which, if the original vegetation, prove that the mounds are about six hundred years old. But many believe that the present generation of trees is a second growth and place the time of construction of these mounds at least twelve hundred years ago.

The strangest of all these antiquities that have given rise to so many different and doubtful theories regarding the pre-Columbian and indigenous population of this country, is a kind of earthen wall that has been found nowhere on the American continent except in Wisconsin. They are evidently of an emblematic character, in shape depicting different kinds of animals, and, according to the views of many students, also describing certain historic events.

Generally they are scattered about, apparently without arrangement, but sometimes they occur with their animal pictures in long, irregular rows as if arrayed in marching order. In the neighborhood of Madison, capital city of Wisconsin, hundreds of earthen walls may be seen, thrown up in various forms and dimensions, some of them round or oblong, some in the shape of an animal.

The erudite archaeologist Schoolcraft[11] regards all these earthworks as nothing more than monuments made by the same race as our present-day Indians. Their chiefs and heroes are frequently named for some animal, such as the fox, the bear, the eagle, or the turtle; a picture of these animals becomes an heraldic emblem or armorial bearing within the family, and the progeny retain it for generations as a sign of their heredity. These signs or animal depictions are also a kind of trademark, in the Indian languages called a totem. A tribe, according to Schoolcraft, could not erect a more durable memorial over an honored and illustrious sachem than one of these emblematic earthen walls and mounds. According to him, they are undoubtedly gigantic graves and have as their only purpose the preservation of the name of some outstanding historical personage.

On the other hand, other excellent scientists, lately engaged in research to shed light, if possible, on the darkness enveloping America's past, have sought to prove that these remarkable earthworks, which occur almost everywhere in Wisconsin, do not always have a sepulchral significance, a theory which recent excavations seem to prove. If these earthworks, they contend, can be ascribed only to the already mentioned custom on the part of the present-day Indian race, how then explain that they occur only in a very limited area and are not to be found everywhere where the totemic system prevails? Owing to this fact, as well as to their antiquity and other considerations, these scholars have come to the conclusion, which actually does not lack probability, that these earthen walls, mounds, and hills, in form evidently resembling certain creatures such as birds, lizards, fish, and all kinds of crawling and four-footed things, constitute a type of hieroglyphic writing which, if we could only find the key to it, would shed much light on the history of the people that formerly lived in these regions. If this theory is correct, it must also be admitted that such a symbolic chronicle, on such a vast scale, closely written on a slate no less than 53,924 square miles in size, is a phenomenon without a parallel in the monumental history of any country.[d]

Among the memorials from ancient times which have been found in Wisconsin are included also the so-called "garden beds," which in our day are regarded as a great curiosity and which in form and construction are quite unlike the examples generally found of Indian agriculture. Everywhere in the United States, where climate and soil have been favorable, the Indians have raised corn, tobacco, and a few other plants, but these cultivated plots have always exhibited a certain carelessness and irregularity in the layout. The "garden beds," on the other hand, are laid out with all the neatness and symmetry that characterize the agriculture of a later age and a far more advanced civilization. They cover great areas on the prairies, where they sometimes cross the circular walls and the symbolic earthen mounds mentioned above; they represent therefore a later period.

Another matter of antiquarian interest is connected with that part of the country located near Lake Superior. The rich copper mines which the white people only recently have begun to work are said to have been known and worked in a far distant past by the aborigines. In the topographical and geological investigations which have been made, traces of such work have been discovered. Men have come upon solid pieces of metal from which smaller pieces have been cut with some heavy instrument. Likewise in the veins of ore themselves great excavations may be met with, which must have cost the Indians incredible labor, considering the imperfect tools used. Masses of such tools have been found now and then lying about the mines. Schoolcraft suggests that these mines may have supplied all the Indians north of the Gulf of Mexico with copper, that this region had been made a sacred and neutral district, and that distant tribes were permitted at given times to send their representatives to get supplies of metal sufficient for their requirements.

Although one of the youngest of the states, Wisconsin is from the point of view of history one of the oldest in the Union. Before the Pilgrims landed at Plymouth Rock, French missionaries had made their way to the Great Lakes, and before Boston was founded they had established missions near Lake Michigan. In 1654 two young traders walked through this country and spent two years among the Indian tribes. The stories they told on their return to Canada induced the Fur Company to extend its business activities into the region. The first European settlement in Wisconsin was made in 1665, when the Jesuit Claude Allouez [12] established a mission on the shores of Lake Superior. After this several people, missionaries as well as laymen, undertook to penetrate the region. The most remarkable of them all was the historically famous, honored, and pious Father Marquette, [13] the first European to reach the Mississippi River. It was not an ambitious hope of founding great cities on the shore of the mighty river that took him upon his venturesome and perilous journey, about which history has written some of its most glorious chapters in the annals of American discoveries. Nor was it the greedy hope of unearthing some of those rich gold mines which many expected to find in the faraway western land. No, it was rather a pious wish to proclaim the gospel of Christ to the children of the wilderness, who up to that time had been dwelling in darkness and the shadow of death.

A few years after Marquette, the no less famed LaSalle, [14] with a few companions, undertook to explore these regions. They finally proceeded as far as the mouth of the Mississippi. From that time on the number of French settlements in Wisconsin increased. It was only the profitable fur trade that made the French living in Canada migrate to this country. Then, as in later years, the French showed themselves of all Europeans the ones that best understood the art of living on friendly terms with the red men. Unlike the British and other nationalities, they have seldom, if ever, had cause to fear the bloody tomahawk. [e]

Wisconsin constituted a part of New France until 1763, when it was ceded to the British Crown, under which it remained, like the entire Northwest, until 1794, when it became part of the American republic. For thirty-one years the condition of the country remained what it had always been. The Indians continued without interference to hunt the deer, set traps for the beaver, and barter their furs in Mackinac and Green Bay for the white traders' baubles or firewater.

Until 1832 the country was hardly more than a habitat for the red men. Only in a few places had Europeans established trading posts, which generally were also small forts. The small log houses, each occupying a space of not more than one or two hundred square feet, were built in rows close to each other and surrounded by palisades. The windows faced inward and the roofs slanted toward the inside. Within this small space the trader or his agent had his storehouse, his shop, and often his own family and the families of his employees. They were never secure against attack by the Indians, and were always prepared to defend themselves bravely within the fortification. The gates were carefully closed, not only at night but also after firewater had been sold to the natives, who were getting a more and more pronounced taste for it. Outside the palisades a few acres of land were generally planted with potatoes and other vegetables, and if relations with the Indians were friendly, these fields were gradually expanded. Other settlers began to make their homes in the country, always in such a way, however, that they could find shelter and protection inside the fortifications of the trading post in case of trouble. Sometimes several families settled in one place, fortified themselves in the same way as the traders, and tilled their soil, their loaded guns resting across the plow, ready for use at the first sign of danger. The stories of these early settlements and the adventurous lives of the early pioneers are in the highest degree rich and exciting. One scarcely knows what to marvel at more, the bravery and boldness of the hardy pioneers or the insatiable greed that always, at least to some extent, lay at the bottom of these perilous ventures.

After 1832 the whites began to take possession of the country more and more. The United States Government succeeded in quieting the disturbances that occasionally arose with the Indian tribes, most of whom had now withdrawn to other hunting grounds. Only a few tribes either had not as yet left the land they had ceded to the Government or ranged annually, on their hunting expeditions, the country still sparsely settled by the whites. Nowadays one hears more rarely of any violence committed, either by the one side or the other.

In the interior, near beautiful Lake Winnebago, are a couple of Indian tribes that have secured all the rights and privileges accorded to United States citizens — the first and so far the only example of its kind. At Green Bay there is a so-called Indian reserve, that is to say, a territory which, when the tribes have ceded their land to the Government, is given to them as a kind of exception, a place of which they are assured the undisturbed possession. This territory is now occupied by the remnants of the once mighty Oneida tribe, which originally possessed a great deal of the land that now comprises the state of New York. These, as well as the Indians at Lake Winnebago, have been converted to Christianity, and are no longer nomadic in their habits, but are energetic and successful farmers. The Oneidas, to a higher degree than the Lake Winnebago Indians, have adopted the manners, customs, and dress of the white people and have nothing in their appearance but their dark skin that recalls the Indian. But unfortunately along with the civilization of the Europeans has gone much also of their vice and sin.

Notes

ᵃ I am speaking here of the present state of Wisconsin, not of the former territory of the same name, which at its organization seems to have been much more extensive. A dispute soon arose with the state of Illinois about an extensive land area, which Congress awarded to Illinois in spite of the fact that it originally had lain within the Wisconsin borders. Some doubt exists also whether the northern peninsula of Michigan ought not logically and legally to belong to Wisconsin, both because of its natural boundaries and by virtue of old territorial limits.

ᵇ It is strange that the white settlers in the backwoods, who, as far as coffee and tea are concerned, make use of the oddest substitutes, do not for want of culivated rice make use of the wild which the country supplies in such abundance and which often serves as the principal food of the red man. In an Indian wigwam I once was offered a few spoonfuls, or rather slices, of a type of porridge made from wild rice, and found it very savory. Cooked by a white woman at her stove, it would no doubt have tasted still better.

ᶜ The greatest of these American sepulchral mounds is found in Ohio. It is 90 feet in height and 825 feet in circumference.

ᵈ Near the Mississippi River an earthen wall has recently been discovered, depicting a great animal with a trunk like that of an elephant or the now extinct mastodon. From this, students have educed the theory that the people who made those symbols belong either to the same era as the gigantic animals, whose bones are sometimes discovered in the Mississippi Valley, or to some people originating in Asia, the homeland of the elephant, and still retaining in their memory the appearance of this animal.

ᵉ The French have intermarried with the Indians more than any other nation. Strangely enough, according to what I have been told and what I have observed for myself, the marriages contracted with Indian women by men of other nationalities have generally, with very few exceptions, proved barren; while, on the other hand, marriages between Indian women and the French have proved so productive that almost an entire new race has grown up in the former French-American possessions.

Chapter 9

TERRITORIAL GOVERNMENT · JUDICIAL POWER · LAND OFFICES

SURVEYING AND DIVIDING LAND · SCHOOL LANDS AND PUBLIC

SCHOOLS · THE PHYSICAL ASPECT AND CHARACTER OF THE COUN-

TRY · THE PRAIRIE · FOREST LAND · OAK OPENINGS · NATURAL

PASTURAGE · THE GEOLOGICAL CHARACTER OF THE COUNTRY

MINERALS · WILD ANIMALS · BIRDS · FISH · CLIMATE

TO THIS brief and concise description of the land where we were about to make our home, it may be proper, for the sake of giving a complete view of the matter, to add something about its government and organization.

According to the laws of the United States, no individual or corporation is permitted to buy land, either in large or small tracts, from the Indian tribes living within the Union and considered subject to it, even though they have not formally ceded the lands they inhabit and possess. When the white population has grown large, or other considerations call for it, a treaty is made between the United States Government and the Indian tribes, by which the Indians surrender their rights to the land they have hitherto possessed in return for a certain price in goods or for other considerations, and agree to leave it within a given time. Next the land is measured and divided into townships and sections. Then it is opened to American or immigrant settlers, who may get the land at stated prices and thus establish settlements or cities. The new possessions that have been obtained in this way are at first organized, with definite boundaries, into territories belonging to the Union. The United States Government appoints a territorial government, subordinate to the President and Congress, with the power to make laws and regulations for the new territories in civil and judicial matters. The Government of the Union has established certain conditions under which the territories may enter the Union as independent states, with a constitution adopted by the people and approved by Congress, and with the same rights and privileges as the older states. To obtain statehood a territory must have, according to a decision made by Congress in 1787, a population of at least 60,000 resident white persons.

When we arrived, Wisconsin had not yet been received into the Union as a state. According to the census of the preceding year the population of this whole vast territory was only 30,945. It has, however, increased considerably during the last year through the unusually large and constantly growing stream of settlers.

The chief administrative officer of the territory is the governor, who is appointed for a term of three years by the President of the United States, this appointment being subject to ratification by the Senate. He is the ex-officio superintendent of Indian affairs within the territory, with a salary of $2,500 a year, drawn from the general treasury of the Union. He is also the commanding officer of the militia and has absolute veto power in the legislative assembly. He holds office entirely at the pleasure of the President and can be removed from office by him at any time. He appoints subordinate officers in accordance with the provisions of the territorial laws and is responsible for the maintenance of law and order.

Next after the governor is the territorial secretary. He is appointed in the same way as the governor, for a period of four years unless removed from office by the President. One of his duties is to record and file all laws and decisions and all executive orders and actions of the governor, and to provide copies of all such public documents for the President and the Speaker of the House of Representatives. He is authorized to assume the duties of the governor in the event of the latter's death, removal from office, resignation, or necessary absence. His salary is fixed at $1,200 a year.

The legislative body consists of the governor, a council of thirteen members elected by the people for two years, and a house of representatives of twenty-six members, elected for a period of one year. These representatives are elected by districts established according to population (exclusive of Indians). The legislative body is empowered to act on all matters related to regular legislation, but it has no power to make laws relative to the sale and disposition of public lands. The public lands remaining unsold cannot be taxed, but those who do not live on or make use of the land they have purchased are taxed like those who have already settled on the land. All laws must be submitted to Congress in Washington for its approval, and unless they are approved and ratified they become null and void. The members of the legislative assembly get $3.00 a day while they are in session plus traveling allowances to and from Madison, the capital. They convene annually the first Monday of December, and sessions may not last more than seventy-five days; or rather, the length of the session depends on the amount of money appropriated by Congress for said purpose.

The judicial power is in the hands of a Supreme Court, District Courts, Probate Courts, and justices of the peace.

The Supreme Court consists of a chief justice and two assistants, who are called into session in Madison once a year. Their salary is $1,800 a year.

The District Court convenes twice a year in each county, under the presidency of one of the members of the Supreme Court. The entire territory is at present divided into three judicial districts.

These two judicial bodies have the right to grant licenses as well as the right of adjudication according to the common law.

Probate judges and justices of the peace are elected by the people. The latter have no judicial power in cases involving real-estate proprietary rights or in other cases where the amount in litigation exceeds fifty dollars.

A delegate to Congress is elected every other year. He is admitted to a seat in the House of Representatives, and has the right to speak, but has no vote on questions before said body.

An attorney and a marshal are appointed by the President for four years, unless removed from office before their regular terms expire.

In addition to these public officers, the legislative body has created other offices specifically necessary to the administration of the territory.[a]

As long as a territory has not acquired statehood, all lands within it are to be regarded as the property of the United States. Hence the Federal Government has in certain districts established land offices, whose officers, appointed by the President, are charged with the duty of selling these unoccupied lands either at public auctions or privately, to give the purchasers valid deeds, and otherwise attend to all affairs connected with the administration and regulation of the public domain. In Wisconsin there are three such land offices, one of which is located in Milwaukee.[b]

To purchase land from private speculators is frequently a risky undertaking for an inexperienced stranger, and the immigrant is best served, unless he wishes to get land that is already under cultivation, by turning to the Land Office, where no one is exposed to cheating and fraud.

Like all other states and new territories in the West, Wisconsin is divided into rectangular pieces of land known as townships and sections. A township is six miles square, and consists of 36 sections, each one containing a square mile, or 640 acres. A section, in its turn, is surveyed into four equal squares, quarter sections, consisting of 160 acres, and each quarter section into four equal squares, each containing 40 acres, which is the smallest unit of land that can be purchased at the Land Office at the price established by Congress, just as sections can be purchased only in lots of 40, 80, 120, or 160 acres. Should, however, any of these squares be cut into by a lake or some other large body of water, a fraction results which is measured up into its true area and which anybody may buy even if its area is less than 40 acres.[c]

Every township has its own definite number, determined by its distance from the southern border of the territory. Ranges of townships are counted east or west from a given meridian, which is determined in accordance with this very practical system of surveying and dividing the land. The sections in a township are counted from the northeast corner and are numbered from one to thirty-six, as may be seen from the illustration.

In each of the four corners of every section, in a tree at the point where the four sections meet, the surveyor hews out not only the number of the section but

N

6	5	4	3	2	+ |NE 1	
7	8	9	10	11	12
18	17	SCHOOL 16 SECTION	15	14	13
19	20	21	22	23	24
30	29	28	27	26	25
31	32	33	34	35	36

W — E

S

also the number of the range and of the township in which it is located. In the center of the section and in the middle of its boundaries trees are also marked indicating the quarter sections. Furthermore, the borderlines of the township, as well as of all the sections located within it, are marked out as far as possible with blazes in the trees along the entire line, from one corner to the other. If the land is prairie or if there are no trees suitable for marking, small posts are driven into the ground and duly marked.

Thus the entire country is surveyed into squares, each one marked as described in the preceding paragraph. Guided by these marks and by a map which can be obtained at a low price in the Land Office and which gives the location of every township and section, anyone can easily find his way through forest and field. The immigrant can roam through the unsettled regions in search of a location for his future home. The map shows which sections and fractions are still unoccupied and unsold, and of this he is further assured as he visits these spots and finds that there is no house or hut on them. When he has finally found a place that suits him, he knows at once in what township, section, or part of a section it is located. All he needs to do is to go to the Land Office and announce his wish to purchase the NE quarter and SE quarter of the NE quarter of Section 33, Township 8, Range 18, or whatever the designation may be.

The Government has recently made it much easier for the new settler to locate and obtain land through the Pre-emption Law passed last month by Congress. Through this law, any person twenty-one years or over who either is a citizen of the United States or has declared his intention of becoming one may, at the minimum price established by Congress, $1.25 per acre, take possession of a quarter section, or, if he prefers, a smaller subdivision of a section, without having to pay for it until it is offered for sale at a public auction, which, however, does not generally take place until a year later. He then has the privilege of purchasing the land, which he is using on deferred payment, at the price agreed upon, even if others may be willing to pay ten times as much for it. However, in order to avail himself of this right he must notify the Land Office what part of a section he wishes to occupy and within thirty days prove that he has made some improvements on it and that he continues to live on that land. These regulations are necessary to prevent land speculators from taking advantage of the law to the detriment of the actual settlers for whose benefit it was passed in order that the country might be settled and cultivated as speedily as possible.[d]

With admirable foresight the Government has taken steps to insure educational opportunities to the coming generation even from the very beginning of the settling of the new country. The sixteenth section in every township, in Wisconsin equal to one thirty-sixth of the entire territorial area, has been set aside for the support of public schools. The intention is not that these sections, although they lie in the center of every township, shall be used for the dwellings of schoolmasters or that schoolhouses shall necessarily be built on them, for the country is, according to the distribution of the population, specially divided into school districts and within one township there may be more than a dozen public school buildings. But after the school lands have been rented out for a time, and as land values rise, they are sold at auction to the highest bidder, the receipts from such sales going to the general school fund. In this way the school lands often bring considerable amounts of money. Strangely enough, I have found that the sixteenth section often is one of the best in the entire township. It happens not infrequently, as for instance in Chicago, where lots now are selling at ten dollars a square foot, that a city grows up and flourishes either in the neighborhood of or on the school land itself, in which case the school districts have at their disposal very abundant funds. In each township a school board is appointed to administer the school land, rent it out for certain years until it can be sold profitably, or otherwise take care of all matters relative to public education.

In addition to these provisions for the maintenance of the schools, every landowning taxpayer is obliged to pay a certain annual tax toward the erection of schoolhouses and teachers' salaries. One of the first undertakings of the new settlers, if, that is to say, they are Americans, for Europeans are frequently more indifferent in these matters, is to build a schoolhouse at some crossroads or other place easily accessible to all. In this territory, still but sparsely settled, numerous schoolhouses have already been put up.

For the purpose of creating a fund for establishing a university, Congress has given the territory two townships, or 46,080 acres, which the legislative assembly is permitted to select at will among the lands not already sold.[e]

These measures taken to promote popular education, in a land where the new settlers have hardly reaped the first harvest from their freshly plowed fields, may give one some conception of how actively and wisely Americans are interested in public education and culture, although often unjustly accused of renouncing every nobler struggle for that after the almighty dollar.

Although Wisconsin, generally speaking, may be regarded as level land, it has large tracts of hilly and rough terrain. West of the Wisconsin River is a long range of hills, the only section of the territory that might be called mountainous. In addition, especially on the wide prairies in the southern part of the territory, there are deep ravines, probably old river beds. These rivers are now entirely dried up, or have been reduced to small creeks. Like the entire western part of the fertile Mississippi Valley, the land in Wisconsin can be divided according to type of soil and vegetation into four distinct classes, which in a unique way strangely vary at times, at times seem to be mingled.

Foremost among these classes is the prairie, which, though predominating, is not so extensive as in Illinois and other western states. The prairie is entirely devoid of every vestige of trees and in its original condition has no growth, not even the smallest bush. It is a vast carpet of grass and flowers in all possible colors, extending as far as the eye can reach. Generally it is bordered by tall timber woods, by which it is framed as a lake is by its shores. The forest land does not seem to lie higher than the prairie but is as a rule a continuation of it. The strange thing is that while trees naturally scatter their seeds all around and new shoots spring up from their roots, the forest nevertheless does not seem to encroach on the prairie. On the other hand, it has been declared that the prairie sometimes replaces the forest.

Many theories have been presented to explain the genesis of these vast grazing lands, which in the American West are truly a strange natural phenomenon. Some maintain that forest and prairie fires, sweeping annually across the land like immense irresistible seas of flame from one end of the wilderness to the other, have in the course of time killed the forests and created these vast expanses, which show no other sign of vegetation than grasses and flowers. Though this theory seems to support what we already have suggested about the expansion of the prairie, it is, however, for a number of reasons far from satisfactory. If such were the case, one would, at least in that part of the prairie closest to the forest lands, note some signs of earlier stands of trees. But there are no such signs. If one digs a few feet into the ground just where the prairie ends and the forest begins, one finds no vestiges of roots or stumps on the prairie side, whereas a few feet away, in the same kind of soil, though perhaps somewhat more porous, the ground is so full of intertwined roots that the axe has to be used before the spade can be. Indian traditions, if one may credit them, also contradict such theories.

Others again imagine that these unforested land areas constitute dried-up swamps or lake bottoms. It is not unlikely that here and there this may be true; but if the hypothesis explains the origin of the low and level prairie, it certainly cannot account for the high or rolling type, where one often finds large, completely unforested hills and ridges, in some cases a hundred feet higher than the forest lands. Like the level prairie the high is overgrown with grass and flowers, and like the forest lands is tillable and fertile.

On my walks through the woods I have myself sometimes quite unexpectedly come across some small prairie, perhaps not more than ten or twelve acres, located in the middle of a forest, surrounded by tall trees as by a high, impenetrable wall. According to the investigations I have been able to make — superficial though they may have been — I have found the soil very much the same and the ground no more swampy in one place than in another. Sometimes I have even found such small prairies lying higher and drier than the surrounding forest land. These small forest-prairies, if I may call them that, are uncommonly attractive, and with their smiling, fresh verdure and rich, many-colored spread of flowers, provide a cheerful contrast to the rather gloomy primeval forest, sparse in flowers and grass, especially when a man has had to work his way for one or two days in the pathless woods between trees and stumps.

Of the rolling prairie one may form a conception by imagining the great Uppsala plain robbed of its few trees and instead studded with big sepulchral mounds, such as Thor's Mound in Old Uppsala,[1] though greater in height and circumference and with a much gentler slope. Many are great admirers of this type of landscape, but in its uncultivated state, with its naked hills and dales, its only growth grass and flowers, it is magnificent, to be sure, but not beautiful. It is like a pretentious but unfinished painting which one is forced to admire. At the same time the eyes tire of looking for something in it which is not yet there. There is light, but no relieving shadow. When the rolling prairie is settled and cultivated, however, it offers a cheerful sight indeed, refreshing as cool springs that with a diamond-like clarity glitter here and there on the hillsides. The farms scattered about in the valleys are surrounded by planted locust groves, gardens, and orchards. Some of the high hills seem to shimmer in the air, completely covered with rich, waving fields of grain. Others again are astir with numerous herds of cattle feeding on the lush grass. Above it all is the mild, clear summer sky, from which a special benediction seems to have streamed down over this vast cornucopia heaped up by nature. Undeniably this is among landscape pictures one of the loveliest to behold.

The level prairie is generally more fertile than the rolling land. It often has small groves of trees, strewn over the wide plain like small isles in coastal waters, or at times a narrow ribbon of woodland winds like a river across the immense meadowland.

The soil of these prairies consists generally of a dark brown, soft loam, often several feet in depth, absolutely free from gravel or stones. It is highly fertile and is generally considered superior to the woodland soil, though it is said that it is worked out faster and needs fertilizer. Yet I have found places where the farmer, to enrich himself as quickly as possible, has sowed his prairie land to wheat eight to ten years in succession without the latest year's harvest being any less bountiful than the first. Underneath the loam is a subsoil of rather tough clay, also suitable for cultivation. It may therefore be said that the top soil is four to five feet deep, perhaps more. The soil of the prairie lends itself better to the cultivation of corn than to that of any other grain.

Especially in southern Wisconsin are to be found very extensive prairies, the more distant parts of which have not been so readily settled and tilled because of their complete lack of timber. All the faster on that account has the prairie land close to the forests and to the groves mentioned above been taken up, especially by backwoodsmen and immigrants who love hunting.

If we classify the land according to type and quality of soil, we next note forest and heavy timberland. Many immigrants, and especially the German, prefer this type of land to the prairie. But the clearing and the preparing it for the plow demand at least ten times as much work as does the prairie land. While with three and sometimes only two horses one can plow up to three acres of virgin land in a single day, it takes at least a week in the forest to hew down the trees, then as long again to pile them together and burn them. Then follows the plowing between the stumps, a slow process that cannot be done with horses, but only with teams of oxen. However, after the trees have been hewn down and burned, it is not necessary to resort to the plow at once. The first year the seed need only be harrowed down among the stumps on the unplowed, ash-covered ground, and it generally yields more then than ever after. As a rule the stumps are left standing. It is said that it does not take more than twelve years for hardwood stumps such as oak, ash, beech, and maple to rot, but as far as I have been able to judge, twice this time is required. At least I found the oak stumps on our own land standing just as solid and well-rooted in the ground after a dozen years as if the trees had just been felled. These stumps make the fields far from attractive, not to speak of the trouble of plowing, harrowing, and especially reaping around them. It is worth noting, however, that in spite of the space they take up, and they often stand close together and cover much of the field area, the settlers still harvest as much wheat and other grains per acre of forest land as on an equal area of prairie land. The topsoil here is nevertheless not in general so deep as on the prairie and consists, like the prairie soil, of a dark brown loam, but with a smaller lime content.

It has been estimated that two or three crops pay for the clearing and cultivation of the ground. The poor immigrant, who is eager to be repaid for his expenditure of toil and money as soon as possible, is accustomed to seed the soil as soon as he is done harvesting. This procedure is continued for years in these regions as well as on the prairie. No doubt there is a kind of vandalism in this impoverishing of the soil, and yet the forest settler is in this respect more excusable than the prairie farmer. The land area which in two weeks the latter can bring under cultivation will require as many years on the forest farm. And when one takes into consideration the poverty of the early settlers, most of whom were ready after a short time to sell the farms they had tilled and with a bigger capital move farther west and there establish themselves on a more solid footing; when one also remembers that this robbing of the soil was carried on in a country where good land is to be had in abundance, where labor is expensive and hard to get, where the marketing centers perhaps still are far away, and the price of the produce is low, then one may well acknowledge that he himself in the same circumstances would probably do likewise. Nevertheless as the population grows, farmers of another class are making their appearance, men with more means than the early settlers and able to give the not entirely worn-out soil more careful attention. The soil so treated will soon, when properly fertilized and cultivated, yield as abundant crops as under its first owner.

The principal, or most common, kind of tree is the oak, which, however, is not so predominant in the heavy timberland as in the more thinly wooded regions. Of the forty kinds of oak growing in the United States, probably more than half are found in Wisconsin. The largest, hardest, and strongest of them all is the white oak, *Quercus alba* [this is not quite correct, since the burr oak, *Quercus macrocarpa*, is generally thought of as the largest of the oak family],[2] which here grows to a height of seventy to eighty feet, with a diameter of four to six feet, measured five feet above the ground. Of the oak family we may also mention the black [shingle] oak, *Quercus imbricaria*, a soft and porous kind of tree which generally grows tall and straight with a slender trunk, easily felled and split and used preferably for making fences. There is also a type of black or, rather, red oak, *Quercus tinctoria* [now known as *Quercus velutina*], somewhat harder and more serviceable than the black [shingle] oak, and containing a rich dye tincture.

Of other trees I wish now to mention only in passing some of the most common: several species of ash, *Fraxinus americana*, *Fraxinus pubescens* [the red ash, now known as *Fraxinus pensylvanica*], *Fraxinus sambucifolia* [the black ash, now known as *Fraxinus nigra*], and others; the common beech, or *Fagus silvestris* [what is known in the United States as *Fagus sylvatica*], several kinds of maple, such as *Acer eriocarpum* [the soft maple, *Acer saccharinum*] and *Acer saccharinum* [properly *Acer saccharum*], from whose sap a most delicious sugar and syrup are produced, about which I shall have more to say later; the linden, or *Tilia americana*; the cherry, *Cerasus borealis* [now known as *Prunus pensylvanica*] and *Cerasus virginiana* [the choke cherry, known today as *Prunus virginiana*], both of beautiful grain and often used in the making of fine furniture and in carpentry. The last trees are not very common in Wisconsin, but I have seen them grow to a height of sixty to seventy feet. From the bark of *Cerasus borealis* [*Prunus pensylvanica*] a bitter, astringent decoction is made, commonly used in the United States, reputedly an effective remedy for pneumonia and other pulmonary diseases.

Numerous kinds of elm also grow here, such as *Ulmus americana*, *Ulmus racemosa* [the rock elm, known today as *Ulmus thomasii*], and *Ulmus fulva* [the slippery elm]. The first named grows to a height of one hundred feet, with a diameter of three to five feet. The beautiful [black or false] acacia, *Robinia Pseudo-Acacia*, here generally known as the locust, is easy to plant and grows fast, for which reason the new settlers on the prairie frequently use it on their farms, planted in small groves, which in a few years supply them with fuel. *Laurus* [*Lindera Benzoin*] and *Sassafras*; the [staghorn] sumac, *Rhus typhina*; and the [poison sumac], *Rhus venenata* [now known as *Rhus vernix*], are also very common.

It would be hopeless to seek to name all the trees, big and small, that grow in the American forests. I wish, however, to mention as among the most useful the ironwood[s], *Carpinus* [hornbeam] and *Ostrya* [hop hornbeam], closely related to our white beech and at first sight not unlike our Swedish birch. This extraordinarily white, strong, and close-textured tree is used for the manufacture of farm implements, wagons, etc. However, it does not grow very high or thick. For the purposes mentioned, and sometimes with better results, the common walnut tree is used. There is an abundance of the black walnut tree here, *Juglans nigra*, from which beautiful furniture and other fine carpentry products are manufactured, as is true also of *Juglans laciniosa* [presumably *Carya laciniosa*, the big shellbark hickory] and *Juglans squamosa* [presumably the *Carya tomentosa*, also a shellbark hickory], all of which grow to a considerable height and thickness and are rich in nuts. It is really sad to see these valuable trees chopped down, to be piled on top of one another and burned. Where trees are not so abundant and where communication with some large city is easier, by means either of better roads or of watercourses, better use is made of these rich natural products. Here the walnut tree is spared, if for no other purpose at least for firewood, for which it is not surpassed by any other tree.

The last named, *Juglans squamosa* [*Carya tomentosa*], in America usually called the hickory, is perhaps the most useful and most durable of all the American woods. Of great solidity and strength, it is used to an even greater extent than ironwood for all kinds of tools, such as axe handles and wheel spokes. These are so neatly wrought that one unfamiliar with the exceptional, almost iron-like strength of this wood might consider it impossible that tools manufactured from it could be used without going to pieces. A common work wagon, for instance, with wheels and other parts of hickory, appears so light that a man might think he could almost carry the whole frame on his shoulders. Yet it stands up, heavily loaded, pulled over rough and uneven roads that in Sweden would be termed impassable for our common farm wagons. This tree is also extraordinarily flexible, so that when heated in boiling water it can be bent and shaped into the crooked scythe handles used in this country, as well as into other agricultural implements. Its nuts are smaller and lighter and have heavier shells than ordinary walnuts, from which they may be easily distinguished by their shape. In the opinion of some they have a better flavor than ordinary walnuts.

Since the hickory grows at a more northerly latitude than the common walnut and in a climate which is almost as cold as the southern part of Sweden, it ought not to be impossible to plant it there, especially in Gottland.[3] A tree more useful to Sweden than the hickory could hardly be imagined. It is true that in general it requires a rich soil, but I have seen it grow on clay soil enriched with lime. Although under these conditions it does not reach a very great height, it grows big enough for the purposes mentioned above.

In addition to these and many other trees, the woods are full of wild fruit trees, apple, plum, etc. The wild grapevine, with its small, juicy, delicious grapes, suitable for preserves, winds its way through the woods, especially near the shores of lakes and rivers, in some places almost covering the big tree trunks.

Among the evergreens, we notice as the most common the American pine, which makes up the great forests of the northern part of the territory but otherwise is found only rarely on the western shore of Lake Michigan and in other parts of Wisconsin. Here one finds also the juniper, the common spruce, and another exceptionally beautiful tree of the species *Abies* known as the hemlock, found especially on the northern shore of Lake Michigan. It grows to a considerable height and with its straight trunk, its spreading top, and its closely grown crown of fine-needled branches is one of the principal beauties of the north woods. In addition, both the red and white cedar grow nearly everywhere, in the northern as well as the southern tracts, by rivers and lakes; the white cedar, with its straight, tall trunk, makes its appearance in marshy regions. The larch tree and a peculiar variation of it, *Larix americana*, commonly known as the tamarack or hackmatack, also grow only in a swampy soil and often cover miles of bog and morass, almost entirely inaccessible in the summertime. The soil in which evergreens grow is generally sandy and not nearly so fertile as that growing other forest trees. Still I have found excellent wheat fields in northern Wisconsin, though the growing of corn hardly pays on this type of soil.

In addition to the prairie and the forest lands we must also take account of a third kind, a class by itself — the land that is known as openings — in a sense a mixture of the other two without being quite a link, or a transition, between them. These openings resemble large and extensive English parks and surpass in natural beauty all other parts of the great West. The trees, which here are mostly oaks, with a mixture of small hickories, are distributed at longer or shorter distances from one another. They are not so big as in the forest regions, but still tall and thick enough to make good saw-timber. The white oak grows sometimes to a height of fifty or sixty feet, and I have found trees four feet in diameter, measured several feet above the ground; trees as big as this, though, are rather rare. The soil, especially where the black oak grows, is not so fertile as prairie and forest land; but where the white oak predominates, for wheat and other grains the soil is, if not better, just as good as the rich loam of the prairie, which is the most suitable for corn growing. This soil is mostly of clay, mixed with sand, in which stones big and small frequently occur. Still there are wide areas entirely free from stones, and in the lower opening lands particularly, the loam is frequently several feet deep.

A special kind of these openings is what is known as the burr-oak land, which, as far as soil and other qualities are concerned, resembles a level prairie planted with a few small oak and hickory trees. These oaks, *Quercus macrocarpa* [burr or mossy-cup oak], which in other places in America are said to be very tall and among the most beautiful and leafiest oaks in the country, are here rough, very low, and generally very crooked in the trunk. So far as I know, they are the least usable and useful of all the trees growing here. Their naked and dwarf-like appearance, as well as the almost complete absence of proper timber, made the early colonists conclude that these regions were most unfertile, and as a result this land was given a name indicating the very opposite of its real condition. The oak that grows here was called burr oak, and the region the Barrens, which, as is well known, means unfruitful and dry lands. Since then, however, men have found out that the burr-oak land is one of the most fertile in the entire West, also healthier than the cultivated prairie and in many other respects preferable to it. As a rule it has good springs of fine, fresh water, and since it is not generally very extensive but adjacent to other openings with plenty of trees, it has at least some supply of timber suitable for fencing, building material, and fuel, which the prairie, rich though it may be in other respects, lacks completely. In comparison with the forest the burr-oak land has this in its favor, that it is more easily cultivated, though it may be true that its soil is less rich and is more easily exhausted than forest land.

The openings are undoubtedly the most attractive regions in the rich and fertile western Mississippi Valley. Tree-clad hills, grass-covered valleys, fruitful plains, small rivers and lakes — everything combines to make this the loveliest region for a settler to make his home in. I must confess, however, that those who select this type of land reveal for the most part more a feeling for the beauty of nature than prudence in economic matters. Therefore, with the exception of the burr-oak openings and a few other places that offer exceptional privileges because of their location, the opening lands have often remained unsettled longer than the prairie and forest lands in the same region.

As a fourth kind of land we may reckon the low-lying, level prairie, or the natural meadow as it is often called, but more cor-rectly, marsh or morass. These swampy regions are found every-where in Wisconsin and are in places very extensive. Many of them are almost inaccessible the greater part of the year. They are found close to the larger lakes particularly, and at high water they are often completely inundated.

The oldest Norwegian settlement in Wisconsin is for the greater part located in the middle of such a swamp. The Norwegians that live there arrived by chance during an unusually dry summer and were charmed by the land, which seemed easily tillable with its rich, deep blackloam, and by the little wooded hills that dotted the plain, promising an abundance of building material and fuel. They settled in a region which is perhaps one of the most unwholesome in all of Wisconsin. Very soon they learned their mistake. The plowed fields soon came to resemble the bottoms of little lakes, in which their houses stood like boathouses surrounded by water. They themselves died in great numbers from fever and other diseases. Out of the original large group of settlers only a few re-main. Most of them have moved elsewhere, and those who are left have moved to the hills, where they support themselves by cattle raising. For this the land is most suitable since it supplies them with plenty of hay and excellent grazing grounds for their animals.

These low meadowlands are often of inestimable value to the new settlers before they have time to raise fodder grasses, such as timothy and clover, a development that is generally long delayed. It is really of no small value to one who has made his home in the woods or on the openings to have close by a piece of marshland or swamp, provided that is, it is not too boggy. Particularly is this desirable near the forest lands, where frequently the cattle would be in want of grazing in the summertime if they did not have access to these swamps. The grass in the woods is often ruined by grasshoppers, which come in such swarms that they almost cover the ground and leave it devastated and as bare as a piece of fallow land, so that it is really sometimes more difficult for the settler to feed his cattle in the summer than in the winter. This condition improves, however, as the land is settled and cultivated.ᶠ In the meantime these low meadows are always convenient to have in the neighborhood. In the spring the cattle find early pasturage there, and during a dry summer the swamp will always have its stand of grass. Very probably these swamps will some day dry up entirely, and the soil there will then certainly be the richest and most fertile in the land. Even now most of them can easily be drained by ditching; the settlers, however, do not bother with such work as long as other good land is available, and the swamps are useful in their present condition.

In some of these swamps or low meadows cranberries grow. Some of these are our ordinary *tranbär* [*Vaccinium Oxycoccus*], some of another species, *Oxycoccum microcarpum* [properly *Oxycoccus macrocarpus*, now known as *Vaccinium macrocarpon*], three to four times as big as our *lingon* [*Vaccinium Vitis-idaea*], but juicier and more pleasantly acid in flavor. They are found in great abundance, and are not picked, but raked from the ground. Examples exist where from a single acre it has been possible to reap as much as a hundred bushels of these berries, which are used in the household like *lingon* in Sweden. Of late people have begun to plant them on higher ground, and this has proved to be most profitable, since they sometimes bring as much as $3.00 per bushel.

From a geological and mineralogical point of view Wisconsin offers a rich field for scientific research. Being only a settler and quite uninitiated in these sciences, I can only state that in the southern part of the territory, Silurian, or transitional, limestone constitutes the first rocky layer underneath the alluvial soil, and that in other places as well there are great limestone quarries, from which great, flat, naturally shaped laminal rocks are obtained, used especially on the woodless prairie for building material and fence making. The lime deposits, which run from the southern part of the territory in a northerly direction, following the entire shore of Lake Michigan, give way inland and along the Mississippi River to a loose sandstone of various colors, in some places almost pure white, elsewhere brown or reddish in color.

In this geological district, in addition to beautiful white marble and gypsum, there are several minerals: iron ore, galena — of which the country has an abundance — lead ore, quartz, limestone, sulfur, and others. The entire part of Wisconsin that lies between Lake Superior to the north and St. Anthony Falls on the Mississippi River, as well as the falls formed by other rivers flowing in a southerly direction, consists mainly of primitive rock, partly granite and hornblende, partly talc, slate, malachite, and other varieties. Within this district are located the copper mines near Lake Superior, probably the richest in the world and apparently inexhaustible. Here also are found septaria, garnets, tournalines, cyanite, limonite, and other minerals. Also found here is red pipestone, or catlinite, which to the Indians has a sacred significance and from which they make tobacco pipes and various kinds of ornaments. This stone when freshly mined is very soft and easily worked, but as it is exposed to the air it hardens quickly and takes on a fine, shining polish.

Zoologically Wisconsin is almost as rich as it is mineralogically. Most of the four-footed animals that exist in the United States are found here, so that it would be easier to list those that are not native to this region than those that are. However, several species have been driven off to remoter and more unsettled tracts by the arrival of the white man. There they will probably remain but a short time until, like the Indians, they will be driven away to the distant and still largely unexplored areas in the wilds of the Far West.

Deer are found in abundance, and the cultivation of the land, instead of frightening them away, seems rather to make them feel more at home, for fields of grain supply them with better pasturage than the meadowlands, which in the heat of summer frequently dry up. Besides, the more the land is settled the less they are disturbed by bears and wolves and other wild beasts that flee from encroaching civilization. Elks formerly existed in great numbers.

Now only rarely does one find the horns of these stately animals on the prairies. The buffalo, likewise, are beginning to withdraw to the other side of the Mississippi River. Around the sources of the Mississippi and west of Lake Superior there are several species of animals that have never been found in the southern part of the territory. Among them are the reindeer, the antelope, *Antilope furcifera* [presumably the pronghorn, *Antilocapra americana*, which is not a true antelope], and the stag, *Cervus canadensis* [also known as the wapiti], the largest animal of the *Cervus* family, sometimes weighing as much as twelve hundred pounds.

The black bear, *Ursus americanus* [now known as *Euarctos americanus*], and *Ursus ferox* [the grizzly bear, today known as *Ursus horribilis*] are still encountered frequently in the forests, where along with the gray wolf, which however is more rare, they are the only really dangerous wild beasts. But it is true of them, as may generally be said of American animals, wild as well as domesticated, that they are not so savage as the same species in Europe. It is unusual to hear of bears or wolves approaching the homes of new settlers and attacking their herds. In the streams and bogs, as well as along the shores of the inland lakes, one still encounters the beaver and the muskrat, *Fiber zibethicus*, though the former is beginning to migrate from his small but carefully constructed house. The woods and oak openings are full of hares, rabbits, raccoons — *Procyon lotor* — weasels, and a great variety of squirrels, from the common squirrel we know in Sweden to the beautiful gray and black *Sciurus* species, which grows to more than a foot in length.

Among game birds we note especially the pheasant and the prairie chicken — *Tetrao umbellus* [presumably the ruffed grouse, *Bonasa umbellus*] and *Tetrao cupido* [now known as *Tympanuchus cupido*] — which are found in great abundance and often enrich the meager board of the settlers with the most sumptuous dishes. The meat, especially of the former, is very tender and savory; it is regarded in the eastern states as a great delicacy and commands therefore a high price. Here, on the other hand, the bird exists in such profusion and is so easily caught that it is possible to get at an exceedingly low price what is no doubt the best-tasting game bird in existence. Many kinds of the grouse family fill the forests, and in the northern part *Tetrao canadensis* [the spruce grouse, now known as *Canachites canadensis*], *Tetrao phasianellus* [the sharp-tailed grouse, known today as *Pedioecetes phasianellus*], and our ordinary ptarmigan, *Tetrao saliceti* [presumably the willow ptarmigan, known today as *Lagopus lagopus*], are found in abundance. Nor are wild turkeys uncommon, but the meat of those that we managed to shoot was not nearly so good as that of the other birds mentioned above. In addition, this territory as well as the rest of the western part of the United States has such an abundance of passenger pigeons, *Columba migratoria* [now known as *Ectopistes migratorius*, although extinct], that the telling of it would sound unbelievable.

When to this is added — not to speak of the numerous small edible birds — the American quail, *Ortyx virginiana* [known today as the bob-white quail, *Colinus virginianus*], which is found in such abundance that it is caught with nets on the prairies, then one may readily realize that while the life of the new settler may have many privations, his palate need not suffer, provided, of course, he has the time and inclination to devote himself to hunting.

In the lakes and rivers innumerable flocks of ducks and wild geese, *Anser canadensis* [presumably the Canada goose, *Branta canadensis*], and other edible water fowl swim about. Among the former we note especially the remarkably beautiful white- and black-speckled *Mergus cucullatus* [presumably *Lophodytes cucullatus*, or the hooded merganser, also known as the little fish duck], which is quite abundant. It was a new experience for us to shoot ducks in trees — those not familiar with conditions in this country may regard this an incredible hunting story. But as they perched in the branches of trees standing on the lake shore, we have picked off more than one *Anas sponsa* [presumably *Aix sponsa*, commonly known as the wood duck], which resorts to the land more frequently than to the water and generally prepares its nest in some hollow tree. Among aquatic birds, we found a few times, though seldom, the pelican, *Pelicanus americanus* [presumably the white pelican, *Pelecanus erythrorhynchos*], which travels up the Mississippi and sometimes strays off into some of its tributaries.

Wisconsin also has its share of reptiles. Snakes are numerous, but only the rattlesnake is dangerously poisonous.

The numerous watercourses almost all abound in fish. On the shores of Lake Michigan there are great quantities of salmon, sturgeon, and trout caught, and especially a savory fish of the species *Coregonus*, known as the whitefish, which is exported to the eastern states. A barrel of this fish is as common and as essential in the homes of the early settlers as are herring and *strömming*[4] in our Swedish country homes. Of the fish abounding in the smaller inland lakes, the black bass deserves mention. It is a big fish of the *Labrax* family, of which sometimes specimens weighing up to twenty and thirty pounds are caught. [This seems a little doubtful; presumably Unonius refers to the white bass, formerly *Labrax multilineatus*, now known as *Lepibema chrysops*. The size of the fish is also questionable.] Of all the lake fish it may not be the most common, but certainly it is the best eating. In addition there are various kinds of perch, bigger and smaller pickerel, carp [presumably some species of the carp family, for the carp as we know it today was not introduced into America until 1877], catfish (or bullhead, a big fish of the *Cottus* family) [incorrect; the bullhead belongs to the *Ameiuridae* family, which only very superficially resembles the *Cottus* family], and many other edible and fine-flavored fish. The Indians in the northern regions, where game is less common, subsist mainly on fish, which is caught easily and in great quantities at the mouths of the rivers.

As for the Wisconsin climate it is, generally speaking, very healthful. The air is pure and ordinarily not contaminated by poisonous vapors such as rise from the earth in other newly cultivated or uncultivated sections of the American West. However, the new settler seldom escapes the fever and ague, which seem to be inseparable from all these new territories. Much depends on where he selects his place of abode and whether or not he plows up the ground around his cottage. The newly plowed-up or overturned turf with its rotting vegetable matter brings about fevers and ague compared to which our ordinary chills in Sweden are child's play. The settler will therefore do well to locate his field some distance from his house.

According to observations made in nine different parts of the territory the mean temperature is between 45° and 54°. The maximum temperature around Milwaukee is 92°, the minimum 12°F.

Perhaps I have been too discursive in describing the general conditions of the country we chose as our future home and have in my description to a certain extent anticipated things to which my attention was called later. I have felt, however, that in this way I could give my readers a clearer conception of the western country than if in the course of my story I were to touch, now and then, on the conditions that serve as the subject matter of these two chapters and that I felt I ought not to pass by. Incomplete though this description is, it may still fulfill its purpose; namely, that at the same time that it is a specific account of Wisconsin, it may also with a few changes serve in some degree to characterize all the new territories in the northwestern Mississippi Valley.

Notes

[a] Although Wisconsin has been in the Union since 1848 and the territorial government consequently has been superseded by its present state government, the excerpts and notes I have given above, written down during our early years in Wisconsin, inasmuch as they apply also to other new territories may not be without interest to those of our readers uninformed about such matters.

These notes are mainly taken from *Wisconsin: Its Geography, etc.*, by I. A. Lapham. [Increase Allen Lapham, *Wisconsin: Its Geography and Topography, History, Geology, and Mineralogy: Together with Brief Sketches of Its Antiquities, Natural History, Soil, Productions, Population and Government* (2nd ed., Milwaukee, 1846). The copy owned by Unonius and now in the library of the Theological Faculty of Uppsala University, Sweden, was given him by Knute A. Peterson in Milwaukee April 13, 1858. Mr. Peterson was the son of Bengt Petterson (Knut Hallström) and had been a fellow student of Unonius at Nashotah.]

[b] The first public land auction in the land district of Milwaukee took place in the early part of 1839, when land was sold to the amount of nearly half a million dollars. In the course of the same year 650,722.8 acres were sold in the entire territory at a price of $819,909.90.

[c] An acre is 43,560 square feet, or nearly 27 Swedish *kappland*.

[d] In spite of the fact that immense sums annually flow into the treasury of the United States through the sale of these vast new possessions ceded to the United States by the Indians for a small price, the profit from these sales is very inconsiderable. The greater part of this money is spent in surveying the country, preparing maps, and paying the salaries of the officials in the land offices. The principal and practically the only gain to the United States is its growing power through the adoption into the federal union of the new states, and after the country has been settled, a larger income.

[e] Up to and including 1854 the value of all the land that Congress had set aside for educational purposes was: for public schools, $48,909,535, and for universities, $4,060,704.

[f] Also in the cultivated forest lands and oak openings, even in the eastern states, grasshoppers often still appear in such numbers that the ground seems alive with the small creatures. This happens mostly in dry summers, about midsummer, but also in the fall, when they ruin the grass and leave no pasturage at all for the

cattle, which are compelled to find their grazing grounds in the swamps. It has been said that Massachusetts and other New England states are sometimes overrun by a kind of grasshopper or locust of a green color, about an inch in length, that ruins entire fields and meadows. Even if it is possible to harvest a small quantity of hay, it is so mixed with the dead bodies of these insects that the cattle refuse to eat it. I myself have seen something similar both in Wisconsin and Illinois. Chickens and turkeys live to a great extent on these insects in the summertime.

WHILE we were waiting for Lange, Carl and I, guns on our shoulders, had the opportunity to take some excursions around the city of Milwaukee. To be armed with guns to take an excursion within a city sounds perhaps a little strange, but we must remember that Milwaukee, like most American cities, had been laid out on a rather large scale and that most of it was still nothing but an uninhabited wilderness; furthermore, a kind of watery wilderness. The shores along the river running through the city, which now is well built up, consisted at that time of inaccessible swamps and morasses, where it was easier to shoot the ducks swimming about by the hundreds among the floating hummocks than to bring them to shore after they had been shot. Fille did not understand birds. The ground consisted of soft mire which allowed neither wading in it nor rowing over it in a canoe. Therefore we had to leave to the hawks and the ravens more of our booty than we were able to bring home as food for ourselves.

We were shown city lots, that is, puddles of mire or water fifty feet wide and a hundred feet long, offered for sale at from fifty to two hundred dollars each. In spite of the great faith we had in the speedy growth and development of American cities, we could not make ourselves believe that purchasing such a lot would not be literally throwing the money into the water or, rather, into the mire. It excited our ridicule and pity to see how some newcomers, whose expectations of the future growth of the city we thought too sanguine, had erected on posts in the swamp itself a sort of small portable wooden shack, connected to firm ground by means of several timbers and boards laid down in the mire, constituting what seemed to us very dangerous bridges to walk on. Time has shown, however, that those newcomers understood better than we the trend of the city's development. But still one must accept things calmly. Though Providence did not will it that we should grow rich in America, it may nevertheless be pleasant enough to recall that we once just missed being so. An opportunity was really offered us at that time. On the very spot where we shot our ducks in 1841, one of the principal hotels of the city has since been built, and in the neighborhood city lots now sell at almost as much for four square yards as we were asked a few years earlier to pay for the entire lot. To be sure, the lots at that time were not firm ground, but a few loads of gravel for filling would not have cost very much.

Milwaukee, however, is not entirely built on a morass. Far from it. On both sides of the river the land rises in terraces from fifty to a hundred feet above the river. Part of the lake front is steep, in some places almost completely perpendicular. On this height, as well as on the terraces mentioned above, several fine buildings had been erected, offering an excellent view of the river and the semicircular bay, which forms a natural, though rather exposed, harbor and anchorage. The city was platted in 1835, when the first settlers located there. The next year the population increased to twelve hundred and has been growing ever since, although not so fast as one might expect considering the excellent location and the fertility of the surrounding country. Since 1841, however, the city has grown considerably and is without question one of the most attractive and well-built cities in the West.[a]

On our arrival there were several small churches, mills, and other water-powered plants, as well as two American and one German printing shop, where papers were being published.

In 1835 only two steamboats and about eighty small sailing vessels arrived at Milwaukee. Last year the number of steamships was 174, and there were about as many sailing vessels.[b] The principal exports of the city are wheat, pork, and furs, as well as lead and copper ores, which are hauled from the mining districts during the winter.

Our friend Lange finally informed us that he was ready to go with us. Early in the morning of Thursday, October 7, we started off on our exploration, duly equipped with guns and hunting bags. Although it was late in the fall and we already had had some nights of frost, the air was mild and summery. For the first ten miles we had to walk through a thick forest, where we saw only a single, little, new-built house, which also served as a kind of inn. The road, which at the time was one of the most frequently traveled in this part of the territory, was in miserable condition. It seemed incredible that anybody could travel over it with a load. Awaiting the laying of a plank road and later the building of railroads in every direction, people paid little attention to road improvements. It is true that so-called pathmasters are appointed in every township, and everyone living in the township is required to give a certain number of days to road work. But that work is generally limited to chopping down a few trees, building bridges across rivers and creeks, and constructing corduroy bridges over the swampiest places, to make the road somewhere near passable.

But I was looking less at the road than at the surrounding woods. Nothing can be compared to an American autumnal forest. It may truly be asked whether in beauty and magnificence it does not surpass the green, fresh forest of summer. The trees, on whose branches the leaves delay, appear in their richest and most variegated colors. All possible tints and shades, from bright red, gleaming crimson, scarlet, purple, and orange, to dark green and dark brown, form a picture one can nowhere else behold. The unique beauty of the American forests in their fall coloring is with justice much talked of and admired. Particularly brilliant and splendid are the leaves of the more tender branches of the maples and poplars. Sometimes a single branch among these spreading, leafy clusters will be seen displaying the richest colors while the leaves on all the other branches still retain their original green. As a result it appears as though big, artistically arranged bouquets of flowers were suspended here and there in the trees, and the road seems to travel through a tall, flowering rose garden rather than through a wilderness already dedicated by the cold autumn winds to destruction. Day by day the picture changes and the leaves are continuously modified in color. The gleaming crimsons are the most enduring, and even later in the fall, when the leaves have fallen from the trees, one sees them as a vari-colored carpet covering the ground or as lifted by the play of the winds, soaring into the air like flowers on wings, still retaining all their glorious shadings. A North American autumn landscape, painted from nature, must always appear exaggerated or altogether created by wild fancy to a European who never has beheld in the real world such an inimitable wealth of color. The shining gold of the American elm mingles in these landscapes with the orange and bright red leaves of the maple and the poplar. The pale yellow of the leaves of the beech and the ironwood, the brown of the linden and the ash, the paling green of the oak, along with the dark green shadings of an occasional pine, cedar, or tamarack, form a mosaic which no one who has not seen it ever can begin to imagine.

Finally we emerged from the thick forest into an "opening land." There, too, the trees were aglow with the same brilliant coloring. We had to walk about thirty miles before reaching the dwelling of Mr. Pearmain,[1] to whom we were to deliver the letter which had been handed us at the Land Office. We hoped to reach the place before dark. That would have been a little difficult, though, if we had not been fortunate enough to catch a ride part of the way in an empty wagon that caught up with us some twelve or thirteen miles from the city. For the first time in my life I had the opportunity to test and admire the strength of the wagons in use here. As a matter of fact, I had occasion during this ride also to admire the stamina of my own limbs, and it seemed a wonder that neither wagon nor passengers were broken to pieces. The wagon was tossed from one stump to another much in the same way as the canalboat had been against the walls of the locks. Now the wheels dived down in some mudhole clear up to the hubs. The owner of the wagon, a brisk new settler from the state of New York, laughed heartily at our inability to keep our balance. For this ride, the only advantage of which was the saving of time, we had to pay well. In these regions no one does anything or gets anything without pay.

Finally we arrived at a log house. It may almost be taken for granted that these small cottages along the main roads most of the time serve as a kind of inns. This was the case here. The long walk and the ride had made us long for a simple meal. This was the first log house I had ever entered. The appearance of the rough, unhewn walls, the two small, low windows, and the floor and roof with their wide cracks was not very inviting. A similar hut, moreover, was soon to become my own dwelling place. Such was the home I was to offer my young wife, who here was to forego almost every comfort which a husband even in moderate circumstances seeks as fast as possible to provide for her that has given up for his sake her beloved parental home.

As one log house is very much like every other, I shall postpone a description of this type of dwelling until I am ready to build my own. When we asked if we might have dinner, the hostess agreed, provided that we were willing to wait till she had baked, for just then she had no bread in the house. Because of my limited experience in household matters and accustomed as I was from Sweden to hear about baking as a laborious and lengthy task, I was afraid we should wait a long while for our dinner, and thought that in the circumstances we might as well continue on our way. Lange assured me, however, that it would not take long. Soon we saw our hostess busy kneading wheat flour and milk in a tin pan. Fire was made in the fireplace. With the aid of some baking powder she made the dough rise, and soon a couple of tin forms were filled with biscuits, which were placed and baked in a so-called reflector. This was a contrivance about two feet long, made of sheet iron, placed in front of the open fire. In this frame meat is fried, bread baked, and smaller dishes are cooked or warmed up by means of the reflection and concentration of the heat from the fire, without coming into direct contact with the flames. In this fashion, in less than half an hour, we had a white, fresh, and very delicious bread for dinner. Other dishes served were fried bacon, boiled eggs, and tea, all of which were prepared while the biscuits were baking. In addition a type of pie or tart was served, a staple dish which the American housewife generally has on hand, but which I for the most part leave untouched in the settlers' log cabins and the western inns.

A household appliance like this reflector is a most useful contrivance where people cannot afford an iron stove but have to satisfy themselves, both for heating and cooking, with a fireplace erected against the wall of the house or made from clay reinforced with various sizes of stones. For want of anything better, a bottomless barrel serves as a chimney. Instead of such a reflector, a large pot with a tight lid is sometimes used. In this the dough is placed and baked into bread after the pot and its contents have been buried in the hot ashes. Through this baking method, strange as it may seem, good and wholesome wheat bread is produced.

Just before dark we arrived at Mr. Pearmain's farm. His home, also located close to the road and somewhat bigger than the previous one we had noticed also laid claim to being a kind of inn, where without difficulty we got supper and lodging for the night. That is, we were given sleeping quarters in an attic to reach which we had to climb up a ladder placed inside the house, clamber through a hole in the ceiling, and, bending forward, make our way to a couple of low beds. Here in a literal sense we had a roof over our heads. Carl had to sleep with a carpenter who was on the premises to build a store. This new structure, together with a sawmill and a gristmill, for which the first unit had been erected at a river connecting two lakes, not to forget the hotel where we now were resting our tired bodies, was no doubt regarded as the beginning of a flourishing future city. The very first evening we were there Pearmain, the carpenter, and the future miller maintained that the favorable location of the place, its water supply, and so forth, would without a question soon make this place another Rochester.

The next day Pearmain conducted us around the neighborhood, which was still uninhabited and unoccupied. We walked through various "openings," which in spots were so covered with trees that they well deserved the name of forest land, although oak was almost the only kind of tree. In such places the soil is tough clay and not nearly so good and fertile as where the woods consist of ash, elm, beech, linden, cherry, and sugar maple. Such trees, intermingled with oaks, indicate the most fertile soil. If the oak or beech predominates, the otherwise rich blackloam is generally mixed more or less with sand or clay. From what we had seen on our way from Milwaukee, we considered our untrained arms hardly able to cope with this kind of land. The prairie, on the other hand, in spite of its rich soil, seemed too much like a naked, grass-grown desert, and the absence of timber on it in a country where, according to what we had learned, a good warm fire in the winter is as much needed as it is in Sweden, discouraged us from selecting it as our homesite. In this neighborhood, moreover, there were only small prairies, already occupied by other settlers. The opening lands, on the other hand, appealed to us very much, and without question this kind of land is the most attractive, even if not the best suited to agriculture. Furthermore, we wanted to make our home near one of those clear, enchanting, small inland lakes which lie like great fountains surrounded by parklike forest lands. In this section we saw a number of such lakes, and more than once we stopped on our way, remarking to our guide that it was hardly worth while going any farther since we wanted to place our home just here. Smiling, however, he guided us farther along and assured us that he should soon show us both more fertile and more beautiful land.

Judging by the tall grass, this region seemed fertile enough. Our guide had brought along his horse, on which he permitted me to ride at times. I noticed as I sat on horseback that some of the blades of grass rose above my head. From this I gathered that they must have been nine to ten feet tall. They were not so lush, however, as tall. Seldom in these openings or in the forest lands does one find the sod as close and attractive as in our Swedish meadowlands.

Just as we were traveling along, admiring the tall grass and the picturesque landscape, dotted with a number of small inland lakes, sometimes separated only by a narrow strip of land, forming a natural bridge between their shores, we were suddenly startled by a rustling noise in the bushes. Not many steps away we saw five or six fine deer. They stopped for a moment to see what could have disturbed them in their peaceful feeding grounds, probably untrodden by man's foot for a long time. Only a moment also would have sufficed for Carl and me to use our guns, but the unexpected sight of these graceful animals, the like of which we had never seen, made us stand quiet in admiration and actually forget we were carrying arms on our shoulders. I believe the beautiful animals could have stood still for a good while further before it would have occurred to us to shoot at them. Pearmain and Lange cried, "Shoot, shoot!" But before we could cock our guns, the light-footed beasts bounded out of shooting range. Soon we were able to see only their high, many-pronged horns above the grass and bushes. "If a Yankee had had your gun just now," said Pearmain, "we should have had venison for dinner." I did not doubt that he was right. Still, we did not regret the unfired bullets, though within ourselves we hoped at some other time to show him that even Swedish hunters understand how to lay low the game of the forest.

Finally we arrived at the shores of the loveliest little lake we had seen in the course of our walk. In Indian language it was called Chenequa, or Pine Lake, since pines, which otherwise do not grow in this part of Wisconsin, are found here along with the red cedar in a couple of places along its shores. Most of these trees have been hewn down, probably by the Indians, who used their easily hollowed-out trunks for canoes. On a small isle we found one of these small boats, left unfinished and partly destroyed by fire.

This spot was one of the prettiest one could ever hope to see. The lake, about two miles long, and branching off into a number of bays and coves, was surrounded almost everywhere by dry, high shores. Only in a couple of places was the ground low and swampy. Close to the lake the ground was somewhat rough, but a short distance away the land was even, and on one side lay a big, perfectly level burr-oak field. Now, we insisted firmly, it was no use to go any farther, especially as the land, in addition to being incredibly beautiful, seemed also to be excellent in every other respect. According to Pearmain's statement, and as far as we ourselves were able to judge, the soil of the burr-oak plain appeared to be of the richest and best quality — a deep blackloam with an admixture of clay. In the opening land next to that plain we found the soil to consist of sandy clay, growing stiffer as we approached the shore.

Since we did not want any of the thousands of prospective settlers roaming about the country looking for homesites to get ahead of us, we decided to return to Milwaukee at once and announce at the Land Office that we each wanted to take under pre-emption a quarter section of land. Pearmain informed us, however, that the section in question, as well as others in the same township, could not be purchased at the Land Office or be occupied under pre-emption right. The situation was that a company had been organized some years earlier for the purpose of constructing a canal from Milwaukee to the Mississippi. To this company Congress had ceded, on certain conditions, all odd-numbered sections along the proposed canal route, and to such a section the piece of land on which we wanted to settle belonged. However, a certain time had been set in which the canal was to be completed, and of that time only two or three years still remained. The work, which had hardly been begun, had stopped long ago, and it seemed almost impossible that the company should ever be able to carry out its contract. Hence it was fairly certain that when the time specified in the contract had expired, these canal lands would revert to the United States and be offered for sale in the regular way. Nevertheless, until that time had expired, the land could not be purchased at the Land Office. As far as the canal company was concerned, no one ever bothered to make any payments to it for this land, since it was regarded as certain that the land would revert to the Government and then be offered at half the price demanded by the canal company. We might therefore take it for granted that we should not have to pay for land thus occupied for a couple of years.[2] Considering our financial status, this was welcome news, although we realized that there would be some uncertainty about our right of ownership, inasmuch as the canal company still had the legal right to sell these sections. Suppose that we, without regarding the company, were to take possession of a piece of land, cultivate it, and build our home on it as though it were our own, what was to prevent some other person after a few months from purchasing it? In this case, would there be anything for us to do but leave our homestead without even being able to claim remuneration for the work we had put into it? Pearmain maintained, however, that we need not fear this eventuality. Many before us had taken possession of land in just this way. In their right of ownership they were protected by what he termed club law, the law, that is, which the people themselves in remote regions had established because of the peculiar conditions under which they were living. According to this law Judge Lynch makes all judicial decisions. No one could prevent the canal company from selling the land, but it was quite possible effectively to prevent the land's being sold to anyone but its present occupant, who had spent time and money making it habitable. All the settlers, whether on land held by Congress or by the canal company, had made a compact to stand by and protect one another against such trespassing. And woe betide anyone who sought to appropriate another man's land! He would do well before taking possession of his purchased ground to obtain the highest possible insurance on his house and life; otherwise neither would be worth much. I know of only one instance where such a thing was attempted, but I shall have more to say of this later on.

There may be divergent views on such a law of terror, but there is much that may be said in its defense. Nobody was the loser by it. Not the Government, for when the privilege of the canal company expired, the land would have to be paid for, and then club law would not protect the settler from having to do his duty. Nor was the canal company the loser, for it had to all practical intents and purposes already lost its rights and would be compelled, when it found itself unable to carry out its agreements, to return to the Government the property tentatively given to it. On the other hand, the rights of the poor settler were protected. He was saved from having to pay double the price of other land without getting any additional privileges. At the same time the community profited, for in this way the land was settled and tilled earlier than otherwise would have been the case.

Inasmuch as others did not fear to settle on this kind of land, we thought we might risk it, all the more because in this way we might count on two or three years of suspended payment, in our circumstances a great privilege. Our capital had been melting away so fast that the combined cash supply of Carl and me was reduced to about four hundred dollars. From this amount we still had to purchase land, build our home, buy at least one team of oxen, a cow, a few pigs, and some essential household articles. In addition, we had to provide food for at least the first winter. How this small amount was to see us through was hard for us or anybody else to see. Here there was no opportunity to borrow money. Notwithstanding all this, we were of good courage, though I cannot deny that with my poetic dreams of a "cottage and a hearth" were mingled in realistic moments some very doubtful intermezzos.

Under these conditions we were happy indeed to cross off from our calculation, at least for the time being, the two hundred dollars — exactly one-half of our present cash — that we had hitherto expected to pay for a quarter section of congressional land. For though we had planned to use our pre-emption rights, these would not have allowed us more than a year to pay, and it was not likely that we should find it any easier in twelve months than now. On the other hand, we might well hope to have improved our finances enough in two or three years to be able to pay for our land. We had at least during this time some harvests to expect, which naturally we could not look for the first year.

Without long deliberation, we decided, therefore, to settle on the shore of the little lake, where both the natural beauty and the good soil promised us a pleasant home and where among oak, beech, and hickory trees, the evergreen pines, untouched by the axe, would always stand as a pleasant reminder of the pine forest of our old homeland. We needed to take no steps to insure our claim except to inform our neighbors that we were planning to make our home here, and as a sign of our intention, start some improvement to indicate that this part of the section had been occupied. Pearmain, as an experienced settler prepared for any eventualities, had brought his axe. As Columbus on first landing in the new world had raised the Castilian flag inscribed with *F & I*, the initials of his sovereigns, so we chopped down a few trees, and into the bark of a couple of others cut a big *C*, signifying "Claimed," a sign that we in our own name had taken possession of the W½ of Section 33, Township 8, Range 18, *in hac altera mundi parte* [in this other part of the world], with full and complete legal right of possession, to be inhabited, settled, and held by us and our descendants forever.

At the same time we looked around for a suitable building site and found such a spot without difficulty close to the shore, with an excellent view over the lake and the land beyond. My only worry at this time was that we had no road to our future home, and as I recalled the great labors expended on roads in Sweden, I feared that great difficulties would face us. Lange, however, knew better. "Cut down the trees," he said, "and drag a couple of logs a few times between the country road and the house; that's all that's needed. Besides, there'll be road enough where you keep driving." In this way this worry also was removed.

We now agreed with Pearmain that Lotten and Christine were to board with him while Carl, Polman, and I — Polman had decided to remain for a while and help us — worked on our log house. Next it would be necessary to buy a team of oxen. These draft animals were indispensable for our work now and in the future, and we reasoned that we might as well purchase a team at once and also a wagon, in order to haul our goods from the city.

Because money is pretty scarce among the new settlers, there is hardly anything, from lands and houses to cattle and farm implements, that they are not willing to sell for cash, provided, of course, they are able to make some profit on the deal. And so when Pearmain's neighbors learned that we were in the market for a team of oxen, we soon had half a dozen to select from. We chose a pair that were rather old and paid sixty dollars for them, probably more than the seller could have got from anyone but a European immigrant, who in order to drive the animals in the way customary here needs a pair steady and well trained. Spak and Wallis, we soon learned, were in steadiness a pair of really exemplary beasts.

The work oxen in this country are generally very obedient and easy to guide. On the prairie, where the soil is easily plowed and free from stumps and roots, the settler is probably better served by horses, if he can afford to buy them. But in the forest and opening lands in all circumstances a team of oxen is wholly indispensable, whereas horses, at least at first, are almost useless for clearing and plowing the land. It is almost impossible to travel with horses in these pathless regions, and still more difficult to plow with them between stumps and roots that constantly stop the plow in its furrow.

The ox harness here is much simpler and, as far as I am a judge, much more serviceable and less tiring to the animals than that used in Sweden. All that is needed is a yoke, a couple of bows, and an iron ring. The yoke is made from a maple block, about four feet long and nine inches thick in the middle. Through this an iron pin is driven, at the lower end of which is an iron ring to which the draft rod of the wagon or plow is hooked. A short distance from the iron ring the yoke is hollowed out and rounded so that it is shaped to the neck of the draft animals. On either side of this rounded space there is a hole, about one and a half inches in diameter, through which both ends of the bow, or collar, which is made in the form of a horseshoe, are passed and fastened with wooden pegs at the upper side of the yoke. If the yoke and the bows are well made so that the former fits the necks of the oxen and the latter their shoulder blades, the beasts are not hurt or chafed by this simple device, through which they pull not only with their withers, but also and principally with their shoulders, on either side of which the bows are fastened very much as the ordinary hames of a harness. Most farmers manufacture their own yokes and bows; the latter are made from small elm or hickory trees, which after being heated in boiling water are easily bent to any shape desired. If one were to buy such a yoke, it would generally cost from two to four dollars. No lines are used, but the oxen are directed by certain words of command — "Gee," to the right; "Haw," to the left; "Whoa," stop — and by the assistance of the whip, which the driver swings over their necks in the direction he wants them to go. In this way they are driven, between trees and stumps, with as much assurance as ever a horse with a pair of reins.

On the way back to Milwaukee Lange gave me a private lesson in driving oxen, for which as in everything else, training and experience are most necessary and in which, without any desire to boast, I may claim that I acquired a remarkable skill. Many a time I wished that my old brothers in Apollo and Thalia [3] could have seen and heard me sitting on my load, exercising my declamatory skill by calling out again and again, with much feeling, "Gee!" "Haw!" "Go along!" gesticulating in the meanwhile with the great whipstock, cracking the lash with full theatrical bravura.

During the long and numerous trips I had to make, especially during those early days of our settlement, I had plenty of time for philosophical reflection, through which I came to the important conclusion that as a remedy for impatience and a violent temper nothing can compare with a few hours of driving oxen. If my temper, which used to be rather hasty and fiery, has grown milder and more tractable in later years, the credit in a large measure is certainly owing to our old draft animals, Spak and Wallis.

Notes

[a] The census of 1850 gives Milwaukee's population as 20,000, and since then it has more than doubled.

[b] How fast American cities grow is indicated by the fact that Milwaukee, as early as 1852, had thirty churches, some of them very well built; namely, three Protestant Episcopal, one Norwegian Lutheran, six German Lutheran and Reformed, three Methodist Episcopal, two Baptist, two Congregational, four Roman Catholic, five Presbyterian, one Universalist, and two Wesleyan Methodist churches. In addition there were several organizations for various purposes: one Bible society, one tract society, two musical organizations, three orphanages, two other charitable organizations, several literary societies, three Masonic lodges, five Odd Fellows lodges, two temperance societies; also banks, insurance companies, etc.

Chapter 11

MOVING TO THE COUNTRY · TRAVEL ON SUNDAY · ARRIVAL AT
DELAFIELD · BOARDING AT PEARMAIN'S · MR. PEARMAIN AND
HIS WIFE · ANOTHER WALK TO PINE LAKE · SELECTION OF BUILD-
ING SITE · BUILDING A TEMPORARY HUT · OUR FIRST CAMPING
THERE · NECESSARY REPAIRS · HAULING HAY

A S SOON as possible we took our oxen on the return journey
to Milwaukee, where Christine meanwhile had got sick — a
condition that delayed our departure for several days. In
the meantime we purchased a lumber wagon for sixty dollars, and
Carl and Polman went with the first load while I remained in the
city to assist the women. Fortunately Christine recovered quickly
so that when Polman returned with the wagon and the oxen, we
were able to start off immediately with the rest of our belongings.
Carl had stayed at Pearmain's to cut some hay, which, though it
was late in the fall, could still be used for fodder.

On Sunday, October 17, at five o'clock in the morning, we left
Milwaukee. Christine, who was still weak from her recent illness,
was placed in the wagon among our boxes, chests, and trunks. Lotten preferred to go on foot, while Polman and I took turns driving
the oxen, an art of which neither of us was as yet master. It went
nevertheless very well, except down hill, where we did not rightly
know how to make the oxen hold back the heavy load. The wagon
went between stumps and stones, roots and hollows, with such
speed that I feared many a time both oxen and it should tumble
over. Finally we met a kind-hearted American who completed the
education we had got from our friend Lange. He drove our oxen
down the next hill, walking close to their heads and gently prod-
ding them with the whip handle as he cried, "Back, Back!" at which
the animals held back with all their strength, making the wagon
roll down hill just as slowly as up another hill a few minutes later.

The rest of the way, following that lesson, we were more proficient in the art of driving oxen.

The trip went nevertheless very slow. The road was so poor that a Swedish drayman would have been astounded at our making any headway over it at all with such a load. By noon we had not made more than ten miles with our slow-footed beasts. There was a lone dwelling standing at this point, and though we naturally had brought our lunch along, I tried to buy there a little milk. But without success. To be sure, they had plenty of milk in the house, but it was Sunday, and the pious people that lived there would not do business on Sunday. I thought, however, that if their consciences did not permit them to sell milk on Sunday, it ought not to have prevented them, out of Christian charity, from giving a couple of strangers a little to quench their thirst. They replied very soberly that it did not rain manna from heaven on the sabbath and those who started out on a trip on Sunday well deserved, even in this life, to accustom themselves to the thirst that is never quenched. At least that was my understanding of the puritanical admonitions they served us in lieu of milk. Since I cannot defend my own failings, neither will I censure too harshly excesses of an opposite kind. But I had some mistrust then, and the same mistrust I have still, of this sort of extravagantly godly display. The good Lord was more merciful, however, than those who called themselves his servants. A little farther along the way we found a spring whose clear water compensated for the milk refused us, as we ate our dinner at a grass-covered board.

This little adventure, nevertheless, began to worry us. If our oxen had been the speediest in the world, it still would have been impossible to make our way to Pearmain's place in a day, perhaps even in two days, considering the condition of the road. I knew we still had a few miles to go before coming to an inn. We could not reach it before dusk, but I had counted on finding lodging there overnight. If now the same Puritanism should be practiced there as where we had been denied a drink of milk, and if we were to be refused lodging, nothing would remain for us but to spend the night in the woods. On these roads it would be impossible to travel in the dark. This might be a serious matter for my wife and for Christine, who was not yet fully recovered from her illness. My anxiety on that score made me regret bitterly that we had started off on a Sunday, although I cannot claim that my regret stemmed from a genuine sense of wrongdoing.

Finally we arrived at the house where we had planned to end our first day's journey, and fortunately our plans worked out. Either the host was a good Samaritan who did not wish to close his door to homeless strangers, or he was one of those that do not trouble themselves about what the elders of Israel ordained. Enough that both we and our draft animals found lodging in return for proper payment.

In the inn were other lodgers as well. The entire building consisted — the attic excepted — of one big room, one end of which was divided by means of a thin board wall into two small bedrooms, or rather alcoves. Instead of doors a couple of curtains had been hung at the doorways, and the rooms were so small that they barely provided room for a double bed with a narrow passage between it and the wall. One of these rooms was occupied by the host and the hostess. The bed in the other room had already been "claimed" by a couple of gentlemen. They displayed, however, the courtesy in America generally shown to women, and giving the room to my wife and Christine, they satisfied themselves with the only remaining bed in the low and chilly attic. Polman and I made our beds on part of the floor not occupied by the two alcoves. All our baggage was left in the wagon, standing in the unfenced yard close to the road. During the night I heard several persons pass by the house and thought it would be a wonder if everything in our wagon was intact when we awoke. But nothing was missing when after a rest as good as can be expected in view of our accommodations and our weariness from the previous day, we early next morning took up our journey.

We had now made our way through the forest, and the rest of the road, which passed through open land, was far better than the part we had already traveled. We now made much better time, and by noon reached Pearmain's newly built house, the location of the future village of Delafield.

This house, in which Lotten and Christine were to spend at least a couple of weeks, was about the same as the one in which we had spent the previous night, but provided with only one bed alcove, reserved for the owners themselves. The women, therefore, had to sleep in the attic, the mode of access and general condition of which I have already described in connection with our former visit. With the aid of blankets and quilts they made a kind of enclosure, within which they could have a little "creep-in" of their own. On the other side of the attic the carpenter, whom I mentioned earlier, had also contrived a kind of shelter for himself. In these sleeping quarters the walls were far from tight, and through the still thinner roof, made of light shingles, the biting autumn wind penetrated, flapping the sleeper's pillow. These conditions made me and my companions determine to get to work on our own cabin as quickly as possible.

The next day, however, we could do nothing more than grind our axes, load the wagon with hay, and get ready such things as were absolutely necessary for Polman's and my camping venture in our own domains. The women baked some wheat bread for us and provided us with food for a few days. Thus equipped, we waited for the morning when our real pioneer life was to begin.

That evening we spent with our host and hostess, who, as I observed already and saw even more plainly in the future, were inclined to profit at our expense. The price demanded for the meals that we men should many times be taking on our trips back and forth to the homestead, as well as the price of board for the women till we should have our own place, was very considerable and, as we later learned, far higher than was customary in this region. All the greater reason, then, why we should not permit our axes to rest. We noticed, however, that in all arrangements Pearmain tried to slow down our progress as much as possible. He wanted to help us with our first load to Pine Lake, but insisted he did not have time to accompany us for a couple of days. Besides, we should have to order lumber in advance at a sawmill, located about seven miles away, and there, too, he promised to accompany us and bring his own oxen, at a price of course, so that we might take two loads of lumber at once and thus save time. However, we would not be detained, but started off the first thing in the morning to fell the first trees for our cabin.

Pearmain and his wife were a rather odd pair and worthy of a paragraph of their own. Their past seemed to be hidden in mystery. The husband had been born in England and had had an education far above his present status as farmer and landlord of an inn. Many things indicated that he had been well-to-do, perhaps wealthy. He had probably been a business man who had failed and who after unfortunate speculations in the old world had decided to try his luck in this new country. After spending a couple of years in the East, he again must have taken advantage of the bankruptcy laws and now, like so many hundreds of others suffering bad luck, had finally retreated to the sparsely populated West to try to repair his fortunes. With a little log house located on the most heavily trafficked road from Milwaukee, he paid little attention to his farm — a fine piece of land, purchased and paid for not in his own name but in the name of one of his non-resident sons to prevent his creditors from gaining possession of it. Most of his time and energy was given to his saloon and inn. He was a man, furthermore, who sought to have a hand in all kinds of communal affairs. He was a rabid Democrat and made harangues at all political rallies. At every election he used to run for some office, but never, as far as I know, with any success. His present wife was his second, but I have my doubts whether he was actually legally married to the woman who now bore his name. He had no children by her, but by his first marriage had several sons and daughters, who, however, had moved out of his house because of the stepmother. A daughter was married and lived in the neighborhood, but she never associated with her parents.

The so-called Mrs. Pearmain was the most original woman I remember ever having seen. She was about forty years old, but as coquettish and affected as any dried-up old maid just about to become a permanent spinster. Her thin face, bearing the marks of time and the hardships of pioneer life, still gave evidence of a lost beauty. Her figure, too, must at one time have been graceful. She still carried her head high, and when she spoke she used many gestures, with easy unconstraint. She still showed a kind of natural grace as she moved about the stove and the simple wooden chairs in the poor hovel for which she also seemed to have exchanged the elegance and pleasures of a once luxurious life. Her manners and appearance put one in mind of a decadent and seedy actress, which, as I learned later, she actually had been while in England, till she departed for America in Pearmain's company.

Her person and history would have given August Blanche[1] ma-

169

terial for an excellent story. Imagine a popular prima donna in her boudoir, surrounded by luxury and abundance, in frivolous madness jesting her way through the fleeting years of youth, draining the champagne cup of joy and pleasure. Then place the same woman in an American log cabin, like a rejected piece of furniture tossed away in a trash closet, herself a mere shabby remnant, yet the only thing bearing witness to past glory and splendor. The sceptre of beauty has been changed into a broom handle. The tender hand that formerly toyed with the golden tassels of the velvet covering of her divan now handles the scrub pail. The cheek whose roses once glistened from the bouquet of champagne now gets its only bloom from the whiskey bottle. The bottle, indeed, was a friend with which Mrs. Pearmain sought more and more to console herself for the loss of life's sunshine. Frequently my wife during her stay in the house had the not very pleasant job of assisting her hostess in her so-called nervous attacks—that is, when she had happened to take a drop too much from the aforementioned fountain of comfort.

Nevertheless, that first evening we found their company agreeable. Both host and hostess were rather talkative, and their conversation served at least as a training course in the English language, in which we were now making more progress.

When we were ready to set out for Pine Lake the next morning Pearmain offered unexpectedly to accompany us. It was necessary, he reasoned, that he go with us to help blaze a road over which we could drive our loads and which was to be our wagon road between his place and our homestead. Carl, who already had spent several days in the country, had got enough information about the local geography to make Pearmain's services superfluous. But we considered it advisable to accept his offer and make use of his experience, although we well knew it would cost us at least a dollar, the regular daily wage at this time of year. In this way my wife also got an opportunity to go along, and we were anxious to show her the place we had selected and to get her help in determining the building site more definitely. On her account Pearmain saddled his horse, from which she was in no danger of being thrown, for he was hardly frisky in nature and in addition was stone blind in both eyes.

Thus we started off, supplied with axes to clear a way for the oxen and wagon as well as to blaze trees to mark the road. Lotten rode behind the wagon on her blind ambling nag. Sometimes she forgot his disability and failed to rein him carefully between bushes and stumps, with the result that a couple of times both horse and rider took a tumble, which fortunately had no more serious result for my wife than a few scratches on her face. After some trouble we reached the public road, which had been laid out along the border line of the section in which our land was located.

I was happy to find Lotten satisfied with the location we had chosen. Like the rest of us she was enthusiastic about the natural beauty of the landscape. We showed her the place we had tenta-tively picked out as our building site, but after looking around awhile and getting her opinion, we selected another as more suit-able, only a short distance away and closer to the shore. The view it had over the lake was, if possible, even more beautiful than the former. It seemed only right and fair that Lotten, who was to have the trouble of arranging everything in the home, also should have something to say about where it was to be located, and we never had reason to regret that we followed her advice and availed ourselves of her good taste and natural wisdom.

She and Pearmain, however, soon had to return. To be sure, the road we had laid out was not more than four miles from Delafield, but the going had been slow. Therefore they had to hurry to reach Pearmain's house before dark, and we who remained had to devise some kind of sleeping place. For this purpose we hewed down a few small trees, some six or seven feet long, and laid them in a square on top of each other. When we had built the walls about four feet high, we placed within them a wide walnut bed that my wife had bought in Milwaukee for five dollars, money she had made by sell-ing horsehair rings. Although it was late in the season, we were not sure we were safe from snakes, and it would not have been good for us to sleep on the cold, damp ground. We had therefore taken the precaution to tie this bed on the hay load along with certain other household articles. After we had furnished our hut in this way, we covered it with a flat roof, consisting of a few poles on which we piled the small supply of hay we had brought with us. We made a kind of door, or, to speak correctly, a hole, in one of the walls, through which we crawled into our hut. The big bed did not leave us any more room than was absolutely necessary for dressing and undressing.

Besides all the other advantages Carl had over Polman and me, he was a fairly capable cook. As an experienced hunter he knew how to accommodate himself to all conditions. We built a fire and got a supper ready, seasoned with an excellent appetite after our unaccustomed labors. Then we crawled into our shelter, the first ever erected by white men on the shores of Pine Lake. A few miles east of us we knew of a couple of other new settlers; to the south was Pearmain, our nearest neighbor, but the west side of the lake was entirely uninhabited, and to the north was a vast expanse of forest in which no white man had ever built his cabin. Certainly there was something romantic in our situation, but it is hardly to be wondered at that loneliness was part of our mood. We were still unacquainted with the wilderness, where our voices could not reach another human abode. We were surrounded — at how great a distance we did not know — by Indians who were still roaming about their old hunting grounds. We were still in a state of tension because of stories we had heard or read, of the perils and adventures of pioneers in the vast waste spaces of the West. Taking all these things into consideration, it was not strange that somber feelings should assail us when the darkness of night fell and we went to rest for the first time in our lonely, makeshift hut. Through its open walls the stars of heaven peeped in, and prompted us to entrust ourselves to His care who, wherever we are, whether we wake or sleep, is round about us and watches over all our ways.

It took me a long time to go to sleep. In my heart kept sounding a lullaby of times past, of a childhood home on a far-off shore, of a mother's bosom left empty and bereft of an only son.

When we woke up early next morning, we found we should have to put our hut in better shape if we were not to invite chills. The cold had been very keen during the night, and before we had warmed our somewhat stiff limbs with a good cup of coffee, we felt rather shivery on the frost-covered ground. The chinks in the wall would have to be filled with clay, dirt thrown up around the walls, and the roof covered with more hay to shelter us in case of rain.

We now discovered in our neighborhood traces of an Indian wigwam, which completely had escaped our attention the preceding evening, and which gave us an idea for a more practical type of construction for our temporary dwelling. It was decided I should go back to Delafield, where we had bought a big haystack, and bring home as big a load of hay as possible. In the meantime Carl and Polman were to work on our hut, and after it was a little improved, start to hew logs for the house.

I started off at once with our oxen, and had no difficulty in finding the road we had cleared and marked the preceding day. Lotten and Christine had slept fairly well in their low attic, but like us complained that it was cold and drafty. There was little time, however, for conversation. I had to borrow a hayrack and as well as I could fit it to my wagon in place of the box, then start off at once to the haystack, located not far from Pearmain's house. There I found a young American, with whose assistance I cut off a corner of the stack so that the remaining part of it was still sheltered against the rain.

In America, where the settlers have not had time yet to build big barns, stables, and sheds, both grain and hay are stacked on the bare ground, the former in the fields and the latter in the meadows or swamps where it has been cut. A fence is built around it to protect it from the cattle. As a rule, the haystacks are long, so that they may be cut off from the top down and hauled home as the hay is required, without subjecting the rest of it to spoilage from snow and rain.

While we were working, my practical young American friend gave me some helpful lessons in the art of stacking hay and loading a hayrack — lessons of which I was very much in need. The hayforks used for this kind of work are, like other American tools and implements, neat and attractive and very convenient. The handle is much longer than ours, and the fork itself is made out of steel with two or three sharp, bent, springy prongs. The tool as a whole is easy to handle and, like many other things, well worthy of being taken as models at home in Sweden.

With this good assistance I soon had my load ready, but to make my way with it on the rough road was another and much harder task. I had to pass a long corduroy bridge laid over a swamp. Across its uneven logs an empty wagon is often in danger of being overturned and broken to pieces; still more so is a heavy load of hay. The top of the load was solidly tied and pressed down with a long pole fastened to the rack by a couple of small iron chains; none the less it swayed back and forth so that I expected at every moment to have the whole load tumble over me. My assistant, who realized the difficulty of managing that part of the road without help, followed me across it. The oxen, who understood very well how to keep to the middle of the road, were made to walk as slowly as possible, and we ourselves walked on either side of the load, steadying it with our hayforks as it jerked and lurched from side to side. Thus we managed to cross the troublesome passage without serious results. How I managed afterwards all alone through the woods seems to this moment a deep mystery, but succeed I did in piloting it between trees and bushes, between stumps and clumps of brushwood. However humiliating it may be to my pride, I still must admit that it was due more to Spak and Wallis than to myself that the load did not topple over.

This trip constituted practically all of my day's work. After I had returned to our hut, which in the meantime had been much improved by my partners, we had time just before dark to unload the hay and pack it both on the roof and around the walls of our hut, so that we might be said to have been living in the middle of a haystack. We raised up several poles around the cone-shaped roof to steady it and prevent it from blowing away, and we closed the door opening with a bundle of hay.

It was well that we took these precautions, for during the night a heavy storm came up, with rain and snow slush. But it was dry and warm in our dark den. We felt sorry, though, for our poor oxen, which, lest they run away, were kept under the yoke all night and fastened to a tree without the least shelter from the storm. Still, they were probably used to this. The new settlers in these regions are strangely careless of their cattle. Both cows and oxen often have to stand outside night and day throughout the cold winter, or else are provided with an open shelter which possibly protects them from snow and rain, but not at all from the cold. But this is true only in places where people have not had a chance to get things into proper shape—which at this time seems to be the condition almost everywhere around here.

Chapter 12

CUTTING LOGS · NEW UPPSALA · THE AMERICAN AXE · CARL
SHOOTS THE FIRST DEER · LOTTEN'S STAY IN DELAFIELD · MEET-
ING WITH FRIMAN · WINNEBAGO INDIANS · A NIGHT IN THEIR
NEIGHBORHOOD · AN UNEXPECTED GUEST FOR BREAKFAST · THE
ABILITY OF INDIANS TO TELL EUROPEANS FROM AMERICANS

NO RAY of daylight awakened us. We found ourselves in
complete darkness. Moreover, we had to be very careful
with fire in our low, easily ignited hut. Carl was the only
one who had a watch with him, and he had forgotten to wind it
the previous evening, so that the only way to find out the time was
to crawl to the door opening and push aside the bundle of hay.
We could see that it was daylight, but there was no sun in the sky
to tell us how late it was. The morning was cold and raw, and the
ground partly covered with snow. Yet it was only the twentieth
of October.

We rekindled our log fire, and after Carl had prepared and we
had eaten a solid breakfast, we set off to work with our axes.

For a log cabin one does not as a rule choose the heaviest trees,
but only those that measure about eighteen inches in diameter.
They also have to be fairly straight. It is sometimes rather hard,
therefore, when the oaks grow far apart, to find proper timber.
Some trees we found close at hand, but most of them we had to
get a long way from our building site. For the cabin we needed
between forty and fifty logs if the attic was not to be too low to
accommodate a room for Carl. In addition we had to have joists
for the floor and ceiling. Not being experienced hewers, as one
may readily suppose, we had to spend several days felling the
needed trees, cutting them into proper lengths, and hauling them
to the building site with our oxen. Because of our need of timber
we had to cut down many tall, beautiful oaks whose branches I

otherwise should have liked to save. Briskly and lustily we nevertheless kept swinging our American axes in the primeval forest, and when the trees fell to the ground we cheered as lustily as at the cry of "Strike" on the bowling alleys in Uppsala.

But speaking of Uppsala, I have forgotten to mention that this was to be the name of our estate in the new world. Here there are many cities and villages named after Paris, London, Rome, and almost every other place of note in the old world. Then why not, on this side of the ocean, perpetuate the name of the memorable and to us beloved city on Fyrisvall? [1] But this, like many other things, proved only one of the young dreams of our pioneer life. A more intimate knowledge of life and conditions here would have convinced us that neither the location nor any other advantages made it likely a city should ever be built on this spot. Although townships are sometimes named in this country after some of their early and influential citizens, or named by them, it was not to be presumed that we should be given the same distinction. Besides it is very unusual for anyone to give a name to his private property. People simply say Mr. Groth's farm, or Mr. Unonius' farm, or just give the number of the section and the name of the township in which it is located. Often a man's home is designated by the river, lake, or prairie where he has settled, as, for instance, it is said he lives at Pine Lake, at Bark River, on the Koshkonong Prairie, or in the Rock River Settlement. Still our place at Pine Lake was marked on some maps as New Upsala. [2] Some people unacquainted with local conditions believed on that account that the name of the person who lived there was Upsal and that the adjective "New" had come about by some mistake, and I was often addressed as Mr. Upsal in the early days. Yet we might perhaps have succeeded in getting the region around our home named as we wished had not the neighborhood been settled after a while by a larger number of Norwegians than Swedes, and after that even by people of other nationalities. As a result other considerations became important and our own destiny took an entirely different turn.

Let us, however, return to our work. After we had felled the trees, we cut them into logs, some eighteen, others twenty-two feet in length. In due time these were hauled and placed in a square around our building plot. Some people who have more time at their disposal and are able to expend more care on the houses smooth the logs on two sides and make them approximately even in thickness, giving the building a better appearance both inside and out. We, on the other hand, like most of the new settlers, had to satisfy ourselves, for the time being, with the rough, unpeeled logs in their natural round shape and could not be too particular if one bark-covered log chanced to bulge out a little farther than the rest.

On the farm the stumps still stand as a memento of my first efforts at handling an axe. They are easily distinguished from the rest because chopped and hacked more unevenly, a clear proof of the inexperienced hand of the workman. Often the sharp, broad-edged axe slipped from the hard trunk, and it was a wonder that I did not cut off my feet or legs. For many years I kept a pair of boots that showed numerous marks of my youthful efforts at the lumberjack's trade. The edge of the soles, the uppers, and the tops were cut through almost everywhere, as if they had been slashed with a sharp knife. It was really a merciful providence that protected my legs from being similarly misused.

But training and persistence accomplish much, and so it was in this instance. I must confess, though, that I never acquired any real accuracy and skill in handling an axe. I was told that I put forth too much effort, not necessary with the excellent axes in use here. The American axe, which is much heavier than those used in Sweden, is more like a small broad-axe. It has just the proper weight, and with its rounded edge, its head a little slanted and not too thick, and its curved hickory handle shaped to fit the hand, it has a swing that makes it bite into the tree more easily, and at the same time it requires less expenditure of force than those used in Sweden. The work goes both faster and lighter than with the latter. It is really something beautiful to see a skillful hewer swinging his shining, broad-edged axe against the tall oaks, from which great wedges fly out under the quick, successive blows. Before one expects it, the tree falls to the ground with a mighty crash. Apparently without needing a moment's rest, the hewer immediately attacks another of the century-old trunks. Many a time I had fun with Norwegian and Swedish immigrants who had brought with them their home-made axes and at first absolutely would not use the American, which in their opinion were too heavy and unwieldy.

But after a short time they were ready to discard their old tools entirely, declaring that work was much easier and less strenuous with American axes.

While at work we generally carried with us our loaded guns, not for defense against any unexpected attacks from either Indians or wild beasts, for in that respect we considered ourselves fairly safe, but for shooting, if possible, some of the abundant game in the woods. Almost from morning till evening we heard Fille's barking, but what he was chasing we never knew. Probably it was deer, but in hunting them he had as little training as we did; nor did we take time for that kind of sport, but were satisfied to get a duck, whenever one happened to swim close to the shore, for a welcome change in our meals, which otherwise were rather monotonous.

I hesitate to tell any hunting stories, which, as is well known, are even less credible than travel descriptions. But since I have never been known as a great hunter, my veracity should be all the greater, especially as I am not the hero of the hunting adventures mentioned in my notes during our early days as settlers.

One day when Carl had gone off from us farther than usual, Polman and I sat resting on the trunk of a tree we had just cut down, leaning against our axes. Suddenly we heard the report of a gun, and immediately afterward a distant shout from Carl and a bark indicating the dog was close to his quarry. We hurried to the spot and found Carl reloading his rifle, declaring that he had wounded a stag which had come running right at him. At the moment the gun was discharged the stag had turned around with a great leap, lifting his white tail high in the air, and swift as an arrow he had taken off into the forest. Immediately afterward Fille had come running. The deer had probably wanted to avoid him by plunging into the lake and swimming over to the other shore, but he was checked by Carl's bullet and turned in another direction. Carl was very certain he had hit the animal; spots of blood on the ground bore him out. We abandoned our logging for the day and decided instead to look for the wounded stag. Fille, however, was no longer barking. We pressed on through bushes and thickets, looking for the stag in valleys and on hills, but with no luck. Twilight came on, and we had to return to our hut. Carl was rather put out because of our failure to find the stag, but insisted that it must be lying dead somewhere in the neighborhood. Fille did not return till late in the evening, and Carl let him in through the door. When he felt of the dog, he assured us that we should have our fill of venison the next day, for Fille, not properly trained, had had the impudence to help himself already.

Early the next morning, after breakfast, of which Fille did not get his share this time, we put our guns on our shoulders and set out to see whether Carl's promise was to be fulfilled. We made the dog show us the way, and, sure enough, after searching for a couple of hours, we finally found the stag lying dead in a copse of small aspens, on a slope leading down to a deep hollow, which afterwards in giving directions we called Deer Hollow. Carl's bullet had been pretty well aimed and had hit the stag in the shoulder, but in spite of his wound he had run almost a mile and had probably kept Fille at bay with his long branching horns till, faint from loss of blood, he had finally given up to his enemy. It was not easy to get out of the hollow with our booty, which weighed nearly two hundred pounds, but having fastened it to a pole we finally carried it in triumph on our shoulders to the hut. It was later my undeserved honor to take our game home to Lotten, who shared it with the Pearmains and with Carl's assistance salted or smoked such parts of the delicate venison as we could not immediately consume.

Lotten had in the meantime not been spending particularly pleasant days. Mrs. Pearmain's "nervous disorder" made the stay in their home less agreeable, especially as the small log house had no room where Lotten and Christine could withdraw and be by themselves. As already remarked, the days were cold and raw, and the rather drafty attic could afford them no place of escape. It was more than enough to have to spend the nights there. Lotten told me that when she woke up one morning she found part of her blanket covered with snow that had penetrated the cracks in the shingle roof during the night. It was a mercy of God that unaccustomed to such hardships, she did not get sick and that Christine, who had hardly recovered from her illness, did not have to take to her bed again.

I told Pearmain that we expected to have all our building logs in place in a couple of days, and I asked him to accompany me to all the settlers in the neighborhood to summon them to the house-raising. It is the custom in these faraway regions for a new settler ready to build his cabin to call on all the neighbors for help so that it may be erected in a hurry, since it is impossible for him to lift the heavy oak logs on top of each other by himself. To assist is regarded as a duty which all must assume and which no one, unless unavoidably prevented, refuses.

Pearmain raised various objections, evidently with a view to prolonging as far as possible the profitable stay of his boarders. However, I overcame his objections by hiring him, his oxen, and his wagon for two days to accompany me to the sawmill, where we had to fetch the lumber ordered for the roof and floor. My suggestion was that we take the opportunity to advise the neighbors living in that direction of the day when we should like their help. As soon as it was a question of some cash remuneration, our good host was ready to be of service, and we agreed that I was to come to Pearmain's the next evening with my wagon and oxen, so that we might start off for the mill early the next morning.

I was just about to return to Pine Lake, taking with me a load of hay to save time, when a stranger stepped up to me and asked without further ado, "What is your name?" I had already become partly accustomed to the curiosity and inquisitiveness apparently a national weakness among Americans. It is fully as bothersome as that encountered in the northern provinces of Sweden, if not more. Still this direct question surprised me in a peculiar way, especially as it seemed to me that some of his English words were pronounced with a distinct Västergötland [3] accent. I was quite right, my ear had not deceived me. The man handed me a letter from Lange. Both it and the man himself informed me that his name was Friman, [4] a native of Västergötland, from which he had emigrated three years earlier. He was temporarily living in southern Wisconsin, near the Illinois border, where he said he had settled down with two of his brothers and was doing rather well. He had happened to have an errand to Milwaukee and had been told of our arrival by Lange. Accordingly he had decided to look up his compatriots. Such an unexpected meeting with a Swede was really enlivening. Friman was a very young man, but apparently already inured to all the difficulties and privations of pioneer life. Rather than stop and rest at Pearmain's, he offered right away to go with me to our hut in the woods, in order to make the acquaintance of "the rest of the gentlemen." This suggestion, which would have pleased me in any circumstances, was all the more welcome now as I needed some support, not for myself but for one side of my load of hay, over the troublesome corduroy bridge and between the stumps in the woods.

The road we had cleared and were the first to drive over is still the one in use between Delafield and Pine Lake. At the southernmost bay of the lake it joins a bigger road to Milwaukee. Where these two roads meet, the terrain becomes more even and less heavily wooded. On one side is Pine Lake, on whose shore one can still glimpse our small log cabin from the road, along which a railroad now runs. On the other side of the road is a burr-oak plain, adjoining a tamarack swamp to the south, forming a rather narrow neck of land which separates Pine Lake from another lake, with the Indian name Nagowicke. Toward dusk, when Friman and I with our load of hay came to the piece of road lying between these two lakes, we saw on the plain ahead of us a scene completely strange to me. At first I almost thought I had taken the wrong road. Instead of an empty and lonely plain, everything was life and movement. Ten or twelve fires were burning a few yards from one another. Around them a number of fantastic shapes were moving. A few horses were cropping the grass, and a number of others were being driven down to the lake to be watered. In the light of the fires between the low burr oaks we soon caught sight of some small tents or huts of a kind, twenty or thirty of them. Even if Friman had not informed me what was up, I could easily have arrived at the explanation. The small huts were Indian wigwams and the people an Indian tribe on a hunting expedition, who had camped there temporarily.

I cannot say that this was a particularly pleasant surprise for one whose scant knowledge of North American Indians had been gathered from Cooper's novels. From the Indian camp to our hut it was only a short distance, and it was not without concern that I thought of us four spending the night close to perhaps a hundred of the wild sons of the forest. What was to prevent them, if not from taking our lives, from taking our goods, especially our guns, an article that the Indian always has a good eye to? They had perhaps come here without any white man's knowing anything about it; they might disappear just as quickly in the morning without being discovered by the thinly scattered white settlers.

Friman verified, to be sure, what I had already heard, that nowadays these savages need not be feared, unless one does them wrong or unless they get hold of whiskey and get drunk, in which case they do not care what they do and sometimes commit outrages. For the moment we had no way of knowing the temper of our neighbors. As we came closer we heard hallooing and shouting, which I suspected at first to be the effect of firewater, but which, as we later learned, were simply the cries with which they collected their horses and drove them down to the water.

Now a couple of almost half-naked Indians came galloping across the road, but they did not seem to pay any attention either to us or to our load. A couple of others, however, sitting close by the road greeted us with *"Bon jour,"* which French words, by them pronounced *boshay*, are generally accepted by all these Indian tribes as a greeting to the white man. It is also used in taking leave, and at the same time is occasionally employed in conversation as a kind of complimentary phrase. We returned the greeting with the same words, after which they gave no further sign of paying any attention to us. Around one of the fires we saw some women and children who, as we passed very close to them, did not even turn around to look at us. On the whole they seemed to be quite unconcerned with us and our doings.

At our hut we found Carl and Polman, who had had no communication either with our red neighbors. They had seen them put up their wigwams nearby, neither party indicating the least inclination to converse or associate with the other. Since the Indians showed no desire to approach us, we felt we should show the same indifference toward them. Besides, we could not tell how a visit on our part would be received. If they were planning to stay in our neighborhood for some time, whether they were peaceful in intent or not, we thought it best to let them make the first approach. Without our knowing it — and Friman was not much more accustomed to dealing with Indians than we — this decision was not only the wisest, but one that got us the respect and good will of the red men. Indians are not lacking in hospitality, but pursued by the white people and driven from their former possessions by them, they seem to view with suspicion the entrance of an unknown white man into their wigwams. They regard such a visit as an indication of curiosity, which makes the white people despicable in their eyes, or they suspect that behind such a visit there is some guile or hidden purpose to gain some advantage at their expense. As they make it a point of honor to hide and control every deep emotion, it is also a matter of pride with them to seem unconcerned about everything that takes place about them, though one may be certain that nothing escapes their attention. Whatever others may think or do, the Indian assumes an air that seems to say, "It is none of my business," and he prefers to attend to his own affairs undisturbed and unnoticed. In the whole character of the Indian there is a certain reticence and reserve — qualities which he also respects in others, regarding them as evidence of self-control.

And so we let the redskins mind their own business and sat down around our own log fire to eat the simple supper Carl had prepared. Friman was a welcome guest, whom we entertained as well as we could. The greatest problem was to provide lodging for him, but Polman gave up his own place in the wide bed to him and made a bed of hay for himself on the ground.

I must admit that we all looked to the night with some misgiving. Fille, who probably would have been the best watch of all of us and sounded alarm at once if anybody approached, had been left in Delafield. Outside the hut we had a couple of big chests in which we kept cooking utensils, tools, and various other necessities; the Indians, who in common opinion are very thievish, could very easily appropriate these to themselves. We feared such an attempt and discussed whether to offer resistance if it was made. Defense on our part might possibly egg them on to greater violence. To be sure, about our bed in the hut we had no less than twenty-one loaded guns and pistols to defend ourselves with, and in addition sabers and axes, but with all that what could we have done against such a superior force of Indians, if they proved hostile?

We delayed long before going to bed. Though the night was chilly it was milder than the night before. No trace was left of the light snow that had fallen. Bright stars sparkled over the calm lake, the shores of which had been lighted for a while by our own fire and those of the Indians. Finally theirs went out, one after another; the human shapes that we had glimpsed among the trees like gloomy, mysterious shadows withdrew into their narrow abodes. Soon we were unable to see a single object in the Indian camp. Where only a little earlier there had been general stir and activity, a gravelike stillness prevailed, broken only now and then by a soft rustling among the withered fallen leaves or some dog's monotonous howling. Complete darkness enveloped the field where nature's wild children, stretched out on the all-motherly earth, slumbered as securely as their white brothers, forgot like them in the bliss of rest the troubles and storms of life's dreary journey. The fire we had kindled was still burning, illuminating the objects nearest our place. The panorama spread before us seemed to me to have a deep, a prophetic meaning: On the one side, the light of culture, civilization, Christianity, by a higher world order destined to persist and spread more and more in these regions; on the other, the last and vanishing shadows of the ancient order of rude force and paganism. There an era and a people that would soon cease to be, a fire of which only ashes would remain; here the first spark presaging a future over which a new "Let there be light" had been pronounced.

At first we thought of each taking an hour's turn at watching, but sleep finally overcame all our fears of the Indians. After a few hours I woke up, and it seemed to me I plainly heard steps outside our hut. I gave Carl a gentle push. He whispered to me that he had been listening to that rustling for some time and was sure it was made by a couple of Indians. Our oxen were tied nearby, and we were afraid they might perhaps make off with them and with our other equipment. However, we thought it best to keep still as long as possible. Everything was quiet awhile, and then we heard the same noise again. There could be no mistake: somebody was walking around our hut and had stopped on the side where our bed was placed. From there he moved on again after a while with slow steps. I was lying nearest to the wall. Carefully I removed some of the hay that we had stuffed into the cracks so as to get a view of what was going on in that direction. It was still dark, but outlined against the fire, which was still glimmering through the ashes we had covered it up with before going to bed, sure enough we saw two Indians, wrapped in their blankets. What they had in mind we could not make out. They did not seem to converse with each other either by word or sign. As far as we could see, they were unarmed. After silently examining first our wagon and then our large chests, they departed as quietly and deliberately as they had come. The object of their visit, which had really made our hearts beat a little faster than usual, remained an unsolved mystery. When we finally crawled out of our haystack in the morning, we found nothing disturbed, nothing lost. Everything was just as we had left it the previous evening.[5]

We were just sitting by the fire eating our breakfast and talking about our nocturnal visitors when suddenly a tall Indian warrior was standing at our side. These people have a most uncanny ability to steal through brush and thicket without a sound. The Indian appeared as though sprung from the ground. Not the least noise had intimated that anyone was approaching. We did not see him until he unexpectedly stood in our midst. When we had recovered from our surprise, Friman greeted him with the usual *"Bon jour, nika"* — "Good morning, my friend."

"Bon jour," was his somewhat curt reply, whereupon he stood silent leaning against his gun, apparently quite unconcerned with us and with everything else about him.

According to what we learned later, this Indian and the party that had been camping near us belonged to the Winnebago tribe, which formerly possessed a part of northern Wisconsin. Of all the Indians that still remain in these parts they are regarded as one of the tribes most savage and most hostile to the white people. Their appearance itself indicates this. In many respects they differ from the neighboring tribes, and according to an old tradition are the descendants of some Mexican nomadic people. Others maintain that these, like most of the tribes in this region, are of Algonquin origin. Their language is harder to understand than the other northern dialects and abounds in burring, guttural sounds, including the *r*, which otherwise seldom occurs in the Algonquin languages. However, the Chippewa dialect is common to them and the other tribes and is the one generally used in conversations with white people and all these other somewhat interrelated Indian groups. According to the erudite Schoolcraft, this dialect, or the Ojibway language, as it is also called, is a kind of court language adopted by them all.

It is hard to get any accurate acquaintance with the character and customs of the Winnebago Indians. They do not seem to stand high in the opinion of either the white people or other Indian tribes. The former regard them with suspicion, and it cannot be denied that in their manners they are more reserved, more uncongenial, more easily provoked to anger and cruelty than other Indians in this region. From what I have seen of this people, however, I should say that their outward peculiarities, on the basis of which a strong prejudice prevails against them, stem rather from an inward, overweening pride than from any real ill will and hostility. Perhaps they feel that they have not yet become so cowed and weakened by the white men as their red brothers in some other tribes. Their appearance testifies to a strength of spirit that cannot brook oppression and injustice and that never can induce them to bow in the dust before their oppressors. Of all the Indians I have seen the Winnebagos are almost the only ones that in some degree measure up to the conception I had formed of the red man from the numerous romantic tales I had read. They are in general taller than most other Indians, and in spite of all the cruelty ascribed to them, their indomitable pride, their unfailing courage, their wild defiance, which are mirrored in their glance and bearing, inspire in me a kind of respect for them. According to what I have learned, they have also to a less degree than other tribes been ruined by firewater.

The name Winnebago, or Winnipeg, means "muddy water"; hence that name has also been given to many lakes in this region. The name adopted by the tribe itself is *Hockungara*, or Troutpeople. They have always enjoyed a great reputation for bravery, and formerly exerted a great influence over the surrounding Indian tribes. In 1812, in the war with England, they took the part of the British against the Americans, and also later proved less than friendly to the latter, who have always viewed them with suspicion and not without reason regarded them as troublesome and dangerous neighbors on their northwestern frontiers. Not until 1833 was it possible to persuade them to sign a pact whereby they ceded to the United States their land in Wisconsin in exchange for a tract in Iowa, west of the Mississippi. But that region they also had to resign to the white people a few years after we came to America. The entire tribe has now been reduced to a few thousand.

The so-called medicine men, who are held in high regard by all Indian tribes and who do not so much pretend to be real doctors as to be wizards and exorcisers of a kind, constitute among the Winnebago Indians a league, or rather a secret order, whose ceremonies and mysteries are known only to the initiates. In some of these ceremonies, as well as in the secret signs the members use among themselves, the Freemasons have imagined that they have found a remarkable similarity to several used in their own order. Whether there is any real basis for this, or whether the resemblance is only accidental or imagined, I shall leave unsaid. Certain it is that among these Indians is an ancient, secret order with several degrees, each of which has its own secrets and identifying signs. One purpose of this order is to give its members mutual support and to aid the poor. Its activities and mysteries are still held entirely sacred and may not in any circumstances be divulged to the uninitiated. Later I hope to give a brief exposition of the Indians' religious beliefs and ceremonial worship in general, including the initiation into their order, insofar as a man can learn about it. I cannot guarantee, though, that this exposition, like much else purportedly known about the Masonic order, is not based more on unreliable reports and guesses than on truly intimate knowledge. This initiation, or at least some part of it, is now said to be open also to those who have not been received into the order. Furthermore, contrary to the custom among the Masons, even women and children are sometimes admitted as members.

The Indian who so unexpectedly interrupted our breakfast was a typical representative of his tribe. If we had seen him the evening before, it is likely that the sight would have kept us awake all night. His face, painted in bright red and black colors which contrasted sharply with the dark brown shading of his skin and formed strange stripes and lines, was stamped with a wild, defiant determination, an awareness of superiority. His glance seemed clearly to say, "I despise the white man."

His head was uncovered, but across his forehead a red ribbon was tied, and into the long, pitch-black, braided hair he had stuck three large eagle feathers, one of which had its edges painted red — the foremost and most honorable distinction given an Indian warrior, one which he may not wear unless he has slain an enemy or fastened to his belt some scalps that he himself has taken. Toward the neck he wore the tail of a black squirrel. Over his shoulders he had thrown a red blanket, which he had wrapped around himself like a robe. When he opened it one could see a blue-striped cotton shirt underneath. His neck, otherwise bare, was encircled with a bead necklace, from which a silver ornament hung down his chest. Above his wrist he wore a couple of bracelets of the same metal, also a sign of his high standing and reputation in his tribe. His ears were adorned with a pair of rings, or rather a couple of large, open-work, silver discs, in which were fastened a few short feathers of different colors. His legs were covered with a kind of long leggings of blue cloth, decorated with a variety of ornaments and tied at the knee with red, beaded garters, having long fringes hanging down from them. On his feet he wore a pair of deerskin moccasins, with a piece of blue cloth sewed across the instep and a square of the same cloth around the heel — all of it adorned very garishly with beads and porcupine quills.

In a many-colored, likewise beaded belt — also a sign that he was one of the chiefs of his tribe — he carried a big hunting knife and a tomahawk, that Indian battle hatchet which all Indians wield with so much speed and dexterity. To the belt was also fastened a kind of pouch or bag, from the entire skin of a mink, lynx, or some other small animal, the hair still on it, and with an opening at the neck closed with a drawstring. This pouch contained steel, tinder, flint, and the Indian's usual supply of tobacco or, for want of it, a kind of herb, kinnikinnick, which sometimes is used as a substitute for that narcotic. His entire array seemed to indicate that he was on his way to some special ceremonial mission rather than on an ordinary hunting expedition. It is possible that he and a part of his tribe were on their way to the nearest Indian Agency to receive their annual payment for the land they had ceded to Congress.

Be that as it may, his mission did not seem to have anything to do with us. Silent and immobile he stood at our side for a long while, until we finally recalled our duty of hospitality and made a sign for him to sit down and share our breakfast. Without saying a word he drank a couple of cups of coffee and ate a little pork and potatoes, whereupon he pointed to his empty *skipetagun*, or pouch, and in a voice more of command than supplication asked for tobacco. We shared with him a little of what we had, and remembering what I had heard of the tobacco pipe as a sign of peace and friendship, I filled a clay pipe (a good thing I did not use my silver-ornamented meerschaum pipe), took a few puffs myself, and handed it to the chief, who put it to his lips with the same frosty calm he had displayed right along. An Indian never displays any emotion or gratitude for favors received. A man may give him the most precious gift, one by which he sets ever so great a store — his outside will reveal not the slightest gratitude. He considers it beneath the red man's dignity to display his feelings in any way. But for all that he is not ungrateful, and forgets as little a favor received as an injustice suffered. Our Winnebago chief arose, wrapped his red blanket about him, and departed without condescending to grant us a single glance or a word of farewell.

A couple of hours later we saw no more of the Indian camp than a few crooked sticks, tied together at the top and stuck in the ground, the remains of their temporarily constructed wigwams.

According to what people told us later, we should be perfectly safe hereafter as far as these Indians were concerned. Their chief had eaten bread and smoked the pipe of peace, if not within the white man's wigwam, yet close to it, and that was enough to assure us of their friendship. Furthermore, they had probably discovered the evening before that we were *Saginash* (a word which really signifies Englishmen, but is also used of Europeans in general) and not *Chomocomon* (Americans). They are always more friendly toward the former than the latter and have a strange ability to distinguish instantly the one from the other, at first glance.

Carl and I once attended a house-raising when a few Potawatami Indians chanced to pass by. One of the Americans present asked them to point out which of us — we were all together about fifteen persons — were *Saginash* and which *Chomocomon*. Carl and I were the only Europeans present. In dress and appearance we did not differ at all from the rest of them, and none of us, with the exception of the aforementioned American, had said a single word, so they could not distinguish one from the other by his dialect. Nonetheless the Indians immediately pointed us out from all the rest, and called us *nisihchin chomocomon* (good white man), whereupon he waved with his hand at the rest of the company saying, "*Caunishin chomocomon*" (not good white man). When that took place we had not yet made the acquaintance of a single member of the Potawatami tribe, and it is quite certain that the person in question had never seen us before, nor probably most of the native Americans present either.

It is quite possible that the Winnebagos, whom I have written about above, would not have left our boxes and equipment quite so untouched if they had not realized, almost by instinct, that we had come from the land beyond the great waters.

While we continued to work on our log cabin, it happened a couple of times that when we returned to our hut we found an Indian lying in the empty wagon box outside it. Though we had no door but the previously mentioned bundle of hay, and the doorway was often left entirely open, we never noticed that anyone had ever entered it or that anything that belonged to us was missing. And yet there were several guns, blankets, and other objects, which Indians seldom hesitate to appropriate when they think they need them and when they feel the owners have more of them than necessary.

Chapter 13

WE WERE now ready, with the assistance of our neighbors, to put up the house. According to my agreement with Pearmain, I set out for the sawmill again with my oxen, and he accompanied me with his draft animals, where each of us got a load of lumber to be used for the floor and the roof of the cabin. We were unable to take very big loads, reckoned by the number of boards, for they were sawed from oaks, were completely raw, and very heavy. To get seasoned building material here was nearly impossible. At the mill in question they had hardly time to saw a few boards daily before settlers hurried there to buy them. No matter how unsuitable the lumber might be, it was used to fill the immediate need. In Milwaukee we might have got pine boards shipped from sawmills on the shores of Michigan and northern Wisconsin, where there are great pine forests, but even these boards had not been given time to dry before they were sold. Moreover, they were three times as expensive as oak boards, and it would have taken considerable time to haul them to our homesite.

All boards are sold by the cubic foot. In this neighborhood the price of oak boards was eight dollars per thousand, every board less than an inch thick, but in cubic feet reckoned as a full inch. Five hundred feet of inch boards was as much as our oxen could pull on the rough road; moreover, at every steep hill we were forced to hitch both teams of oxen first to one load and then to the other, our slow progress being retarded all the more. The distance between Delafield and the sawmill was about six miles, between the mill and Pine Lake about eight, but though we had started out at sunrise we did not reach our hut till late in the evening.

On this trip I had an opportunity to take another look at the neighboring country, which was really extraordinarily beautiful. On the way from Delafield we had to travel over a small, level piece of prairie called Summit, where most of the land seemed to be already settled and where a number of fields and newly cultivated acres indicated that farming was already somewhat advanced. Around several houses I noticed not only gardens but also in a couple of places apple and peach trees that promised to bear fruit in a year or two. Everywhere the country was studded with the prettiest lakes, connected by narrow and not very deep creeks.

At a place called Oconomowoc, which even at that time laid claim to being a small village, a sawmill and a flour mill had just been erected by a Milwaukee company, which no doubt found these industries a rather good source of income. The manager was living in a good-sized frame house, built of pine boards. With its gleaming white coat of paint, green shutters, veranda, and grill work, it looked very fine by the side of the rough, clumsy, and not very inviting log cabins. The interior of the house agreed with its exterior, as far as I was able to ascertain during my brief visit there. There was nothing in it to remind us that we were in the Far West, which Americans in the East are used to thinking of as a complete wilderness where one is deprived of all the comforts of life and where there is no trace of taste or culture. Here I saw carpeted floors, polished furniture, and an elegant bookcase, and I not only saw but heard a melodious pianoforte, from which a young lady got up when we entered the room. The manager himself, Mr. F.,[1] seemed to be a complete gentleman, probably a man who had enjoyed prosperity in the East but on account of some business failure had been compelled to give up his establishment and with a few remnants of his old wealth retire to these remote regions. He received me very courteously, but I saw at once that as long as we ourselves lived in a log cabin where everything bore the stamp of pioneer simplicity and poverty, we could look for no social intercourse with him and his family.

It is true that life in a new settlement tends to eradicate class distinctions, or rather distinctions based on wealth, which, say what you will about equality, still inevitably separate one class from another. But one finds also many, like Mr. F., who assume toward the laboring class and those in humble circumstances a markedly aristocratic attitude which lets the latter know that equality in civil rights does not eradicate the inequality that otherwise exists between them. Out of doors and in the relations that human beings have with one another in their outward common life, this is not so marked. An old saying has it that "No one is a lord at sea," and so it seems here, too, at certain times. I saw Mr. F. together with the common people at the mill; I saw him and many others of his social status mingling with them at elections and similar events. On such occasions there was nothing except possibly their finer coats to differentiate him and his group from the rest. The one saw in the backwoodsman, and the other in the gentleman, nothing but a citizen with whom he was on a footing of perfect equality. But in private matters and in social life it was quite otherwise. There both knew their places. There was a gulf between them that the one did not claim, and the other did not grant, the right to cross.

At the time of which I am writing, Oconomowoc had, in addition to the manager's home and the two mills, only a few log houses, which, though located close to the lumber mill, confirmed the old adage that the blacksmith's horses and the shoemaker's wife are the poorest shod. These small cabins were really among the most unattractive in the neighborhood. The roofs were poor, and on the uneven floor one seemed to walk as on some kind of keyboard. In addition, there were a smithy and a carpenter shop, where beds, tables, and chairs were manufactured from walnut, cherry, and other less expensive woods. These were for settlers in easier circumstances, not obliged, like ourselves, to make with their own hands a good many of their household essentials.

The surroundings consisted of closely grown, tall forests, where at the time of my first visit only a few recent arrivals had settled. A mile west of the mills the land was entirely unsettled and vacant, and those already in the neighborhood were saving the late-comers some trouble by cutting down the best and most useful trees. The place, which has since grown into an attractive and prosperous village, is located between three lakes and right on the shores of one of them. LaBelle Lake, the largest of these, is three miles long and one and a half miles wide, with an extraordinarily beautiful island almost in the very center of its crystal-clear, mirror-like expanse. It is surrounded by high, wooded shores.

On our trip to the mill and back to Pine Lake we stopped at every home and asked for assistance at the house-raising which was to take place two days later. Only a few excused themselves as being unavoidably prevented from coming. Most of them promised to be there and also to notify their next-door neighbors whom we had not had the opportunity to visit. Almost all of them not only were perfectly willing but even showed real eagerness to give the newcomers help, which everybody seemed to consider it a point of honor not to refuse. Far from showing any displeasure at such a call, which involved walking, axe on shoulder, eight, ten, or even more miles from their homes and neglecting their own urgent affairs, the settlers appeared to take pleasure in coming to the aid of the strangers. They seemed to think, "The more the merrier," and were pleased as schoolboys at the arrival of new companions, who make the game faster and more exciting.

When we returned to our hay hut at Pine Lake we were greatly surprised to find my wife and Christine there. They had walked over in the company of Friman, who although he had that morning followed me to Delafield to proceed at once to Milwaukee, had after reconsidering the matter decided to stay another couple of days and lend a hand with the building of our house. In bundles and baskets they had brought along fresh bread and various other additions to our food supply, which was beginning to get rather low. Not having expected us to be so late, they had counted on going back to Delafield with Pearmain and his oxen. It began to grow dark, and they hesitated whether to venture back over the little-known road or stay in our hut overnight. If they did the latter, the men would, of course, have to vacate it in their favor.

But finally Pearmain and I arrived with our loads. Carl's activity as cook had this time been assisted by more experienced hands, and we enjoyed an excellent supper, consisting of venison and other good things, around our log fire, where nothing suggested that any of us felt depressed by the hardships and privations of pioneer life. I only wished I might have been able to send home to friends and relatives a sketch of our camp life in the wilderness. Would they have recognized in the brave young woman standing by my side, calmly looking out into the lonely shadows of the night and into the future she faced in this new country, the frail young girl of Uppsala, better trained for a peaceful, quiet, undisturbed life than for wandering about in the wild woods of America as the wife of a pioneer farmer? Pearmain had been half-minded to stay overnight in our hut. Now, however, there was nothing to do, after he had unloaded his wagon, but to leave a couple of boards for Lotten and Christine to sit on and set out again into the darkness over the rough road. Wrapped in blankets and sheepskin coats, the women seated themselves in the bottom of the wagon, and as fast as the team of tired oxen were able, they proceeded to Delafield.

Finally the day came when with the aid of our neighbors we were to put up the framework of our house, after which we hoped soon to finish the simple structure and move into it. Since we were not much used to the work, it had taken us eight days to cut and haul the material for our future dwelling. A couple of Americans accustomed to pioneer life probably could have done it all in less than half the time. But now we had everything in order except for a sufficient supply of lumber and ceiling joists. To speed the work, we preferred to buy the latter at the mill rather than hew them out by hand. The logs lay ready in a square around the building site. Ready too were a number of handspikes, slender, smooth trees for leaning against the walls, over which the top logs could be slid into place, and a number of strong forked branches to use in lifting up the logs. Everything was in order, including something quite essential on such occasions, a simple repast for the workers.

It was the twenty-ninth of October,[2] and the day, though rather chilly, was as clear and beautiful as a man could have wished for at this time of the year. If it had rained, as we had very much feared, it would have delayed us several days, for Americans never work out of doors in rainy weather. It must be something of uncommonly great importance to induce them to do that, and when a day for house-raising is set, there is always the provision "unless it rains." A rainstorm would have made it necessary for us to make another trip to the neighbors and call them for a later day. And what would have been worse, such a delay would have added dollars to Pearmain's bill for the women's room and board, a bill we were certain he would make big enough as it was. Our constantly shrinking capital and our longing to leave our haystack shelter for something roomier and more comfortable made us rather anxious when we made our weather observations in the morning. About eleven o'clock in the forenoon, the first of our neighbors arrived. Without waiting for further reinforcements, they started at once on the first layer of logs, into which we recently had hewed notches to fit the cross-timbers. The company increased more and more until finally, counting ourselves, we were twenty-three persons at work. This was a very respectable working force, and it was not long before the skeleton of the house was ready. The first two logs on the longer side were laid right on the ground, here and there supported with stones and pieces of wood to make them lie in an approximately horizontal position. On these, four or five feet apart, the cross-timbers, or floor sills, were laid, their upper side having been peeled and leveled off. A man now posted himself at every corner to notch and fit the logs into each other.

When a log house is being built, the logs are not fitted and pressed close together as in Swedish log houses. At both ends, on the upper and under side, notches are made so that the logs will lie fairly solid on top of each other, and with the corners at approximately the same height above the ground. Between each round of logs there is thus left, depending on the supply of logs, openings up to five or six inches, to be closed after the logs have been put in place, in a way I shall describe later. So it continues, layer after layer. Those who do not work with their axes and at the corners help to roll the logs, which, since they are of oak and freshly cut, are very heavy, and that is the main reason why the assistance of the neighbors is called for. When the wall has risen some distance from the ground, the men have to exert all their strength, even, as in this case, where the working force is not inconsiderable. Not infrequently accidents happen on these occasions. One of the forks with which the logs are being lifted may break, or someone may be a little careless—for on such occasions, as on many others, everything has to be done in great haste and hurry—and a log may fall down and hurt one of those standing nearby. That happened once to our friend Carl, who came near being killed at such a house-raising; fortunately he escaped with a hard blow on his shoulder, which incapacitated him for work for a long time.

When we had come to the height necessary for the main room, a few peeled cross-timbers were fitted to support the ceiling, and on them were laid a few more layers of logs still so as to provide for an attic room in addition to the main room on the first floor.

In this way the walls of a log house are generally erected in a few hours. By four o'clock in the afternoon the work on our house had been completed, and in addition our friends had helped us saw out a door opening and two other openings on either side of that for windows. There stood now the skeleton of our palace, 12 feet high, 22 feet long, and 18 feet wide. However plain and lacking in promise of comfort it may have appeared, it was the beginning of *our* home, built from logs we had cut ourselves, and so in a special sense the work of our own hands. I doubt that any wealthy property owner could have viewed with more satisfaction the construction of the walls of his four-story stone mansion than we now did the rough, unpeeled walls of our cabin.

The work had proceeded cheerfully and heartily. Those whose job it was to lift the logs had plenty of time to tell one funny story after another. Many adventures were told from early pioneer days. Jokes, witticisms, and laughter were the order of the day. A jug of whiskey had been placed by the side of a pail of fresh spring water with a teacup ready at hand to be used in mixing a strengthening drink. When we took leave of one another, no one was drunk although there had been plenty of the whiskey, to which everyone was free to help himself as he wished, and to which we kept urging our guests from time to time, according to the good old Swedish custom.

I cannot omit mentioning also that at no time, among all the jokes and quips and stories, and with all the lack of cultivation that sometimes revealed itself in the conversation, was one indecent expression used or a single story told that could not have been if women had been present. Not more than a couple of times did I hear any oaths, which the laboring class otherwise use very freely and without which some would seem to believe that no work can be accomplished. I will certainly not say that things always happen as I have described them here, for I myself at house-raisings have at times experienced the opposite. But one thing I believe I can affirm, and that is that much of what is indecent in speech and behavior, of which America has its fair share, as well as much of the brazen immorality in evidence, is imported goods. With the exception of us who were Swedes, all that took part in the house-raising were native Americans. Many of them had come from remote regions in the state of New York, where people in general have a high standard of morality, industry, and good order.

The mores, customs, and the very atmosphere in recently settled areas of America depend often to a great extent upon those that have been the first to settle there. Their greater experience and longer citizenship create for them a certain respect and give them a certain influence upon those that follow. With the exception of Milwaukee, where a great number of Germans have settled, and a few other places mainly settled by Europeans, Wisconsin was from the beginning settled and thereafter occupied mainly by native Americans. These were in the real meaning of the word members of the better social class, not because of financial standing or education, but because of inherent qualities of nobility, idealism, and goodness, in addition to which, of course, temporary strokes of good fortune may have fallen to their lot. The results of this are evident to this day. Despite the fact that the population at the moment is rather mixed and that Europe and the eastern states have contributed some elements not of the very best, Wisconsin has in the main been able to retain the character of its earliest settlers. We find here a morality, order, and respect for the law that many feel are not possible in the newly settled areas of western America.

Pearmain had prepared us for the eventuality that most of those present at our house-raising would offer for sale agricultural products of every kind, and he warned us to look out for swindling Americans. He himself was willing to supply all our needs at a cheap price. We had already, however, begun to realize that he was just the person to beware of, and when one man offered us flour, another potatoes, another cows and pigs, and so on, we bought small supplies of the things we needed for our household. In fact, there wasn't a person there who didn't have something to sell us. Most of them wanted to sell for cash, but many of our neighbors, whose wardrobes seemed to be rather shabby and worn-out, were almost as eager to barter clothing for their provisions. Since we in proportion had much less cash and many more clothes than we needed, this was something to keep in mind. We promised our neighbors that as soon as our house was finished and we were better settled, we would engage in barter. Already that evening we made a good deal with one of our sheepskin coats, which we traded for two big, fat pigs, ten bushels of corn, and several bushels of potatoes and rutabagas, the total worth about eighteen dollars, almost four times what the coat had cost us. The buyer promised to deliver all these things to our new cottage after two weeks.

When the work was finished, we drank to the health of our neighbors, and it fell to my lot to thank them in a little oration, carried on in a mixture of Swedish and English that aroused much laughter. The filled teacup passed from hand to hand. The rest of the refreshments, simple and consisting only of a few sandwiches and a kind of ginger cookie, were eaten, and we took leave of one another like good friends and faithful neighbors.

But that did not end the day's work for us. We had already learned the meaning of the sentence "Time is money," and the less we had of the latter, the more necessary it was to spend the former well. The openings sawed out for the door and the windows had to be attended to, if the wall, now consisting of loose pieces of logs, was to be kept from tumbling down. From a few planed pieces of plank we made door and window posts. That is, we sawed the planks into suitable lengths, fitted them into the openings, and by means of a heavy auger fastened them to the wall, thus giving it added strength. The window openings we made to fit a couple of glass window panes we had brought with us from Milwaukee.

The work advanced quickly for a couple of days, though persistent rainy weather somewhat hampered us. The boards we had

got were enough to make the roof, which, however, nailed together out of completely uncured material, could not be anything
but makeshift. But we could not afford a roof of shingles, which
here is the best material, provided they are made of pine. Though
we lived at Pine Lake, the few pines that had escaped destruction
at the hands of the Indians were hardly big enough to use. Besides
they were dear to us as reminders of the pinewoods of our northern
homeland, and we wished to spare their branches. If we had insisted on a shingle roof we should either have had to get the shingles
in Milwaukee and haul them home, or make our own oaken
shingles and so delay the completion of the house. Moreover, uncured oak shingles are hardly any better than fresh oak boards.
They bend and crack after a short time and become an inadequate
shelter against wind and rain. As far as going to Milwaukee was
concerned, I was soon to learn by personal experience that at this
time of year, after all the rain that had fallen, it was no easy matter anyhow to drive a load from there.

Laying the roof, though a simple enough process, did not prove
as speedy as our haste demanded. We had been able to get only
cut nails, and to pound them in demanded, like everything else in
this world, a certain skill which none of us had as yet acquired. If
you miss the nail with the hammer, or hit it the least bit on the
slant, it bends, and it cannot be straightened out, but breaks. Indeed,
it was almost as great a test of our patience as was ox-driving to
lie on the slanting roof and drive in nails of this kind into the hard
oak boards. In the process I am sure more than a pound of nails
broke off and rolled to the ground. Besides this, the fingers of our
left hands suffered numerous bangs and bruises because of the
inexperience of the right in using a hammer.

Finally we did get the roof in place, after which we also boarded
in the gables and fitted a couple of small windows into them to
admit light to the attic. Now our boards were almost gone, and
I had a couple of trips to the sawmill in prospect to get material
for the floors in the main room and in the attic. For the time being,
however, that had to wait.

Carl fell sick with yellow jaundice. Though this disease did not
seem to be dangerous, we thought it prudent to take him to Delafield, though he would be just as much subjected to cold and draft

in Pearmain's attic as in our hut at Pine Lake. But at least he could get better care there. Consulting Hartman's *Home Physician*,[3] and using the small supply of medicines we had brought with us, we hoped soon to see him recover. But a temporary stop was put to the work on the house, where his hand and experience were needed.

Polman and I (Friman had returned home immediately after the house-raising) thought we might tackle the job of the mason and fireplace builder and contrive a kind of fireplace like the ones constructed in, or rather at the side of, the most primitive log cabins. These are generally built in the following fashion: In one end of the house a sufficiently big opening is cut, into which a plank frame is fitted and fastened to the logs where they have been sawed off. Beyond this frame the fireplace is built out of bricks or cobble stones, if these are available. If not, as is generally the case, a wall of small logs is built outside the opening in the wall, and about ten or twelve inches from it another. Between these two walls wet clay is packed as solidly as possible to the height necessary for the fireplace and the chimney, although, as I have already remarked, a bottomless barrel is sometimes made to serve as the chimney. When this has been done, the inner wall is removed. The hardened, packed clay then makes the wall of a passable fireplace, which, if there is a sufficient supply of firewood, can warm up a room completely, although it is little to be recommended as a kitchen stove. The outer wall around the fireplace is not removed, but is left standing to support it. Such fireplaces are more durable than might be supposed, and if anything goes wrong with them, they are easily repaired. There are also certain other methods of building fireplaces, such as raising outside the opening in the wall a four-post framework on which are nailed thin slats, sticks, or twigs, covered on the inside and outside with heavy mortar.

We consulted with each other about the best way to build this highly important part of our new dwelling. Realizing the great inconvenience to the women of having only such a fireplace for preparing food and for other housekeeping requirements, I suggested that we buy an iron cookstove together with all the necessary kettles, pots, and pans. We could buy it in Milwaukee, where one of us would have to go anyway for nails and other necessities that could not be got near at hand. For this purpose I offered to go with the oxen and the wagon. On my return it would be necessary simply to put in the stove and make a hole in the roof for the stovepipe. After that we could immediately make a fire, and I saw no reason why the family could not at once move into our new home. It is true the openings between the logs had not yet been made tight, but we had a good supply of quilts and blankets to hang up around the walls, and with a good iron stove I thought that both Lotten and Carl, even if he did not recover very soon, would not have so hard a time as in Pearmain's cold and drafty attic, where they were exposed to both rain and drifting snow.

We all agreed that the plan was good, and the only question was whether our money supply could stand the drain. We counted our resources. Out of the four hundred dollars that remained on our arrival in Milwaukee, hardly more than half was left. We had bought a wagon and oxen. We should still have to buy a cow, food for the winter, more lumber, and certain other necessities. And we had to pay Pearmain's bill, which would no doubt be considerable. An iron stove big enough to heat our cottage and serve to cook with, along with pipe and other equipment, would cost something over thirty dollars. After these expenditures there would not be very much cash left. But we still had a few sheepskin coats and other wearing apparel that, situated as we were at present, we could very well spare. These we could easily barter for flour, potatoes, and other food staples. Furthermore, we had more guns than we needed, and if the need became really great Lotten and I had from our homes a little silverware. Although it might well be reckoned a superfluity in our log house, we hesitated to part with it because of the memories attached to it; but if no other way was open even that could be sold. The upshot of it all was that we thought we could buy our iron stove, which, though not an absolute necessity, still would add much to the comfort and cleanliness of our home and, what was still more important, make the work of my wife and Christine much easier. For the sake of that it would really pay to make a sacrifice, even if afterwards we must in other things economize as much as possible. It was therefore decided that as soon as it could be done I was to set out for Milwaukee.

When informed of this plan Pearmain offered, as usual on such expeditions, to accompany me in the hope of earning a few dollars by helping, and as usual I found I needed his assistance to some degree. True, I was not expecting to take on a bigger load than I could handle with the aid of my draft animals, but it seemed a good idea to have in my company another man with a team of oxen and a wagon, and when Pearmain said he had to call for some goods in the city, I had nothing to say against his offer. It was decided that we were to set out in three days.

Meanwhile to make as good use as possible of our time, Polman and I returned to our cabin to work on the house. The first thing was to tighten the walls. As I have already said, when a log house is erected, there remain big cracks between the logs, which have only shallow notches at the corners where they are placed on top of each other. To tighten these cracks, first of all lengths of black oak are cut off, or better still, aspen or some other soft wood which is easily split. These are made into blocks about two or three feet long and split into smaller pieces according to the width of the cracks into which they are to be fitted. They are then pounded in from the inside with the head of an axe. This is known as chinking. When all the cracks in the walls have been chinked in this manner and all the bigger openings have been filled, there are still a number of smaller cracks and holes. These are tightened from the outside either with common lime mortar, if such is available, or, as we had to do the job, with a hastily prepared mortar made of clay dug from one's own land and mixed with water and finely chopped straw or hay. With this mortar all the cracks between the logs and the wedges that have been driven between them are filled. Thus the wedges sit as tight as if walled in with masonry. The wall is evened off still more and tightened on the outside between the round logs. This operation is called mudding. When the walls and the corners have been carefully chinked and mudded in this fashion, all that is needed is a good roof on the cottage to make it completely warm and draft-free, though the building, even when completed, hardly can be judged a creation of architectural beauty.

The pioneer settler must accept this type of simple dwelling for the first few years and perhaps longer, and however plain and uninviting it may seem even in comparison with small farm homes in Sweden, I know that life's true joy is not excluded from it. In such a dwelling, industry and contentment create a happiness that makes one forget the unpeeled, rough walls with their chinking and mudding as well as many of the hardships inseparable from life within them. During the shifting fortunes of our own life, we have dwelt under higher ceilings and within walls of greater beauty, where we have been privileged to enjoy the comforts we were accustomed to in our youth. Most of these we had to do without in the low cabin at Pine Lake; yet after many years our thoughts still wander back with special fondness to that cabin as to our happiest home, as to the shelter where we spent our most carefree years, where in the midst of all our toil and, if you will, hardships, we were blessed with peace and joy. In the midst of life's storms, memory has often made us long to return to it and made us regret that we ever gave it up, our first, own, defective, but serene home. Involuntarily my thoughts stray back to it even now, though in my description I still have not even completed the cabin and we consequently have not yet moved in. But I seem to be standing once more, axe in hand, driving wedges into the walls; or covered with a heavy leather apron, mixing the mortar and daubing it into the cracks, in the glad hope of having our own home ready in a few days, the old dream of a cottage and a hearth fulfilled.

The chinking and mudding nevertheless took time, and Polman and I had not yet finished tightening all the walls when, according to my agreement with Pearmain, I had to yoke my oxen, hitch them to the wagon, and start off for Milwaukee to pick up the stove and other necessities.

This proved one of the most troublesome trips I had ever undertaken. The rain had been falling in rivers for the past several weeks, and had made the roads almost impassable, especially in the forest regions, where the loose soil was so water soaked that it was like driving in a newly plowed and unditched field. The only difference was that here there were hollows and pools of water which seemed to call for a boat rather than a lumber wagon as a means of transportation. To cross the corduroy bridges we now had to use about the same method as Munchausen[4] when with only a short rope he climbed down from the moon, for time and again we had to take material from one bridge to patch up another. Some of the loose logs or poles used to construct these bridges across swamps and low places had been washed away by the water. After we had proceeded with the wagons a certain distance across the bridges we would come to a chasm that had to be filled in. For the time being, we had to take the material to repair them from the portion of the bridge which we had already crossed. The next traveler over the same road, coming from the opposite direction, would have to carry or roll back the logs to their former place. It is unwise to travel over such roads without being supplied with an axe, and it was a good thing that both Pearmain and I had brought ours along. We had to use them often enough, sometimes to fell small trees by the roadside, sometimes to repair the bridges. It was a wonder that our oxen managed to cross without breaking their legs, and had it not been for the stove that was now the unavoidable condition of our moving into our cabin, probably I for my part should have returned before we had covered half the way. Though we had no load on our way to the city, only the empty wagons, it still took us two and a half days to cover the twenty-seven miles between Delafield and Milwaukee.

Upon our arrival there we stopped at a hotel where the landlord was also a general in the militia. With this title he was honored all the time, when he was serving his guests at the table as well as when otherwise attending to their needs in his capacity as host. It struck me as highly ridiculous when Pearmain addressed him quite unceremoniously and without showing any particular respect, "General, please drive our oxen into the yard and give them some hay," and when the general, who did not at the moment have any of his servants at hand, himself drove the oxen into a yard he had specially fenced in for the welcoming and provisioning of his paying guests. The performance reminded me of the citizen-general Pantaleon in Atterbom's *The Isle of Bliss*,[5] although nothing else here corresponded to the poet's description of his parody-republic.

It is undoubtedly true that the citizens of this model republic have in general just as great a weakness for titles and other distinctions as those living under a monarchy. In directing letters it is held most important to affix "Honorable" before the name or "Esquire" following it, and these titles of distinction are often used to and about persons whose place in society entitles them to neither the one nor the other. The same is true of the titles Captain, Major,

Colonel, or General. It makes no difference if one is busy at the shoemaker's last, with the tailor's needle, at the bar of an inn, or behind the plow and the hoe—the military rank must be recognized. And if decorations were permitted to be granted or received, it is quite certain we should find Generals A, B, C, D & Co. just as anxious to have tokens of distinction pinned on their threadbare tail coats, holey at the elbow, as they now are to be addressed by their honorary military titles. It has always been a mystery to me where the subalterns and privates are to be found. One seldom hears of them, whereas one is always meeting officers of regiment grade, from captains and majors without number to colonels and generals in legion. If one could assume that each of these gentlemen commanded at least one lieutenant and a few privates, the United States would be maintaining an army ten times bigger than that of Xerxes.

In the hotel where we were staying we found a number of travelers, some of them immigrant newcomers and some who had been in the territory for several years. Most of the latter were farmers and settlers from more or less distant parts who, like ourselves, had come to Milwaukee to buy things almost unprocurable anywhere else. Very few had anything to sell; their freshly cultivated farms were in general small enough for them to sell locally what they did not need themselves, disposing of it among neighbors and new arrivals. To judge by their looks, that is to say, their dress, most of these gentlemen would not be thought very respectable, for few of them had on anything but patched and ragged clothes, but the hound is not to be judged by the hair in these circumstances. In the new western country clothes are very costly, and sometimes worn-out garments cannot be replaced by new. It is not uncommon, therefore, to see a farmer, after his regular working coat no longer hangs together, go plowing in the field dressed in a blue or black tail coat with a silk lining, a remnant from an earlier and more elegant era in his life. That garment must serve for all purposes as long as it lasts. But whatever the outer dress, the cleanliness of the linen is always a pleasant contrast, and it makes one forget the outer shabbiness.

An unpleasant aspect of these hotels is that a guest is not shown to his room at once; indeed he may not be able to get such accommodations at all. He is shown into a little cubicle, and there he may undertake the tidying-up process spoken of before, using the common towel, soap, and washbowl, generally the first things the traveler looks for when he enters a hotel. If he wants to rest, he has no alternative but to throw himself down in a basement room where, as on this occasion, twenty to thirty persons may be seated round the heated stove. Though most of them are unacquainted with each other, they form a kind of closed group in which all freely express themselves on all sorts of subjects. In this new country there is no standing on ceremony. One begins speaking to his neighbor even without knowing his name or where he is from, and in a few minutes is deep in conversation. This is carried on as freely and with as great animation as if the speakers had been acquainted for years and were accustomed often to exchange views. If I hear two persons discussing a subject of general interest, I may safely stand by and listen to them and myself express my own views on the subject.

Political matters were on this occasion as usual the principal theme, and I had here my first opportunity to admire the extraordinary ease with which the American expresses himself. As a rule he is undeniably a born speaker, and on all questions that concern conditions in his country, its constitution and institutions, he generally displays great knowledge and keenness no matter how ignorant and uncultivated he may be otherwise. This is principally due to the free schools that have been established everywhere, in which citizens are educated from their early youth to take part in the government of their country and vote on all questions. As the heir to the throne in a hereditary monarchy is educated and trained with a view to the high office he is some day to fill, so every American youth — who in reality, whether in high position or low, whether poor or rich, is an heir to the throne of the sovereign people — is trained to exercise with earnestness and political insight his power and influence as a citizen in a free social order. I listened with keen interest to discussions on questions dealing both with federal and territorial matters. These were treated with a clarity and orderliness of thought which, to judge by the outward appearance of those who constituted the members of this transient political club, one scarcely would have expected.

Our business, however, was neither political nor social. My immediate job was to purchase a kitchen stove, which, together with some iron pots, copper kettles, coffee pot, and a few tin forms, cost thirty-five dollars. Fortunately, the shrinkage in our cash made by these purchases was partly compensated for by the sale of a sheepskin coat I had left in Lange's store, which he had sold for not less than twenty dollars. I bought also a barrel of salt, a few dry pine boards for a door, and several other articles. We were all ready to leave the city next day with our load when something unexpected happened. Pearmain's oxen, not so sedate as Wallis and Spak, had taken it into their heads to jump over the low enclosure in which they had been shut up and had run away into the woods. Pearmain had to borrow a horse to go and look for them, and I was compelled to remain with the citizen-general and wait for his return. Our return trip was delayed two days by this, and my hotel bill increased accordingly.

It happens very frequently that cattle run away from their owners in this fashion, even though they have been let out to graze on his own unfenced grounds. Especially in spring and fall they seek better grazing elsewhere, and when the whole country is open to them and they are not restricted by fences or gates, naturally it is only by pure good luck that they can be found. Many a man has spent as much as a week hunting his cattle. Pearmain's animals had fortunately started off toward home, and after a long search he finally found them feeding in a swamp a little distance from the road.

In the meantime the roads had grown worse and worse. With our considerable, though not unreasonably heavy loads, we could not drive far in a day. The road through the woods was hilly, and up the bigger hills we had to hitch both of our teams first to one and then to the other of the wagons. It was really the most tedious work I had ever done in my life, not to mention the fact that in appearance it made me exactly like most of the other dwellers in this part of the country. We made better time nevertheless than some other settlers we heard of, who lived in the northern part of Indiana. They had been traveling constantly for four days, but yet had lodged in the same inn for four nights too. Every day they got no farther with their loads than made it possible for them to return to the inn where they had spent the previous night, and where the small number of travelers was made up for by the opportunity of entertaining so much longer those who did come. For nearly four days we too had to toil through mire and mud, sometimes tearing down, sometimes building up the corduroy roads, but by the morning of the fourth day we finally had covered the twenty-seven miles and reached Pearmain's house.

This was the eleventh of November, exactly half a year since we had left old Uppsala, and we decided in spite of Pearmain's protests and arguments, that this was also to be the day for moving into what we wanted to call our New Uppsala. Carl in the meantime had luckily recovered from his jaundice — I will not say whether because of his strong constitution, the medicines I had given him, or the yellow silk Lotten had had him eat, said to be a sure cure for that ailment. In any event, he had so far improved that he thought he might risk the trip to Pine Lake. On the other hand, Polman, while working on our house, had fallen from a scaffolding and broken one of his ribs; none the less he declared himself willing to be placed on the load to ride to our uncompleted dwelling. Lotten and Christine longed to get away from Pearmain's attic and have a chance to bestir themselves round their own stove. I did not even unhitch my animals, therefore, but after the load had been increased with both dead and live weight, and after a tender farewell from Mrs. Pearmain, who amid many tears and with much dramatic effect embraced her "dear Mrs. Unonius," we set off in the hope of being under our own roof by evening. These four miles, though the road was far from good, were nevertheless far better than the road from Milwaukee, and had the advantage of being new and not driven very much. So it came about that we really succeeded in reaching our home by nightfall.

Our home! How much lies in the words, though in our case, they meant a small unfinished cabin without floor, without a door, without chairs, table, or any other piece of furniture — only an empty room with great openings here and there between the rough logs. Still it was home — the first *own* home a man has after life's first sorrow drives the child across the parental threshold to be a stranger in the world. It was our own home, built by our own hands, in a strange land, which nevertheless just because of it took on the coloring of home. It was home — a home we had longed for during the trials of a long journey and many brief sojourns, now in one place, now in another. To be sure it lacked every outward comfort, was wanting in every convenience that the most insignificant dwellings generally offer, and yet it was home, and as we entered it, it seemed rich in all its poverty, rich in love, rich in friendship, rich in trust in God for His peace and blessing under that low roof.

I must describe more in detail this first evening in our new home. Our first job was to install the stove I had brought from the city, and this did not take many minutes. By our united efforts it was lifted from the wagon and carried into the house, where it was placed a couple of feet from one of the walls. The stovepipes were fitted into each other. We sawed an opening in the roof and over it placed a piece of sheet iron with a hole in the middle; through this we put the pipe so that it extended a couple of feet above the roof and thus made unnecessary any other chimney. In this way the pipe was steadied, and even though it was heated to a high temperature the roof could not catch fire. After this was done, we lit a fire, much needed too, for the evening was chilly and the wind blew through all the cracks that had not yet been filled. We placed a few loose boards close together around the stove as a provisional floor. We also laid a couple of boards over the shallow pit, a couple of feet deep and a few feet square, that we had dug in the middle of the room. This we planned to enlarge still more and use as a cellar during the winter until we had a chance to make a better and more practical one. Chests and trunks were carried in, and as far as time permitted, the bedclothes and some of the things that we had used in our temporary hut, located a short distance from our new home.

While Carl and I were busy with this and while we were tying up our oxen and chopping as much wood as was needed to keep the fire burning during the night, Lotten and Christine unpacked such things as were immediately needed. A big trunk was converted into a sort of pantry, which was put to use at once in providing our plain evening meal. When Carl and I entered the cottage after finishing our chores, the simple meal was ready, set out, for lack of better arrangement, on the boards that had been

placed over the cellar opening. Into this opening we now stepped
down to sit at the table. It must be admitted that we might have
supped in a more comfortable way, but hardly with a better appetite, and, I should like to add, scarcely with greater merriment.

If a stranger had looked into the small cottage — and that would
not have been difficult, through the cracks in the walls or through
the door opening closed off by no shutter — he would have seen a
group of people sitting in a hollow in the middle of the room
with a few boards between them, on which were lined up a jar
of butter, wheat rolls, plates of cheese, summer sausage, pork, and
potatoes. He would have noticed in the room articles of a most
heterogeneous kind — chests, bedclothes, barrels, pans and kettles,
tools, articles of clothing, food stuffs — all lighted by the faint glow
of a lantern hanging from a nail on the wall. But in this first scene
of an American pioneer drama, if he had paid close attention to
the persons enacting it, he would have seen more. He would have
seen in every eye evidence of happiness and a brave determination
to face every fortune without flinching. It was a feeling of this
being home that made me and my wife, at least, ignore every hardship we were experiencing at the time or ever expected to experience in our new home.

But for all this we were not in the new home forgetful of the
old. The fact that exactly half a year had passed since we had left
our relatives and friends recalled it vividly to our minds, and the
New Uppsala, with all our joy at having reached the end of our
journey, with all our bright hopes for prosperity and good fortune, had still a tear of regret for the old home with its beloved
and sacred memories.

Among these memories, I do not know how it happened, there
came vividly to my mind the old, magnificent temple at home, with
the picture of Christ above the altar, and the peace of grace and
reconciliation dwelling underneath its lofty arches. Alas, here was
something the new home lacked; here was something which the
happy home-feeling spoken of could not supply, a regret without
a corresponding compensation — a reminder that we were *away*
and not *at home*. In the neighborhood of our home stood no Christian temple with its tolling bells solemnly inviting us to listen to
the holy words of revelation. In no house of God here should we

be admonished to worship the Almighty, an admonition we needed so much but had often thoughtlessly ignored and held of little value. In the wilderness we should find no Holy Table at which to kneel when our hearts hungered and thirsted for other food than what our well-watered meadows and fields could supply. Our separation from these things became very real to my soul; the realization of it awakened in me and in all of us some of those better, graver thoughts that at times in the midst of life's stir and sorrow come to us out of our inner world. They wander like the wind, whose voice we hear, but whence it cometh or whither it goeth we do not know. The need of establishing an altar at home when we had no opportunity of public divine worship stood plainly before us. We felt the need of approaching God — a need more insistent than I had ever before known. We brought out the hymnal and prayer book, and before we gave ourselves to rest we dedicated our new home with a heartfelt prayer to God for His blessing upon it. Feeling that

> Everywhere the heavens surround us,
> Everywhere's the self-same God,

we went to sleep in the common bed we had hastily prepared on the makeshift floor around the stove.

Chapter 14

MORE WORK ON THE HOUSE AND ITS FURNISHINGS · VISIT WITH
MR. W[ARREN] · BUILDING A BARN · FLYING SQUIRRELS · BIRD
HUNTING · INDIAN SUMMER · PRAIRIE FIRES

THE first days after we had moved into our log cabin we spent finishing it and getting ourselves settled. We tore down the old haystack hut, no longer needed, and moved the bed into the room in our new home which thereafter was to be the bedroom, the parlor, and the dining room — in a word our only room, for it was a long time before the attic, where Carl and Polman had their sleeping quarters, could be called one. I still had to make a couple of trips to the mill to get a supply of boards for the floor and some other necessities. Furthermore we had another load of things to bring from Delafield, so that my time at first was very much occupied with hauling, while Polman and Carl, after they got well, were kept busy with inside work.

Gradually the walls were made tight and snug in the way already described, and a bank of earth to cover the lowest round of logs was spaded up around the house to prevent a floor draft. From raw, unplaned lumber we laid floors both in the cottage and the attic, to which we had access by a ladder through an opening in one corner of the room. We dug the cellar a little deeper and made an entry, or rather descent, closed with a lid, in approximately the middle of the floor. It was a long time before we found time to make a door. In its place we used one of our big chests, which served as a table in the daytime; in the evening we lifted it up in the doorway so that when the lid was opened there was at least a barrier if someone should get a notion to enter our house in the night. But we had little reason to fear such an eventuality; we had lived here several weeks without seeing a single human being other than the neighbors who brought us the corn and other farm products for which we had bargained.

213

For want of chairs we made a few small benches from unplaned pieces of boards, with holes bored into their corners for legs of hickory to be fitted into. In addition we carved specially for Lotten's use a kind of easy chair, made out of a thick, hollow oak stump, which was rather hard to move from place to place but proved fairly comfortable. In form and appearance it somewhat resembled the chairs used by the hucksters at Munkbron [1] in Stockholm. In the walls of the cabin we bored a few holes into which we fitted pegs of various sizes on which to place boards for shelves. On one wall we put a few kitchen shelves on either side of the stove. On the opposite wall we put shelves for the modest library we had brought with us from Sweden, and on the wall next to the door another for tools and similar equipment. Around most of these shelves and also the windows, Lotten put up small curtains. Our own bed and Christine's were similarly provided with calico draperies. A few pictures were hung on the walls, and the low cottage began to take on a more pleasing and homelike appearance. The woman's hand could even here, with the small means at its disposal, so arrange everything that the plainness of the simple, rough furnishings was forgotten. Indeed it went almost unnoticed in the gleam of light and peace spread over things by her without whom a man even in the wealthiest and most luxurious house does not have a home.

The chilly nights finally made it necessary to provide another door than the big chest, which did not entirely cover the opening, but left too much room for the wind when it blew from the lake. The reason we had so long postponed this detail was that we had forgotten, while in Milwaukee, to supply ourselves with lock and hinges. It was impossible to get the necessary hardware in our neighborhood, and to drive or walk the long way into the city just for that seemed to us not worth while.

One day I went to call on Mr. W[arren],[2] a farmer living four miles away, who according to report, had a good cow for sale. Since I did not understand such transactions very well, Christine, who had the widest experience of all of us in these matters, went with me. Mr. W[arren] had lived in the neighborhood several years. He had a big family, twelve children, I believe, among whom were several full-grown boys. With their assistance he had managed to get his farm well cultivated and had an abundance of cattle and all kinds of farm produce. A large barn indicated that he was reaping bigger crops from his fields than any of his neighbors, but in spite of everything his house, though somewhat bigger and better furnished than ours, was still of the primitive pioneer style with chinked and mudded, though peeled and evened, log walls.

The door to his house attracted our attention as we entered. It had neither lock nor hinges in the ordinary sense of the word, but for lock a wooden latch, and instead of iron hinges a contrivance made also from wood and somewhat like the hinges generally used on barn and shed doors in the country. One end of the braces — I can find no better word for them — was nailed clear across the door, connecting its boards; through the other end, which was somewhat wider, a hole had been bored, admitting a wooden hook nailed to the doorpost, about which the door turned as on an ordinary pair of hinges.

Here was proof that necessity is the mother of invention. Nowhere can one find better evidence of this truth than in the pioneer settlements of the American West. I believe it is Arfwedson who says in his travel narratives: "Put a Yankee with a horse and an axe on a country road, and he will go into the woods and make a sled of his own invention." Put him in the wilderness, and he will build a house, in which every small detail is the work of his own hands. In a masterly way he can with his own hands and out of such material as he happens to have available make all sorts of things that are generally bought in the stores but which he lacks money or opportunity to buy, or both. So wood is made to do in place of iron, old barrels serve as chimneys, wooden stumps as easy chairs, and so forth. American energy is manifested in these comparatively trivial matters as well as in more important inventions. There is nothing a genuine American believes he cannot accomplish, even if he has had no previous experience in it, if necessity or his own advantage urges him to the undertaking. He will not permit himself to stand helpless, and he generally succeeds when he really tries. "I don't know how to do that," is an expression that seldom, if ever, is found in the vocabulary of an American.

The wooden hinges and latch on Mr. W[arren]'s door taught me that one should never say of a thing, "I can't do it," until an effort has been made. Where there's a will, there's a way. Though an inexperienced carpenter, better to try to make a pair of wooden hinges than to lie freezing through the cold nights back of a wooden chest. When I came home I told Carl what I had seen, and the next day we had a fairly good door for our cottage at no cost except our own labor. Without Carl's assistance, however, I might have had to try several times before I succeeded. Without any experience in work of this kind, I discovered how important it is for an immigrant to know a little of the carpenter's trade, or rather, to know a little of everything. Most important, however, if one is unfortunate enough not to know anything, is it to seek to be like the Americans and never let oneself be discouraged from making an attempt even at things that formerly were completely strange.

We now had our cottage as much in order as was possible under existing conditions, but outdoors there were a number of things that had to be done before winter set in in earnest. Our herd of cattle still consisted of only two old oxen, Spak and Wallis, and an excellent cow, the biggest and finest looking animal of its kind I had ever seen, purchased for twenty dollars from Mr. W[arren]. Even if we had had the means to buy more cattle it would have been unwise to do so, since for the first year we should have to buy all the fodder needed for the winter. But small though our herd was, it still needed a roof over it during the cold winter months. We couldn't in that respect bring ourselves to follow the example of the American settlers, who even when the temperature is down to twenty degrees below zero, let their cattle either stay outside or crawl into an open shed, entirely inadequate to shelter them from the cold. It is strange that the cattle do not freeze to death more often than they actually do. But that cows under such conditions fail to produce any milk and that oxen are completely unusable in the spring are quite natural.

As well as we could, we built a temporary barn of about the same type as the haystack we had lived in till we moved into the log house. We were unable, however, to get it ready before the cold season had advanced so far that in the mornings a heavy layer of ice and snow covered the backs of the shivering cattle. This touched the kindly heart especially of Christine, and she was the one that labored most earnestly, for the sake of her cow, to get the barn ready, with the result that finally a shelter was provided such as the cow and the oxen had probably never before enjoyed. In addition to these creatures we had some pigs and chickens that also needed shelter. All this gave us plenty of work for a while.

Close to the house, almost too close in fact, there stood a big, old oak tree which we decided to chop down and to split up the trunk of for use on these buildings. The tree proved hollow, and when it fell to the ground a great number of small animals came from its trunk, some of them flying, some running from branch to branch. They seemed to be blinded by the daylight, and we had no trouble in catching them. They were flying squirrels (*Pteromys volans*, or *volucella*) [presumably *Glaucomys volans*], pretty little animals with a delicate brownish-yellow skin that extends clear to their feet. Between their fore and hind legs is a thin membrane which when drawn taut enables them in jumping from a high place to sail rather far through the air, using their flat tails as a kind of rudder. These squirrels are exceedingly lively and active at twilight and after dark. The sunshine seems to affect their eyes so as to make them almost blind. Generally they live near human dwellings and are easily tamed. We kept one that after a few days got so tame he would jump in and out of the cottage and eat from our hands, but he finally fell victim to the voracity of our cat.

During all this work, though it left us no time for hunting, still we sometimes managed to get better game than flying squirrels. We always had our loaded guns with us, and when our hands needed to rest from the axe they reached for the gun instead, which generally provided us with a few wild pigeons or pheasants for dinner. Both of these birds were found here in abundance, though pigeons became more and more scarce as winter approached. Still it happened often that flocks of them came and settled in nearby trees without being disturbed by the noise of our axes.

Pheasants frequently announced their presence by means of a sound which we did not recognize at first, but which we learned later was made by the strange way they have of beating their wings. It is a vibrant sound, almost like that of a distant drum, and in calm weather can be heard a mile away. It is made by the males, generally during the mating season, but is sometimes heard also in the autumn and winter. If one imitates the sound by beating a bladder or a taut skin, the male is said to imagine that there is a rival in the neighborhood and hasten to the fight, thus becoming an easy prey for the hunter's bullet. I never have tried this method of catching these fine-flavored game birds and dare not recommend it as sure and infallible. But I learned another method of getting within gunshot of them.

During my numerous hauling expeditions I almost always heard or saw these birds close to the road. If I stopped my oxen and tried to slip up to them, they generally flew away before I got close enough and so I failed to get my game. Once, contrary to my habit, I had left my gun at home. As I went through an oak opening I saw several pheasants sitting in the trees close to the road. In spite of the rattling of the wagon and my shouting to the oxen they were not frightened away, but remained sitting in their tree, stretching forth their long necks, listening as if wondering what was going on. In the midst of all this bustle I came within a few steps of them and could hardly have missed if I had had a gun with me. On another occasion when I was out driving and, as usual, saw some pheasants sitting in the trees, I remembered this, and instead of trying to steal up on them, I let the oxen go along, and kept shouting loudly my usual "Gee!" and "Haw!" In this way I came within easy gunshot.

I found out later that these birds are somewhat like rabbits, which, when one whistles, stop to figure out what is happening, or like deer, which, when one bleats like a sheep, stop too. If a person is trying to slip up to them, they appear to sense the danger and are frightened away, but if he approaches them quickly, shouting or singing, he can generally come within gunshot of them and, if they are not given too much time, shoot them. Especially is this true when driving, in which event the oxen or horses attract their attention rather than the hunter. And so it was that I seldom came home from the mill with a load of boards or from otherwise driving my oxen without bringing at least one pheasant with me. Carl was the first to shoot one of these birds, which we had never seen before. As ignorant about American ornithology as about conditions in general, we did not know whether or not it was an edible bird, and so hesitated to eat it. But we reasoned that it would not hurt to try. So Lotten prepared it like an ordinary Swedish game bird, and we found it a real delicacy. Afterward, when other food was scarce, it saved us from ever leaving the table with our hunger unsatisfied.

Indian summer came a little later than usual this year. Of all of the seasons, this is the most pleasant in America. It is a kind of late summer which sometimes begins in October, sometimes as late as in November, and lasts sometimes into December. It comes generally after the first snow has fallen and the frost has clothed the autumn forests in brilliant colors. Once again the air becomes as mild and temperate as on the fairest spring and summer days. The weather is calm and still; the atmosphere, veiled with a heavy haze like smoke, has in fact a faint smoky odor not unlike what is caused by an extensive forest fire, but milder; far from being disagreeable, it is very pleasant. This haze is sometimes so dense that it almost darkens the sun, which, when visible, assumes a blood-red hue and appears to the eye as through a smoked glass.

This kind of after-summer with its strange smoky odor is a phenomenon characteristic of the North American continent. Hitherto no satisfactory explanation has been given for the smoky haze with which the atmosphere is saturated. Some have actually insisted it comes from prairie fires, which at this time of year burn over vast stretches of the sparsely populated regions of the western part of the country, especially of the Far West, where the Indians still rule. These fires are said to roll like a sea of flames across their hunting grounds and forests, advancing unhindered for perhaps a thousand miles. But this explanation has for several reasons been found as unsatisfactory as every other.

All I can say on the basis of my own experience with Indian summer and its heavy haze is that it is most pleasant and perhaps the time of year when one can best enjoy life in the country here and the glories of nature. The mosquitoes, those pests that torture the settlers in the summertime both at work and at rest and that make it almost impossible for him really to enjoy life out of doors, have now been killed by the preceding cold weather. The harvests have been reaped; the newly seeded fields lie once again in the green of springtime. The ground and the trees, which otherwise give signs of approaching winter, taken together with the summery air one is breathing, make one hesitate to say what season it really is. It seems a blend of all of them, or perhaps it would be truer to say that America has not only four seasons, but a fifth, Indian summer. The new door to our cottage was hardly ever closed in the daytime, and the kitchen stove, when it absolutely had to be fired, drove us all out to eat our meals on the grassy sward underneath the tall oak trees.

We divided our days in this fashion: about seven or eight o'clock in the morning, after we had attended to our ordinary chores, like wood chopping, and after we had eaten breakfast, we went to our regular work, which we kept on with till four in the afternoon. Then we ate our dinner, which was also our evening meal, with splendid appetite. The remainder of the day we rested, studied English, took care of the cattle, attended to other chores, and spent hours with one another in happy conversation till, after evening prayer, we went to bed early to be refreshed and fit for the next day's work. This was a life that agreed very well with all of us. With a feeling of regret I have many times since remembered those days. The hardships we had to undergo we really did not feel very much. To be sure, certain worries began to assail us as we thought of our meager funds, and when we considered the necessity of obtaining before next spring, plow, harrow, and other farming implements; but we observed how other new settlers managed almost without money, and as long as the Lord granted us health, strength, and the will to work, we hoped to be able to do likewise.

Something that in the beginning frightened us very much was the prairie fires, so called although they are not limited to the immense grass deserts and plains, but just as often attack forest and oak-opening lands. The descriptions we had read in certain romantic stories of America, according to which they were supposed to resemble our Swedish forest fires, but be still more destructive, made us a little panicky when in the evenings we saw the red glow in the sky coming closer and closer. Finally we could see not only the glow of the fire but in the distance even the very flames that here and there raced up the tall trees, from whose tops they shone like beacons in the night. Within a circumference which was growing progressively narrower we found ourselves surrounded by those fiery pillars; ever more clearly we heard in the distance the fearful roaring, like the rumbling of a constant thunder, while the atmosphere grew thicker and thicker. We feared that our cottage would soon be consumed by the flames and that we ourselves should have a hard time to escape.

A short distance from our house was a narrow neck of land, or rather a peninsula, separated from the mainland by a swamp which at that time of year was almost covered with water, and we reasoned that we might drive our cattle over there if the fire came too close to us. First, however, we considered it best to investigate, and Carl and I set out one morning in the direction where the fire seemed to be closest. We had not gone far before we met an American who probably was walking about trying to find a suitable place to settle down. He smiled at our fear of the fire and said that whereas it could be dangerous enough in the pine forests, there was no reason to be afraid of it in these regions, if we only knew how to take care of fences and haystacks.

It was high time that our fears should be quieted, for otherwise we might have given ourselves much needless trouble. When these fires get a good start and have had time to spread in some extensive forest or on some prairie (they need not extend over more than a few miles), the air is naturally much rarified and the wind begins to blow until it develops into a regular hurricane. That was how it was now. With the speed of an arrow the vast mass of fire was hurling itself down from the hills. The tall grass and the brush, from which the leaves had not yet dropped, were changed into a billowing sea of fire; half-rotted trees fell to the ground with resounding crashes; deer and other animals sprang away terrified from the roaring flames; the winged multitudes of the air flew through the heavy whirls of smoke. It really appeared as if the hour had come when "the heavens being on fire shall be dissolved, and the elements shall melt with fervent heat." But with all this surging the fire did not penetrate below the surface of the earth, but only devoured the dry leaves and vegetation on its surface. The road along which the grass was not so high was enough to slow down its progress, and though it skipped across, it was again slowed down at the burr-oak plain which was next to us, an area in which there was no brush but only dry grass to feed on. Around our cottage and the hay-covered shed we had erected to shelter our cattle, the ground was already so trampled down and in a way so plowed up by the logs we had hauled for our buildings that when the fire finally reached our place we had no trouble in putting it out.

These fires, which generally are lighted by Indians to make it easier for them during the winter to hunt buffalo, deer, and other game, are nevertheless not always harmless to the settlers. Where the brushwood is abundant and the grass is thick and has not been grazed off, they can easily burn down haystacks and fences, and even, unless great care is exercised, their homes. A man should therefore never neglect, when there is no wind and he can control a fire, to kindle one himself in the dry grass around the stacks and buildings and let it burn for some yards around these places as a protection from prairie fires. It is still better to plow a few furrows around them. This is necessary especially along fences, which more than anything else are exposed to the fire's ravages.

If these precautions are taken, prairie fires, no matter how fright-ful they appear, do no harm, but are on the contrary, in the opinion of many, useful for the hunt and good for the ground itself. For this reason not only Indians, but white people as well, sometimes let this destructive element loose to race across areas for hundreds of miles till it is stopped by some watercourse or much traveled road. There are many, however, who do not share this view. To set such fires, very beautiful illuminating the dark night, is now forbidden by law, and any person doing so is answerable for the damage caused. It is a standing law that is yearly broken, however, in the sparsely settled regions of the country, spring and fall.

ONE morning when Carl and I were busy feeding the cattle, we were surprised to hear a rooster crowing a short distance away. The presence of this domestic bird, we reasoned, must signify the proximity of a human dwelling, and we gathered from it that we had got a neighbor at closer range than any of the scattered settlers we had discovered on our walks in the vicinity. No matter how satisfied we were in our seclusion, we were happy to hear these signs of other human beings settling in our neighborhood. We decided to go out on an expedition of discovery in the direction from which we had heard the rooster crow, and to try to get some game for dinner.

After walking about a mile, we found that we had not been mistaken. Somebody was chopping in the woods. A tree crashed to the ground, and the sound of the axe strokes led us in a few minutes to the place where the work was going on. In the lonely wilderness were other human beings besides ourselves. On the other side of a little creek or brook, which nevertheless here was called a river, we discovered two men, hacking away, as well as women and children. They were an entire pioneer family that had bivouacked here and were busy providing a shelter for themselves. We called across to them, and they pointed to the trunk of a tree that had been felled across the river, which made it possible to cross dry-shod to the other side.

Many of these watercourses, even the bigger ones that on our maps are designated as river, are shallow enough in many places to wade across. Nor are most of them very wide, in many cases just a few yards. In this new country, where little progress has been made in the construction of bridges and roads, it is necessary, to get across, either to balance oneself on the trunk of some fallen tree, as we did now, or to wade. The wagon road may end on one shore and resume on the other, so that one has no alternative but to drive right down into the river, whose muddy bottom is sometimes very difficult to cross. The shallow water, on the other hand, offers only a slight obstacle to getting to the opposite side. It is only the length of these streams that qualifies them as rivers. Even many of those that are navigable and on which steamship traffic is very lively, as for instance the upper Mississippi, have channels only four or five feet deep in some places. When a person sees them for the first time, without knowing their great length, he is apt to regard them as only small creeks or nondescript streams and fail to realize he is face to face with one of the famous rivers contributing so much to the mercantile prosperity and industrial progress of the country.

The narrow Bark River, which we encountered here, is nowhere navigable, but is nevertheless of inestimable value to the region through which it winds, because of the excellent opportunities it offers for mills and other industrial plants. After joining together several lakes, it flows out through them into a bigger river known as Rock River, which is navigable for some distance in the state of Illinois and empties into the Mississippi 165 miles south of the Wisconsin border. Thus we had, in a sense, hardly a mile from our cottage, communication by water with almost all the new states and territories in the West, and it would not have been impossible to travel by canoe all the way from there to New Orleans.

But we did not have in mind an excursion of that length, only a trip over to our new neighbors, who were separated from us by a stone's throw across the narrow river. Crossing over was easily accomplished by means of trunks of trees that had been felled in opposite directions from both shores of the river. There we found a whole family: man, wife, and at least half a dozen children, and the husband's brother, a vigorous youth of some seventeen or nineteen years of age.

Mr. S.[1] and his wife, both members of the laboring class, were born — or as it is put, I believe, in the curious phraseology of the western states, "raised" — in Vermont. When a new settler is asked where he hails from, he is likely to answer that he comes from this state or that, but that he was originally "raised," that is, born and bred, in some other place. To "raise" a stock of cattle means to engage in cattle breeding, and in the same way married people are said to have "raised" a big family, that is, to have brought into the world and reared many children. So, having been "raised" in Vermont, thus being Yankees, Mr. S. and his wife had moved to Ohio when that state, which is now rather fully settled, began to be occupied by white people. From there they had moved to southern Michigan, and after they had managed to build and cultivate a small farm there, they had sold it and migrated to Indiana. They had now moved on into Wisconsin to hew out a new home, encouraged by the talk about its rich and abundant soil.

This homesite too would perhaps finally be exchanged for another in some hitherto unknown territory beyond the Mississippi, God knows where. The man belonged to that singular class of Americans, who constitute a kind of outposts of civilization, and who in proportion as settlers increase and the land is more and more cultivated, get to feeling crowded for elbow room and must absolutely move from one thinly populated territory to another. Of them it is true, as Cooper puts it so strikingly in one of his novels, that heaven itself would lose its attraction if they only knew of some other place farther west. What little they get for one farm, which is generally not cultivated very extensively, is likely to be used up while they look for another and before they have managed to get settled again. They are always in the process of beginning afresh with the same scanty means as before.

However, when our new neighbor took possession of his claim he seemed to be better situated than we. In addition to a team of splendid oxen, he brought with him to his new home two excellent milch cows, a number of pigs, and, as our ears had already notified us, certain domestic creatures of the feathered kind. Over his roomy wagon he had raised a tent, in which the entire family had been lodged during the long trip and which now served them as a temporary dwelling. Several bright nomad faces peered at us from the wagon as if rejoicing over the added space under the tent now that the small supply of pots and pans and other needful household articles had been unloaded and placed in the burned-off grass around a crackling log fire.

Mr. S. and his family understood better than we the life of a new settler and had had more experience in making a temporary home in the wilderness without extra expense. There was no question here of boarding wife and children in some neighboring log inn till a permanent home was ready; nor did they waste any time in building a temporary shelter while they were working on a better house. They set to work at once building a shanty, for which the husband and his brother were busy hewing down some small and not too heavy trees. Although they believed they would be able to erect their simple abode all by themselves, they accepted the assistance we offered them with thanks. We on our side had the opportunity to learn much from the speed and vigor with which the work was pursued by these true backwoodsmen, and from the skill with which they made up for the lack of such materials as we had thought essential for building a house.

What is known as a shanty is the plainest of all the varieties of houses that one finds in the new territories, and also the easiest to erect. The front is made somewhat higher than the back; these are connected by a slanting roof which, when neither boards nor shingles are available, is covered with gutters made from linden logs split and hollowed out with an axe. These gutters are laid with the hollowed side upward, as close as possible to the top log on the front side of the house, so that they slant down to the lower wall in the rear. Other hollowed-out logs are laid over these with the hollowed side down, so as to cover the cracks between the lower gutters, the edges of which rest against the concave surface above. In this way no rain can enter the building. To preserve heat the roof may further be tightened with such mortar as has already been described. For the floor also, linden or black-oak logs are utilized; they are split in the middle and their edges evened with the axe so that they may fit reasonably close to each other. The round side of the split log is of course laid on the ground, and the upper, flat side is somewhat evened with a broad axe as time and opportunity permit. The floor thus formed at least has the advantage of being solid and does not warp so easily as does a floor made from uncured oak boards. Nails and boards are also saved. Mr. S. had his shanty ready in a couple of days, at no cost except a few shillings for a window frame with four small panes of glass, which, together with a door supplied with wooden hinges and a latch, completed the simple dwelling.

We might have saved ourselves much expense if we had learned a little sooner the lessons we got here in the architecture of a pioneer dwelling. Especially in the matter of the roof we were sorry not to have been able to make use of the method of construction just described.

The family whose acquaintance we made here formed a curious contrast to another that we found on a walk through the neighborhood a few days later a little farther away. They, too, were among our nearest neighbors. The material resources of both families seemed to be about the same, although the log house of the one had some of the conveniences that the shanty of the other lacked. But most striking was the difference in culture and education between the people themselves. In the one case the husband was an uncultured and uneducated backwoodsman, strong, hardened and experienced in all the difficulties and circumstances of frontier life. He was nevertheless not lacking in a certain social ease and, considering his place in society, had a kind of breeding generally characterizing even the laboring classes in America. One may say what one will about the local manners and customs that grate on cultured Europeans and from which they generally draw very faulty conclusions, but as far as the persons in question were concerned, it was clear that as members of a civilized community they stood on a very low plane. The wife, probably even more ignorant and uncultured than her husband, revealed in her person something of an amazon nature. Each day she smoked her clay pipe, loaded with strong virginia, cut into fine shavings from her husband's tobacco twists. Her patched calico dress was the only sign of femininity about her; otherwise it would have been very hard to discover anything in her appearance and behavior identifying her as a member of the fair sex. With the exception of some old papers and a few dirty and torn school readers, there was nothing in their shanty to suggest any literary activity.

In the other cottage the husband, in spite of his worn coat and the hard work to which he had to devote most of his time, was a complete gentleman. A high degree of cultivation and a better upbringing manifested themselves in his entire personality. It might be said that it shone forth not only from his brown and weather-beaten face, but even through the holes at his elbows. The manner in which his wife asked us to sit down on a wooden bench by the stove was the same as if she had invited us to sit down on a well-upholstered sofa in an elegantly furnished drawing room. Even in the log house, where she had to attend to work generally done by servants, she retained the character of a lady. Some books and sheets of music, relics from other days, along with a guitar without a missing string, lay on a piece of furniture that was something between a table and a chair in one of the corners of the room. In her conversation with us about Sweden she revealed that she was acquainted not only with the works of Fredrika Bremer, the novelist, but also with the names of Linnaeus [2] and Berzelius,[3] and was not unfamiliar with the later history of our country. This family had lived in one of the eastern states until the year before, and the husband had been a well-known and respected business man. But at a time when it might be taken almost for granted that in any of the large cities nine out of ten businesses would go bankrupt, he too had been ruined and, accompanied by his wife and two children, had now come to this place. Here his only possession was the quarter section they were occupying, which he had purchased in his children's names in order that his creditors might not get possession of it.

I have placed these two families side by side to illustrate the different degrees of civilization that exist in a population in which one is as good as another. Wealth is the only mark of rank, the only thing that in itself serves to erect a wall of boundary between the lower and the so-called better classes; for even education and culture, if not accompanied by riches, must nevertheless on the outside carry the stamp of a standard of living better than the average if they are not to be put on the same level. Mr. S. in the shanty is a gentleman of equal standing with Mr. F.,[4] the gentleman in the log house. Mrs. S., smoking her clay pipe, pays a visit to Mrs. F., who will do well to let the guitar rest and as a subject of conversation choose something other than Linnaeus and General Bernadotte.[5]

Unquestionably these conditions are sometimes irksome to people like Mrs. F. and her husband, compelled by unfortunate circumstances to step down from the plane where in spite of reduced finances they might rightfully have retained a place. A family of the educated class in Sweden living in some faraway corner of the land often has difficulty finding a suitable social group. How much more is this true here where democratic equality, which I certainly do not object to, tends to break down between the various strata of society the dividing walls raised by intelligence and a higher degree of cultivation. Here the dollar alone is able to erect and maintain such walls, something which ought not to be. Yet at the same time, however embarrassed a man may feel by the complete removal of class lines to which he has been accustomed in the old country, or by the new lines drawn here, it cannot be denied that the democratic equality prevailing is under present conditions beneficial to the masses in the new community as well as to the community itself in its process of development. It is not intelligence and cultivation, though they may have crept into a shanty ever so poor, that are lost in and become absorbed by vulgarity and ignorance, but the very opposite. With a new generation the better fruits of equality mature, and the advancing community continues to take shape and acquire more order. Though still in a state of growth, it gathers nourishment from this equality for the future improvement of culture and civilization.

For the time being, however, we did not have the opportunity to profit by either class of neighbors. In general it was only business that gave occasion for mutual visits. We still had to get food supplies for the winter and were fortunate enough not to have to pay for everything in cash. Several necessities we procured through trade. Carl bartered a black tail coat, which he thought he might very well spare in his present milieu, for a fat hog, which otherwise would have cost five and a half dollars, and in addition several bushels of corn and potatoes — the whole worth about twelve dollars, four riksdaler more in Swedish money than he had paid for the coat four years earlier, a gain of one riksdaler for each year he had worn it. Since we had a far bigger wardrobe than we needed for the time being, and since most of our neighbors were in need of such goods, we made occasional trades of this kind to the satisfaction of all concerned. Articles of clothing being valued very high, we at least were not the losers in these deals.

A process which was entirely new to all of us except Christine was slaughtering. Generally hogs are killed by shooting, or else they are stuck with a knife and permitted to run about till they bleed to death. Blood and entrails are generally not preserved; sausage making except by professional slaughterers is a thing of which people know nothing. Furthermore, to eat blood is regarded as an abomination, and Acts 15:29 is quoted as an authority against it. In this country every American would push away a plate of blood bread, though I have noticed that where they have come in contact with Europeans, and in denominations where they are gradually adopting the customs and modes of life practiced by the Germans, they do not spurn a good helping of black pudding.

Once when unexpectedly we had one of our neighbors as guest at dinner, Lotten had nothing to offer him except fried blood bread. He ate it with relish, just as in general Swedish cooking and Swedish dishes have pleased those to whom we have had the joy of showing our hospitality, and he was particularly eager to determine the nature of the savory dish we had served him. When we finally told him, he was not at all pleased, but remarked instead that next time he would be very careful before he accepted food or drink in our house.

At our slaughtering we proceeded according to our Swedish customs, which, I must confess, were entirely new to me. Whatever might be said about the poetry of our pastoral life, it would not by any means include this operation, at which I was obliged to assist with unaccustomed hand. The slaughtered hog bore many a sign, too, of my inexpertness at the barber's trade. But those to whose lot it fell to convert into head cheese, sausage, and so on, what our inexperienced hands had butchered, knew their business much better. On these occasions American custom demands that a few pounds of fresh meat be sent as a present to the nearest neighbors.

This courtesy is always returned, and had several times already been shown to us.

The woods and oak glades teem with herds of half-wild hogs which, although really not without owners, are left practically without care. It is sometimes difficult to tell to whom they belong. In some cases the owner himself does not know. The hogs are let out in the spring to forage for themselves and when in the fall it is thought they are properly fattened from the abundant supply of acorns, the owner will go and look for them. The hogs are then generally slaughtered without additional fattening. The owner is not always certain, however, to find his entire herd, which in the meantime may have increased in number. The offspring of such animals are sometimes discovered in such a wild state that many new settlers are not troubled in conscience when they appropriate and shoot them. This procedure, nevertheless, is not considered ethical and can occasion much contention and hard feeling between neighbors, for the animal in reality is some other man's property, to which now and then he may be able to prove ownership. At any rate, we thought it best not to engage in this kind of hunt, but satisfied ourselves with such meat as we had full right to call our own.

The beautiful Indian summer soon passed, and winter began in earnest, with piercing cold. The change in temperature was very sudden. After a day of almost summery air, the thermometer fell till in not more than two or three days it read below zero. By December 3 the ice on Pine Lake was so strong that we could skate on it, a pleasure I had not expected in this country, but for which Carl, more forward looking than I, was prepared. We took turns using a pair of skates he had brought along from Sweden, and made our first tour around the lake on the shore of which we had built our cottage.

Since we were without a boat, we had been unable to investigate it and its surrounding shores. We now found that the other side consisted of white-oak openings, and that it was hilly and not nearly so good and fertile as where we had settled. By sheer luck we had chanced upon the best part. On its shores we found no dwelling but our own, and we therefore had the pleasure of knowing that we were, at least for the time being, sole masters of its apparently rich fishing waters. At the upper end of the lake there was a pretty island of a few acres, which, except for its outermost shore line, was totally inaccessible because of its abundant vegetation. Among the big oak, beech, maple, and cedar trees which were growing close to each other, an impenetrable jungle of brushwood had grown up, owing no doubt to the fact that the island had never been swept by fire and had probably never been disturbed by a pathfinder's axe. Among the tightly interwoven branches of a tall tree, a couple of eagles, the largest I had ever seen, had built their aerie, from which they came hovering over us as if warning us not to encroach on the domain over which they hitherto had been undisputed lords.

One day when the ice lay smooth and mirror-clear on Pine Lake, with whose beautiful surroundings we had now familiarized ourselves, we were surprised, while at work, by an unusual noise. Suddenly four stags rushed close by us at full speed and out on the lake. They were followed in almost the same instant by an Indian. He caught up with the speedy animals, which, because their hoofs slipped on the shiny ice, could not get away from their pursuer. With surprising agility and sureness of foot on the slippery surface he cut off the hind leg of one after the other of the stags and laid them low. Then he put a speedy end to them with his hunting knife. All this was just the work of a few moments, and we had hardly had time to recover from our surprise at this unusual hunting scene before the Indian, as calm as if he had caught a mere fly, stood there surrounded by his rich booty.

The mighty hunter was one of the chiefs of the Potawatami tribe, and the first Indian with whom we had the opportunity to become really acquainted. Having invited him into the white man's wigwam, we entertained as well as we could afford. During his visit he showed more affability and gratitude than the Winnebago Indian who had earlier honored us with his presence. He examined all our guns with great care. None of them seemed to satisfy him, however, except the splendid rifle that had formerly belonged to King Fredrik [6] and had afterward come into Carl's possession. This gun he wanted, and he was willing to "swap" — an Anglo-Indian word for trade — the stags for it. He pointed to them, promising to give us more game to boot. Carl, however, would not part with his good rifle at any price. Some target practice was arranged for, though, in which our Indian acquaintance took part with evident pleasure.

Carl was a rather beautiful free-hand shot. The Indian, on the other hand, when his turn came, steadied himself against a tree, and aimed long and carefully before discharging what was for him an unaccustomed weapon. When he did shoot, however, he made a bull's-eye on the target which we had hastily constructed out of a sheet of paper.

Several times we had the opportunity of seeing that Indians, no matter how good shots they are, seldom shoot free-hand but always, if possible, seek support for the gun, if in no other way, against the knee. If they see a deer within gunshot, before taking aim, supported against tree or bush, they generally try to stop the animal by means of a strange sound, something like the bleating of a sheep, and seldom shoot it while it is running.

Kee-wah-goosh-kum was on a hunting trip along with some other members of his tribe and had camped a couple of miles north of our cabin. He promised to pay us another call and asked us to lend him a couple of dollars till he returned. Despite the low state of our treasury, we lent him the money, not so much in the hope of having it returned, which we thought rather doubtful, as in the wish to be on a friendly footing with our red neighbors. It proved, however, that Kee-wah-goosh-kum was not a bad risk. When he returned to hunt a couple of months later, he paid his debt. Later I had reason to be thankful for our friendly relations, when he saved me from a serious predicament.

The winter wore on. Great masses of snow began to fall. By the middle of December we had real northern sledding. During this season we busied ourselves with cutting down and splitting trees for fence rails. For that purpose we preferred black oak, which was easier both to chop down and to split. The straight trunks are cut off in lengths of ten feet or, more generally, twelve, and by means of wooden or iron wedges and a big mallet are split into fence rails about four to six inches on the heavier side. These are laid zigzag on top of one another so that one length crosses the other about six to eight inches from the end, an angle of about twenty-five degrees from the straight fence line thus being formed. A fence consisting of seven or eight ordinary rails in height is generally sufficient. For a good fence, however, one not easily broken down, it is necessary to pound a rod into the ground on each side of the corner so as to make a crotch and then to place another length of heavier rails across each crotch for real stability. Fences of this kind are the most common on wooded land in the West and are the least expensive and easiest to construct. The progress of the work depends, of course, on the quality of the trees, but under ordinary conditions a good workman should be able to fell the trees, cut them up into proper lengths, and split about two hundred rails a day. If the logs are hauled in advance and placed at a proper distance from each other about the place that is to be fenced in, the fencing is made much easier and a considerable area can be completed in a day.

This is one of the new settler's first and most important jobs. He ought to prepare enough fence rails during the first winter to enable him to fence in not only the ground he is planning to make into fields but also, if possible, pasture for his cattle. Otherwise they are likely to run wild and cost him several days in hunting for them. He will be fortunate, in fact, to locate them at all in a sparsely settled region. Sometimes they are even lost entirely or are picked up far away, possibly in some other state, where it depends on the honesty of the finder whether a notice of the find is published in the papers. Even so it is expensive both in terms of time and money to have the cattle restored to the original owner. In view of such eventualities, it is strange that new settlers are so careless in this respect. During spring and fall one receives almost daily visits from people who are wandering about from one section to another hunting for their cattle.

In cutting rails it is necessary to select suitable trees; otherwise one is likely to waste time and labor. If possible the trees should be straight and tall and the lower trunk free from knots. Notwithstanding care, the trunk may twist a few feet from the ground, and hence be useless for fence rails or, at any rate, difficult and slow to split. Even a trained eye can easily be mistaken about the trees that are to be selected and felled. It is certainly very disappointing to an axeman, after he has hewn down a tree four to six feet in diameter from which he expects to get a couple of hundred rails, to discover that it is entirely useless for his purpose or that the splitting, which ought to be the easiest part of the job, proves the most tiring. It is therefore important, especially in the larger trees, to find out which way the grain runs in the trunk. Where the trunk is blazed, the grain may run straight up and down, and yet a few feet higher as in most trees turn clockwise around the trunk. In this case the log, after being cut off, is hard to split in two, and after it has been, additional trouble is encountered in splitting the parts because they are twisted like corkscrews. Many of the pieces are entirely useless, and the rest are crooked and little suited to making fences. If the grain turns a little counterclockwise it generally makes less difference. The higher part of the trunk is in this case less twisted than when the grain runs in the other direction.

Except on forest lands, however, the settler seldom has any choice. In the sparsely wooded oak openings he must not be too particular about his material, and must frequently use trees he would reject on more heavily wooded land. We were fortunate enough to find sufficient trees suitable for rails, partly on our own land, partly on neighboring land of Uncle Sam's, from which settlers generally do not scruple to take good timber trees for their own needs. We succeeded in cutting from easily split trees a supply of rails that under less favorable conditions, considering our unaccustomed arms, would have taken far more time to produce. The hardest work, at least for me, was to chop down the trees, and my high Swedish boots gave many plain indications that I was not a skillful axeman. Feet and legs were preserved in an almost miraculous manner, although it happened again and again that the axe slipped and cut through the cloth-lined boot, clear to the socks on my feet.

In cutting rails the settler on oak-opening land should be very sparing of the wood and should not follow the example of the forest people who, after the trees have been felled for rail splitting, make great piles of the timber they do not use and burn it. Still less should the trees felled in clearing the land be wasted. Even smaller branches should be utilized. In a country where our excellent Swedish fireplaces are unknown and for the most part impractical and where during the winter months a fire must be kept going constantly in the stove lest the room be chilled off at once, a great deal of fuel is used, and on such lands the settler has seldom more wood than he needs for this as well as other purposes. While the country around us was scarce in good timber, we on our section had a number of tall oak trees which promised to become a good future source of income. A sawmill was under construction in Delafield, and we had already been called to assist at the raising of another still closer to us. So part of our winter's work consisted in hauling logs to these sawmills, and we were provident enough to save for fuel the parts of the trees that could not be used in other ways.

However, we still had no working sawmill closer than Oconomowoc, and I had to make trips there with our oxen to bring home what we needed in the way of boards and similar materials. There was also a blacksmith shop there, where I had Spak and Wallis shod to perform their work better. Without shoes it would have been practically impossible to use them on the hard-frozen ground, which was sometimes covered with a sheet of ice.

These trips were, if not the hardest, still the most tedious of all the labors that accompanied our early life as settlers. They were also the occasions of minor adventures which in part inured us to the efforts and self-denials that further awaited us, in part adjusted us to the customs and manners of the country and to hitherto unfamiliar conditions.

During these trips we also succeeded in making an occasional barter for some of the necessities that because of our shortage of money we could not have obtained in any other way. We should scarcely have known otherwise how to manage during the winter, without any income as we were, and obliged to use all our energies to clear and work our own land. In this way our Helsingör fur coats, which in truth were worth gold, brought us an additional supply of hay and corn for our cattle as well as flour and vegetables for ourselves. With a sufficient supply of such goods we were secured against want, at least for the immediate future. As far as coffee and other groceries are concerned, we sometimes had to restrict ourselves. Roasted wheat was made at times to serve instead of genuine mocca, and we had to train ourselves to use a kind of syrup in place of sugar.

All these things were borne with patience if not with contentment, but the thing that was hardest to do without, and for which I was not able to find a substitute, was snuff. As a persistent user of snuff, I looked forward with a sense of dread to the day when I might be deprived entirely of this luxury, and I regarded the deprivation as one of the most difficult trials to which I could ever be subjected. It didn't help any to stave off my nose with half portions. The habit was strong, the small supply I had brought with me from Sweden was almost gone, and a new supply was not to be had for fur coats, double-barreled guns, or even money. But the American atmosphere must have inspired and encouraged the power of invention even in one who otherwise cannot boast of exceptional inventiveness. I could not get snuff, but on the other hand I was able to obtain a few small packages of black, long-leaved smoking tobacco. I dried it on the stove, ground it in the coffee mill, dampened it with a solution of refined potash, and set it on the stove in a closed vessel to ferment. Herr Schwartz,[7] like Cantzler and Co.,[8] may laugh at my method of snuff making, but be it known to all and sundry that the snuff from my factory was the best in the entire region, altogether worthy of praise — still proving that where there is a will there is a way.

Finally Christmas came, that holiday which from our earliest childhood we had been accustomed to spend in the family circle, with friends and relatives now far separated from us. On such occasions a person remembers the past more clearly than ever before; careful comparisons are made between the past and the present; yet the present derives its wealth of content from the past. Certainly it might appear that the first Christmas Eve we spent in our poor log cabin was poor in the outward materials of rejoicing; but it was all the richer in the memories that we were happy to recall in our talk with one another, memories of goodness and love from the time when Mother's hand lit the Christmas candles for the children playing about the gift-laden tree, and Father's voice sought to awaken in the innocent heart a holy longing to be guided always by the Bethlehem star.

But neither did our Christmas lack its outward joy. During the evenings Carl had been working on a dining table, a really fine piece of oak furniture, which he had fortunately just completed by Christmas Eve. It became a welcome gift to Lotten; yes, and to all of us. Now we did not have to eat our Christmas rice porridge from the lid of a chest, none too convenient an arrangement. I had bought a couple of plain but neatly painted wooden chairs on one of my recent trips to Oconomowoc and had kept them hidden in the hayloft. Now they were brought out, and together with a common rocking chair, which is seldom missing in even the simplest American log house, they were placed beside the plainly decorated Christmas table. A meerschaum pipe, a gift from last year's Christmas Eve from my brother O[ldberg],[9] was now filled ceremoniously with good Swedish tobacco, hoarded especially for this occasion. Christine had cooked a splended rice porridge. In fact, nothing was lacking except the traditional *lutfisk*,[10] and except—alas, one and another tear, vainly held back, testified indeed to more than one "except," but at any rate, in our poor, humble, yet festive settler's cabin, love, peace, and contentment had lit their Christmas candles. In spite of all that was missing, we realized that this, our first Christmas Eve in an alien land, had also its own blessing and its own joy.

Christmas Day came, but no bells awakened us with their solemn call to worship, and no brightly lighted temple invited us to join our voices in a common "All hail to thee, O blessed morn." After concluding our family worship, Carl and I made a hasty visit to Delafield. There was nothing there that bore witness to the great Christian holiday. Men were working to put up the sawmill and flour mill, and as on every other day everybody was busy at his worldy activities. The Pearmains, who were born in England, had no doubt been baptized into the Anglican High Church, and had reckoned themselves among its members; like many others, though, they had forgotten, when not reminded by outward church observances, the inner significance of the season. Two Irishmen, residents of Delafield, members of the Roman Catholic Church, were the only ones who were observing the day that for ages had been held sacred as commemorating the birth of our Savior.

Early in the morning, accompanied by their families, they had set out for one of the plain chapels that often are no more than big log houses. Whereas Protestantism, divided internally, has difficulty in persuading its members scattered through the wilderness to come together in a house dedicated to the glory of God, the Roman Catholic religion is seldom without a church in any faraway settlement where it has even just a few adherents. In these uninhabited regions, where everything testifies more and more to the advancement of human industry, where, in a word, so much is said of the world and the things that are in the world, I have been surprised to find small unpretentious buildings erected in the lonely woodlands or on the wide prairies, with their cross-adorned roofs a witness to Him through whom the promise of a better world has been given us. The emblem of the cross, because of its abuse by the Roman Church, is almost detested by ultra-Protestant sects. Hence it is an almost infallible sign that the building which carries it is a Roman Catholic chapel. As one looks at the surrounding enclosure a little more closely, one observes perhaps here and there a little hillock and here and there a simple monument that indicates a holy and sacred resting place for the dead. Generally it takes a long time for adherents of other faiths to think of setting aside a bit of ground for this purpose. Their dead are often interred without ceremony on some hillside or in a field where their moldering bones after a few years may be plowed up by a new owner.

I have no sympathy with Roman Catholicism and have a settled repugnance against its errors. But I honor the zeal and solicitude with which, even under the most unfavorable conditions, it seeks to establish and preserve holy things from the destructive influence of opposite religious excesses and religious indifference. With the exception of this church, only the Protestant Episcopal and some Lutheran churches in this country observe Christmas and other church festivals. These holidays, along with almost all other venerable and age-old ecclesiastical usages, have been banished by the Puritans and their offspring.

According to Puritanism — that worm-eaten creeping growth which, winding itself under the sunny vaults of Christendom, has sought to crowd out the altar and change the sanctuary into a gloomy prison — it was forbidden to keep sacred the day that from earliest times has been observed in memory of Christ's birth. It proved difficult, however, to abolish a holy day so much a part of the very life of the family, and though the message of great joy was not preached in a festively adorned church, there were voices in many homes that kept proclaiming it. The higher significance of Christmas Day was hence to some extent retained in the intimacy of the family's expression of festivity and joy. Then the Puritans, who during the days of their so-called persecution loudly demanded tolerance and freedom of conscience but after coming to power, equaled Philip II and Torquemada[a] in intolerance and the restraint of conscience, decreed with a papal severity that an end be put also to this kind of observance of Christmas, that December 25 be observed as a national day of penance and fasting. In New England it was not observed like this for very long, but the purpose was achieved. Among the ultra-Protestant sects in America, Christmas Day is kept like an ordinary workday, with the exception perhaps that many people have retained the age-old custom of eating roast turkey and plum pudding at dinner. So in this case as in many others we have an example of how the sects in their misdirected zeal are the enemies of the church. They are like the old enemies of Jerusalem who when they saw the Holy City and its holy beauty were seized by a wild, destructive zeal and cried, "Let us break it to the ground."

Note

[a] There has been a tendency to ascribe to the Puritans, or the so-called Pilgrims who were the first colonists of New England, the honor of having established the religious tolerance and freedom of conscience which at present prevail in the North American republic. No mistake could be greater than that. The same persons who demanded from Charles II[11] freedom of conscience for themselves and free religious exercise were deaf, dumb, and blind when there was later a question of granting the same liberty to others. When they left England to settle in America, their purpose was not in any sense to establish and maintain religious liberty in their new homeland. One of their own historians, Hutchinson, declares that such freedom was regarded as a sin and would bring the curse of heaven upon the country. Therefore they hanged Quakers, banished Baptists, and made numbers of the Anglican Church languish in prison. In every way they exercised a political and spiritual oppression which anyone who takes the time to study their history will find quite enough to deprive them of the halo of sainthood that men strangely enough, even in our own age, have sought to adorn them with. They were a sect that began by proving their loyalty to a lawful king and their reverence for God by killing the one and desecrating the temples of the other.

Chapter 16

THE YEAR 1842 BEGINS · ALMANACS · POLMAN AS PRACTICING

PHYSICIAN · PHYSICIANS IN THE WEST · SOCIAL LIFE · VISITS AND

RETURN VISITS · PEARMAIN'S SUICIDE · A BRIEF WIDOWHOOD

MATRIMONIAL ALLIANCES · MARRIAGE CEREMONIES · ABUN-

DANCE OF GAME · VISIT BY OLD ACQUAINTANCES · MISSIONARIES

OF THE PROTESTANT EPISCOPAL CHURCH · OUR FIRST ACQUAINT-

ANCE WITH THE REVEREND MR. BRECK · ATTENDING OUR FIRST

PUBLIC WORSHIP

THE old year came to an end, and a new began. The old Swedish almanac, outwardly ever the same, related to old Father Time's own visage, had to be laid aside as of no further use. It was with a sigh of regret we said farewell to this little book, which as far as I could remember had come every year in its own well-remembered format, reminding us of the flight of time and of the continuing work of the Royal Swedish Academy of Science.[1] Now it had to be exchanged for another, one of the thousands of publications of the kind put out in America and distributed free of charge. The American almanac is a small brochure in which the part that really belongs to an almanac occupies little space while the rest of it is dedicated to the strangest things under the sun. A doctor, for instance, who has invented a new patent medicine, publishes and distributes an almanac in which the wonder-working pill, decoction, salve, or mouthwash is puffed and trumpeted abroad in the most extraordinary manner. Under every month there is a story of some remarkable cure it has brought about. Some pages are filled with anecdotes, advice, and certificates made out by various kinds of people testifying to the wonder-working power of the medicine, people who have tried other cures and medicines in vain, who finally, through the use of this discovery, have been completely healed. The names of the persons mentioned in these chronicles may sometimes be hard to locate within the boundaries of the United States; many certificates, on the other hand, carry well-known and honorable names, but no one takes the trouble to ascertain whether they are genuine. Furthermore, the brochure is illustrated with various woodcuts setting forth most convincingly the appearance of the patient before and after taking the medicine.

In addition to these medical almanacs, there are countless others of the most varied content. Dealers, manufacturers, owners of patents, etc., employ this method to advertise their wares and inventions. The scheme is advertising on the grand scale and is a practical way of making oneself remembered every day by the purchasing public. The hardware dealer distributes in his stores a special almanac illustrated with drawings of improved stoves and tools that he offers for sale. Even tailors, shoemakers, hatters, and others offer their illustrated contributions to these calendars, which at times are just as amusing as the creations in Sweden parading the word "poetic" in their titles.[2]

The new year began with weather that even for a son of the North seemed sharply cold. A few times the thermometer pointed to minus 20 or even 22 degrees. However, the cold spells did not last long, at the most two or three days, after which milder weather followed. At the end of January the weather was so warm that we had to keep windows and door open in our cabin. Then one of those sudden changes in temperature came that are so common in America. Most of February was so cold and blustery that there were days when we could not work outdoors. If the morning's milk was placed on the table near the window, it froze in a few minutes, and we had to keep the stove almost red hot to keep from freezing stiff ourselves. To some extent the imperfect roof was responsible for this, for generally a log cabin is about the warmest building one could wish for; but as the raw wooden roof dried, it shrank and let the cold air through. We realized we should have to get a better roof before another winter. During the first days of March the snow disappeared, and by the third of that month there was not a trace of the deep drifts which had piled up during the months preceding. On the eighth of March prairie fires began to be in evidence, and on the nineteenth they were raging over that part of Pine Lake which had escaped their ravages in the fall. The last few days of March we had full winter again; the ground was covered with snow; the wind was as chilly and penetrating as it had been in February; but after the seventh of April we could work the soil.

In the meantime Polman had left us to try his luck at a career that agreed better with his previous studies and experience. Assuming the title of doctor, he settled in a community that was more thickly settled, a few miles away,[3] and began to practice as a physician. In that profession he was fully as well qualified as many others who were classified as medical doctors. Unfortunately many of those gentlemen are nothing but charlatans and quacks. I have reference here to those in out-of-the-way corners, for America is not lacking in skillful physicians, and even in the new cities of the Far West there are many practitioners who, I have reason to believe, compare favorably with their professional brethren in Europe.[a] Here, too, however, it is hard to distingush between real physicians and those that have promoted themselves to that dignity. Many of them have assumed the profession of healing just from whim or for profit, possessing a certain daring and possibly also certain gifts of a medical sort. Misfortune that it is to become sick at all, it is doubly one under such conditions. A person I have seen going about working as a mason served for a couple of months as an assistant in a drugstore in Milwaukee, whereupon he laid aside the trowel, got himself some medical books, and assumed the title of doctor. That profession gave him a living till financial conditions changed and possibly made it more profitable for him once more to don his mason's apron or to try something else.

The speed with which people here change their life calling and the slight preparation generally needed to leave one calling for another are really surprising, especially to one that has been accustomed to our Swedish guild-ordinances. If liberty in the one case seems too circumscribed, it may well be thought too unlimited in the other. A man who today is a mason may tomorrow be a doctor, the next day a cobbler, and still another day a sailor, druggist, waiter, or schoolmaster. Certainly distinct inconveniences arise from this situation; yet undeniably this unlimited freedom is exactly one of the important reasons why America has advanced with such tremendous speed. It has indeed given opportunity for many humbugs to flourish, but at the same time it has called forth many able men and has spurred them on to greater efforts.

Hitherto we had not maintained much social intercourse with our neighbors. Only a couple of times had we made or received visits. On these occasions, that is, when the women accompanied us, we rode on a big work sled or dray pulled by oxen — a none too agreeable way of paying calls. Besides, visiting demanded more time than we could well spare from our rail splitting, hauling logs to the mill, and other necessary activities.

Mrs. Pearmain and a couple of other "ladies" from Delafield came once to spend a Sunday afternoon with us. Arrayed in silk dresses and bedecked with all manner of gems and gewgaws, they came journeying in the aforementioned fashion, sitting wrapped up in blankets and quilts on chairs that had been placed on the dray. Their costume made in truth a strange contrast both to their means of transportation and to the house that was honored by their visit. In our cabin with its rough, unpeeled walls and its nondescript furnishings of chest and wooden chairs, they sat like gaudy peacocks lodging under the timbers of a barn floor. But such is the custom even in these pioneer settlements. Here too women retain their taste for trinkets and fineries, which hardly harmonize with the garb worn by their husbands and men in general. The husband in his underwear adorned with patches of variegated colors, with holes at his elbows and a ragged straw hat on his head, stands by the side of his spouse like a barn lantern by the side of a gilt parlor lamp. Even in the poorest log houses the wardrobe of the women testifies to the luxury that in the big cities and among the wealthy threatens to undermine the native simplicity of manners and social life.

The entertainment on such visits with pioneer neighbors is completely simple, and elaborate preparations are not expected. It is not required as in Sweden to make a fine spread even beyond what one can afford. The table and what is placed on it are what matters least. People do not visit one another to eat, and the hostess may keep her guests company and not have to busy herself providing food and drink. The most important thing is to provide, along with

Unonius' original home at Pine Lake, Wisconsin. Painting by unknown artist

Carl Gustaf Groth, distant relative of
Unonius, another pioneer

Carl Wilhelm Polman, one of the original
settlers at Pine Lake

coffee or tea, some good, fresh wheat bread, the usual small round biscuits baked with milk, and a little jam, cake, or pie, of which there is almost always a supply in the house.

One day while the sleighing was good, we decided as a family to pay our neighbors in Delafield a return visit, but in order not to waste any time, we arranged to take along a couple of logs for the mill that was being built. The logs lay lashed to the dray with an iron chain, and seated on either side of them were Lotten and Christine, parading their long unused holiday dresses. Carl and I took turns driving the oxen. This was the first time we had all been away from the cabin, which, notwithstanding, we left without any other fastening than its wooden latch. With all the crudeness of backwoods life on the frontier, and in spite of the unpolished manners of which Americans have been accused, they never enter another man's house or room without first knocking on the door. Even the lower classes observe this custom in their intercourse with others, and even in the poorest log cabin it would be regarded as bad manners to enter without first announcing one's presence in this fashion and waiting for permission to enter, expressed by a "Come in." Anyone omitting this courtesy before entering a private home might get the same reception as one of my acquaintances, a Norwegian doctor, who, having entered a gentleman's room in his usual informal way without rapping on the door, was greeted with a box on the ear and thrown down the stairs.

We reached Delafield without meeting a single person and were therefore totally unprepared for the shocking news that reached us on our arrival at the door of Pearmain's house. We had just been jesting about Mrs. Pearmain and had wondered if she would give evidence of her usual "nervous disorder," when a workman [4] living in the village came out of his house and informed us that Pearmain had shot himself that very morning. The surprising nature of this piece of news was increased by the fact that the suicide had been committed with one of my pistols, which he had asked to borrow a few days before and which, without suspecting how he was going to use it, I had told him to keep as a memento.

Under these conditions there was nothing for us to do but to postpone our call, and after we had unloaded our logs we returned home in a somber mood. Despite all his faults and his efforts to enrich himself at our expense, he was the one among our neighbors that we had been best able to communicate with, and we had him to thank for much very useful advice and information. He was without doubt a far better person than his wife, on whom I considered it my duty to pay a call of condolence a couple of days later. I found her altogether prostrated with grief, expressing her sorrow with the most tragical pathos.

A couple of weeks later Pearmain's few possessions were sold at a public auction. The tavern business was taken over by another, and so was the widow. Mrs. Pearmain was married the same evening to an adventurer from one of the eastern states, and we never saw her again.[5]

This was the first example we had of the frivolous, not to say scandalous, manner into which so-called marriages are entered. There is no law in America that forbids one mate to remarry within an hour of the death of the other. True enough, few are in such a hurry as Mrs. Pearmain, but it is nothing unusual for a wife or husband to get another companion a few weeks after the spouse's death. Even among educated classes one often hears the one mate speak of the other as his "companion" or "partner," a term that under existing conditions and as marriage is conceived of by many here, is really more appropriate than husband and wife. The one is in many cases just an associate of the other, and if the union is broken through the death of one of its members, financial considerations rather than the heart determine whether another is soon to be received into the firm.

No previous banns are required.[6] The formalities for entering into marriage differ in different states. In Wisconsin the only condition is that the husband declare under oath before an official or magistrate that there is no lawful reason why he cannot be married. He then obtains for himself and his "partner" a marriage license, which authorizes any clergyman within the state, any justice of the peace, or any other magistrate to unite them in marriage. In some states not even an oath or license is required. It is enough that both parties appear before any witnesses they may get and declare that they take each other for husband and wife.

A few years ago in New York a noted jurist married a woman celebrated for her culture and talents, but still more famous as a proponent of the emancipation of women, one of the new lights Miss Bremer in her book on America points to as to a beacon for humanity and in whom she sees signs of the coming perfection of society in moral relations. The marriage ceremony, if one may call it that, was performed by the bride and bridegroom themselves, and carried out in the following manner: The two parties to the transaction took each other by the hand, and in a little talk the bridegroom called upon the wedding guests to serve as witnesses to the fact that he therewith took for his wife Miss ——— standing by his side. "I do not bind and pledge myself by any vows," he said, "to fidelity and an indissoluble union, but I hope we shall live together happily." The emancipated woman then proceeded to make the same declaration, whereupon they received congratulations as husband and wife. A written certificate to the effect that they had been united in marriage was drawn up and duly signed by the witnesses. Thereupon it was sent for recording to the public officer whose duty it is to keep a record of all marriages entered into in his district.

This was all that was required to establish a civil marriage. The conclusion that may be drawn from this is evident: the same authority that establishes a marriage must naturally have also the right to dissolve it. Matters, however, have not progressed so far as that, although the signs in which Miss Bremer sees "the perfecting of all things" certainly point in that direction. But, praise God, in America there are also other signs presaging better days than might be expected from the socialistic ideas, the phalansteries, and the "woman's right" craze, as well as other more or less anti-Christian movements and associations—in a word, from all that moral, philosophical, religious, and many times undeniably clever humbug which under the guise of promoting social betterment has awakened the sympathy and admiration of the aforementioned Swedish writer.

Like the marriage in New York described above, the civil marriage ceremony is in general carried out in a very summary fashion. It is altogether a juridical act, often without prayer or any kind of ritual to put a religious stamp upon it.

The two lovers enter the office of a justice of the peace.

"What is your business?" he asks.

"We want to get married."

The justice, seating himself at his desk, turning to the man: "What is your name?"

"Peter Thompson."

The justice, turning to the woman: "And yours?"

"Sally Johnson."

The justice: "Peter Thompson, do you take Sally Johnson as your wife?"

"Yes."

"Sally Johnson, do you take Peter Thompson as your husband?"

"Yes."

The justice, rising from his desk: "Inasmuch as you have now made this declaration, I hereby pronounce you husband and wife. This is your marriage certificate."

The bridegroom presses a few dollars into the magistrate's hand or, not uncommonly, asks him first very nonchalantly how much he owes. Thereupon Peter and Sally march home, pleased at being able to take to their neighbors and friends, and possibly also to their immediate families, the unexpected news that they are now husband and wife.

With rail splitting and other labors, the winter passed by. Every so often we shot a prairie chicken or a deer to add welcome variety to a table none too rich in it. After the departure of Kee-wah-goosh-kum and his tribe the deer had returned in great numbers and often wandered close to the house. One day when Carl and I were away for a load of hay, Lotten noticed a herd of deer coming across the ice, aiming directly for our cabin. Close to the house, between four trees which grew close together, we had nailed up some boards and made for ourselves a kind of crib in which to keep our supply of corn. The whole herd made directly for the crib, which was only a few steps from our threshold. Lotten picked up a gun and fired through the door, the first shot she had ever discharged. If in her haste she had not picked a bird gun loaded with small shot instead of a rifle, it is likely that even with her inexpert hand she would have either killed or at least wounded one of the animals.

But let no sport-loving fellow countryman be led to emigrate because of such hunting tales. The time is past, at least in Wisconsin and surrounding states, when herds of deer would come trooping up to the door. However good the hunting may be, no person of small means should think of trying to make his living in this way. It is well enough for the new settler in his spare hours— and these are not many — to walk about through the woods and hunt in order to add to his food supply, but beyond that he is wasting time that could be used to better advantage. In these sparsely settled regions he would find it difficult to dispose of anything that he could not use for his own larder.

Spring was already on the way when we were surprised by a visit which I must to a certain extent regard as the first of those signposts leading to the momentous change that in the future was to occur in our life.

When we had boarded the steamer that was to take us from New York to Albany, we had made the acquaintance of a Mr. N[anscawen],[7] an Englishman who with his lovely wife was on a trip to the Far West. I do not know how it happened, but on the crowded steamer where we were entirely surrounded by strangers, we seemed drawn to each other so that during the few hours we spent together there arose between us a mutual trust. At that time we couldn't very well speak to each other, but for all that we felt as though we were well acquainted. The young wives especially were deeply attracted to each other, and what they could not express in words, they communicated in the silent language of mutual sympathy. Women appear to have an inbred gift of perception which makes them more easily and often with more truth than we men apprehend another person's character as well as condition of life. At that time my wife hardly understood a word of English, and yet she knew, when she went to sleep by the side of her new friend, that she was an American lady from New Jersey, that she had been married to Mr. N[anscawen] only a few weeks, and had now left father, mother, and home to accompany her husband to some faraway corner in the West, where he already had built a home in anticipation of their marriage. But what neither my wife nor any of the rest of us could understand was the name of the place where they were to make their home. So much we did understand, that they were going to Wisconsin, and this may well have been the first time our thoughts were awakened to the possibility of steering our way there instead of to Illinois.

At Albany we were separated from Mr. and Mrs. N[anscawen], who left at once on a river boat for Buffalo, and on our arrival there they were ready to leave on a sailing vessel. In Detroit we met them again for a few moments and again, to our great pleasure, in Milwaukee, but that was before we had decided in what part of the new territory to make our home. However, Mr. N[anscawen], having made certain inquiries, thought he might find us somewhere around Pine Lake, whereupon he and his wife set out one day to look for us. Asking for the Swedish settlement, which was now becoming rather well known in the neighborhood, they found us at last, and we gave them a hearty welcome.

Mr. N[anscawen] informed us that they were living only twelve miles away, in the small village of Prairieville, later named Waukesha, where they had a farm. In that place three young missionaries of the Protestant Episcopal Church had been stationed since the preceding fall, and were extending their activities for several miles into the neighborhood. At Summit, only a few miles from our home, they had recently begun to hold services, and Mr. N[anscawen] and his wife, both members of that church, urged us to attend. Acquainted at least to some degree with the English High Church, which we regarded as closely related to the Swedish Church, we thought this really good news, and we decided not to miss the first opportunity offered to take part in public worship, the high spiritual content of which we had long been missing. Mr. N[anscawen] prepared us, however, to look first for a visit from one of the missionaries. They too had heard of some Swedes that had settled in the neighborhood and had told Mr. N[anscawen] they considered it their duty to look us up.

It was only a few days later that the Reverend J. Lloyd Breck [8] paid us a call. From the very first his personality made an impression that I shall never forget. His entire being revealed the Christian and the zealous minister of the gospel. In his soulful eyes I could read a strong faith coupled with a firm steadfastness and an unyielding courage based on trust in God. He would brook no hindrance in the pursuit of his sacred calling, but would calmly meet every danger, even death if necessary, in proclaiming the gospel and extending the kingdom of Christ. It was impossible to see him without feeling oneself attracted to him through both love and esteem. With a most youthful and to a certain degree even jovial appearance, without any of that forced, artificial gloom which a species of religiosity often considers the essential sign of piety, there was in him a dignified seriousness that let one and all understand he had laid to heart Paul's admonition to Timothy, "Let no one despise thy youth." The kindly, unaffected friendliness which characterized him would never permit anyone to forget that his mission was to command, teach, and be an example to others in word and personal communion. One might well conceive that in his work he might be contradicted, but never that he could be insulted.

Born into a respected and well-to-do family in Pennsylvania and with many wealthy and influential relations, he could certainly in any other calling than the priestly have made for himself a position more secure and advantageous in a worldly sense. But a powerful inward urge had led him to enter the ministry, and though in this calling, which in America always entails much self-denial and sacrifice, it might have been to his advantage to remain in an eastern diocese, he had chosen the western wilderness as his field of labor. He was prepared to face hardships and sacrifices that were certain as well as to encounter a spirit of contradiction which, though not specially directed against the church he represented, is nevertheless more keenly felt in this region than in the eastern states with their ordered, older, and more serenely progressive congregations.

Half a year before this time Mr. Breck had been ordained deacon in the Protestant Episcopal Church and had set out at once for this part of Wisconsin. This church, with an insufficient number of ministers, had not hitherto been able to extend its work here. On his mission he was accompanied by two other men, the Reverend W. Adams [9] and the Reverend J. Hobart,[10] who had been graduated with him from the General Theological Seminary [b] and had at the same time been ordained into the diaconate. These consecrated men, full of zeal for the advancement of the kingdom of Christ, here sought out the scattered members of their church and brought them together in small congregations. Furthermore, within a district of more than two hundred miles in circumference, they sought in every way to fulfill the command of the Master to "go out and teach all nations."

These men were missionaries, by which term one must understand not only those sent out to convert the heathen, but also those that labor in far places among white people in the United States' own territory or in places where the church has only a few members and consequently needs more support than these scattered few can offer. Even in the big cities, such missionaries are appointed and supported by their respective missionary societies for various purposes. There are in New York and other cities missionaries whose duty it is to look up and assist the poor, and especially those who have failed for some reason or other to join any church. Again, there are seamen's missionaries, whose field of labor is the ships and the wharves; also missionaries among the Germans and among the laboring population in industrial communities. The Protestant Episcopal Church and the work under its jurisdiction is thus separated into two divisions, each with its own separate treasury, the foreign mission and the domestic mission, the latter of which also supports as far as possible pastors in small and struggling churches.

On his very first visit, Mr. Breck led our conversation into religious channels. He asked whether we were among the numerous immigrants who, having arrived in America and left the church of their fatherland behind, had left behind also its faith and confession. We told him that we were seeking through private worship in our home to conserve the heritage that had been given us and in this way as far as possible to nourish and keep in our hearts the godliness enjoined upon us whether within or outside an ordered church denomination as a sacred duty. He urged us to maintain our family altar, but showed us at the same time the inadequacy of this form of worship when it is not revived and watered by the stream that proceeds from the fountains of life within the church. In our homeland we had through holy baptism been received as members of Christ's church; we must not now separate ourselves from it. Since God, even in this faraway corner of the world, had sent forth the gospel for the salvation of sinners, and since by His grace His church had been planted here, it was our duty not to keep ourselves apart from it but to become true and active members within it. The Anglo-American and the Swedish churches were both branches of the holy universal church of Christ; they were both founded on the communion and the teaching of the holy apostles and built upon the eternal rock. Their confessions might show certain differences, but these were differences of opinion rather than of faith. Both had through the episcopal office maintained a valid apostolic priesthood, without which no true church can exist. In his conversation Mr. Breck also touched on the former Swedish churches in New Sweden on the shores of the Delaware River and on the mutually friendly relations that had existed between them and the Anglican Church till, no longer able to get ministers from home, they had finally been entirely incorporated into the Episcopal Church in America.

This was the sum and substance of the first conversation I had with this man, with whom I was afterwards to be associated through the closest bonds of friendship and fraternity. The amiability of the man himself and his engaging ways made his simple words and admonitions, on purpose kept plain, and notwithstanding our still limited English easily understood, leave a deep impression on me. They planted in me the first seed from which were to grow theological views that more and more ripened into real convictions. The only thing I could not quite grasp and about which at that time I differed with him was the strong emphasis placed on the episcopal office. Also I did not trouble myself much or beat my brains over things in either the Swedish Church or the Anglican that I considered only accidental, contingent upon the institutions and the general civil setup of those lands. What might be good and practical in those countries seemed to me here where church and state are entirely separated and independent of one another to be a matter of no concern.

At our invitation, Mr. Breck decided to spend the night with us. He had ridden far that day, and when we apologized for the poor accommodations we had to offer, he assured us he should sleep very well by Carl's side under the ridgepole of our attic. Before we went to bed, he conducted evening devotions with us as is customary in America when a minister is guest in the home. Likewise in the morning before we went to our work. During prayer he knelt, but being unaccustomed to a mode of worship entirely out of use in Sweden, we could not make ourselves follow his example. I asked myself why. Was it the power of habit or was it an unwillingness based on prejudice that kept me even outwardly from bowing down before God to glorify Him in my body and my spirit?

Something that seemed unusual to us also was that our new acquaintance, in addition to the family worship morning and evening, quietly engaged in private devotion, kneeling at his bedside before going to bed in the evening and immediately upon arising in the morning. He did this without any ostentation and without any sentimentalities spoken either before or afterward. It was wholly natural with him, like one of the daily customs that circumstances did not now permit him to perform in the prescribed fashion of going into his chamber and closing the door. I felt myself involuntarily attracted to the godly man and regarded him with veneration. An inner voice told me that in his prayers were included the strangers that now were living near him in his country. When he went away he left us some of the books and tracts he carried in his saddlebag: Scougal's excellent treatise *The Life of God in the Soul of Man*[11] and two copies of the Book of Common Prayer as adopted by and used in the American church.

A couple of Sundays after this visit, when we knew that Mr. Breck was to preach in Summit, we set out early to attend the service. Because the distance was a little too great for Lotten to walk back and forth, we traveled in the usual pioneer manner, behind our oxen. The day was bright and clear. The first green shoots of spring were sprouting from the layer of ashes left by the prairie fire of the preceding fall. No faded, half-rotting leaves from last year covered the ground; it seemed to have been specially swept for Flora's coming. Everything had a holiday appearance, which harmonized with that particularly glad mood one feels in the country when, freed from customary domestic duties and toils, one is on the way to God's house.

We did not really, of course, arrive at church here. In these new rural communities it is the schoolhouse rather than the church that rallies the entire community. In religious matters minds are divided, and among forty or fifty families of settlers perhaps no two may be found willing to unite in a common worship. For the time being the schoolhouse has to serve as a church until the denominations represented in the neighborhood become strong enough to erect specific buildings for the purpose. Other communities that do not have the means to build have to content themselves, perhaps with no prospect of anything better, with agreements among themselves and itinerant preachers about the use of the schoolhouse. One group will meet in the forenoon, another in the early afternoon, the third one Sunday, the fourth the next Sunday, the fifth at four o'clock, the sixth at seven in the evening, and so forth, so that all day Sunday groups succeed each other like regiments at the changing of the guard, and the different ministers and congregations meet each other on the threshold. Occasionally people will be found who, without my likening them to Phanuel's daughter [12] or the people of Athens, who "spent their time in nothing else, but either to tell, or to hear some new thing," seem to want to remain in the provisional temple night and day and so go through a regular course in contemporary church history.

The small schoolhouse in which Mr. Breck was to conduct the service was one of those ordinary, simple structures of which the new communities make use, and in the building of which all the people in the district cooperate. It was an ordinary log house, some twenty-four feet long and a couple of feet less wide. With its uneven corners and unpeeled log walls, its small windows placed high up, close under the eaves, to keep the children from being distracted by whatever was going on outside, its poorly laid and defective shingle roof, and in one wall its rickety, unpainted door, it looked more like an unattractive barn than a building erected for the education of the young. The interior was almost as uninviting as the exterior, though the logs there had been peeled and evened off. The building naturally consisted of only one room, hardly more than eight feet in height. In the middle of the floor stood a big portable iron stove. Heating at full capacity, it would have turned the low-ceilinged room with thirty to forty children in it into a regular Finnish steambath if the great cracks in roof, walls, and floor had not supplied a constant change of air. From the stove an iron pipe extended right up through the roof, and on each side of the stove, as close to it as possible, were two solid oak tables which, like the benches that flanked them, carried the marks of the irresistible yearning of young America to put pocket knives to use. A few maps and charts hung on the walls. At one end of the room were a table and a rough wooden chair for the teacher. At the door a water bucket with a tin cup floating in it completed the furnishings of the room. Anything less designed to encourage a worshipful attitude can hardly be imagined.

Settlers and their families, walking and riding, arrived one after another. Some came, like ourselves, driving oxen; others, in better circumstances, came with horses and conveyances of many different varieties. The women, decked out in showy hats and varicolored silk dresses, sat lined up on boards and chairs in the long work wagons.

In a country that offers no opportunities for attending any public amusement and where, even if they were available, many would consider them forbidden on religious grounds, the meetings on Sunday furnish almost the only chance a young girl has to go out a little and show herself to the world. I will not venture to say whether in other circumstances she would be just as careful not to miss a service. It is a very curious thing to hear the charming sex in the shops of little towns beseeching the merchant to bring out from his scanty supply of silk, calico, and muslin some piece of goods suitable — not for a ball or visiting gown or anything of that sort — there is no question of such a thing — but for a new dress to "go to meeting" in.

Quite a respectable gathering was on hand on this occasion, and not only the benches but the tables were filled almost to capacity. Before the service began there was no great display of devotion. The unchurchly surroundings may have been the excuse for people's behaving as if they had come together for amusement or for some political meeting rather than for worship. They talked and laughed with one another unceremoniously, especially the women, while many of the men pulled out their knives and passed the time either by adding to the schoolboys' wood carvings on tables and seats or, if space permitted, by opening the blade at a right angle and throwing the knife into the air in such a way that as it struck the floor it buried its point in the wood. As far as I was concerned, I freely confess that my mind focused on these and similar activities almost to the exclusion of the more serious things that ought to have engaged my attention.

A few persons exhibited a spirit suited to the occasion. Having knelt in devotion before they took their places, they occupied themselves during the time that preceded the service with reading their prayer books. They were apparently members of the church according to whose ritual and confession the service was to be held. Strangely enough, when members of one religious denomination attend service in a church of another, they seldom if ever accommodate themselves to the forms of that particular church. Even if these correspond fully with those of their own church, they feel free to dispense with them. For instance, if a Methodist or a member of some other sect, accustomed to kneel at prayer in his own church, goes to a Prostestant Episcopal service where the same custom prevails, he generally remains seated both during prayer and confessions. The common custom in America — a custom that as far as I know only the Lutherans deviate from — is to stand while singing the praise of God. People for the most part always do this even when attending a strange church. Yet none the less, if Presbyterians or Congregationalists, in their own service very particular in this respect, go to an Episcopal service, they generally remain seated in perfect comfort during the singing of *Gloria in Excelsis*, *Gloria Patri*, *Te Deum Laudamus*, or some anthem word for word taken from the Psalms of David and rendered not in Latin, but in English, which all understand. They stand up together, however, during the singing of an ordinary hymn, of which unfortunately there are many that a public service could well do without. It is as if these human compositions deserve to be shown a greater reverence than the hymns of praise to God taken from His own revealed Word.

Finally Mr. Breck came. The knives were put away, the conversation ended, and the service began. His own spiritual attitude appeared to communicate itself to all of us.

This was the first time I had ever attended an Anglo-American church service as well as my first acquaintance with the Book of Common Prayer. The church ritual is found in its totality in this book together with the Epistles, the Gospels, the Psalms, and hymns. As well as I could, I followed the service with the aid of the copy that Mr. Breck had recently given me. It appeared to be a form of worship that well merited the name "common."

As is well known, the congregation here takes a greater part in the service than in any other Protestant church, where the minister is all too much the only acting person and the sole reader, the occupation of the congregation being largely just listening to his words. When I heard the congregation loudly joining in the words of the Confession and the Creed — where the minister in the name of everyone does not say, "We believe," but one and all declare their "I believe in God Almighty"— when I heard all as with one voice intoning the "Our Father" and with a devout "Amen" endorsing all the other church prayers, it fell at first on my unaccustomed ear like a disturbing mumble. It was not long, however, before I found something really solemn in this communal worship, just as my own religious devoutness awakened and stirred as I took part in it. What especially impressed me was the beautiful and perfect form in which the Litany occurs in the Episcopal ritual, where the kneeling congregation devoutly breathes forth the prayer "Lord, have mercy upon us." Anything that pierces more to the heart can hardly be imagined than when after the minister's words, transporting in their melody and beauty in English, "In all time of our tribulation; in all time of our prosperity; in the hour of death, and in the day of judgment," the entire congregation responds with "Good Lord, deliver us." This, along with every other part of the common prayer, in which each petition is laid upon the lips of the members of the congregation, made such an impression on me that I completely forgot the low, insignificant, and grimy schoolhouse, where there was nothing otherwise to awaken religious feelings and move the spirit to devotion.

Yet with all this I cannot deny, accustomed as I was to regarding the sermon as the main part of the service, that I thought the preceding altar service rather lengthy, though I could not decide either then or later what part of it I should have liked to eliminate. Prayer, anthems, and Scripture readings succeeded each other so appropriately that a truly religious spirit should not have grown tired. Still, in the American as well as in the English High Church, three services, originally separate, have been combined into one — Morning Prayer, the Litany, and High Mass. In the Prayer Book of the American church these have been made somewhat briefer than in the English. After the Litany a psalm is sung, whereupon the minister takes his place before the altar. After he has read a prayer, he turns to the congregation, which in the meantime has knelt, and reads the Decalogue exactly as found in Exodus, the twentieth chapter. The fourth verse, which by the Lutheran Church has been regarded as an amplification of the First Commandment and for that reason has been excluded from its catechism, is here given as the Second Commandment; what in the Swedish Catechism is given as the Second Commandment is here made the Third, and so forth, until the seventeenth verse, which is not here divided into two commandments but is presented as one, the Tenth. The first table hence consists of the first four commandments, and the second of the following six, counting from what we consider the Fourth, and combining the Ninth and Tenth Commandments into one.

This form of High Mass, the ante-communion service, which is peculiar to the Episcopal Church, cannot but make a deep and powerful impression on anyone who attends it with some feeling of devoutness. These sacred commandments, set forth to us in a temple, must involuntarily awaken the sinner to self-examination and bring him to a lively consciousness of having broken them in thought, word, and deed. They must make heart and tongue break out in the prayer in which the congregation upon the restatement of each of these commandments joins: "Lord, have mercy upon us, and write all these thy laws in our hearts, we beseech thee." The law is brought in here with the strength of "a schoolmaster to bring us to Christ." After a brief prayer and the Collect for the day, the Gospel is proclaimed according to the texts that have been selected for every Sunday and holy day. These and the Epistles and the Gospels as well as the preceding Collects are, with a few exceptions, the same as in our Swedish Book of Prayer.

In the Episcopal Church, however, the minister is not limited to these texts, which are read before the altar, but has freedom in his choice of topics, although the division of the church year is almost always observed, at least in the morning service. It was observed today, the first Sunday after Easter, when, without exactly treating the day's Gospel, the preacher in his sermon directed our thoughts to the church feast just observed as well as to the new soon coming.

After the service I had a chance to speak a few words with Mr. Breck, who conveyed the pleasing news that he and the other two missionaries were planning to build homes in our neighborhood because it was more central for their missionary work. For that purpose they had already purchased a section only three miles from us, in one of the most beautiful regions in Wisconsin. Their aim was to build a chapel and found an educational institution, for which already some money had been collected among members of the Episcopal Church in the eastern states.

Notes

[a] According to the census of 1850 there were in the United States 36 medical institutes, 10 of them in the western states. The number of professors engaged in those institutions was 247, and the number of students 4,947. It is reasonable to suppose that between 1,300 and 1,400 graduate as medical doctors each year. This seems a big number; yet it is far from enough to satisfy the needs in such a big country with its constantly growing population. No wonder, then, that quack doctors fill the gap in many localities and are called upon in times of need.

[b] It is called the General Theological Seminary, though it is not a general institution of learning in the sense that its students are trained to go out as preachers of religion in any of the various religious denominations. Each denomination has its own schools and seminaries for that purpose. The General Theological Seminary in New York is exclusively an institution of the Protestant Episcopal Church; it is called General because it is not like many institutions of that kind connected with any bishopric, but is controlled and governed by the Protestant Episcopal Church as a whole, and all its bishops and certain appointees from each bishopric serve as its trustees.

Chapter 17

CULTIVATING THE LAND · PLOWS · RAISING CORN · THE YIELD

DIFFERENT KINDS · BROOMCORN · THE WIDE USEFULNESS OF

CORN · DIFFICULTY OF RAISING IT · CHIPMUNKS AND GOPHERS

RAISING POTATOES · MELONS · TOMATOES

ALTHOUGH spring is not the best time to plow new soil, we had to get a few acres under cultivation for planting corn, potatoes, and other vegetables if we were to have anything to live on another winter. It would not be worth while to plant any other crops on soil broken early in the spring — on oak-opening land, at any rate, where the soil is harder and more mixed with clay than on prairie and forest land. On forest land particularly it sometimes happens that settlers who have come in the fall and have to get an early yield from their ground reap a considerable harvest from wheat sown between the stumps early in the spring, on ground cleared during the winter. In this case the ground is not plowed, but the seed is harrowed down in the loose blackloam.

Our finances did not allow us to buy a breaking plow, but even had we been able to afford one, we could hardly have used it, since on oak-opening land pulling it would have required at least four or five teams of draft animals. We therefore had to hire a man who had both plow and oxen and who went around plowing for others. Sometimes several poor settlers buy a plow in common, and by hitching their oxen together they assist each other in breaking the land. However, we were able to get such cooperation only to a limited degree.

The usual price for breaking an acre of ground is three to four dollars, depending on the character of the soil. This cash payment was reduced, however, both because we helped with the work ourselves and used our own oxen and because we also pledged ourselves to give in exchange certain days of labor with men and draft animals.

The breaking plows in use here are of many kinds, and to give a full description of them would require too much time and space. The most common type, which was the one used to cut the first furrow of the earth that was to give us our daily bread, is shaped like the Swedish Överum-plow,[1] but both the body and its various parts are much bigger and turn a far wider strip of sod. Furthermore, the colter of the American breaking plow is sometimes welded to the share. This is true of plows used on hard-broken land. In other models colter and share are connected in such a way that the share, which has a very sharp point, is fitted into a hole at the lower end of the colter, so that it can be removed if desired. It generally is when the ground is stony, but then much more power is needed to pull the plow. The breaking plow is in addition frequently supplied with a small wheel, running between two horseshoe-shaped irons fastened one on each side of the plow beam a few inches from the clevis. This wheel, which can be raised or lowered at will according to the desired depth of the furrow, undeniably gives more stability to the plow, and even when the plowman does not give full attention to his work, makes the plowing more regular.

Plows are numbered according to their size. Every part in the same series is standardized, so that if any part is broken it is possible to obtain from the factory another to replace it. All the wooden parts are made by machinery; the body of the plow is made from cast iron. The moldboard of cast iron is sometimes covered with steel. The iron used for this purpose is of the best quality, and in some factories is made from a mixture of various kinds and tempered by "chilling," a new method that makes it very strong and durable. Plows made from this kind of iron last at least twice as long as those manufactured from common cast iron. The moldboard and other parts are carefully ground and polished, and the entire implement is attractive as well as durable. The price naturally varies with the size. In the eastern states plows cost from nine to thirteen dollars; in the West they are, like everything else, much more expensive and may cost as much as twenty dollars.

Like all other tools and equipment in use here, plows are constructed with a view to making physical labor easier. The plowman walks very erect, and if the plow is properly adjusted and the ring in which the draft chain is fastened has been correctly fitted to the clevis, he does not have to use much physical strength to press and keep the plow in the ground. The job, however, requires a good deal of experience and attention. The most difficult thing is to adjust the plow itself and to keep the clevis at a proper angle to the plow beam, on doing which the width of the turf to be turned depends, and to adjust the ring at a proper height so that the length of the draft chain fits the evenness or unevenness of the ground.

Once these things have been done, the plow can be driven on even prairie land by a half-grown boy, provided he is strong enough to turn it at the end of the furrow. In fact, on such land I have seen long furrows plowed with no one holding the plow. There has been only a boy to drive the team of four horses needed to supply power enough to break the virgin soil. If the plow has a keen edge, it can turn over a strip of turf from twenty-two to thirty-six inches wide and from two to three inches deep.

In hardly any situation does man more strikingly stand forth as lord over nature than when he is converting the wild and wide prairie into a fertile field. The bottom of the furrow and the top of the upturned turf are as smooth as if they had been cut with a sharp knife. The length of the whole field, one plowed turf strip lies even and unbroken at the side of another. Not a green sprig is seen, not a weed, not a root, stone, or stump; nothing but the rich, fertile fields, ever widening under the settler's hands, ready for seed and golden harvest.

On the prairie a man with four horses can plow about two acres a day; with more draft animals, perhaps three. On ordinary oak-opening land it does not go so fast; sometimes he cannot manage more than one acre. With the exception of the burr-oak openings, it is not possible, either, to turn over as wide a strip of sod on this kind of ground as on the prairie. The same kind of plow can be used on the one kind of land as on the other, but whereas it is possible on the prairie to place the clevis on a straight line with the beam, it is necessary on oak-opening land, if a big plow is used, to turn the clevis at an angle and by that means as well as by the direction of the plow regulate the width of the furrow. Everything depends, however, on the type of ground and the number of draft animals used. On new oak-opening ground the plow frequently strikes roots which it cannot cut off. The plowman must therefore always keep an axe handy. Many a time, also, he must turn the turf up by hand whenever the plow has not been able to cut through it or invert it completely. For the plow used in breaking our land, which made a furrow from eighteen to twenty inches in width, five teams of strong oxen were required, though in burr-oak openings more free from roots, four or perhaps even three teams might be enough.

If in driving the oxen we had exercised our lungs before, we now had to strain them to their uttermost capacity. Supplied with a great whip, having a two-yard-long hickory handle and a whip-cord, pleated from deerskin, long enough to reach both the foremost and hindmost animals as we walked at a short distance from the clevis, Carl and I took turns at the by no means idyllic labor of driving oxen. It was not so easy as one might suppose, especially as we had to deal with five teams of long-horned critters that were at once lazy and headstrong. The oxen to the right had to be kept walking in the furrow; for that reason the most experienced and best-trained animals were placed in lead-position. However, that did not prevent now one, now another, of the teams that followed from turning aside. The whip had to be kept in almost constant motion while the driver himself had to shout and shriek the words of command necessary to successful ox-driving. Yet the resulting soreness of arms and hoarseness of voice mattered little set against the joy of at last plowing and sowing our own land (alas, still not paid for), with a hope of future harvests. As we well knew that the first yield from ground plowed this spring would in all likelihood not be very great, we did not break more than four acres, postponing until later in the summer, before the grass should have gone to seed, the breaking of a larger area for fall planting.

In the early part of May we planted about half of the plowed area in corn. This rich and useful grain, though it may not be peculiar to the North American continent, is more important here than in any other country and has attracted the admiration of all Europe. This wonderful cereal is native to America and is commonly known here as Indian corn because the aborigines were already planting it and using it for food when Europeans first arrived. To the latter it is said to have been completely unknown. It is still the food staple of the red man as it was in ancient times. For the white settler, of all the products of this rich and fertile land it is, at least in the beginning, the most important and the one to which he gives his earliest work and attention. Of all the grains it is the most cultivated in America and the one that gives the richest yield. According to the statistical tables of 1850 the corn crop that year yielded 592,071,104 bushels,[2] more than twice the combined quantities of wheat, rye, barley, oats, and buckwheat.

The section of Wisconsin where we had settled, however, was, like all the northern and northwestern states, less suitable for corn raising than the southern and especially the central regions, where a warmer climate and a richer, more porous type of soil produce species of corn that will not ripen farther north. With the exception of the burr-oak plains and the river valleys, opening lands are not as a rule so well suited to corn growing as forest land is, and especially the prairie. Yet even here the settler cannot afford to neglect corn, even though he may have to satisfy himself with less of a yield and smaller ears than where soil and climate are better suited. His crop will in any event well repay him for his toil, the grain is useful in so many ways.

The straw, or stalk, if it is proper to call by that what looks more like the trunk of a young tree, grows often to a height of twelve feet and more on suitable soil. As the plant grows, it forms a kind of joints or knobs about a foot apart, from which big, broad leaves grow out two by two on each side, the outer covering consisting of a continuation of the stalk. After it grows a little higher, the leaves begin to bend outward till they are completely flattened out, their tips hanging downward by the side of the stalk. When it is fully developed, there grows out of its top a cluster of flowers, blue, red, and green, consisting of a number of fine, thread-like fibers, covered with numerous male flowers, which hang down like a bushy tuft or tassel. In time, in four, five, or more places on the stalk, small cone-shaped heads appear. These heads, or ears, sheathed in tightly grown, light green leaves forming the husk, continue to grow to a foot in length and sometimes more. As they grow and ripen, the husks keep opening and finally dry up. From their tips during the flowering season grow out countless numbers of female blossoms in several different shades, in appearance like fine silken threads; they cling to the kernels inside the husk, and as the grain ripens dry up and fall off. At the time when the corn is tasseling and its bushy crown surrenders its pollen to the wind to be carried about, a tall-grown cornfield is without question both the most beautiful and most magnificent sight that can reward the farmer's labor, blessed by Him who makes all things grow. When a man, having watered and tended the plants, small and delicate at first, finally sees them developing in such richness and color, he is almost ready to believe that God has lifted the curse He pronounced upon the earth because of man's sin, and he forgets the briars and thistles it was condemned to produce.

The ear consists of a heavy, fibrous cob around which the kernels grow in regular rows; these run from top to base, with smaller or wider gaps between them. The color of the corn is generally yellow, although there are species that put forth white, red, and brown ears. The kernels close to the base are the largest and fullest; at the middle of the ear they become somewhat smaller, and at the top they are very small. On ears of the bigger kinds of corn, one may count twenty-four and even thirty-six rows of kernels running side by side from top to base, each row containing from thirty to forty kernels. The ears of the smaller kinds have generally eight rows, seldom less, but sometimes even twelve. Corn of eight rows is raised even in Canada, and rather commonly and successfully on the shores of Lake Superior, where the climate is just as cold as in central Sweden, if not colder. Even corn of twelve to fifteen rows is raised very generally in the northern states, where it is planted in the middle of May, if not earlier. Sometimes, however, it is not planted until the first days in June and is harvested as early as the end of August. A warm Swedish summer with its long days ought to permit this useful cereal to ripen. May it not be that the failure of efforts to raise corn in Sweden have been due to the fact that the seeds obtained were unsuited to a northerly and colder climate?

If I venture to say that a tall, well-cared-for cornfield is the most attractive and glorious field of grain one can behold, also probably no soil exists anywhere else in the world able to produce anything that in beauty, richness, and I will even add usefulness, can rival an American ear of corn. There are instances where a single cornstalk has produced up to ten or twelve ears. If we suppose that each ear contains at least three hundred kernels, we have in such a case three thousand kernels from a single seed. So many ears as this to a stalk is, however, exceptional. But the result will be about the same if we imagine three ears to the stalk, each one containing eight hundred kernels, not at all an uncommon number in the bigger kinds of corn. I have been told that at county fairs ears of corn have been exhibited a foot in length, ten inches in circumference, two pounds in weight, and containing fourteen hundred kernels, of which the largest were three-fourths of an inch long. In the region where we had settled it was not uncommon to find ears of corn containing five hundred kernels or more.

Corn is planted in straight rows, two and a half to three feet apart, with about three feet between each hill. In the South, where corn grows considerably taller, the rows are kept farther apart and more space is left between hills. In planting, the implement used is the hoe, common everywhere in America and employed with energy and skill. This is a very simple but really excellent piece of farm equipment and one among the many that might well be used as models in Sweden. Both in the small potato field and in the garden it would prove most useful. It is really strange that it has not taken the place of the clumsy hoes and shovels used so sparingly by us for softening the soil and ridding it of weeds. An American farmer could not do without his hoe, and in the summertime there is no implement he uses more assiduously.

In every other or every third row one or two pumpkin seeds are also planted, which grow fast and yield immense pumpkins. Specimens up to two hundred and two hundred and fifty pounds have been exhibited. From a cornfield of a single acre it is possible to reap eight to ten fully loaded wagons of pumpkins. Without taking any extra land, therefore, or exerting any special effort, one can obtain this very convenient cattle feed. When the corn is about an inch high, it is hoed and weeded at the same time. This hoeing and weeding is repeated at the beginning of the flowering period. On bigger fields this work, which requires much time and labor, is done with a kind of harrow, a small plow or cultivator as it is called.

After the corn has ripened, it can be left standing in the field for a long time without being damaged. Still, it is of advantage to cut off the stalks before they get too dry so that they may be used as fodder. In harvesting, either the ears are broken off, after which the stalks are cut down, or the stalks are cut with the corn still on them, after which they are piled up in shocks. After they have dried thoroughly, the so-called husking takes place, in which the ears are broken off and twisted out of their husks. Then the stalks are stacked to be kept for cattle fodder. It is not necessary, though, to hurry with this work, for neither the corn nor the stalks are harmed by standing in shocks on the field. At the husking neighbors often help one another. Ordinarily they are then regaled with all the delicacies that a farm can offer, especially pumpkin pie, which is a favorite dish among Americans. These gatherings, which somewhat resemble our harvest feasts, are oftentimes very hilarious and lively, and offer the young people opportunities for different sports and games all too few in this country, which in general offers as good as nothing in the way of community life and its attendant festivities and amusements.

The yield from an acre of corn, on which about four quarts of seed are used, is in ordinary years from 50 to 70 bushels, depending on the quality of the soil. In good years, even in Wisconsin, the yield is sometimes 100 bushels to the acre. But in Ohio and Illinois, where the soil and climate are more favorable, 120 bushels to the acre is not at all unusual. There are even instances when an acre has yielded as much as 190 bushels.

I am afraid that my description of this unexcelled cereal crop, which is so useful to new settlers in America and on which their existence, at least during the first and second years, so much depends, already has become too lengthy. Yet I cannot deny myself the pleasure of saying a few words in this context about a couple of strange species of this grain and their wide use.

Of corn in general there are many kinds, differing mainly in the number of rows to the cob and the size and shape of the grain. In the state of Illinois alone not less than twelve different kinds are planted. One of these, Wyandot corn, has been highly praised because of its rich yield and the high quality of the meal produced from it. The seed was procured only a few years ago from the Wyandot Indians. Planted in Illinois, it yields 150 bushels to the acre. A single grain laid into the ground forms a mass of rootlike fibers, often as big as an ordinary hat, and from this mass of roots four to nine sprouts or stems grow up, each of them bearing from one to five ears. There is evidence that a single seed has yielded as many as 8,000 kernels. A few bushels of this corn was brought a couple of years ago to a fair in Chicago and there sold for 25 cents an ear.

Among the more unusual varieties of corn, raised in smaller quantities more for table eating than anything else, sweet corn, or sugar corn, should be mentioned. It contains a considerable amount of the phosphates and of sugar, but less starch than ordinary corn. When cooked fresh, before the corn has had time to ripen, it is very delicious. Even when dried, it can be used for certain dishes.

A traveler on the railroads in America almost invariably becomes acquainted with another kind of corn, known as popcorn or pearl corn, *Zea caragua* [*Zea mays*, var. *tunicata*], which small children offer for sale at all stations. This is really a Central- or South-American kind of grain, yet quite common in the United States, where it is used only when roasted. The ears are much smaller than those of ordinary corn, with small, blood-red grains, rich in oil. Children amuse themselves with them on winter evenings, just as we enjoy cracking nuts. The small, round kernels are placed in a frying pan and sprinkled with salt or sugar. In a little while they swell and burst with a light crackle, taking on a mealy, white appearance, and then are very good to eat.

Among the corns broomcorn may be reckoned to a certain extent, *Sorghum saccharatum* [*Sorghum vulgare*, var. *technicum*]. At first sight it resembles ordinary corn. It is almost of the same height and has as heavy a stalk, but its leaves are narrower and it has a branched and bushy top, the only part of it put to use. When the seed begins to appear, the long head, or branched top, where the seeds are located, is bent down at a right angle, about two feet from the top. In that way the stem is broken off so that the sap can rise no farther, and when the end has dried it is cut off. After that the seeds are separated from the end cut off, and the straws left are sorted and tied together with steel or brass wires and fastened to sticks specially prepared for the purpose. In suitable soil the raising of broomcorn is a very profitable industry. In America no other brooms are used than these, which are excellent and answer the requirements very well. Large factories have been established, where brooms are made by the thousands, some of them with artistically painted handles and in other respects so well made and attractive that though generally carefully hidden away, they would not be at all unsightly in the living room or hall.

As for the uses of ordinary corn, they are so varied and so numerous that one may safely say most of the efforts at settling the West and the South would be impracticable if it were not for this unexcelled grain. To be sure, it is not best for bread, although warm, freshly baked corn bread served with butter is very good. It looks like a thick gingerbread patty and commonly is the principal breakfast dish, especially in the West. Not only the corn but also the meal prepared from it may be used for cooking in many other ways. While the corn is ripening, and before the kernels have hardened, ordinary corn may be cooked like sugar corn; when eaten with fresh butter, it is a real delicacy and not unlike our *släpärter*.[3]

But it is mainly as cattle feed that corn has proved most serviceable and for that reason invaluable to the settler. All cattle eat it, and even horses. For fattening hogs nothing is better. It has been said that the meat of corn-fed swine is too porous, but the large annual export of pork and ham to Europe, where they are in great demand, would seem to prove both the quality of the products and the usefulness of corn for fattening. Cattle eat it with great relish. Along with the kernels, they generally eat the cob, which in itself contains a good food substance. Therefore, it is the custom in some mills to grind the entire ear — cob as well as kernels — to produce a meal, good and nourishing used as grits. The stalks, unless allowed to stand too long and dry up in the field, are also excellent cattle fodder. In many places it is customary, while the ears are ripening, to cut off the upper part of the tall stalk together with its leaves and use it as fodder. For every bushel of corn, one gets about twenty pounds of such fodder, which like all the remaining stalk is most nourishing, especially for milch cows. The stalk has a rich sugar content and, while growing, is very succulent. Hence in some places syrup and sugar are cooked from it. Though these are put to household use, I have not found them particularly good. Even the thin, light green leaves which surround the ears are useful. They may be shredded into fine fibers and used to fill mattresses. Such shuck-mattresses, very common, especially in the West, are next to those stuffed with horsehair the best in the market.

Corn plays such an important role in the life of the new settlers that one can hardly form a conception of pioneer life in America without visualizing a corn patch, a hoe, a corn crib (in appearance usually like the basket of a coal cart), chewed-off cobs scattered around the house, and inside the house ears hanging on the walls to dry, ears in the kettle, and ears on the table. Perhaps I have been rather redundant on that account in my description of this cereal grain. At this point in my story it was the daily subject of our thoughts; more than anything else it demanded our time and labors, and in addition caused us much worry and serious anxiety. For excellent and productive though this grain may be, its cultivation demands, perhaps more than does anything else, the settler's care and time, and is frequently accompanied with many difficulties and reverses.

Of all the different kinds of grain fields, the cornfield is most exposed to hazards that bring the settler's work to nothing and destroy his hopes of a harvest. The violent storms so common in America may easily break the brittle and heavy-weighted stems or crush them to the ground. After that he can hope for no harvest, or at least for one far less than might otherwise be reaped. In the northern states there are often heavy frosts, to which corn more than any other kind of grain is sensitive. The settlers in these regions are therefore very careful to select corn that ripens quickly. Even as early as September one cannot be safe from frosts, which without being very severe may totally destroy corn planted late and not completely ripened. Added to these risks are the worms and other insects that seem to take greater pleasure in corn than in most other plants and not seldom inflict great damage. Furthermore, countless small birds infest cornfields, especially blackbirds, *Quiscalus versicolor* [now known as the bronzed grackle, *Quiscalus quiscala*], which sometimes seem to descend by the millions. To be sure, they devour a great many destructive insects, but they demand from the growing corn too great a remuneration for the service rendered.

But the worst scourge is a kind of small squirrels, chipmunks and gophers by name, *Tamias striatus* and *Spermophilus tredecim-lineatus* [the latter known today as *Citellus tredecimlineatus*], which to a farmer are more destructive than wolves or bears. Throughout our whole life as farmers they were regular pests. They dig small holes under fences and in the field and there they make their nests, from which, if they become really settled, it is almost impossible to dislodge them. Within a very small area one may discover hundreds of such holes, from which they come in tribes to raid the newly seeded cornfield. As soon as the corn sprouts, before the seed has fully rotted and just when it is in the process of taking root, they move from hill to hill all over the field, dig up one plant after another, and then either eat the kernel at once or carry it off to their underground storehouses, where one will often turn up great quantities while plowing. Thus in two or three nights they may completely destroy entire cornfields so that not a single plant is left. The farmer must therefore either reseed the field, if it is not too late in the season for that, or use it that year for some other purpose. It may even happen that large fields, prepared with much care and labor, must be left idle till next planting time.

The forest and oak-opening lands more than the prairie are subject to these pests. One can hardly think of anything more depressing for a farmer or new settler than to come out in the morning and find one sprouting corn hill after another lying rooted up and withered on the ground. Even though we could not have counted in any circumstances on a rich corn harvest during our first year, we were sorry to learn that these little creatures did everything in their power to make it still smaller. It did not help to serve them enough arsenic to dispose of an entire army. True enough, piles of dead bodies lay about on the ground, but so also — image of the devastated hopes of many a settler — did the uprooted, withered corn plants from which we had expected golden ears and better living conditions.

The balance of our small tract now under cultivation we used for planting potatoes and other vegetables. The former we put in at the same time as we plowed the ground, in the furrow beneath the turned-over sod. When potatoes are put in in this way, if they are well hoed afterward, a considerable harvest may be looked for even the first year although, as in our case, the fresh-broken, clay-mixed, and as yet unpulverized earth in the oak openings yields less than the black mold of the forest land and the prairie. From eight to ten bushels of potatoes are planted on one acre, which on old soil should yield 150, 200, or even 300 bushels. Rumor had it that a farmer not far from us had harvested 600 bushels to the acre. But that may have been one of those exaggerated, not to say preposterous, stories through which the settlers of a new territory sometimes noise abroad its extraordinary fruitfulness and advantages — in a word, a rather common method of puffing the country in order to get it settled and fully populated as soon as possible.

Our spring work consisted, among other things, of digging a garden patch around our cabin, but since the ground as yet was not altogether suitable for gardening, we planted in one corner of the field where the earth was more friable and mixed with black-loam watermelons, *Cucurbita citrullus* [today known as *Citrullus vulgaris*], other melons, cucumbers, and a number of garden vegetables, which even the first summer gave us a good harvest. Melons are of different kinds and grow readily in the fields without requiring much care. Naturally they ripen more perfectly here than in Sweden, and in general one does not need to use sugar to be able to eat them with relish.

Another very common garden food in America and one that the settler hardly ever fails to provide space for in his field is the tomato, or love apple, which, strangely enough, is rarely grown in Sweden. Even if it is not possible to grow it out of doors, to grow it in greenhouses ought to pay. I believe that even in the middle and southern parts of Sweden, if the plants were started in a hot-bed, they could be replanted outside. Since they are very productive, a few plants are enough for the needs of the home. Among fruits the tomato is one of the most wholesome and most useful. In America it is much used, either raw, when it is generally eaten as a kind of salad with vinegar, salt, pepper, and sugar; or stewed, when it is a fine addition to meat dishes. It is also much used preserved in vinegar for pickles. A splendid catchup is made from it, and as jam it is very delicious, though not equal to tropical fruits. I am sure that if the usefulness and versatility of the tomato were better known in Sweden, a few failures would not be permitted to discourage people from planting it, even though it might require greater care than is usually given to garden plants.

Chapter 18

PASSENGER PIGEONS · DUCKS · *Ellida* · FISHING · BEE HUNTS
AND BEE TREES · MOSQUITOES · ARRIVAL OF SWEDES · IMMI-
GRANTS WHO ARE NOT LABORERS · SCANDINAVIAN MEETINGS
LETTER FROM SWEDEN · CRUEL DISAPPOINTMENTS

EARLY in the spring we were visited by pigeons, *Columba
migratoria* [*Ectopistes migratorius*], in almost incredible numbers. These beautiful birds, not quite so big as European wood
pigeons, are of a bluish-gray color, the side, neck, and breast feathers being of iridescent green, purple, and gold. The tail is cloven
and, like the bill, black. They are seldom seen alone or in pairs, but
come in great flocks, spring and fall, almost everywhere on the
American continent east of the Rocky Mountains. The extraordinarily great numbers in which they fly together from one place
to another border upon the fabulous. Those who have not seen the
sight are inclined to doubt the descriptions they have heard or
read, but from my own observation I can testify that in this respect
no description can be carried too far.

These pigeons choose as their stopping places especially such
tracts as are rich in beech mast and acorns, that is, within an area
of a few hundred miles, for it is said they can fly a mile a minute.
The pay little attention to whether the climate is colder or milder
except as the quantity of their available food is affected, and only
for this reason do they change their haunts in spite of the way in
which they are being destroyed. Men hunt them with guns and
nets, as good as rake them down from the branches with long
poles, burn sulfur under them, cut down the trees where they
roost, and in every other conceivable way slaughter them by the
thousands. Sometimes they remain for years in the same locality,
from which they fly away only to seek food elsewhere. When it
grows scant there, they return to their old feeding grounds, which

in the meantime have grown up again. When they roost in an easily accessible region, entire wagons and boats are often loaded with them, and there have been instances when herds of swine have been driven a hundred miles and more to such a place to fatten them on the pigeons that every morning are found fallen to the ground.

In the evening the sky is often darkened by these birds as at an eclipse of the sun; there is a whirring noise through which the firing of a gun could not be heard, and the very air is set in motion by the flapping of their wings. Hundreds of flocks arrive, one after the other, each one innumerable. Untroubled by the slaughter that is taking place among them, they settle down in the branches of the trees. Those that are killed at this time of day or during the night are left lying until morning, when the flocks have flown to some other place, for it often happens that they roost in such numbers in a tree that great limbs are overloaded and break off, endangering anyone underneath. Wolves, foxes, lynxes, cougars, bears, raccoons, opossums, and skunks have regular feasts, and after them come the eagles, the hawks, and the vultures. In the meantime the hunters, having gathered as much of the booty as they want, have driven their swine to the woods to share in the treat.

Since it is altogether the food supply that determines the flight of these birds from one place to another, a flight occurs at no given time, although according to what I thought I observed, commonly the beginning of spring and the early fall are the times when the greatest numbers arrive in the regions of western America where we had settled. Their speed makes it possible for them to traverse and scout great areas, and their sight is so keen that in flight they can distinguish with certainty the land's resources in the food they are seeking. When they pass over an inviting stretch, they swoop swiftly toward the ground, but in an instant soar to a higher level if they notice that the ground is barren.

Audubon,[1] the great naturalist, once sought to number the flocks of pigeons that passed over his head in a single hour. In a short while he had counted 163, but gave it up as he noted the impossibility of keeping count of them. "The very noonday light," he said, "was obscured as by an eclipse of the sun, and the continued buzz of wings made me drowsy. For three days one flock kept following another, and they flew so high that they could not be reached with the best rifle. If a hawk sought to break into a flock, at once, like a torrent, and with a noise like thunder, they rushed into a compact mass, and darted forward in undulating and angular lines, descended and swept close over the earth with inconceivable velocity, whereupon they mounted perpendicularly so as to resemble a vast column shooting skyward. Once they had risen high in the air again, their closely massed ranks were seen to rise, sink, and writhe like the coils of a gigantic serpent. These movements are executed not only by the flock that has been attacked, but all the others that follow perform exactly the same evolutions although the astounded hawk long since has beat a retreat.

"When these immense flocks in the course of their evolutions turn their backs, one sees above him something resembling a great, glistening sheet of azure and a moment later a mass of rich deep purple. Compelled by hunger to descend to the ground, they search for acorns among the forest's withered leaves; the next flock sweeps like a sea billow over the one that has just landed, and the whole mass of birds seems still on the wing. In a few minutes they have gathered up over a wide area every small seed that can serve them as food, after which they rest in the trees for a while. But at sundown they return to their roosting place, though this may be hundreds of miles distant."

One might suppose that such a mass of birds would settle down on the fields and entirely destroy the growing seed, but that is not the case. In seed time they may be a bit troublesome, but I understand that they seldom if ever attack the ripening grain.

The description quoted above has been taken from *The Agricultural Report of the Commissioners of Patents* for 1856. My own observations to a great extent have verified it. The pigeons came to us in the spring, as the quails in olden times to the Israelites in the wilderness, and provided a welcome change in our diet, which for some time had been more than usually meager. Their meat is somewhat dark. The young especially are a real delicacy. At first we used our guns, and succeeded at times in killing as many as twenty or more with one shot. Many a time, when they were sitting in the trees, we were able to shoot those on one branch and then reload and shoot those roosting on another in the same tree. Finally, however, we decided to save our powder. Instead, we took

Mrs. Bengt Petterson (Knut Hallström), for many years known as "the grandmother" of the Pine Lake Settlement

Mrs. Polycarpus von Schneidau, who arrived at the Pine Lake Settlement in 1842 together with her husband

Gustaf Unonius in clerical garb. This picture was taken in Milwaukee in 1849, four years after he had been ordained.

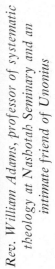

Rev. William Adams, professor of systematic theology at Nashotah Seminary and an intimate friend of Unonius

a live pigeon and tied its feet to a small piece of board; when it flapped it swings it attracted others, of which we were able to catch hundreds with a clapnet.

The more the country is settled and cultivated, the less it is visited by the flocks of pigeons, and those that do come are not nearly so numerous as those in the more faraway and unsettled parts. During our first years in Wisconsin it happened frequently that a countless flock would settle down in the trees growing very close to our cabin, and their flapping and cooing could keep us awake all night.

Just as the woods overflowed with pigeons, so did the lake with ducks and other waterfowl, though perhaps not to the same degree. We succeeded in shooting several of a blue-winged species, equal to mallards in being undoubtedly among the finest-flavored of all the numerous game birds in which this country is so rich.

For duck shooting as well as fishing, a boat was essential. Busy with many other things, we had little time to try our hand at boat building, a craft we were absolutely inexperienced in besides. We therefore made a trade with a farmer who lived a few miles away, by which we got a boat, a hollowed-out oak log, a canoe, or whatever one wants to call the floating thingumajig that might rather have been taken for a trough if it hadn't been on the water. It served its purpose, after a fashion, where one didn't have to worry about being surprised by storms or heavy seas. Yet a certain amount of care was required to take it home over one of the big neighboring lakes, connected with our own only by a bog as impassable on foot as by boat. With a so-called paddle, similar to a small shovel, instead of oars, I had to convey myself, Indian fashion, by alternate strokes first on one side and then on the other, about six miles along the lake shore till I reached a river, from one point on which the frail craft could be transported by land to Pine Lake. At the time when I called for the boat I also bought a dozen hens, which, packed in a bushel basket, I had to carry on my head the remainder of the way. There was a cackling and a commotion that, not to speak of the weight of the burden, might have dizzied a better head than my own. But I had my reward when I got home and found almost as many eggs as chickens in the basket.

With *Ellida*,[2]—that was the name of our new Viking craft — we began a fishing campaign the like of which has rarely been equaled. Probably no white man ever before had fished in this lake, and the red man must have disdained its wealth. It was like taking fish from a well-filled corf. Only a few yards from the shore was a shoal, where all we had to do was to cast out our hooks and in a few minutes we had plenty for a meal, even if the household had been twice as big as ours. In the evenings we went spearing fish, and then Ellida was generally loaded to capacity with perch, pickerel, and other big fish. What we were unable to eat, salt down, or dry in the sun, we fed to the hogs. Many were of a kind good only for this. Such was a type of gar fish found here in great abundance, some weighing as much as twenty pounds or more. They were so hard they had to be cut to pieces with an axe, and after the hogs at last had tired of their fish diet, it was more nuisance than profit when by mistake we sometimes caught them with our spears.

This was great sport, though, during the evenings. In addition to the fine fishing we enjoyed the beautiful, various landscape, which as we gently glided through bays and inlets with their inviting shores and new-leaved oak trees, was illumined by the cedar torch in the boat. While spearing fish, we sometimes caught a muskrat that came sliding through the water attracted by our flaming torch. The proper way to catch these animals, however, is with traps or snares so that the skin, for which there is always a good market, may be unharmed. Along the shores of Pine Lake a number of muskrats had built their homes, especially in the swampy places, where we found one row after another of their small, painstakingly and skillfully constructed houses. The inhabitants were for a long time complete strangers to us, until the Indians that came to hunt in the winter informed us of their value.

But for that year at least it was too late to turn their information to account. The Indians had almost exterminated them. Armed with long, forked spears, they went from one little nest, in which several muskrats generally lived together, to the other, stuck through the roof quickly, and not infrequently succeeded in catching three or four animals at a thrust. The skins do not indeed bring so much money as they did years ago, but Indians and professional hunters still find it profitable annually to cause the same devastation with spears and snares among the muskrats as among the beavers, now more and more fled to remote parts of the West. Indians eat these animals, and professional hunters, too, declare that the back part and the long, naked, ratlike tail are very delicate. We were fortunate enough, however, never to be so hard up for other kinds of food that we had to resort to such means to satisfy our hunger.

At this time of year the deer were thin, and we thought it best to let them alone. Perhaps, though, if we had not been so well supplied with fish and fowl, we might not have shown so much conscience when in our walks through the woods we sometimes came to places where the pressed-down grass indicated they had made their beds there for the night, from which spots it would not have been difficult to follow their tracks. In the new territory there were at this time no game laws, but it did not take long before laws were passed forbidding the shooting of deer, prairie chickens, pheasants, and other game birds during and immediately following the mating season. This law is now strictly enforced and observed even in the remotest parts of the western states.

But there is another kind of hunt to which the settler, provided he has the time and experience for it, devotes many spare hours, and though it may not immediately repay him for his trouble it pays off abundantly later in the autumn. I refer to bee hunting. In the western forests there are innumerable swarms of wild bees, though like the deer, beaver, and other game, these, too, withdraw farther and farther away as the white man pushes along with plow and axe. When we arrived in Wisconsin, however, it was not unusual for a settler to find in the oak openings trees with hollow trunks, in the tops of which bees had formed hives, where they had maintained themselves for many years and multiplied many times, sucking nectar and gathering stores from wild Flora's rich and prodigal bosom. Many frontier dwellers who have lived for a long time in the wild woods and are accustomed to taking note of everything that may serve them for subsistence have a wonderful ability to follow the flight of the bees to the bee trees. As a dog sniffs the trail of a wild animal, so they seem able as if by instinct to smell the way of the bees to their hives. Often where wild bees have been seen, a piece of honeycomb is fastened as a bait in some bush, about which swarms of them soon gather. After they have collected what booty they can, they fly in a straight line to their home. By carefully noting the direction they take, one can follow them all the way to the bee tree.

If that is of such a kind and so located that the part of the trunk occupied by the bees can be cut off and taken home, the bees are left in peace until winter, when tree, hive, and all are transported to the settler's home. The finder must carve his name or leave some other mark of ownership on the tree, however, which means that only he may cut it down. This right of possession is always respected by the settlers. Since hunting and fishing are a *commune bonum*, it matters nothing that the bee tree has been found on some other man's land. The tree itself belongs to the owner of the ground, but not the swarm of bees. He can forbid the chopping down of the tree, but if the bee hunter can find some other means of taking possession, he is free to do so. Should the owner himself decide to cut down the tree, he must, according to pioneer law, leave wax and honey untouched. Generally a detail of that kind is settled by common agreement. A hollow tree is of little value, and as a rule Americans are not niggardly.

During the first part of the summer Carl and I discovered by chance a great, hollow oak which, as far as we could judge, was a gigantic beehive. We were not mistaken. We saw at once that by its nature the tree could not be felled or sawed off without the beehive's being destroyed at the same time. Hence the swarm of bees could not be saved. We tested the crooked trunk with an auger in several places and found that far down from the opening at the top there was, or would be in the fall, a real storehouse of honey. For the present we just cut our mark in the tree and left it standing till a more appropriate time.

In due season we went there with our axes, to have it proved to us that America truly and literally is a land flowing with milk and honey. Lotten and Christine came to our aid with pails, pots, pans, and any other vessels we could ladle our sweet treasure into. And it was necessary to have such things in readiness. With a terrific crash the tree plunged to the ground, the bent top buried itself deep in the earth, a big part of the trunk splintered to pieces, and we had to start scooping up the honey with might and main whether or not bees, bark, and bits of wood came along with the honeycombs, most of which had been broken in the fall. We had protected ourselves with veils and gloves, and had taken all possible precautions; notwithstanding, we were still to learn that just as every rose has its thorns, so there is no sweetness without bitterness. The poor bees by the millions buzzed about our heads, settled in clumps on our veils and clothes to seek revenge — nobody could blame them — for human rapacity and cruelty. As we saw the havoc we had made, we felt in our hearts a sting that smarted almost more than those made by the small, infuriated insects.

For days later we saw swarms of bees flying about the ruins of their former hive tree, like a homeless family searching the burned-out ruins of their former dwelling for a few remnants of the possessions gathered by industry and toil. The honey, however, provided a welcome change from brown syrup, and part of the wax we sold in Milwaukee for real cash, which was becoming scarcer and scarcer in our household.

Only once again did we succeed in finding a bee tree, which we hoped to take home to Pine Lake with the swarm of bees intact. This, too, we marked with our initials, but when winter came and we went to get it, we found it already cut down. Several European immigrants had settled on the land in our neighborhood, and old pioneer law began to be less strictly respected than before. One of them, a Norwegian who interpreted in his own way the meaning of personal liberty, had regarded as fair game what the American on whose land we had made our first find would not so much as have touched without our knowledge, considering it against all right and justice to do so.

But if forest and water offered us plenty to eat, we ourselves were made to serve as food for the millions of mosquitoes that began to make their appearance. I believe I pronounced too hasty a judgment once before in declaring them to be no worse than our Swedish mosquitoes. The suffering they caused us was indescribable. Our faces, disfigured by their bites, could hardly have been recognized by our best friends. On land and water, while hunting or fishing, plowing or sowing, by day and by night, they tortured us. Their stings may not have pierced our boots as some people claim they do, but ordinary garments were inadequate protection against them. We made smudges in and around our cabin, but in vain: the European blood must still have been in our veins. The only means of protecting ourselves, at least during the night, was to surround our beds with mosquito netting of a coarse material or haircloth specially woven for the purpose. Such netting is in America as indispensable in a bedroom in summertime as a blanket in winter. It did not cost more than a dollar or two, but even this sum had begun to be rather hard to find in our house. By the time we finally succeeded in getting this necessity, the summer was already far advanced and we ourselves half devoured.

I heartily recommend this kind of netting for use in the rural districts of Sweden, where mosquitoes may also be very annoying. Under so coarse a netting there is no noticeable increase in heat, and when a man knows he is completely protected from the bite of mosquitoes, their buzzing music is a not unpleasant lullaby.

One day when Carl and I had gone our separate ways into the woods to look for the cattle, whose propensity to stray cost us much trouble and time, I unexpectedly met four strangers wandering about. The map that one of them had in his hand, the cane that another carried, with a little spade instead of the regular cap at the tip in order to examine the nature of the soil, and the general equipment of the company showed they belonged to that great army of immigrants that was pouring into Wisconsin now that traffic had been resumed on the Great Lakes, having heard of the fertile soil and the other local advantages for which the state was becoming widely known.

It is with the western territories as with many another thing in this world: they must be tooted about to be rightly appreciated, and Wisconsin in this respect had just come into its own. "There is no better country in the world," it was said, and people hurried from east, north, and south to take possession of it, leaving behind them vast, unsettled, fertile areas in Michigan, Indiana, and Illinois. The puffs of newspapermen, speculators, and landowners had succeeded splendidly. For some time now people of different garbs and tongues had been paying us almost daily calls as they roamed through the neighborhood.

Hardly had I had time to greet the four strangers before one of them said: "We are now on Section 33, aren't we? You are one of the Swedes living here, I guess." I guessed so too, for as a Yankee put it to me one time, "This is a great country for guessing, I guess." People guess that the sun is shining when in full midday clarity it is bright above them, and in perfect keeping with common usage a man may reply to the question whether he is a Swede, "I guess so." So I guessed quite correctly that I was a Swede, and an intuition told me that I might also safely guess I had compatriots before me. The person who had addressed me, however, was an American. After he had been duly advised of my nationality, he left the conversation to the other three. These were a Baron Thott of Skåne,[3] Mr. E. Bergwall,[4] from Gothenburg, and Mr. Wadman,[5] from Norrköping, all of whom I heartily welcomed to a frugal meal in our simple cabin. Here I am afraid we were rather discourteous in leaving their American companion perhaps too much to himself, to hold his own meditations upon the language and the manners of Swedes. But it was a long time since we had seen a countryman, and since our first arrival there had been no one able, as were these men directly come from across the Atlantic, to bring us a greeting from our beloved fatherland. It was a day of genuine joy to us.

Thott and the American, who was a well-educated man from the state of New York but who there had gone bankrupt, each bought a piece of land for cash only a few miles from us. Bergwall, whose means were rather limited, took a claim, hoping to be able to pay for it later through labor. Wadman, trained in business, went to Milwaukee to seek employment.

We were surprised finally also by the arrival of Ivar Hagberg. After working for a farmer in Ohio to get a thorough grounding in American farming methods, he had spent some time in Cincinnati, where among other things he had been employed in — hell. A former Swedish officer [6] had settled in Cincinnati and had started a kind of museum consisting of various "marvelous rarities" and curiosities. Among these was a mechanical contrivance with moving figures depicting hell, which was said to have caused a great sensation and attracted many spectators. In producing thunder, lightning, and brimstone and in keeping the evil spirits in motion, he was assisted by another Swede, who, however, could not fill all the different roles in the performance. So Hagberg was engaged for a time to clean the lamps in Gehenna and perform other similar jobs. The owner of the museum is reported to have made a very good business of hell and had it to thank for his becoming a wealthy man.

For our traveling companion and friend from old Uppsala, the New had, of course, both home and land. With united strength we worked now at our farming, of which, however, Hagberg was not to enjoy the harvest. After he had been with us only a few weeks, he was called back to Sweden on some private business. The pain of separation was eased by the hope we all shared that he would soon return. But that was not to be. Loaded with a thousand greetings to fatherland and relatives, he left us, never to plow the land again that we had planned to share with him.[7]

In his place we secured a faithful friend in the person of B. Petterson,[8] an elderly countryman who had spent some time in America, but who, crushed by reverses, disappointments, and sorrows, had hitherto sought a home in vain. Yet the foreign land had really no home to offer him as long as wife and child, to whom he was attached by the tenderest bonds, were separated from him. Haunted by misfortunes, he had had to leave them in Sweden and set out alone for the new world, where he thought he should soon be able to earn enough money to finance their journey across the ocean. Up to this time he had found himself deceived in these hopes. He was one of the many who only in exceptional cases can make a success in America. As a former official in Sweden, he was unaccustomed to manual labor and was besides rather old when he emigrated. Although a man of education and culture, he discovered that with those qualifications alone he could not make a living here.

And so it is in general with European immigrants. Those who belong to the educated class and are either unaccustomed to or entirely incapable of physical labor can hardly do anything unwiser than emigrate, unless there are special conditions that assure them of success. In fact, I know of nothing, with possibly the exception of business, innkeeping, or the like, that they can engage in and retain about the same social position they had before coming to America. But even this has difficulties and requires at least some capital, which usually immigrants of this class lack. Even if they have some, it does not help them much unless they are trained businessmen. Generally they use up in various ventures what little they have, till finally they have to exert themselves in the physical labor they are unused to. Unacquainted with the language and the conditions of this country, they often fall into the clutches of swindlers, who lure them into undertakings in which they are likely to lose their small capital. Again, such enterprises often lead to lawsuits and court trials. The immigrant, when he discovers that he has been duped, will resort to the law, but even if he is able to recover something of what he lost, the high legal costs will make him poorer than ever. Finally he is entirely destitute, and as I have suggested already, he will have to turn to manual labor.

Yet here, too, he will meet nearly insurmountable difficulties. He knows no trade and is too old to become an apprentice. If he has landed in the West, where the axe is the tool with which most of the work is done, by wood chopping or similar hard labor he must earn a day's pay, bound to be insignificant because of his limited working capacity. At the luckiest he may get a job as waiter in some hotel, if he is not driven to enlist as a soldier or become a roustabout on a steamboat. It is not at all uncommon to find former Swedish officers and others of equal social rank submitting to beginning at the bottom — a bottom that unfortunately seldom or never carries with it any prospect of advancement.

Our friend Petterson had gone through many troubles of this kind, but endowed with more wisdom and perseverance than most Europeans display under such conditions, he undertook, though advanced in age, to learn a trade. He chose shoemaking as one of the most profitable. With what little money he still had he paid for a training course in a shop in Ohio [9] and learned thoroughly all the operations in making shoes, from nailing and patching and shaping of the uppers to the most intricate details. By application and perseverance he gained a skill that would no doubt have earned him a modest livelihood in any city had he possessed means enough to start a fair-sized shop. At his age, and situated as he had been, it was hard for him to go to work for someone else; therefore he decided to take the few tools he had and go West, where in some faraway spot, without too much competition, he hoped to earn a living and at the same time be his own master.

The fact that we were his fellow countrymen attracted him to our cottage, where he began as a guest but shortly became an honored member of the family. In a corner of the attic he established a tiny shop and soon had all the work he could handle. His personal history in the old country was such that he had thought it expedient to assume another name. But whatever wrong he may have done there, if ever a man atoned for an error through patience in trials and through humility amidst personal misfortunes, he was that man. Fair in all his dealings, he won the respect of all that came to know him. Before long an intimate friendship sprang up between us. His advice in times of trouble proved to be based on wisdom ripened by experience. His genuine devotion to us soon entitled him to the place of an elder brother in our family circle, a relationship which even after the lapse of many years we recall with deep feeling.

In addition to the above-mentioned countrymen, several others — Swedes, Danes, and Norwegians — settled in our neighborhood. A few letters I had written to Sweden had been published in Swedish papers and later translated and published in Denmark. They had directed the attention of prospective emigrants to our small colony. Day after day we had new callers, and not infrequently our little cabin quite unexpectedly became the scene of Scandinavian gatherings with representatives from Livonia, Finland, and the three northern kingdoms. Everything may not have gone so jovially and festively as at our student gatherings in Copenhagen and Uppsala. There were no set speeches here. But still there was no lack of talking, and though joy was not nourished by foaming cups and at loaded tables, things were none the less lively on that account. They began to look livelier too around our settlement. Some of the Scandinavians settled fairly close to us. Some of them, though, belonged to the class we have just described, and they soon went elsewhere to try their fortunes.

A lieutenant B[öttiger],[10] whose family I had known in Sweden, was one of those who came to tussle with the hardships of pioneer life. No way was open to him but to exchange his gold-braided uniform for the workingman's jacket, and his sword for the hoe and the spade. For a while he remained with us at Pine Lake and helped with the work. Though it was not light for him, he made it lighter for us by his constant good humor and high spirits. He invariably knew how to spread cheerfulness about him whether at work or during hours of relaxation. It was truly almost impossible to feel depressed in his company. We taught him to drive our oxen, which he sometimes commanded in the most comical manner, as if ordering about a company of recruits on a Swedish drill field, and he could give to the monotonous words of command a certain poetic and musical lilt to which the four-legged barnyard battalion seemed not insensible. Possessing a melodious voice, he had stored in his memory a great number of Swedish songs and ballads. At one of our neighbors he managed to find an old guitar which had been hidden away in a corner and on which the housewife, compelled to do all her own work, heavy or light, seldom had time to exercise her fingers. This instrument he borrowed, fitted it with strings as well as he could, and sometimes in the evenings, after the day's work was done, he would entertain us with beloved, well-remembered tunes from home, from Geijer,[11] Lindblad,[12] and Nordblom,[13] and songs of others, among which were several for which his own brother [14] had written the words, vividly calling up memories of former days.

In addition to personal visits we were favored with letters from others who were still in their homeland but had it in mind to emigrate, but who before doing so wanted to consult us about details. There were thousands of questions they wanted us to answer. The first letter we got of this kind is connected with a little adventure which I feel impelled to relate for the guidance of others who may feel inclined to write about personal matters to total strangers in the new world.

For a long time we had heard nothing from the members of our family in Sweden, and we were impatiently waiting for a letter. We had reason to suppose it would also contain a draft for a small sum of money, which in our present economic situation we desperately wanted for the purchase of more cattle and other necessities. One day I received notice from the post office in Milwaukee that an important foreign letter had arrived, which would be delivered on payment of the postage due. The rejoicing in the cabin was general. The letter could surely be none other than the one we were expecting, and whether it contained money or not, it would certainly bring us greetings and news from those in the homeland lying closest to our hearts.

Carl's work was always more indispensable at home than mine;

so as usual when a trip had to be made, it fell to my lot to go to Milwaukee. True, the mail carrier might have been authorized to bring us the letter, but we needed a few things from the city, and in addition we really did not have the small amount needed to pay the postage. The farmer's bank had long ago suspended payments and was totally empty. The shoemaker's bank was in the same sad state of affairs: our brother Petterson had spent his last dollar on leather and shoe nails. No military bank had ever been established in New Uppsala, for poor Lieutenant B[öttiger]'s capital had been barely sufficient to cover his traveling expenses. In vain we searched our former money box and the drawer in the shoemaker's desk; the pockets of the well-worn uniform were turned inside out: all was fruitless. Besides a couple of twelve-skilling [15] coins we could find only a few copper pennies. The postage of the letter would undoubtedly amount to at least a dollar. It was at last thought best for me to go to the city and scrape up this amount, which could be repaid as soon as I had the letter in hand. I could hardly control my impatience and wait till the next morning. We made a list in the meantime of a number of little things to be bought in the city — things that, though generally regarded as household essentials, had been lacking in our home for a long time. We rejoiced in anticipation of sugar instead of syrup, and of real coffee in place of roasted wheat. I was also to buy scythes for the haying now in the offing, as well as a number of other necessities.

With a lunch in my traveling bag I set out at daybreak. It was a beautiful summer morning. Thousands of small, blue-feathered magpies were chattering gaily in the grain fields; kingbirds in the top branches of the oaks with their peculiar but melodious tones made up a chorus that sounded far and wide; flocks of red-winged blackbirds hopped twittering along the garden fences, expecting to get their share of the rich harvest; refreshed by the morning dew, flowers in all imaginable colors were turning their calyxes to the sun; the parklike hills and vales of the oak openings, through which could be glimpsed the clear, serene mirror of the lake, reminded me of the fair tracts and wide-spreading oaks of Djurgården.[16] Thoughts of home and the greetings I expected before long to receive speeded my steps. Before the sun had reached its noonday height I was standing on the sandy ridge from which opens up a glorious view of the city in the valley below, its houses and other buildings being constructed bigger and bigger, handsomer and handsomer. Through the city the river, filled with sailing craft and steamboats, wound its way to Lake Michigan, that giant wellhead, that sounding inland sea, its boundless, watery expanse forming toward the east a glittering frame around the terraced city with its sunlit orchards.

On my arrival in Milwaukee I went to look for my Danish friend K[iaer],[17] hoping to persuade him to lend me the money I needed. Since he was not in his store at the time and would not be there for an hour, there was of course no use in going to the post office. While waiting for him, I went to a hotel, our regular stopping place when we were in the city, and sought to while away the time with a good meal, which in spite of the lunch I had brought with me I really needed after a walk of thirty miles. This was not the regular time for serving meals, but thanks to the kindness of fair Ingeborg I was given certain refreshments which I promised to pay for on my return. Finally I found K[iaer], and with a couple of dollars in my pocket I ran, rather than walked, to the post office.

I got my letter, but was astonished to find that it was addressed in a strange hand and that the post stamp read Halmstad,[18] a city where I had no acquaintances. With sad forebodings I opened it. It was from a person entirely unknown to me, a king's chamberlain, a Lieutenant L[indsfelt],[19] who wrote to get certain information about America as well as advice relative to his prospective emigration. Never in my life, as far as I can recall, have I been so disappointed, and had I been able to lay my hands on the king's chamberlain, I am sure I should have addressed him in most uncourtly language. To send a letter of private concern from Sweden to a person entirely unknown to him in the American interior and then make the addressee pay the heavy postage! — it was an imposition, to put it mildly. Angered beyond measure, I threw his letter into the street. Downcast that my hopes of news from mother, relatives, and friends, of coffee and sugar too, had in an instant come to nothing, I hardly knew what to do. Of course I could do nothing but return home, where they were waiting for me impatiently. I was ashamed to appear again at K[iaer]'s. The payment of the hotel bill I left to a more convenient time — my first tavern bill in the new world. Without speaking to anyone, and with heavy steps, I went out of the city, and returned the same way I had come.

Nature, which a short while before had been bathed in morning sunlight, now seemed to bear the stamp of my own heaviness: burned by the hot sun, it lay faint and strengthless, with feverish pores yearning for the cool, refreshing dew of night. The birds' chirping was silenced, the fragrance of the flowers was gone, the green of the hills had paled, and the oaks, their crowns moved by no wind, their leaves drooping, seemed sunk in a noonday sleep. The mosquitoes alone appeared to be fully alive. Several farmers I didn't know drove past me, but I was afraid to ask for a ride lest they should want to be paid. Tired and worn out, I lay down on a shady wooded hill to rest a while during the worst of the heat; but gnats, grasshoppers, and long, green snakes, which, though their bite is not dangerous, are not pleasant bedfellows and which slither and writhe by the dozen about the wayfarer's feet at almost every step, combined to make my rest period brief and none too refreshing. Finally evening came and then darkness, but since I had come to a well-known neighborhood I was able to take a few short cuts to save time. Passing through a forest, I saw here and there small clearings where settlers had piled up the giant trees and set fire to them. The mighty, flaming pyres, some nearby, others at a greater distance, lit up the dark night and spread far and wide over the peaceful landscape a brightness that drove back the shadows without and within me. The grand spectacle made me forget both the king's chamberlain and other irritations.

After walking about fifty-four miles in less than twenty-four hours — the longest walk I have ever made or expect to make — I arrived at our cottage. All were awakened by my unexpectedly early return. But after they had recovered from the surprise caused by the equally unexpected outcome of my expedition, the angry grief at having our hopes so betrayed dissolved in a hearty laugh, in which I could not but share.

Chapter 19

CUTTING HAY · SWAMP MEADOWS · A FARMER'S GENTLEMANLY

BEHAVIOR · SCYTHE AND CRADLE · DIFFERENT RESULTS FROM

WORK · RATTLESNAKES · CURES FOR THEIR BITE · A SWEDISH

SNAKE CHARMER · BIVOUACKING ON THE SWAMP MEADOW · THE

ARRIVAL OF AN OLD ACQUAINTANCE FROM SWEDEN · FURTHER

ADDITIONS TO THE SWEDISH SETTLEMENT

THE disappointment which has just been related was offset a hundredfold by another letter from our fatherland, of which the very handwriting on the envelope and the well-known postage stamp were enough to make the images of home more vivid in our hearts.

We got also, however, several letters of the same kind as Mr. L[indsfelt]'s, from which we may well hope that future settlers who like ourselves have neither time nor money to spare may mercifully be preserved.

On July 27, we began haying, in my opinion the hardest and most trying work in which up to now we had been compelled to engage. This work is not, I believe, harder than corresponding labor in Sweden; rather it is easier, because of the better and more practical tools in use here. But what makes it especially oppressive for an inexperienced laborer is the burning heat, the blood-sucking mosquitoes, and the difficulty, while busy at this work, of getting good, fresh spring water.

Since it generally takes several years for a settler to harvest cultivated fodder, he must get his supply of hay in swamps and on marshy natural meadows. The prairie dweller is in this respect, as in several others, far better off than the settler in the woodlands and on oak openings. The wild grass, which grows even on the high prairies, offers good mowing, whereas naturally it is altogether impossible to use a scythe on uncleared forest land, and neither there nor on the oak openings is there any real grassy sward. True, the grass in such places sometimes grows to a surprising height, but it is coarse and so sparse that it does not pay to spend time mowing it. A settler on such land must look for some swamp or lowland in the neighborhood, where he will often find grasses that make good, nourishing cattle fodder. The sedge grasses growing in such places are without question among the best kinds of hay available. These spots, however, are often far away. This makes the haying itself as well as the hauling very difficult, the latter of which on wet swamps must wait till wintertime.

These swamps, however useful, not to say indispensable, to the settler, are usually the lands to be sold last of all. If they are very extensive, as they generally are around lakes and rivers, they are used as common lands, for which no one pays anything to the Government. But if they are of smaller size, the rule "First come, first served" is generally followed. A few strokes of the scythe will insure the ground against subsequent encroachment, and the swamp, which as little belongs to one man as another, is still regarded and respected as the legal possession of the first comer. Generally attention is also paid to the location of the meadow. The settler whose land is nearest to it ordinarily is left in possession, and it would be considered highly unethical and incompatible with the character of gentleman that everyone here aspires to have to dispute a neighbor's property rights.

Fortunately for us there was not far from our land a rather extensive and unbought swamp which every summer for several years had been mowed by another settler. Here grew excellent sedge grass. We had certainly pitched upon it as our meadow, but at the same time feared that the person who had been using it would continue to claim it on the ground of prior use. He did, in fact, show up before we had begun our haying. "For several years before you settled on this land," he said, "I have been cutting the grass on the swamp at Pine Lake near your property. I imagine you want to cut the hay on that swamp yourself, but I just wanted to make sure. In case you don't want it, I naturally intend to use it as before."

Informed that we had indeed had our eyes on that swamp, which furthermore would be insufficient for our own needs since we had recently added two cows and their calves to our herd, he answered only with his "I guess so." Without any objections he thus gave up a privilege which had been very useful to him, the loss of which now would probably cause him considerable inconvenience. Though insignificant in itself, his act was that of a real gentleman. It typifies the romance of frontier life and the living conditions and social relations in the West. Yet many have imagined complete lawlessness to be the rule there, and might the only right to be respected. This observation, however, applies mainly to regions that have been settled exclusively by Americans, or where Americans constitute the overwhelming majority. The greater the number of European immigrants, the less, unfortunately, does it hold true.

The American scythe is both longer and broader than that used in Sweden, far more practical in construction, and in spite of its greater weight also far easier to handle. The scythe proper is about forty-five inches long and two inches wide. The snath is made from hickory. As shown by the accompanying drawing, it curves somewhat inward from the blade to the nether handle, namely, that for the right hand. From there to the left-hand handle it curves considerably outward. The remaining part, or the helve end, curves slightly inward again. These curves in the snath as well as its length mean that the mower does not have to lean forward and bend his back so much as when the snath is straight. He is able to walk almost erect. Together with the easy swing of the entire implement, this makes the work not half so heavy and tiring. The handles are movable; they can be brought closer together or made farther apart, or they may be turned to the other side of the snath, to which they are fastened by a couple of screws or small iron wedges.

In connection with the foregoing description of the scythe, I trust I may be permitted to add a few words about the singular implements used in harvesting grain. I shall have to ask the indulgence of those of my readers who are not farmers for spending so much time on agricultural matters. I am sorry not to be able to weave into this story any adventures and descriptions more general in interest, but in fidelity to truth I cannot give to our pioneer life a coloring it did not have. The activities that occupied almost all of our time and the conditions that as good as exclusively perforce claimed our entire attention are all that we have to talk about from this period.

The cradles, as they are called, are in themselves remarkable enough, and our Swedish farmers would no doubt think twice before adopting a harvesting implement at first sight so unshapely and heavy. None the less, even this piece of equipment is designed both to ease and speed up the work, a purpose it fully achieves, at least in the forest regions and in the oak-opening lands, where the lately invented reapers, or harvesting machines, cannot be used.

Referring to the accompanying drawing, I venture to give a detailed description of this implement, in the hope of possibly turn-

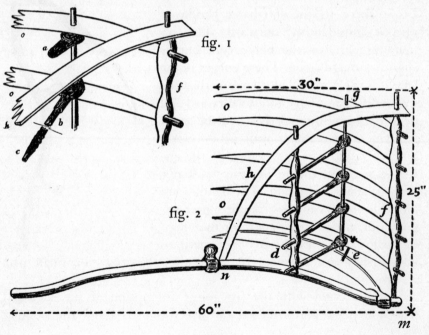

ing the attention of some Swedish farmers to it. On the basis of my own experience, after careful attention to the methods of harvesting here and in the old country, as well as to the results of the labor performed in a given time, I can safely assert that a farmer whose economic resources or the characteristics of whose soil do not permit him to use a harvesting machine never can find a better and more practical implement for the speedy and even harvesting of his grain.

The snath is five feet long, curved and furnished with a movable handle. The basket, or cradle, is generally made from maple or hickory, but sometimes from iron. It consists of five teeth, or ribs, *o,o* (fig. 1), running parallel to the scythe. They are 38 inches long, with one end fastened tightly to a round crosstree, *f*, issuing from and attached to the snath at point *m* (fig. 2). At the other end of the crosstree there is a bow, *h*, joined to the snath at point *n*. To keep the teeth in their proper position above the scythe and to give the entire cradle proper strength, the teeth are connected by a round rib, *g*, which is supplied with metal rings and sockets, *a* (fig. 1), into which a set of small rods, *b*, made with threads, *c*, are screwed into pole *d* (fig. 2). In addition, the cradle is attached to the scythe by means of a short peg, *e*, in order to keep it always at a constant distance. When the grain is cut, it falls on the teeth of the cradle, and at each swing of the scythe a cutting is laid aside in a small bundle ready to be gathered together and bound into sheaves. A person skillful in the use of this implement is able to cut two or three acres a day, whether of wheat, rye, barley, or oats, and it should be noted that a workday during harvest time in the western states of America is far shorter than in Sweden. Here the outdoor work does not begin till after breakfast, and it generally ends in the neighborhood of six o'clock, certainly not later than seven, in the evening.

In the matter of work I must note in passing how native Americans differ from most European immigrants. I have often had occasion to see the former at work with, for example, Swedes and Norwegians. It is hard to tell when the American is really working. He appears to be merely playing with his implements. If anyone by chance passes by, he may spend a long while in conversation with him. Communal affairs and questions of the day are discussed with a vigor that might lead one to imagine that this was his real work, and that axe, scythe, plow, or the ever busy knife was something held just to keep the hands occupied. The immigrant workman, on the other hand, keeps everlastingly at it, works almost without cessation, silent and sober, seldom rests, undoubtedly uses more muscular power, and yet in the end accomplishes far less.

No doubt the greater handiness of the American at the labor-saving implements to which the strangers have not as yet become accustomed is largely responsible; yet the European never seems to learn to use these with the same ease and effectiveness. When it comes to lifting heavy objects or doing other work requiring physical strength, the Swede and the Norwegian, at least, are far superior to the American, but in everything else the latter develops an agility and ease in which the others cannot equal him. Likewise in the results of the work they are his inferior. Things keep moving under his hand, though it is difficult to say how. Perhaps the others do their work better and in most cases with greater care, certainly something to value more highly than a "go-ahead system" carried too far. But in any event we cannot deny that we ourselves, together with the tools we use, show generally a certain clumsiness.

But to return to our haying: it progressed as well as our energies permitted, unaccustomed as we were to it. In this labor Christine proved a good helper, frequently trading the rake for the scythe, in which exchange I must confess the work by no means suffered. Even Lotten assisted with the raking, cocking, and stacking. In this fashion we succeeded, though rainy weather greatly delayed our work, in harvesting from the swamp lying closest to us a stack containing some four tons of hay. This, however, would not be nearly enough, for we were hoping to get another team of oxen in the fall. We had, therefore, to get more hay from a swamp that was about three miles from our home. There in the burning heat of the sun we really came to experience the toilsome nature of our work. The ground was soft and miry, and we found it hard to use our oxen. Some of the cocks had to be carried to the stack. At every step between hummocks we sank deep into the muddy water. That water, mixed with a little ill-tasting whiskey, was the only drink we had to quench our thirst with in this country otherwise so rich in clear natural springs.

What especially made this labor unpleasant was the great number of snakes that swarmed here as in all other low places in the still little cultivated country. In general, however, they are reportedly not poisonous, with the exception of the rattlesnake, with which we were also to become acquainted.

About this snake people commonly have strange notions. In reality it is far from corresponding to the conception one gets of it from most books of travel. I am speaking now of the rattlesnake as it is found in the northwestern territories, but I have reason to believe that it is very similar to those found in the eastern and southern states, in spite of all the wonderful tales that are told about it. The rattle, whose warning sounds are supposed to be heard at a considerable distance, consists only of a small cartilaginous membrane in the tail, divided into a double row of sections smaller than ordinary peas and connected with each other by a series of joints. It is these joints that when the snake moves cause the rattling sound, which is seldom heard until one is close to the snake, and hardly even then. The first of these rattles develops when the snake is three years old, and after that a new one is added annually. The biggest rattlesnake I saw, which we killed without any difficulty, was hardly more than four feet long and had eight rattles.

From what I have been told, snakes scarcely ever grow any bigger in these regions, where in general they are far more rare than is generally supposed, and where one hardly ever hears of people or cattle being bitten by them. This is rather strange, for in low-lying places one is never quite sure of not meeting these dangerous reptiles, and such places are the very ones the cattle seek out most frequently because of their rich grazing, just as the settlers have to resort to them to cut and gather their hay. I shall not deny that as we walked through the mire in the dense, tall grass, which did not permit us to see more than a few inches ahead of us, the idea that a rattlesnake might be close by disturbed me. The least rustling of the grass made me imagine I heard a snake's warning rattle, and I would hurriedly put my foot back. We were finally, however, actually to hear one, but not until we were hard upon the reptile. Even then we were scarcely aware of its warning, and did not know it was a rattler until we had killed it.

It was when we were raking some grass we had mowed, we noticed on top of the pile something we thought at first was a dry branch, come there by chance. Soon, however, we observed that it was a big snake lying altogether motionless. Without any trouble we killed it with our hay forks. We saw then that it was a rattle-snake, not quite so big as the one just mentioned; its six rattles we cut off as a memento of our first meeting with one of these danger-ous creatures. From what I have learned, they seldom attack any-one, are generally very slow in their movements, and frequently lie stock-still on the ground, so that they may easily be taken for a dry branch. The danger then consists in coming too close to them or stepping on them. It is said that in the summertime they are so full of poison they are unable to see. Whether or not that is so, I do not know, but what is certain is that the rattlesnakes we killed did not seem to notice our presence until we gave them the fatal blow. The stories of their ability to charm are pure fables. What on the other hand is no fable is the deadly nature of their poison. Their bite, should ever so small a portion of their poison enter the blood, is invariably fatal unless some remedy is under-taken at once. Of the cures that have been reported those used by the Indians are probably the most effective. A big quantity of strong cognac or rum is a certain cure if drunk immediately, and it is said that one who has been bitten by a rattlesnake can drink half a gal-lon of cognac without feeling intoxicated.

Carl told me of an incident which he had witnessed with his own eyes, and I am therefore able to vouch for its truth. It may serve as proof of what has been said, and as an example also of the almost phenomenal power some persons exercise over snakes. If snakes do not have the power to charm people, people, apparently, certainly have the power to charm them.

A Swedish Baron X[1] had, like so many others, set off for Cali-fornia to dig for gold. One day while sitting on the ground resting from his labors, he saw a big snake come slithering toward him. He saw at once that it was not of a poisonous species, and so he sat quite still to see what it would do, keeping his eyes steadily on it. When the snake noticed X, it, too, fastened its eyes on him and be-came motionless. After a while X found this mutual staring some-what strange; so he approached the snake carefully, thinking it would seek to escape, but it remained motionless. Finally he was standing right close to it, but it made no move. Then it occurred to him that he must have some power over the snake and that it was unable to do him any harm. He caught it by the neck, and after he had fixed his gaze upon it for yet a while, he put it back on the ground. It appeared to be absolutely tame, crawled over his hand, and twined itself around his arm without harming him in the least.

This power he had so unexpectedly discovered he possessed made him try other experiments in snake charming, always with the same result. He now took rattlesnakes and other poisonous reptiles, and after subjecting them a few moments to his magnetic power, if one may call it that, they proved completely tame and harmless. Finally it occurred to him that it would be more profitable to devote himself to snake charming than to gold digging in California. He traveled around with his snake menagerie and announced that he was prepared to display his power over any wild and poisonous snake that might be caught. These performances proved most profitable. In the meantime he studied the snakes from every angle, collected a number of stories illustrating the characteristics of the various species, and since everything in America has to be done with lectures, he gave at his performances regular talks on the anatomy of the snakes and related matters.

One day a big, newly captured, completely wild rattlesnake was delivered to him. To the great delight of his spectators he charmed it in his usual way and opened its jaws with a small stick, which he left there so that anyone that wanted to come close might examine its teeth and so on. While he was explaining his subject, he kept playing with his finger between the jaws of the snake, and without thinking, he pulled away the stick which separated its jaws. Naturally the snake closed them, and so — whether voluntarily or not on the part of the snake it is impossible to say — his finger was bitten. The teeth penetrated deep into the flesh. In an instant he tossed the snake aside and ran to a restaurant that fortunately was close by. He grasped a decanter of cognac and emptied it almost in one gulp. He ordered another, and continued to drink as much as he could hold. As a result he was saved from almost certain death. The intoxicating liquor did not seem to have its usual effect on him, unless the rather high fever he had for a few days might have been caused by it. That might just as easily, though, have been caused by the snake bite. After a while he was able to continue his exhibitions and lectures.

During the haying, Carl and I camped for several nights near the swamp, where we discovered an uncompleted, abandoned cottage. Such unfinished buildings are frequently found in the new territories. Some settler may select a piece of ground and erect on it a hastily contrived claim shanty to prove the land has been occupied. Before the shack is ready, or even after he has been living there for some time, he may change his mind, abandon his claim, and settle in another place he has discovered in the meanwhile that pleases him better. Where there is a great abundance of unoccupied land, and one section vies with another in beauty and fertility, many people in their choice of land are as undecided as a child that has to choose one from a great number of colorful toys.

We had now come to the end of August, and the nights in the open hut at the swamp would have been very romantic had it not been for those pestiferous mosquitoes. Here under the open sky they were nevertheless not much worse than under the roof of our own cabin at Pine Lake. It has been said that one can get used to everything under the sun; yet I challenge anyone to get used to this scourge. Their favorite haunts are near swamps and other low places, and it was fortunate for us that it was the time of year when they begin to diminish in number and in part lose their poisonous vigor. During the clear, mild August nights they could certainly for a time prevent our limbs, wearied by the day's toil, from being refreshed by sleep, but we tried not to get angry inasmuch as they conferred at least one benefit. In the peace and stillnesss of the night we were kept awake a little longer to enjoy the beauty of nature and, lifting our eyes to the sky, sown with thousands of lights, to repeat within ourselves the question, "Who hath created these things and caused countless stars to appear?"

The abandoned hut, of which we took possession for several nights, had neither roof, door, nor windows, and the cracks in the walls had been left in their original condition. We therefore had almost as good a view through the walls as above us. Before us lay the wide meadow with its haycocks rising here and there, like rocks in the skerries, testifying to the past day's labor; beyond that a rather large lake, whose slumbering waves were girdled far off by the purplish horizon. Richly hung with their clusters of small grapes, the wild grapevines, which wind around the trees, especially near river and lake shores, filled the air around us with a sweet, tropical fragrance. The earth, too, had its stars, which it pleased the eye, not closed in sleep, to watch — small fireflies that like lightning in the summer night flitted about between the branches. With their bright, phosphorescent glow they often produce a veritable shower of fire that for an instant lights up leaves, flowers, and other small objects approached by their sparkling wings.

In full harmony with all this we heard now and then the plaintive notes of the whippoorwill, a little bird that has been given this name because of the monotonous but far from unmusical warbling resembling this word combination that for hours after sunset it repeats again and again. With this song mingled also the often equally monotonous calls of other nocturnal birds, which, if they could not properly be termed harmonious, yet in the stillness of the night sweetly and gratefully lay upon the mind and lulled the weary heart to rest. Under these conditions, despite the mosquitoes, to lie in an open hut these beautiful summer nights carried with it a pleasure all its own. Few, I believe, can spend the night under the open sky and give themselves up to unbroken sleep. Every now and then the sleeper is disturbed, how or by what he doesn't know, and yet upon awakening he feels he has rested well. The fresh air he breathes, the solemn stillness and quiet of the night, the peace that on the air's vibrations descends from the habitations of light above — all these things are more strengthening and refreshing to body and soul alike than an unbroken sleep.

In these meditations, however, we were one night disturbed, and that in a very unpleasant way. One evening at sunset we noticed that the dying rays of the sun were indeed subdued by a heavy cloud bank, but we had been deceived so often by the signs from which one is supposed to be able to forecast the weather that this time we paid no attention to the old tokens. Just as everything in this new country seems to follow a different law and order from what prevails socially and politically in the old world, so in America outward nature itself seems to display a capricious independence of ordinary weather signs. The most violent and unexpected changes take place again and again. At the very time one feels justified in looking for fair weather, all of a sudden a violent shower breaks over head, or the other way about — clear evidence that the old signs cannot be relied on, something that begins now to puzzle even meteorologists beyond the ocean.

Undisturbed, then, by the cloud bank in the west, we went that night to rest on our bed of grass under our roof of stars, in the hope of clear weather as on previous nights. Hardly had we closed our eyes, though, before we were awakened by a violent gust of wind which, howling through the cracks in the house, or rather enclosure, threatened to tear apart the uncemented logs. Soon a full-fledged hurricane was raging. Not a star was visible in the sky; everything about us was impenetrable darkness. Suddenly a sharp flash of lightning burst from the clouds and for an instant wrapped the entire landscape like a sheet of flame. Almost at the same moment a clap of thunder reverberated above our heads, re-echoing from the wooded hills that on our side framed the meadow. It was one of those sudden electrical discharges that accompany a hurricane and that, at least in northern Europe, have nothing to equal them in violence, whether of storm, lightning, or thunder.

A few times before, to be sure, we had witnessed a similar uproar of the elements, but never as now experienced the combined solemnity and terror of the spectacle. I have heard people make sport of those who are afraid of thunder; they try to dispel the gravity of mind that, not necessarily joined with fear, more or less seizes us when we listen to the thunder pealing. I am certain nevertheless that no one could have listened to the voice from the clouds on this occasion without a deep feeling of dread. Flash after flash of lightning shot by; rolling and crashing, one thunderclap after another dinned, not just from one point in the firmament but from a thousand. Meanwhile the storm was raging with increasing vehemence, snapping off the tops of ancient oaks and whirling them like chips through the air, snatching up whole trees by the roots and hurling them to the ground with a crash that mingled with the thunderbolts made these all the more terrifying. It was a strife on earth and in air that for a few moments left us without counsel what to do.

Soon the rain began to pour down in streams. Rather than sit or lie drenched under the open sky, fearing every moment that the walls would tumble down over our heads or that some of the overhanging trees would crush us in their fall, we decided to return to Pine Lake as quickly as possible, although the trip would not be without peril and trouble. The wagon and tools we left in the swamp meadow, where by the flashes of the storm we seemed to see the haycocks, the result of the sweat and toil of previous days, snatched up by the wind and scattered. Our poor oxen, which shivering lay huddled close to the hut, we thought it advisable, however, to take with us, not knowing where otherwise we might find them afterward. Driving them ahead of us, we hurried as fast as we could between trees, thickets, and bushes, sometimes undecided about our direction. Until we reached a traveled road, we had nothing to guide us but the few tracks our wagon had left behind it, which, being obliterated now by the falling rain, could be traced only with difficulty in the glare of the frequent lightning flashes. To the right and left of us one tree after another crashed to the ground.

Once we were on our way there was nothing for us to do but push ahead stoutly, with the same blind and half-intoxicated zeal to go on that I imagine drives soldiers forward through a rain of bullets on the battlefield. It was fortunate indeed that we reached our cabin as quickly as we did. With all its imperfections it offered us a more welcome shelter than any stately palace could have done. Uneasiness about us, more than the storm, had kept our people awake. Hardly had their minds been set at rest by our arrival when the tempest increased in violence still more. Like weak, spent sailors tossed upon the beach by the ocean waves, we could thank God for a wonderful salvation.

Not till the next day could we form any true conception of the awful desolation wrought by the wild hurricane. Not only were fences broken down, but in several places rails had been broken off and tossed far into the woods. Large trees had been toppled over and were now blocking the path we had traveled during the night;

others were standing, their naked poles splintered by lightning, like admonitory ghosts speaking of the perishability of all things. When we returned to the meadow we found only a few fragments of the former claim shanty. Before it had lacked a roof! Now it also lacked walls! We learned that for a straight stretch of nearly twenty miles the storm had swept away everything in its path. The roofs of several houses had been torn off; dwellings themselves as well as barns and other buildings had in some places been carried away by the wind. Most of the hay we had been mowing was probably hanging in the treetops across the lake. Only a small part of it lay in the water between the hummocks in the swamp. After this, we had little inclination to spend our nights there. For the remainder of the haying period we returned every evening to our own house, spared by the storm.

A short time later, one evening when after our day's work Carl and I had taken Ellida and rowed out into the small bay just outside our windows to take from our rich storehouse, that is to say, the lake, some fresh fish for our evening meal, we noticed a gentleman come riding to our cabin who, as we thought, talked to Lotten in Swedish. When she called us to come home, we were met on the shore by a stately young man whose entire bearing suggested a Swedish officer. It was P. von Schneidau,[2] an ex-lieutenant in the Svea Artillery Regiment. In our younger days he and I had met at a dance, where we had got on familiar footing, but as frequently happens, there had been little opportunity to follow up the friendship. For fourteen years we had not met; but we recognized each other at once and recalled the occasion when we first became acquainted. It seemed very strange to meet after so many years and under such entirely different conditions.

A few words were enough to explain his unexpected arrival. He was one of those whom I should least of all have expected to emigrate to America and settle down as a colonist, something for which he was completely unsuited. When I learned of his plans and the circumstances connected with his emigration, I was both happy and sorry to meet him. He had read the letter of mine that had been published in some papers, and like myself had gone with his young bride to build himself a cottage in the wilderness. I felt a pang of regret as I realized that through my descriptions, which I had never intended to encourage emigration, I had perhaps been the innocent cause of a decision I feared he would soon come to regret.

My own experience had already taught me that pioneer life in the western sections of America, whereas it offered great advantages to common laborers and artisans, had nothing to offer young officials, military officers, and poor students. Persons reared under different social conditions, and for the most part spoiled by them, need a more than usually strong will power not to succumb to the troubles and hardships that meet them here. The new life requires above all physical strength, though that may not hitherto have been much developed, and health that will stand up not only under the lack of the most ordinary conveniences of refined living but also in the battle with want and hunger, if necessary. As far as we ourselves were concerned, we had reason to thank God that up to that time we had been granted not only health and strength but also courage to bear the trials of which we realized we had as yet experienced only the beginning. But Schneidau, the former ordnance officer in the service of His Majesty the King; the sought-after cavalier at all the balls of the capital city, unaccustomed to troubles and worries except such as at times may shadow a happy, youthful garrison life; with a health already impaired by his long ocean voyage — I confess it was not without deep disquietude that I invited him to enter our cabin, the pattern of his own future home.

Soon his wife and brother-in-law arrived, both of them already the personification of exaggerated and disappointed hopes of what was to be had from America. There was something both comical and sad in the way they gave expression to their displeasure. Mrs. Schneidau declared definitely that she was going back to Sweden without delay. She had thought of our "estate," as she was pleased to term our small farm, as something comparable to a well-built country estate in Sweden. A half-spoken reproach that we had not managed to provide a better road from Milwaukee resolved itself into a cry of horror and dismay when she learned that this was our living quarters and that she would have to spend the night there. Turning her eyes to the rough, unpeeled logs and our own rough, unkempt exteriors — for it must be confessed that in our working clothes and with chins that had not known a razor for several months, we were hardly in a position to make a good impression on an elegant Stockholm lady — she burst into a flood of tears, took my wife by the arm, and exclaimed: "Mrs. Unonius, you surely cannot be happy here. Come, let us get up into the wagon and go our way and leave the men that have got us into this miserable mess to look after themselves." In vain Lotten sought to calm her. It was only with difficulty that we could persuade her to cross our threshold. There, as bad luck would have it, our friend Petterson, with his tall stature, his long, heavy, matted black beard, his dark visage and his leather shoemaker's apron, approached her, and with a subdued cry of "Robbers!" she ran for the door.

Schneidau was the one that took things calmly, fully determined to make the best of the situation, as he said, assuring us that his wife would do likewise. But that eventuality seemed most doubtful. The poor man was really to be pitied. His wife's condition meanwhile made it necessary to meet her caprices with caution and consideration, mental excitability not infrequently accompanying her particular state. Considering everything, it was hardly to be wondered at that her temper got the best of her in these new circumstances, for her so completely strange and unexpected.

We tried, nevertheless, to accommodate our guests as well as we could in our little cabin. The single, ground-floor room was placed at the disposal of the women; we men, six in number, took up quarters in the attic, on beds improvised from fur coats, sacks, hay, old carpets, and anything else that Christine could in haste lay hands on to serve as mattress or covering. Schneidau declared that he should sleep as soundly here as formerly on the sofa in the king's antechamber. His wife, on the other hand, would not go to bed, insisting that there was nothing to prevent us in the attic from looking at them through the cracks between the boards. In that observation she was quite correct. The light, which otherwise she would have wanted to burn all night, now had to be put out because of this inconvenience, of which we vainly assured her we would not take advantage. Christine was told to lock the door carefully, and when she explained that we never, either night or day, closed it except by a wooden latch, which was opened as easily from without as within, there was new disturbance on the first floor. Then, oh heavens! a cat was discovered in the house, and he had to be expelled without mercy. To add to the bad luck, during the night a heavy rainstorm came up, and since our poor, warped wooden roof leaked, being no tighter than the first-floor ceiling, it became necessary, both in the upper and lower lodgings, to move our beds to the lee side — a maneuver we had become accustomed to during the summer, but which completely ruined the sleep of our guests.

Chapter 20

LOTTEN SICK · GUESTS IN OUR HOME · LAND SPECULATORS · OB-
SERVATIONS ON FREDRIKA BREMER'S *Homes in the New World*
SCHNEIDAU BUYS LAND AND SETTLES ON IT · BERGWALL BUILDS
HIS HOME · A COURT CASE · A SIXTY-YEAR-OLD IMMIGRANT
BRIEF NOTES ON OTHER SWEDISH IMMIGRANTS

MORE than a month passed by, with hard work and not without considerable domestic anxieties. Lotten became seriously ill. Fortunately we had, besides Polman, another skillful physician in our neighborhood; through their combined efforts she was finally restored to the point where she could get out of bed and do some of the lighter housework.

In the meantime, our cabin was a full-fledged inn; one Swede after another came and went. There were times when we had as many as eighteen people in the house. How we were able to provide lodging for all of them is to this hour more than I can explain; but an old adage says that where there is harmony there is no lack of space and we certainly did everything in our power to make the former stretch out the latter. But our house was taxed to its capacity, limited as it was to a single room, eighteen feet by twenty-two, and an attic of the same area, where the steeply sloping roof made it necessary to crawl from one bed to another and where a man was able to stand upright only under the ridge. When we consider that this space was made to lodge no fewer than eighteen persons, "ladies" and "gentlemen," some of them accustomed to luxurious apartments and well-furnished guest rooms, while one belonged to a class used to no other conveniences than those of a humble cottage, praise is due the pioneer ingenuity able to manage under all conditions. Some of the newly arrived Swedes settled in our neighborhood.

Schneidau as well as his wife and brother-in-law lived with us for several weeks. All this time he suffered from a leg complaint which made it difficult for him to walk about the neighborhood to choose a site for his future home. In the meantime his wife calmed down. Lotten may largely take the credit for this, who by her patience and cheerful spirit set her a good example in how to endure the privations which one and all must share. Perhaps, however, this would have availed as little as anything else with the spoiled, but at heart good, "lady from the capital city," had Lotten herself not got sick. Then her better and nobler feelings came to the surface. In watching the sufferings of another, she forgot her own troubles. At the sickbed, whether in a palace or a cottage, it is always the woman who is at home, and as her kind, tender influence makes itself felt there, the good angel in her own soul speaks to her and she is unable to withstand its voice. As she busied herself about Lotten's sickbed, Mrs. Schneidau seemed to forget her own disappointments and came to feel at home in the log cabin she at first had thought so odious. The tender hand that had probably never before been seen around a kitchen stove now lent itself willingly to assist Christine in the cooking of soups and similar things. From the cooking of dishes for the patient she was gradually led to prepare other food, so that all of a sudden, probably without realizing herself what had happened, Mrs. Schneidau, with a white kitchen apron covering her modern muslin dress, was to be found standing watching the potato pot and the bacon in the frying pan and speaking kindly both to "robbers" and other folk.

Schneidau finally bought a quarter section of land from an American who a few weeks before, probably as a speculation, had built a small cabin at the south end of Pine Lake, hoping to sell his claim to some Swede anxious to settle near his own countrymen.

Such land speculations occur often, with great profit to those who love to roam from one place to another and who have a perfect passion for trading houses and plots of land, much as farm laborers in Sweden trade watches at the county fairs. They practice their business particularly among German immigrants, who like to settle as close together as possible and form a compact community of their own, seeking to organize even in this country a

little patch of *das grosse Vaterland*. If three or four German families have settled close together, one may be certain that they have
done so hoping to attract many times that number of neighbors
within a year. The American, with his locomotive nature, grasps
the opportunity to build a shack either within or close to the little
settlement, tills a couple of acres of land, makes believe he is about
to clear and break still more in order to settle down, which may
no more be his plan than to settle on the moon. In the meantime
he busies himself with hunting and with trapping muskrats, and
when the next caravan of immigrants comes along, he sells his
claim to some German glad to pay more than its worth to settle
near those with whom he can empty his stein of beer in the fashion
of the old country.

To insist upon buying a farm or otherwise making a living just
where acquaintances and relatives have settled is, I have often noticed, a mistake common among our Swedish settlers too. It seems
as if the one place and nowhere else is America to them. The late-
comers naturally find the best land taken by others; yet rather than
go a few miles farther away, where a thousand times better land is
available and where there may also be better opportunities of a
livelihood, they elect, for the sake of being close to their countrymen, to dig in among hills, hollows, and rocks. In this there is of
course something creditable; that the Swede has not forgotten the
old country and that he loves it are proved by his love for his
countrymen. From the economic standpoint, however, such a procedure is rather unwise. It may be true that settling among unknown people has its elements of hardship for a time. It is not easy
to live among those whose language and customs are unfamiliar.
But for all that, I have observed that Swedes who make their homes
in the midst of a completely American settlement or in some section where they have no opportunity to associate with many of
their countrymen, generally improve their condition and become
independent sooner than those who, coming at the same time and
with about the same means, insist on settling among immigrant folk
of their own nationality.

As far as Schneidau is concerned, though, as long as he was set
on trying his hand at farming, he could hardly have made a better
choice than he did when he bought his quarter section with what-

ever improvements were on it for the sum of a couple of hundred dollars. The location was most attractive, and the soil good, consisting mainly of a level, easily broken burr-oak plain just as fertile as our own, which was generally regarded as the most beautiful and best along the shores of Pine Lake.

In case the reader has read Fredrika Bremer's *Homes in the New World*, a book of much merit in many respects, I feel obliged at this point to make a few remarks on what she says there about the Swedish settlement at Pine Lake, a description contradictory to much of my own. The distinguished author says of it: "It was a region of inland lakes, as fair and romantic as one could imagine, a replica of a Swedish lake region. And it is understandable that it so charmed the first settlers that without taking time to examine the character of the soil, they determined to found a New Sweden, and build a New Uppsala! . . . With the exception of Bergwall's farm, all the land around Pine Lake seemed to be of a poor quality. . . . We traveled along the wooded shores, which in their resplendent fall colors mirrored themselves in the unruffled lake. Here, on a high point jutting out into the lake, covered by leafy groves, was the site of New Uppsala, planned by Unonius and his friends when they first came to this fair region and were charmed by its beauty . . . fair in a Swedish way, for dark pines mingled with deciduous trees, and the woods extended down to the shore of the lake just as at our lakes, where Necken[1] sits in the moonlight, playing his harp, singing his songs under the shade of the trees."[a]

I must express my gratitude to the eminent authoress for her description of the beauty of the region, the site of my former home, dear always to remembrance, and for the flattering way in which she describes the good taste of me and my countrymen in choosing it. It is with this as with everything she has been able to apprehend: it is true, it is pretty — no one could have said it better. But in her account of the characteristics of the soil, as well as in other important explanations, or, more correctly, reflections, I am afraid she did not really know what she was talking about. Bergwall's farm, however fertile, was far from being the most fertile in the Swedish settlement at Pine Lake. We had the first choice, and it certainly was not the beauty of the region alone that determined it among the many we had the opportunity to make. Even if I should admit that I myself at that time had much less ability than Miss Bremer to judge the quality of the land, it should be made clear that Carl, not without previous agricultural experience, knew more of this matter than both Miss Bremer and I put together. In justice to him he should be cleared from the imputation of a lack of judgment which even his love of nature could not have excused.

Our soil was conceded generally to be the very best and the most fertile offered anywhere. The same judgment was expressed also about the quarter section Schneidau bought. Its soundness is best proved by the high prices later paid for these farms at the various times they changed hands. I have already stated that oak openings as a rule are not so fertile as the prairie and forest lands. But even the oak openings, often preferable to the prairie for raising wheat, possess certain qualities which the prairies and the forest lands lack. For instance, they are more easily tilled than the forest lands and do not, like the prairies, lack timber.

I might add much more besides contravening Miss Bremer's description of the former Swedish settlement at Pine Lake and the manner of life there. I am sorry to have to say that the brilliant writer has so veiled the truth with poetic fancy that it is perfectly unrecognizable to one who like me happened to be intimately acquainted with these conditions and who himself lived the life she is describing. She talks about us as though, having got our houses in order, we did nothing else afterward and lived each day as if it were our last. Had Miss Bremer come to Pine Lake seven or eight years earlier, she would have discovered that there was little enough feasting among "the Swedish gentry." Moreover the settlers would have had very little opportunity to entertain their famous countrywoman in the manner of her visit a few years later to the community. She might not have had occasion to look for a candle snuffer on the bedside table, because there would have been no candle to snuff. Sometimes, though very seldom, we did come together for Christmas celebrations or midsummer dances, but the entertainment was plain enough. The abundance, if there was any, came from the woods and the lake; the remainder, for the most part consisting of contributions of produce from the various homes, bore witness to poverty. Personally, I cannot recall more than two or three occasions when cash contributions to cover expenses were even considered.

But these are insignificant mistakes, which would never have been remarked upon if they had not given many an entirely wrong conception of pioneer life — a life I myself was a part of and of which I have attempted an inadequate description. They may freely be forgiven Miss Bremer for the sake of the truth, commendable both where she approves and disapproves, of her description of the men, women, and homes in the new world. Those who, like myself, have learned to know, love, esteem, and honor them in their better manifestations cannot but rejoice heartily that she makes amends for the false and unfair judgments of most other writers on America. But alas, all the more must one regret that her sympathy for, and reasoning about, phalansterianism, Shakers, women's-rights associations, yes, even Mormonism, and everything of the sort — things that judicious Americans regard as more or less noxious weeds sown by the enemy into good ground — almost destroy the good and favorable impression these descriptions otherwise would make on an impartial reader. It requires little judgment and discernment to see how much of what with good intentions she paints in the most beautiful colors is in reality nothing but pure humbug, often even something worse. Finding her description and her judgment untrustworthy in one thing, the reader is likely to mistrust her in others, where, nevertheless, besides other merits, she has the great one of being fully reliable.

If the piece of land that Schneidau purchased was good, the little cottage that stood on it was all the poorer. It had been erected in an unattractive spot close to the public road and consisted, like ours, of only one room, but much smaller, lower, and in all ways more uncomfortable. The floor had been constructed from loose sawed slabs laid side by side. Close to the door was a kind of window opening, about a foot square, which, with the exception of cracks in the roof and the walls, was the only place where daylight managed to make its way into the dark room. The attic was designed for creeping rather than walking. But this miserable hovel was to serve as a home for Schneidau and his wife for the rest of the year as well as for the winter. Schneidau was for a long time an invalid and sensitive to drafts and cold, and his wife was about to become a mother. He soon made arrangements, however, for building a better and more comfortable house. Like everything else about the farm, this work had to be done by hired laborers, among them Bergwall, who soon learned to handle briskly and skillfully both hatchet and axe.

Having good health and great physical power united to a certain natural handiness, Bergwall, compelled to work for others, had acclimated himself completely to his new status in life. Instead of building a dwelling, he dug himself one. After the fashion of the ancient Nordics he sought, namely, to prepare a dugout. For this, however, he needed, besides certain household articles, others he was unable to get without money, of which he had almost none. Yet through diligence, forethought, and an admirable ability to accommodate himself to existing conditions as well as to endure struggles and privations that in his happier days he had known only by name, he was able in time to acquire the necessary tools and materials for his dugout and its furnishings. He was one of the few immigrants I knew during my years in America who were able to accommodate themselves to their hard lot after being accustomed to comparative wealth in earlier days. Here he devoted himself to the hardest kind of toil with the same happy spirit, the same light-hearted humor he had formerly displayed in the days of his prosperity. He was satisfied with everything; the trees that grew on the hills around *Vänhem* [the home of friends], the name he had given his dwelling, were bigger and better, he insisted, than in any other place; the spring he had discovered on his land had clearer and better-tasting water; the dugout, at which he spent one or two days a week while working for Schneidau, became to his mind the warmest and most comfortable dwelling in the entire Pine Lake region. However meager and insignificant it may have appeared to others, there was no one who was able to say with more satisfaction and self-assurance, "Everywhere it is good, but there is no place like home."

J[acobsso]n, too, Schneidau's brother-in-law, planned to become a farmer and built a small structure on a claim next to his relatives'. There, however, he became more of a country merchant than a farmer. The former occupation was indeed more in line with his abilities and antecedents than the latter, for which he, like most persons of his racial background, had no experience and little aptitude. In Milwaukee he obtained a small stock of goods suitable for a country store along the public road, but he did not succeed in making much of the business. After a time he sold everything, store, stock and land, and returned to Sweden.

Thott had also built a small cabin, but farther from us than the rest of the Swedes. Many republican Americans, with their aversion to old-world institutions, are nevertheless inclined to attach at times an almost childish importance and significance to the aristocratic titles in use over there. It had been rumored abroad that Thott was a baron. That was enough to give him entrance into a more elite circle both in the country and the city than the rest of us poor plebeians and laborers enjoyed. He, too, had formerly been a lieutenant in a Swedish regiment and was one of those who had to learn through bitter experience how incomparably harder are the difficulties of pioneer life than those of a military encampment. Being a native of Skåne,[2] he naturally had to have a horse; so he bought a smart pacer, on which he sometimes rode about and called on us and other neighbors. In the meantime he had hired a French-Canadian at thirty dollars a month to serve as interpreter and to care for his farm.

One day Thott and B[öttige]r[3] were subpoenaed to appear before the justice of the peace as witnesses in a court case. Neither of the lieutenants knew any English, and B[öttige]r was in addition just as ignorant of French. The judge turned to B[öttige]r, read the oath, asked him to kiss the Bible in acknowledgment of said oath, and told him to state what he knew of the case. B[öttige]r shook his head to signify that he did not know what it was all about. The judge appointed M. Colet, Thott's servant, to act as interpreter. M. Colet translated the judge's words to Thott in French; he in turn interpreted them in Swedish to B[öttige]r, whereupon the latter's reply and testimony had to be transmitted to the justice in the same roundabout manner. So the questions and answers went from man to man for some time, to the huge enjoyment of the spectators and to the bewilderment of the justice, who found it hard to get the connection of it all in this Babylonian confusion. The case threatened to become somewhat lengthy, whereupon B[öttige]r decided to put an end to it in his own comical way, at least as far as his own part in it was concerned. With the soberest and solemnest mien in the world he began a long harangue. The justice listened for a while with patience to "the tongue of honorable men and heroes,"[4] but finally asked M. Colet to find out what it was all about. Thott, who in the meantime had been convulsed with laughter, hardly knew what to say. What B[öttige]r had said was not translatable. The merriment spread to the rest of them; both the justice and the spectators began to find the procedure ridiculous; and certainly they would have had thought it funnier still had they been able to understand B[öttige]r's oration.

Thott did not stay with his farming very long. The yield of the small area of land that had been tilled was not enough to pay M. Colet's wages. After a year he sold his farm and went farther north into Wisconsin. There after many shifting fortunes he secured some kind of civil appointment, and finally died in impoverished circumstances.

Among the countrymen who visited us about this time or were stopping in our neighborhood, I remember a sixty-year-old immigrant named Ihrmark,[5] who along with a few other Swedes finally settled in Illinois. There he certainly owned good land, but nevertheless he was always highly dissatisfied with his situation.

When we first landed in Milwaukee, I wrote a letter to Sweden, where it was published in the papers. In that letter I was unwise enough to advise future emigrants to take with them not only tools but also heavy equipment, even the framework of wagons, if possible. Ihrmark followed my advice and took along a clumsy Swedish work wagon which, after he had paid all the transportation costs to the West, proved entirely unfit for practical use and was generally looked upon as a great curiosity.

Carried away by their first impressions of conditions that are entirely new to them, immigrants generally in their letters home give descriptions and volunteer information and advice which, owing to their limited knowledge of the country, may prove anything but reliable. It would be well if friends and relatives in Sweden, encouraged by such letters to emigrate, were not to regard such stories and such advice as gospel truth. No doubt the immigrants write what for the moment seems indeed true, but there is not one in a hundred that in a short time, after getting better acquainted with conditions, will not have changed his opinions and found himself mistaken in his earlier reports. So it was with my advice in the matter of taking along tools and other equipment. An emigrant can do nothing more unwise than to load himself down with such things. The cost of transportation often exceeds their value, and before long he will put them aside for others that are more practical. Ihrmark's old farm wagon lay for a long time heavy on my conscience, and I hope it was the only one, as I believe it was the first of its kind, to roll along the roads in America. Of Ihrmark's later fortunes I have had no definite information. At his age and in his circumstances the hardships in the strange land must have been doubly heavy. According to one rumor his days there were soon ended, in the realization no doubt that he might have spent his declining years with less trouble in his fatherland.

In his company came another compatriot, O. Dreutzer,[6] from Göteborg, who settled with his family in Ihrmark's neighborhood. He was one of those who seemed better fitted for life in the West, though not in the capacity of farmer. Fully conversant with the English language, he had the ability to push his way to the front in the world, and for that reason the confines of a pioneer cottage were too limited for him. It was not long before he settled in Milwaukee, where he started a hotel business and kept a Scandinavian boardinghouse. Sometimes fortune smiled on him, sometimes not; at times he succeeded through his activities in political campaigns in winning a certain standing; at others there was an end both to his influence and his resources. He was a man who certainly could easily get into predicaments, but who nevertheless knew always how to get out of them. Some years later he tried his luck once again as a settler far off in Wisconsin, where he also opened a store and tried to start a Swedish settlement. Rumor has it that he was successful in both of these undertakings. In the new colony he managed to get himself elected justice of the peace. This gave him a taste for law, and when last I heard from him, he had become a prosperous lawyer, no doubt owing to his penchant for lawsuits. The great number of Norwegians who settled in that section, which afterwards became one of the largest and most populous Norwegian settlements in the state, doubtless contributed not a little to his success. The taste for litigation and legal processes, which, from what I have heard, are common in Norway, seems in the immigrants from that country to have further developed on American soil. They are everlastingly engaged in disputes with one another and their neighbors, and it does not take a Norwegian long to start an action which in costs to both parties far exceeds the value of the matter in dispute. I have heard American lawyers in the judicial districts where many of the inhabitants are Norwegian say that most of their income derives from them. It would not surprise me if Dreutzer's success as a jurist was related to that propensity among his Norwegian neighbors.

I cannot refrain from speaking of another Swede, Wester[7] by name, one of the many who for a time were our guests at New Uppsala. I was later to meet him several times in the course of his eventful life, which is not without its own interest. He had been a rag collector in Sweden, but the first time he visited our colony he was planning to become a minister, and had already begun to preach in private homes in the Norwegian settlements. Shortly after his arrival in New York, he came in contact with a well-known Swedish shipwright, who maintained that he had once, while lying under a pile of lumber, received, like Paul, a revelation from above to go out and preach the gospel. At his services he never failed to tell of his own wonderful conversion. Gripped by his preaching, Wester experienced a religious awakening, was converted, and considered himself called to the same kind of service. With great ardor he joined his spiritual father's denomination, the Methodist, by which sect he seems to have been engaged as an exhorter, class leader, or something of the sort, with a special view toward laboring among the Scandinavians in the West, whither he proceeded shortly after his conversion.

Probably it was in his capacity as missionary, that is, to influence us religiously, that he paid us his call; unfortunately he had little success. One evening, however, he took the opportunity to read for our edification one of his long sermons. As we listened, we had all we could do to maintain our seriousness. It was of the kind of which it is hard to decide whether the writing of it or the listening to it is a greater misuse of God's name. Let it be enough that the only impression his sermon made on us was to deepen our conviction that Wester was better suited to pick rags than to preach the gospel. Besides, there was something in the man himself that clearly told us this was a form of activity he would not be likely to remain in for long, that a reaction would soon set in and cool off his hot zeal. With this he thought himself to be fired more completely than he really was; it expressed itself mainly in bitter diatribes against the Swedish clergy, which he pronounced destitute of all true Christianity. Though completely uncultivated and ignorant, he appeared, though not as a preacher, to be what Americans call a smart man, that is, clever, canny, eager to make money despite all his piety, missing no opportunity to achieve that end. An inner voice told us that though this might not have been clear to himself, Methodism and preaching were to him only a means to rise in the world, and if he were not able to profit by them, he would gain his goal in some other way.

Soon it became evident that we were not mistaken about him. A brother in the faith with whom he had associated himself, to whom he had given his full confidence, together with whom he had attended all kinds of camp meetings and prayer meetings, and whom he had regarded as a real saint, fleeced him finally of all the little that he had, which he had been anxious to increase in any way. This was a hard blow to Wester and, if you will, still more so to Methodism, which thereby lost a zealous laborer. But even if that had not happened, he probably would not have remained faithful to them; the event merely speeded his fall.

Wester once said, quite openly, "Now I want no God but the dollar, and for him I will labor." Not being either inclined or accustomed to hard physical labor, he learned the barber's trade, and went to New Orleans, where he had been told it was easy to make money. There he set up a barber shop, with an advertisement reading, "How keen's the steel of Sweden; come let us test its edge." [8] But those that came to test it were few indeed. Wester soon found it to his advantage to put his razors in his pocket and set out for Illinois. There he became acquainted with Erik Jansson [9] and his company, who had just arrived from Sweden. He joined that sect, whether with an eye to business — for his finances were at a low ebb — or through reawakened religious convictions I leave unsaid.

Enough that he joined the communistic group at Bishop Hill, where he had, at least for the time being, food and raiment.

One of his duties was to shave the famous prophet. This man, very eager to increase the population of his colony, at times, like King Frederick of Prussia, got the notion of being a matchmaker. Wester was strong and stately in appearance, and one morning, after he had fulfilled his duty as the prophet's barber, he received orders forthwith to marry a brisk and lively girl from Hälsingland.[10] Wester thanked him for his fatherly interest, but declared that he was not prepared to obey his order. Erik Jansson insisted sternly on blind obedience to all his wishes. Wester, however, felt that church discipline ought not to go so far as to impose a mate. His refusal was interpreted as insubordination and rebellion against the divine power and authority of the prophet, and for that crime he was thrown into jail and given a starvation cure. He was, in his way, very fond of his food; along with Mammon his belly was his god. He did not want to marry, for the simple reason that he already was, a detail he had decided not to divulge to the prophet, nor did he dare to tell him now. Yet in some way he must have food, and liberty as well.

To attain this end he started to preach. It was reported to Jansson that the spirit had fallen on one of the prisoners, who was proclaiming wonderful things of his own sinlessness and that of the rest of those who had the true faith. It was decided that next Sunday he was to appear publicly and speak to the congregation. He spoke with great power, and was fed. After a couple of days he turned his back on Bishop Hill, leaving the prophet to shave himself and to select another husband for the lass of Hälsingland.

Next he established a barber shop in Galesburg, a small city not far from Erik Jansson's colony. Shortly afterward there was a schism within the sect; Erik Jansson was forsaken by many of his adherents, and these resorted to Wester, whose preaching had given them the impression that he was a man richly endowed with the gifts of the spirit and that he had been called to become a mighty prophet in the new Israel. But Wester, heartily weary of the whole crowd, and feeling that it was his calling to ply his shaving brush rather than to serve in an apostolic office, told them in good Swedish to go to — Hälsingland,[11] informing them that it was hunger and not high inspiration that had driven him to appear among them as a prophet.

After that for several years we heard nothing further of Wester and what he was doing. Finally we were informed that he was living in Princeton, a flourishing little town in Illinois, where, in addition to his barbering, he also ran a small store. The business increased more and more, and one day we were surprised to find in one of the papers of the city a pompous advertisement, printed in big and varied type, now in short, now in longer lines, which I reproduce here as a typical specimen of American advertising.

WESTER

begs to announce to the citizens of Princeton and its environs that he has sold out his old stock, paid his debts, and has now started with an entirely new stock, superior to all others west of Chicago, though he still sells at the same prices as during the last seven years, that is, cheaper than anyone else. My stock consists of ready-made clothes, boots, shoes, hats, and caps, all kinds of articles belonging to a gentleman's wardrobe, Yankee notions,[b] handbags, pocketbooks, knives, Colt's revolvers, pistols, double-barreled guns and all kinds of hunting equipment, groceries, cigars, chewing and smoking tobacco, candies, etc. I have built an addition to my house and there established tailoring, shoemaking, and gunsmithing shops, so that if you are looking for goods not kept in stock, I am ready with the greatest pleasure to take your orders, and my work will speak for itself.

I want to tell you the secret of how I am able to sell my clothing so much cheaper than anyone else. What I tell you is the truth and nothing but the truth. I am in favor of free trade and of seamen's rights, and that means that I take good care of what I do in regard to duties on my imported goods. You know I am a Swede. In Sweden there is a small city of about 20,000 inhabitants called Norrköping. The only manufacture of that city is cloth — the best cloth in existence. You know that in this country we reckon by dollars, but in Sweden they reckon by riksdaler, of which it takes four to equal an American dollar. Now in Sweden I can buy as much for a riksdaler as I can for a dollar in America. When I buy my cloth in Norrköping, I naturally get four yards for what one yard costs here. No wonder that I can sell my clothes cheaper than anyone else, and still make money! When my Swedish iron is shipped to this country, there is always enough room left in the ship for the cloth I import. As for my shoes, let me state that I buy my sole leather in Rio Janeiro after it has been tanned in Brazil, and my calfskin in Paris. Through my connections with Mr. Rothschild, who always discounts my bills and supplies me with business advice, I assure you I shall pull through these difficult financial times. If you have faith like a mustard seed, then come to me and buy your goods! Believe, and you shall be saved!

E. Wester.

Notes

ᵃ Vol. II, Letter 25.

ᵇ It is hard to explain what is really meant by that term, unless it is trinkets of various kinds, fancy goods, and assortments of small articles such as peddlers carry around in their boxes or bags.

Chapter 21

CLAIM JUMPING · A PUBLIC MEETING · APPLICATION OF THE
LYNCH LAW · BUILDING REPAIRS · A SURGICAL OPERATION
ROOFING WITH SHINGLES · EARLY WINTER · NEIGHBORLY HELP-
FULNESS · AN ADDITION TO THE FAMILY · NASHOTAH · THE
BEGINNING OF A MISSION SCHOOL · INFANT BAPTISM · GENERAL
NEGLECT OF IT · THE GENERAL ATTITUDE IN THIS RESPECT
AMONG PRESBYTERIANS AND LUTHERANS

U P TO this time we had taken no part in current political activities, which nevertheless were discussed with the same
earnestness at meetings in the small schoolhouses here as
ever in Faneuil Hall in Boston or in a great public hall in New York.
Often we had found notices nailed to some tree close to the public
road announcing such meetings, and had had private invitations to
attend them, especially from zealous partisans of the Democratic
party apparently eager to convert us to their political faith. Notwithstanding these solicitations we had not as yet even applied for
United States citizenship. This would not have prevented us,
though, from taking part in various communal affairs and from
voting in the local elections. But we did not consider ourselves
well enough informed in these matters to be willing to take active
part in them. Who were to become justices of the peace, road
inspectors, constables, tax collectors, and so forth, did not much
concern us. We were protected as to person and property and felt
fully satisfied with our government, or, rather, we hardly noticed
that we had any.

Foreigners are generally inclined to engage in political disputes
long before they know what things are all about, and the rashness
with which they make use of a citizenship they have gained all too

soon is without question harmful to the country. The American republic will no doubt sooner or later find it necessary to change its naturalization laws. The Germans and especially the Irish have hardly had time to get a roof over their heads before they begin to busy themselves with political affairs of all kinds, become eager partisans, get their hands into everything, and cause no end of trouble and disorder — all of which could be avoided if Americans were left to govern the country alone. Accustomed perhaps to being of little or no importance before, in a more liberal social order they feel all-important, and the spirit of opposition that led them to political radicalism at home now induces them to oppose almost everything proposed by sane and wise Americans for the good of the country. Many a time I have heard Germans who hardly understood the simplest English sentences say, "We are not going to let the Americans rule over us." Their false conception of liberty and citizenship and that of the Irish gave me an absolute distaste for all politics, and neither then nor later did I meddle with it except in questions where my duty bade me appear quietly and calmly at the ballot box.

I love the democratic social order where the majesty of the people really is a majesty before which a man can stand with the same veneration, yes, with even more, than before a royal throne; and I believe that the American people, left to themselves, will one day reveal that majesty to the world. But when one sees European immigrants assume the democratic toga, which on their shoulders easily becomes the fool's motley; when one hears them speak of freedom and with an air of authority pronounce judgment on the most weighty social questions, of which they have not the least comprehension, being mere tools in the hands of selfish partisans, then one can hardly help smiling at the thought of the kind of republic most European countries would be blessed with were these modern apostles of freedom to have their way. A popular government in Europe would undoubtedly prove very different from what it is in America. Whereas the latter is developing more and more an innate power to construct and build, the former — to judge by signs here — would be excellent in tearing down and destroying things and in fighting the opposition but altogether useless, yes, even dangerous, when it was a question of construction.

As for my application for naturalization, I delayed a long time, I hardly know why. I had no thought then of returning to my native country, but with all my well-known radicalism when I was there, and with all my notions of liberty, I was still haunted by the oath of allegiance which once as a Swedish citizen I had given the ruler of Sweden, and it went a little against my feelings to file my application to become a naturalized citizen of the United States and according to the established formulation swear to "renounce all allegiance and loyalty to every foreign potentate, monarch, state or authority whatsoever, and especially Charles XIV John, King of Sweden and Norway."

Nevertheless one cannot completely ignore public affairs, especially when something is afoot in which one is personally interested. So we went one day to attend a town meeting, that is, a meeting of all the landowners within the township.

I have already described the kind of land of which we, like many other new settlers, had taken possession; how Congress had ceded it as a subvention to a canal company for building a canal which was never constructed, and how all the settlers on it refused to pay for it while its ownership was so unsettled. As has also been mentioned, all the squatters on these lands had entered into an agreement to stand by one another until the manner of payment had been determined upon and to protect one another in their possession of the land. This compact provided, among other things, that we would prevent anyone else from buying the lands on which we had settled and made improvements. Such a protective compact had also been agreed to by those who had settled on ordinary Congress land, and though they had no interest in the matter except to get the land settled and cultivated as quickly as possible, they also considered it their duty to prevent anyone from jumping another man's claim, that is to say, from buying the piece of land another person had taken possession of though he had not yet paid for it.

Now it happened that an American who apparently had more money than most newcomers had moved here from one of the eastern states and had bought a quarter section that had not up to that time been settled, and paid the price demanded by the canal company. To this no one had any objection since he was encroaching on nobody's rights. We merely laughed at him for wasting good money. But when he also after a time bought eighty acres adjoining his quarter on which a poor immigrant shortly before had settled under the protection of the club law and on which he was just building a cabin, that was quite another story.

Owing to this development and the dispute arising from it, a call went out to all the settlers in the township to meet in the schoolhouse. Almost all of us Swedes were there at the appointed time. The gathering was large, and in the weatherbeaten faces of some of the backwoodsmen there was an expression of wrath and determination that suggested they had already made up their minds in a way boding no good to the culprit. Others, apparently quite calm, had seated themselves close to the red-hot stove, and the low room was soon filled with stifling heat and the smell of burnt leather. Some Americans are accustomed, when it is cold, to putting their feet almost into the fire. Enter a hotel or some other public place in the wintertime and you will find them rocking in their chairs, as many as possible crowding around the stove, their feet resting upon it. The snow underneath the soles of their shoes will melt and sizzle on the hot sheet iron, and from the singed boots rises one pillar of smoke beside another, making a sweet smell at least for the cobbler, if not for anyone else.

As usual, the jackknives were busy, in the handling of which the men in the West have acquired considerable skill. The urge to whittle is apparently irresistible. An ordinary stick of wood in the hands of a skillful whittler goes through one transformation after another, taking the form of now a cone, now a cube, now a pyramid, now some other geometric figure, till the entire stick has been reduced to chips. Let us not imagine, though, that this is merely idle pastime. Oftentimes while a man's jackknife is busy, his head is full of deep thoughts, and just when one might fancy he has no thought for anything but his shining blade or his stick, he may be hatching a plan for a profitable deal. While matters of business are being discussed, the whittling becomes merely a mutual byplay through which one party seeks to gain insight into the mind of the other. The way in which the stick and the knife are being used may serve as a thermometer for the experienced eye to discover the plus or minus degrees of the whittler's frame of mind. When a deal is in prospect between two parties and one of them stops whittling, closes his knife, and puts it in his pocket, one may be certain that either his negotiations have brought the other party to the point where he wants him or he himself has made a decision from which it would be useless to try to budge him.

On this occasion the broad-bladed knives of various dimensions seemed to me bared less for whittling than for stabbing some opponent through the chest. The chips were flying from one bench to another with more than ordinary vigor; in the movements of the hands there was something ominous, and the gleaming knife blade as well as the face of each whittler appeared to reflect a judgment already pronounced in accordance with the lynch law's stern justice.

In a short while the meeting was called to order in the regular way. One man arose and moved, in a few words, that Mr. S[kinner][1] be made the chairman of the meeting. Mr. S[kinner] was a farmer, well-to-do, but like most of those present uneducated. He was one of the oldest settlers in the neighborhood, and a man of great influence and high reputation in the community. Recently he had been elected justice of the peace and still held that office. He accepted the chairmanship and took his place back of the schoolmaster's table at one end of the room, expressed his thanks for the honor bestowed on him, and asked the meeting to proceed to elect a secretary. Another man arose and moved that Mr. Unonius be elected to fill that office. But Mr. Unonius asked to be excused from this position of trust because he was not accustomed to keeping the minutes of such meetings. Thereupon another man was elected and took his place by the side of the chairman. Everything was done in perfect parliamentary order. Next, the chairman declared the meeting duly organized, explained in a few words its purpose, and invited those in attendance to express themselves on the subject before them.

A tall, strong-built farmer, a perfect example of the genuine backwoodsman, arose. In his dark face and sharply marked features could be read the record of an unremitting but freely chosen struggle with wild nature; of a strength hardened by many years of troubles and privations cheerfully and courageously borne; of a resoluteness and presence of mind attesting dangers undergone

327

among the wild beasts and wild sons of the prairie and the forest. In a word, in his bearing and appearance was written the whole life history of a frontiersman. His clothing was half that of a white, half that of a red man. A hunting shirt of red flannel girded by a broad leather belt, was visible under the wide tunic that extended to his knees — a garment that had been made from a blue blanket and so constructed that its broad black borders formed a kind of hem or decoration at the bottom and at the lapels. On his feet he wore a pair of deerskin moccasins, and extending up to his knees a pair of tight leggings from the same material. In his hand he held a long rifle, which no doubt had often been put to use and had long been his faithful companion in a richly adventurous life.

After greeting the chairman with the customary "Mr. President and Gentlemen," he developed in a coherent, orderly address, presented with natural ease and fluency, the subject of the canal lands. He sought to show that the canal company had never done anything but cheat both Congress, which had voted public funds for performing work the company was evidently neither able nor willing to carry through, and the individual settlers, who in the hope of corresponding advantages had paid a higher price for that land than the law provided; that under these conditions it was nothing less than a fraud for the Government to continue to demand a higher price for this land than for any other; that the people had a perfect right to oppose such a proceeding; but that the land in the meantime ought not to be left idle and unpopulated when daily new crowds of immigrants, "a respectable class of native citizens and foreigners," were arriving to build for themselves happy homes and in a few years lift this "glorious territory to one of the greatest and most important states in the union."

He next developed each settler's legal and moral right to the claim he had chosen with intent and purpose to make on it his home, calling it "the greatest piece of rascality" that ever could be perpetrated that anybody should secretly proceed to buy the same; and he sincerely hoped that now that such an unjust deed had been done, they all might stick together as one man and establish an example of stern justice so that they might for the future be protected from such encroachments.

His speech was interspersed with idioms peculiar to the West, and other strong expressions often employed in American oratory, like "the duty of every citizen to guard the sacred freedom for which our fathers bled and died, and to protect each other in our enjoyment thereof."

The chairman submitted to the meeting whether it would not be necessary, before making any decision, first to have it shown and proved beyond a doubt that the man accused of having "jumped" another man's claim was really guilty of that crime. At once, serving both as prosecutors and witnesses, one after another rose up and explained all the circumstances connected with the matter. The accused man appeared to have in the whole gathering not a single person to speak in his defense, unless one might so regard the chairman and several others who calmly and apparently with complete impartiality set forth questions for the purpose of fully clarifying and proving the case. The result of the trial was that the accused was declared guilty. Thereupon the question came up of the nature of the punishment to be imposed.

An Irishman, a genuine paddy, dressed in ragged and dirty clothes, who seated in a corner, swinging his body to and fro, had by repeated puffings given the meeting to understand that he was preparing to make "a speech," asked for the floor. As if ready for a boxing bout, he got up and unburdened himself of what was on his mind in the characteristic style and brogue of the renowned sons of the beautiful Erin. He noted that his beloved adopted fatherland and its free institutions were in grave peril unless such misconduct as that in question were to be punished severely. For his part he urged that the house of the culprit be burned and the man himself be tarred and feathered, adding that he would be damned if he would not assist in carrying out that sentence.

Some of those present thought the measures suggested by the honorable gentleman rather severe, but there was a general inclination nevertheless to consider favorably the burning of the claim jumper's house. There is no telling what might have happened had not our countryman Petterson in his usual quiet and judicious manner asked for the floor and proposed another approach to the matter.

He observed that minds were greatly inflamed, and to avoid any act of violence, of which the consequences might be very serious, he proposed another punishment. Though stern and corrective, it involved no violence, and once inflicted on the culprit, could not lead to countersteps by the real representatives of the law or give occasion to a suit against those who had imposed it. He suggested that the accused be placed under a kind of interdict: that no one was to speak to him, have any intercourse with him, or visit him in his house, and if he came to the threshold of any other man's, he was not to be admitted. No one was to buy from him or sell anything to him. In short, he was to be regarded as an excommunicated man, avoided and shunned by all, till he had atoned for his error and deeded the land in question to the man to whom it really belonged. For this he was to be paid the legal price when the dispute concerning the canal lands finally had been settled.

His suggestion won the approval of the meeting. It contained an element of novelty; it could even be published in the papers as a warning to other claim jumpers; it would lend a kind of respectability to the entire community. Petterson was complimented as a clever, just, and wise judge under the lynch law. To be sure, the proposal did not please the Irishman and his friends. Fire and violence would have agreed far better with their volatile and fiery spirits, and tarring and feathering would to them have been as exciting a spectacle as a bullfight to a Spaniard. For once, though, they had to forego the pleasure. Petterson's proposal was adopted and recorded in the minutes as unanimously approved, with the amendment that whosoever might be found breaking the agreement and entering into any kind of intercourse whatsoever with the interdicted man was to be regarded as guilty along with him and to be visited with the same punishment.

The decision of the meeting was carried out, with the result that the wrongdoer soon found it advisable to give the opposite party full restitution for the loss he had suffered.

As we had expected, the first year's harvest on the fresh-tilled ground did not prove very rich. But we consoled ourselves with "better luck next time," after the ground should have been softened up and we have been able to take more effective measures against the corn-destroying gophers. The small crop was soon harvested, and not without serious anxiety we saw ahead the coming winter and year, in which we should have to buy all cereal food and many other things besides for ourselves and our cattle. Our fields, however, had been enlarged by a few acres which were sown to winter wheat.

Both the living house and the barn needed repairs. Certain circumstances made it necessary that Lotten soon be provided with a room of her own, one warmer in winter and better than the one hitherto used in the daytime by all of us as our common living room. We therefore built a small addition to our cabin, and over all of it we laid a new shingle roof. We proceeded in this fashion: we tore off the old board roof on one side of the house, and after it had been replaced with shingles, we repeated the process on the other side. In this way we had as we went along some shelter on one side of the house, though insufficient against rain and storms. My state of anxiety during this time cannot be described. It was only by divine grace that Lotten, frail, strengthless, and in the condition she was in, was able to stand all these privations.

Besides her we had another sick person in the house, a student named Björkander [2] from Västergötland, who together with a couple of other Swedes had taken possession of a piece of ground in our neighborhood. While they were cutting and hauling logs for their cabins, they lived in a hut made out of brushwood. Owing to carelessness and over-exertion Björkander fell ill. His illness, serious in itself, was made still more so by the nature of the instruments used in a surgical operation performed on him. One can imagine for oneself what they were like when a rough whetstone and my old razor strop were employed to sharpen them. I hope I need never again witness such torture.

"What do you imagine Professor Bergstrand [3] in Uppsala would say if he were present at the operation?" I asked Polman, who was assisting the physician who had been called in to perform the surgery.

"He would have kicked both of us out," was Polman's reply.

What is certain is that even if he had not ousted the two surgeons he certainly would have thrown out their instruments. Meanwhile we bade farewell in this life to poor Björkander, who courageously went to meet his fate. Yet in spite of the cutting, carving, and sewing, he recovered in due time, and the successful operation,

331

which was rumored far and wide in the neighborhood, gave Polman and the other physician a great reputation as surgeons.

Björkander, however, remained sick in bed in our attic for a long time. Since it was impossible to remove him from there, we tried to protect him from drafts and rain as well as we could by hanging blankets and skins around his bed.

Our shingles cost us many sacrifices and even much time, for we had to buy them in Milwaukee, where they were shipped in from the inexhaustible pine and cedar forests on the northern shores of Lake Michigan. These shingles are generally eighteen inches long and vary in width from four to ten inches. At the upper end they are very thin while at the lower they are about a quarter of an inch thick. They are sold in bundles, now at a much higher price than then. Every bundle contains five hundred shingles, with the thin ends laid on top of each other and pressed together hard in the center by a frame which keeps them together and prevents them from warping as they are drying in the sun. The roofs are not laid as in Sweden, where narrow splints are placed in several layers on top of each other, but in single straight rows, with great care taken to see that the chinks between the shingles are always at the middle of the shingle underneath. In this way row after row, together with the small nails used to fasten the shingles to the horizontally running furring strips, is completely covered by the succeeding layer. These roofs, commonly used, sometimes even in the big cities, look very neat and trim, and prove very durable. The shingles are neither tarred nor painted, but are left in their natural color.

For roofing and other building work we were obliged to get help, among others from a former Swedish sailor who was spending some time in our neighborhood and whose assistance proved most welcome. This man, like so many of his trade, had upon arriving in an American port several years ago deserted his ship and without the least knowledge at first of the country and its language, had traveled and shifted about from one place to another. Sometimes he had worked in New Orleans, sometimes in New York, sometimes in the West. When he had worked long enough in one place to collect a month's wages, he would spend them in traveling to some other place.

For such perambulating laborers harvest time is a golden season when wages are high and farmers have difficulty in getting the help they need. I hardly know what sort of man it would be that could not count on employment and earnings then. After working on various farms our Swedish sailor had now earned a sum of ready cash for travel and was preparing, not to pack up his possessions, for he had no baggage to pack, but as usual to depart for some other market. When he heard of the Swedish settlement at Pine Lake, he decided, however, for the sake of our common nationality, to remain a bit longer than he generally did in one place.

As far as this man was concerned, he belonged to the numerous class of European immigrants who, reared in humble circumstances and accustomed to a subordinate place in society, consider themselves here perfect masters, or rather they recognize no masters at all. According to their notion, true liberty consists in doing what one wants to and in any way one pleases. Equality, to their minds, means nothing but obliterating all class distinctions. When W.[4] spoke Swedish it made no difference to him whether he addressed barons or journeymen, maids or matrons: all were addressed by the same intimate *du*,[5] which he, like many others, considered a literal translation of the English *you*. Religiously, he had a strong leaning to Mormonism, which was beginning to win a number of adherents in this section of the country.

With the assistance of this man and a couple of other workmen, we managed to get our roof relaid, and to our great joy were enabled even in rainy weather to walk dry-shod on our living-room floor, likewise relaid and tightened. The addition, of which mention has been made, consisted of a small, light, pleasant room, with the interior of the logs evened and lined with boards. Two small windows were also installed. The floor was laid with dry linden boards sawed from logs that we ourselves had cut and hauled to the sawmill. Through this addition the attic was also enlarged and made roomier. A regular stairway was built to take the place of the ladder from which everyone of us had at one time or another fallen down and almost broken our legs. The small conveniences that these and other improvements afforded, insignificant as they may appear, had for us an inestimable value because of the inconveniences we had known. What it meant to

333

sleep under a tight roof and walk on a steady floor only a man can completely appreciate who frequently has been wet by leaking rain and snow or who has been in danger of tumbling headlong over rough boards.

We came near paying dearly for waiting with our building project till so late in the fall. This year Indian summer came earlier than usual and did not last long. Then winter began with a severity and violence such as had never been known in this section. As early as November 10 we not only had perfect sledding, but in spots the snow lay as much as two feet deep. Fortunately we had by that time managed to get our addition ready, and Lotten was safely ensconced in a comparatively warm room. The hewing and pounding at the corners and walls had loosened much of the chinking and mudding in the older cabin, however, and made it fall out, and before we were able to close up the openings, one of those sudden changes in temperature occurred. In less than twenty-four hours the thermometer dropped from more than thirty degrees above to fourteen below zero. Using boiling water we sought to mix some mortar to tighten the cracks as far as possible. But as late as November 27, when the critical hour came for Lotten, the outer room was so cold that the milk froze on the table where, clad in fur coats, we sat eating our evening meal.

As long as I live I shall never forget that night, which we hardly thought Lotten would live through. More than anything else it made me realize the anxieties and dangers of pioneer life, when one's previous mode of living has not sufficiently inured one to hardship. How often I thought of the old home and the maternal care which there would have been given her who now herself was to become a mother for the first time, far separated from all her nearest relatives, without the assistance of any woman experienced in such matters, lying in a lonely cabin in the wilderness, barely protected from the cold night wind, which with a frightful vehemence whipped around the corners and made it necessary the whole time to keep the stove red hot.

To get out of doors in such weather was no child's play. The snow had whirled together into deep drifts, and most people would have insisted that the road, even in ordinary circumstances difficult to travel, was now entirely impassable. In the coal-black night, lighted by no star, we heard the storm breaking off the ice-covered branches of trees; but in spite of everything Carl took his lantern and set out for the homes of two settlers living close together about a mile from our house. Here a couple of American families had settled during the summer. The women had visited my wife a couple of times and had volunteered to help when the time should come that was now filling us all with anxious worry. Carl went, therefore, to look for them and ask them to come to our aid, but could we expect them to start out afoot on such a night and in such cold as this?

These women nowise belonged to the educated, or the so-called better, class. Rather, in their conversation they many times gave evidence of both vulgarity and lack of feeling. One might have thought them a feminine version of the principal trait in the American character as that is commonly conceived, namely, selfishness, indifference to anything not to one's own interest or profit, unconcern for the misery and misfortunes of others unless relieving them would somehow be to one's own advantage. Yet under the hard surface there was hidden here, as appeared upon many another occasion, a warm, perfectly unselfish sympathy for others; and not only sympathy, but decision, resolution, sacrifice — qualities perhaps more pronounced in American women than among any other people. Of these we were now to have our first evidence, the first of many which we recall always with humble gratitude and respect.

There is a general notion abroad that Americans as a rule take no interest in anything but money. "Where two or three talk together," we read in travel stories by Hauswolff and other tourists of his kind, "be it in saloon, church, street, theater, or market place — in a word, anywhere within the republic — one is certain to hear among the first expressions to reach one's ear the magical word *dollar*, the motto of the American people, the only divinity that in reality they worship. It occupies them to the exclusion of every other concern."

No judgment could be more unjust. Granted that the word *dollar* is often heard in the street and in public places; but is that so strange in a country where the things that characterize our age wherever society is organized — business, industry, and a life of

335

affairs in which the individual's interests are more and more inseparable from the general — have had an opportunity more than elsewhere to flourish and develop? To be sure, "whereof the heart is
full the mouth speaketh," but if we are to give that statement a
universal application, what about our own native country? What
is to be thought the watchword of our people, and what god shall
it be said we worship? Listen to two or three of our own countrymen meeting in a house, the street, or the market place, and not
in one out of a hundred times will there fail to be heard among
the first words an oath, an invocation of the devil, a prayer to
whole legions of evil spirits. Are we to judge the Swedish people
in everything from this bad national habit, not to say national sin?
If not, let the Americans speak of their dollars! They like to make
them, that is true, but often they take as much pleasure in giving
them away as in earning them. No nation is less greedy than the
American. A really worth-while cause can generally count on the
support of an American; a destitute or needy person seldom turns
away empty-handed from his door; and when doing a good deed
is in question, no one is more willing than he to sacrifice time and
labor, to him the same thing as money, which otherwise he might
appear to spend exclusively in building up the temple of his own
fortune. So I, at least have come to know the American, with all
his great faults — and what people is without them? — with all his
inclination to luxury and extravagance, with all his desire for gain,
and with all the levity with which he sometimes throws himself
into the most daring speculations, like a gambler always doubling
his stake to gain more yet, till he finally loses all and ruins both
himself and others.

The American woman as well as the man engages in practical
affairs more here than in any other country, and therefore it seems
many times that she is cold, calculating, and alien from all tender
feelings. But where another weeps and complains, she acts; where
another only expresses pity for an unfortunate, "Too bad about
the poor fellow!" she may not utter a single word, but if she can,
she goes and helps the one in need. So it is also in religious matters.
True enough, one finds in America much, yes, very much, false
and sentimental religious display. Yet whatever there is that may
be justly condemned — however many are the religious errors,

often even horrible and morally shocking ones — nevertheless one witnesses there in the whole general trend a true practical Christianity, "that faith which worketh by love."

A notable example of this was given by the aforementioned women on the occasion that I have just been speaking of. They left their men at home alone to take care of the small children, and without hesitation followed Carl into the dark, stormy, cold night, walking through snowdrifts waist-deep, to the dwelling of almost complete strangers, to perform their duty as true Christian mothers. Carl declared that this was the hardest walk he had ever taken in his life, and he could not but admire his companions not only for not turning back at their very first steps, but still more for persisting in toiling on to their goal.

In anticipation of what was to take place Polman had kindly remained with us for a few days. Next to God I have him and the courageous women to thank that my wife survived that night and that I had the joy the next morning as a father of holding a beloved child in my arms.[6] For several hours during the night Polman thought the one outcome was to be as little hoped for as the other.

The cold in Wisconsin may become as keen as in the central part of Sweden, but it is seldom of long duration. After two or at most three days there is generally a turn to milder weather. So it was in this instance, and we made good use of the change by finishing our repairs. Farmer, physician, shoemaker, sailor — each in his place was busy at it.

Some months earlier Mr. Breck, of whom I have already made mention, along with two other missionaries of the Protestant Episcopal Church, had moved to a place only about three miles from our home. There, in an enchanting spot, on the shore of one of the beautiful lakes that here lie close to each other, they had built their unpretentious dwelling with their own hands. A section of land had been purchased for the church; there they were planning to build a chapel and establish a school, and from this as a central point extend their missionary labors.[7]

A prevailing notion about ministers in the Far West — the pioneer preachers, if I may call them that — is that they are mostly uncultivated, ignorant persons from the lower classes who, unsuited to any other calling or often unfortunate financially, have chosen the ministry, as one chooses any other trade, for the sake of a livelihood. There is an idea that they are men who could not be expected to succeed in a better civilized, better organized community where there would be greater demand for culture and education; they therefore have selected as their field of labor the faraway forests or prairies, where the wild Indians have had to make room for a class of whites that in customs and culture are not far above them. It is nevertheless an entirely false conception. It may be true that America has sects whose preachers are, in a manner of speaking, picked up from the street. Whether they appear in a New York meeting house or in a settler's cabin, they betray the same lack of both humanistic and theological training, alleging that the call and the enlightenment of the spirit are all that is required for the work they have taken upon themselves to do. But in general this is not so, at least in that denomination with which Providence ordained I should be intimately related. The three missionaries at Nashotah were the best evidence of this. What I have already said of Mr. Breck holds good also for the other two. Their standing in the community, their family connections, the complete education they had enjoyed, and the knowledge they had acquired would surely have opened the way to an easier and economically more profitable place in one of the eastern states. But their own inward prompting and calling had impelled them to settle in what was practically a wilderness, there to fight, with toil and renunciation, the good fight of faith, and under conditions far from favorable and encouraging do the work of Him that had sent them.

A few times before I had found occasion to visit them, and I now set out for their ministerial settlement to ask that one of them might administer Christian baptism to my newborn child. As on my first visit, they were still their own servants, doing their own housekeeping. It was most refreshing to have an opportunity to converse with them and to enter their newly plastered and tastefully furnished living quarters, where everything was extremely simple. A couple of plain writing tables, a half dozen black-painted wooden chairs, and a big bookcase — really the only decoration in the room — in which a few hundred well-bound volumes were lined up, made me feel that I had been removed to a neat, pleasant student chamber in Uppsala, as one of these used to be funished. This was their reception room, and at the same time their common sitting and dining room; so far it was also their church, in which they read the morning and evening prayers prescribed by the Anglo-American ritual, though these were seldom attended by others than themselves. A few yards from their house, however, building materials had been collected and a beginning made toward a chapel to be erected as soon as the weather permitted.

Nearby was one of those small Indian mounds that, where they have not been cut up and leveled by the white man's plow, may perhaps in a few years be the only memorials of the original inhabitants of the country. Who was resting under this one? Nobody knows. Perhaps it hid the remains of a former mighty chief, of a great tribe now like himself vanished from the earth or driven from the graves of their fathers, fleeing farther toward the setting sun, to go out, to die in its last rays. The ministers had had a fence built around the little mound, that in the shadow of the cross-surmounted Christian temple the bones of the heathen might molder in peace, till all that are in the grave shall hear the voice of the Son of God.

Mr. Breck took me around the level oak land close to the shore of the small lake. Even in its winter dress the lake was beautiful, surrounded by a frame of oak-covered hills and valleys. Between these, now that the trees were bare, could be seen eight other lakes, some of them from one-half to two miles in length, the otherwise mirror-like waters of which were locked now under snow-covered ice.

As Mr. Breck and the other ministers showed me the beautiful locality, they acquainted me with their plans for future buildings. Here a farmhouse was to be erected, there a building to house kitchen and dining room, there another to serve as a dormitory for future students, there an auditorium, and so on.

There are examples enough, one might almost say daily, of cities with their factories, great hotels, and well-stocked stores springing up between the tree stumps as if by witchcraft. I was inclined to doubt, however, that the extension of the kingdom of Christ and the establishment of church institutions would be a miracle as easy to accomplish as the building of a mercantile and industrial kingdom. In the latter sphere the wilderness would soon blossom like a rose; but was it likely that in the former the same growth would come to pass? But if "all things are possible to them that believe," there was really reason to hope that the plans of these missionaries would be realized, and that the church bell already suspended from a branch of an ancient oak would with its iron tongue soon proclaim to the surrounding countryside the daily hours of prayer. Then a host of young men would gather here in a consecrated temple to obtain power and grace to go forth into the world and proclaim the gospel of peace far and wide after they had completed their training.

From a worldly point of view the prospects for the success of such an undertaking did not appear particularly bright. In this section they had met with little or no sympathy, at least of a kind that would lead to financial support. The members of the Episcopal Church living in the neighborhood were few and poor, and like most of their neighbors they had settled in the West because they had no wealth. Against this church, furthermore, there prevailed then, as always among people generally, many prejudices. These expressed themselves often in an animosity more quarrelsome and bitter than what at times discovers itself among other groups of different faiths. The episcopal government and its public confession that "the Church of England, to which the Protestant Episcopal Church in these States is indebted under God for her first foundation and a long continuance of nurturing care and protection" [a] make it regarded in many places as an English state institution, or at least an anti-democratic institution, which, though the United States is independent, persists in maintaining its loyalty to the former mother country. Added to this are the traditions of older American sects whose less well-informed adherents imagine that the English Church is essentially the same as the Roman Church except for the pope. All they know of its long history is the stories of constraint and persecution it is supposed to have practiced according to the histories published by these sects. Hence they look with suspicion and prejudice on its American daughter-church, which, however, is flourishing more and more.

A spirit of prejudice is especially prevalent in the West, where, even were financial conditions more favorable, the three young missionaries could not hope to win much immediate encouragement for their work. Their hope for support was entirely in voluntary contributions by local churches in the East, but of such contributions they had absolutely no guarantee. In a country where everything that is to be done to promote religion and the Church is dependent on contributions, for which the individual members are constantly receiving appeals, the success of an undertaking depends on the interest of these individuals in the cause. It is practically impossible, therefore, to count on any definite amount, especially when a new project such as this is planned. Poor and almost empty-handed, these three worthy ministers had begun this fine undertaking, at considerable sacrifice to themselves, without knowing where they were to get funds to carry out their plans. Of one thing they were assured: it was to be carried out in the name of the Lord.

This undertaking was entirely a venture in faith, just as they had based their entire life and future on a strong, immovable trust in God. I could only with admiration listen to the story of their labors for the future institution which by faith they saw already established in the wilderness. It was a story told in Christian humility and with no trace of human pride or vainglory. Yet my feeling was not merely one of admiration for the human tools. Through their example my own heart was strengthened in my faith in Him who had chosen them to lay the foundation of a work that in His own good time He would grant them the means to finish. An inward voice told me then that the small seed sown here would be watered by the rain of heaven and protected by Him who gives growth, and would develop into a glorious tree, supplying fruit and protection to those who should resort to it from all lands.

A few days later Mr. Breck came to our cabin as I had asked him to. The Scandinavian settlement was not too large to make it possible for all to gather there to share our joy at the birth of the first Swedish-American child, and to serve as witnesses at his baptism, the first infant baptism, as far as I know, to be administered in that region.[8] At least, according to Mr. Breck, neither he nor either of his fellow ministers had been called upon in this part of their missionary district to officiate at such a rite, which he declared was one that more than any other filled his heart with joy and thanksgiving.

In passing it is worth mentioning here that infant baptism not only is in general postponed too long but has gradually been neglected altogether, even by Christian sects that according to their own confessions accept it as, if not a necessary, at least a proper rite. The Methodists and the Presbyterians, for instance, who according to their original forms of confession, still retained at least in the letter, ought not to be lax or indifferent with regard to infant baptism, are in practice more and more approaching the Baptists in this matter. That they should do so is a natural consequence both of the Calvinistic doctrine of election and of the low estimation of the sacrament itself that is becoming more and more evident in the pedobaptist denominations, according to which Christian baptism is not a washing of regeneration, and consequently not a sacrament at all, but an empty ceremony.

Some have accepted a theory recently propounded by a theologian of great reputation. He holds that in the heart of the child there is written a law against which even in its earliest years it can sin intentionally, that even before its birth it may belong to those destined to eternal damnation. From this it naturally follows that a child must not be baptized until it has given evidence of repentance and conversion. Others again have accepted the popular Pelagianism to the effect that since a child is not born with a sinful nature, it is not in need of baptism for the forgiveness of sin. This doctrine, though diametrically opposed to the former, leads to the same result, the neglect of infant baptism. Again, there are those who faithfully and consistently cling to the Calvinistic doctrine of elect children as well as elect angels and older people. Since it is difficult, if not impossible, to determine whether or not a child belongs to the elect, this belief must necessarily diminish, as it has already fearfully done, the number of baptized children within the denominations that have accepted it, and must at length lead to a condition under which infant baptism among them will be entirely discontinued.

Furthermore, there are those who have fallen into the error of the Quakers who believe in a mystical, spiritual, invisible church. This heresy, which goes hand in hand with the new doctrine of holiness, has likewise spread; if consistently carried to its consequences, it, too, must undermine the doctrine of infant baptism and ultimately perhaps obliterate the last traces of it. Finally, infant baptism is crowded out by the kind of liberalism which considers it wrong to influence the religious faith of the child, holding it should be let alone till its mind has been developed far enough to enable it to make its choice among the sects, or, in other words, between Paul and Confucius, Christ and Belial. The neglect of infant baptism springing from this view is very common, not only among those who have not yet made their own choice and therefore have not joined any church congregation, but even among those who, professing to be church members, still consider it inconsistent with true Christian love to prefer one denomination to another and who maintain that they ought not in any way to seek to influence the religious views of anyone, not even their own children.

As far as the Presbyterian denominations are concerned, both common experience and statistics indicate that if infant baptism continues to be ignored in the future as it has been in the past fifty years, a hundred years from now the Presbyterian Church in America will no longer be a pedobaptist denomination. In reality it is already a semi-Baptist one. The ratio of the annual number of infant baptisms to its total membership is approximately one to twenty-five. In large churches of several hundred members the ministers often do not report more than six infant baptisms in the course of a year, in some cases only one.[b] Among other causes of the decline of infant baptisms among the Presbyterian congregations is the common practice of baptizing children only of parents admitted to Holy Communion. Since there are many who have been baptized in their early years into this denomination, and continue to profess belonging to it though they frequently bar themselves from the table of the Lord through indifference and still more frequently through their misdirected or deficient training, more than three-fourths of the children born within these churches are thus denied participation in the grace of baptism. To punish parents in their children; because the parents have sinned to refuse to the children for whom Christ has suffered death the only sacrament they are capable of receiving; to excommunicate them in this fashion, so to speak, from the atoning grace in Christ — that is a cruelty that even the Roman Catholic Church in its most tyrannical periods would have hesitated to exercise, being reserved for those who annually at Plymouth Rock celebrate the victory of light, liberty, and tolerance over all spiritual oppression and so-called clerical domination.

It would be well if those in Sweden who have recently begun to show such a preference and sympathy for Presbyterianism, both because of its church organization and because of the higher spiritual life said to flourish within its portals — it would be well if they were to note carefully these and other conditions prevailing in a country where Presbyterianism, entirely independent of the state and free from secular interference, has sat safely beneath its own fig tree, without hindrance working out the natural consequences of its system.

The Protestant Episcopal Church is practically the only Protestant church in America which on the basis of the Scriptures and historical Christianity, has retained the primitive doctrine of the holy sacrament of baptism and the primitive custom of consecrating the children thereby. It has earnestly combated the increasing neglect of it and the numerous false doctrines abroad regarding it. True, the doctrine and the practice of infant baptism are supported by a few local Lutheran churches; but as a general rule one may say that even the Lutheran Church in America, like many others, has departed from its original usage and confession. The General Lutheran Synod has declared that the articles of the Augsburg Confession relative to baptism as essential to salvation and relative to the imputation of original sin are among those not accepted and recognized by the Lutheran Church in America. According to one of its most distinguished theologians, there is not at this time more than one in five hundred of the members of this church that has accepted or ever will accept Luther's teaching in this respect.[c] As a natural consequence infant baptism is frequently neglected among its members, though not so commonly as among Presbyterian denominations.

In the Episcopal Church the beautiful custom of administering infant baptism at a public service before the entire congregation has been maintained. Exceptions to the custom are made only in frontier regions where the scattered members are few and have not yet been organized into a regular congregation or where, as in our neighborhood, no church building has been erected. Naturally an exception is also made where the child is ill. In such a case the minister administers private baptism, which later on, however, if the child recovers, is confirmed and attested before the congregation, when the sponsors are present to give their sacred pledges and in the name of the child make the promises asked for in the baptismal covenant. This custom is entirely proper. It prevents what is so common among us, the social gathering and the feasting that are entirely inconsistent with an occasion of such importance and solemnity, yet by many regarded as almost the most essential element of it. Through the diversion for which they give an opportunity, they tend to exclude among the sponsors and witnesses every consideration of the deep significance of the sacred act and of their own baptismal covenant, of which this baptism ought to remind them, inviting self-examination upon whether or not they have abided in it. Such baptismal and sponsorship feasts are not customary in America. Still, I was too much a slave to the usages common in my fatherland to permit an occasion of this kind to pass by without such entertainment as our economic conditions permitted.

Notes

[a] Introduction to the Book of Common Prayer used in the American Protestant Episcopal Church.

[b] When at a later time I was pastor for one year in an American church, there was in my congregation a young, well-educated lawyer who attended our services regularly, although he had joined no religious denomination. He told me that he was not baptized and that his father, in whose house he had been reared till he was twelve years old, had been a minister in the Presbyterian Church.

[c] Dr. S. S. Schmucker, professor of theology in the theological seminary of the Lutheran General Synod at Gettysburg, Pennsylvania. In support of his statement we refer to his book *The American Lutheran Church, Doctrinally and Practically Delineated*, as well as to statements of other authors about the Lutheran Church in America.

ONE day our old acquaintance Kee-wah-goosh-kum entered
our home quite unexpectedly. Several months had elapsed
since his last visit, when Carl, yielding to his insistent request, had lent him his rifle, which he had been coveting for a long
time. According to his promise the rifle was to be returned in a few
weeks. The time, however, had passed by, and we had heard nothing
from him. Carl began to believe that his royal rifle had become too
great a treasure in the armory of His Indian Majesty to permit the
return of it thence to its rightful owner. Now it was proved, though,
that the red man had not deceived his white brother's trust. Kee-wah-
goosh-kum returned the rifle in good shape, with its royal crown,
name, and other brass ornaments even more shining and polished
than when he had received it. With a few words, half of which
we could not understand, he sought to explain the reason for his
long absence. We could not make out whether he merely had
been on a hunt in some faraway wilderness or whether he had been
sounding his war whoop in the forest against hostile tribes. The

way in which he pointed to the gun and to the tomahawk in his belt could have indicated the one thing as well as the other. Possibly King Fredrik's rifle had been used in more dangerous pastimes than formerly at the royal pleasure hunts on Lovön.[1]

Once again the Indian chief with part of his tribe had pitched his camp a few miles north of Pine Lake, where he remained longer this time than usual. During his stay we got to be on such a friendly footing with each other that we went on a hunting party together — a favor that an Indian seldom shows a white man.

The Great Spirit, they say, has taught white men to live without hunting and has taught them to make all they need. To Indians on the other hand, he has taught nothing but hunting. Hunting was showed to them as their only means of livelihood. They must hunt if they are not to starve to death. White men, they say, have therefore no right to hunt.

It was easy to see that there was an abundance of deer in the neighborhood, and we promised ourselves rich rewards under the direction of so experienced a hunter. The ground, though, was covered with deep snow, so that it was impossible to make much progress either in the woods or on the plain without snowshoes. Kee-wah-goosh-kum therefore supplied us each with a pair, made from narrow hickory splints bent together at the ends in an elliptical shape, like the bows used in playing shuttlecock, but much bigger. As with them thongs or laces are pulled crosswise from one side to the other of the frames. The foot is put within a leather strap and rests on a couple of cross pieces, which also serve to make the shoe firm and steady. Those unaccustomed to this type of footgear are inclined to be somewhat clumsy and ungainly in their movements. In an attempt to walk with the shoes, I realized why the Indian warrior from his early childhood is made to walk with his feet straight forward. If my heels sometimes tangled with each other so that I tumbled in the snowdrift, it was a result of the dancing lessons I took once upon a time from old man Ambrosiani.[2]

After walking for an hour, Kee-wah-goosh-kum told us to separate and go in different directions, which meant that the hunt was now to begin. A small lake in the woods was appointed as our meeting place. There, he made us understand, he was to meet with a few other Indians, who had already set out for the place and were now serving as links in the hunting chain he was trying to have us form. This was a disappointment to me; for the great and the only pleasure I had anticipated from the whole hunt was to be in the company of the Indian and witness the skill with which he doubtless would locate the game and then shoot it. But this our chief would not permit. With signs which we understood better than his words, he indicated the direction each one of us was to take, and told us, if we discovered any deer tracks, to follow them, try to catch up with the animals, and do our best. If a fresh track is discovered, to follow is not very difficult even for an inexperienced hunter, provided he does not tire. In the deep snow it is hard for the deer to escape their pursuers. Their small feet and slender, delicate legs sink deep into the snowdrifts, preventing them from leaping as easily and swiftly as usual. The hunter on his snowshoes is then able to get close to them. The Indians, who are used to this kind of hunting, save their ammunition on such occasions, throw themselves upon their quarry, and cut off the sinews of their hind legs.

The reason why the Indian would not continue the hunt in our company may have been that he did not wish to initiate us into his hunting secrets, or else that he considered us perfect greenhorns who did not understand the job we had undertaken. Whatever the reason, we felt that for the sake of our friendship we must follow his directions. Bergwall, who like a mighty hunter found himself greatly interested in the sport, started off in one direction, Carl in another, and it fell to my lot to walk across a small ice-covered lake to try my luck on the other shore. Which way the chief went was hard to say. In a few moments he disappeared like another spirit of the woods.

It is one thing to hunt rabbits on fresh-fallen snow in Sweden, but to race deer on snowshoes in the wilderness is a pleasure that from now on I shall gladly let others enjoy. Though I lose my reputation as a hunter, I must still confess the truth, not put the blame on bad luck as is customary after a fruitless hunt. To be sure, I found tracks — deep tracks — and it seemed to me that the deer had had as much trouble making their way through the snow as I on my shuttlecock bows; but in spite of that, they kept their distance. I noted with satisfaction, however, that most of the tracks led in the direction where my hunting companions were posted, and I hoped in the course of time to drive the quarry right into their arms. The end of the hunt proved that in this respect I may not have been entirely useless.

I was nevertheless not to be quite without my share of the game. Dragging a lynx that had come lumbering along only a few steps from me, and carrying a couple of pheasants in my hunting bag (which I was afraid to show my Indian friends, who would, no doubt, have considered it beneath their dignity, except in necessity, to waste powder on such tiny game), I was the first to arrive at our meeting place. Now and then I heard gunshots in the distance. While waiting for my companions, I made a fire and skinned the lynx, and, tired out, sat down to rest and recover my strength for the return march. Though we had a considerable distance to walk, I still preferred putting on my snowshoes and starting for home to spending the night in the woods or in an Indian wigwam.

Not so my companions, who came one by one, all of them in good humor. They were all in favor of bivouacking around the campfire in order to start their hunt again early in the morning. Carl, who rarely if ever returned empty-handed from a hunt, had succeeded in killing a buck, Indian fashion, after first cutting off the tendons of its hind legs — an adventure in the snowdrifts he had found very stimulating, though one arm and shoulder for a long time carried blue marks as a memento of his adventure. Bergwall, in true Swedish hunting fashion, had aimed his trusty rifle at two deer. His first shot had brought down one, one of the biggest we had seen, weighing at least 220 pounds. His second had merely wounded the quarry, which Kee-wah-goosh-kum managed to bring to the ground. How many he and the rest of the Indians had killed we did not find out. Very probably, however, their bags were a good deal bigger than that of the rest of us put together. For our part, we were well satisfied with the result of the hunt.

However romantic it might have been to spend the night in the woods with our red friends, we finally agreed to return home. The sun had set by the time we had finished our evening meal around the campfire. In our Swedish hunting bags, which the Indians found amusing and thought very strange — they called them *skipetaguns* — we had brought along a little food which they in particular enjoyed very much. Even the hunting bottle was part of our supply, and for the first and last time I treated an Indian to whiskey. We all shared it equally. The amount we had with us was no more than each one could stand or than he needed after the exertions of the hunt and in the cold winter night. It was also the only time I can recall when this liquor, otherwise loathsome and vile to my taste, had ever impressed me as tolerably palatable as we drank it diluted with snow water and sweetened with sugar. But the Indians expressed their satisfaction with the undiluted drink by a protracted and emphatic "Ugh!" whereupon they started off on their march in deep silence. The night was so clear and starlit that even we might have found our way out of the woods without difficulty. As the Indians knew better how to find the easiest and shortest route, however, we let Keewah-goosh-kum walk ahead, the rest of us following, as is customary when the Indians are on the march, in single file. The silence finally became so boring that Bergwall began to sing in his deep and full voice one of the hunting songs of his friend Wadman,[3] whereupon the three of us made the forest re-echo with Atterbom's beautiful Hunters' Song and found with Florio that "even hunting and winter have their glories." [4]

A couple of days later we paid a visit to the Indian encampment. Up to that time we had watched it only from a distance. The first thing that attracted our attention was several small brown human beings who, in spite of the biting cold, were jumping stark naked from one fallen tree trunk to another or clambering and twining themselves around the snowy branches. Had it been summer, we might have imagined ourselves removed to the wilds of Africa among a flock of monkeys. What the dance of the naked children among the snowdrifts was all about, whether they were merely playing or were searching for some scraps of food for themselves or the lean, shivering horses keeping them company, we could not make out. When they jumped down to the ground, they tossed down in front of them a few big flat pieces of bark, on which they walked to avoid stepping into the snow with their bare feet. Before we knew it, we were surrounded by a flock of these small human snow sparrows, who without a doubt regarded us with greater curiosity than we them. Between the children and their patches of bark, we made our way to the nearest wigwam.

The camp consisted of about twenty of those movable dwellings, erected without any visible order in this as yet unsettled part of the forest. Some of them appeared to have been constructed with greater care than others. But all were such that it would not take many minutes either to make or break camp. To make one a few long, slender tree trunks, or poles, were placed in a circle, stuck about two inches into the ground, with their tops bent inward and fastened together so as to leave a round opening between them. Over these poles were laid either big pieces of bark or mats plaited from reeds or bast, so constructed and placed over each other that they excluded, if not cold and drafts, at least rain and snow. These tents resembled ordinary beehives, with an opening at the top to allow the smoke to escape from the fireplace at the center. There, too, we found a number of small children crawling in and out through the tent openings, in appearance as lean and hungry as the dogs with whom they were sharing their miserable food. These dogs looked just as strange as their owners and like them as though they belonged to a barbaric race — small, long-haired creatures, the shape of their heads something between that of a wolf and of a fox, rather than an ordinary dog's. These and the children were the only ones that seemed to pay any special attention to our arrival.

At first we saw no men. A number of women were busy cutting down some linden and small walnut trees, whose tender branches and buds often constitute in winter the only food for their horses. We stopped for a while to watch these creatures, also small and insignificant-looking, who during the cold winter had to spend day and night under the open sky. Now they were carefully watching every stroke of the axes, wielded with skill by the women, who appeared to be strong and well accustomed to this kind of work. As soon as a tree fell to the ground the horses rushed forward to feed from its top.

We found only women working, for the woman is the one that performs the work in an Indian camp. The man hunts and fights; when he returns to his wigwam he devotes himself to his naturally lazy and idle life. The woman is his slave and has to serve him.

Even the game he shoots in the woods she must bring home on her back or in any other way she can. As they move about from place to place, it also falls to her lot to carry on her shoulders whatever utensils are needed for cooking or used otherwise in the wigwam, if a place cannot be found for them on the back of the horse. Like the horse, she is a draft animal, and hers is not always the lightest burden. The man carries only his gun and other hunting equipment. When the tribe encamps, it is the woman that has to shovel away the snow, pitch the tent, gather fuel, and make the fire. Not till all this is done, following her long, wearisome walk, may she sit down and thaw out her moccasins. When they break camp, it is her duty to pack together the mats, hides, and provisions, and place them together with the children either on the horse's back or her own.

We realized we could look for no invitation to enter. An Indian knows no ceremony. He is not wanting in hospitality, but if a person does not enter his wigwam unbidden, he will be left outside in the cold. No one bids a stranger welcome. Once within the wigwam, he takes whatever place may be found. If the guest is hungry and has a taste for half-raw meat, he is welcome to cut a chunk from the slabs hanging in the tent or help himself to something from the boiling pot. No one urges him to do so; but no one objects when he helps himself to what is available, no matter how scant the supply.

We lifted up one of the mats I have mentioned, fastened at its upper end to a cross piece and draped in front of the doorway, and went, or rather crawled, into one of the tents. Inside, the snow had been carefully swept away from the ground, which was covered with deer or buffalo skins. In the middle of the tent was a small path, or aisle, on either side of which the members of the family had their resting places. In an Indian wigwam, which is generally the home of from six to eight persons, not counting the children, each one has his definite place, sacred to himself, on which no one else is permitted to encroach. In the middle of the tent is the fireplace, from which ascends a suffocating smoke. At this time it would have made it impossible for us to remain long in that hovel, which in every way was miserable and unclean.

Just as a person, in general, is known by his home life, so only from the life in the wigwam can one learn to know these children of the wilderness. The reticence that the Indian always observes cannot in his own dwelling, as it does when he is on the hunt or is a guest in a white man's house, prevent a close observer from catching a glimpse of his inner life. Though he himself persists in keeping perfectly silent, the objects he is surrounded with and the conditions of his natural environment speak. Within the wigwam we found a number of human beings, some of them seated, some lying prone around the fire, resting on their elbows. Some were wrapped in dirty and in many cases ragged blankets; others were stark naked. In their entire personality, both men and women gave expression to that dullness of spirit and tendency to drift characteristic of the Mongolian race. The men were not so tall as those of the Winnebago tribe, nor did they have so bold and manly an appearance. The facial type, however, was the same, and in spite of the craggy face and the dull look, even here, as in all Indians, was a flame in the eyes that seemed able not to warm but just to consume. Watching an Indian's eyes one feels as if standing before a dead volcano which, however, may be ready for a new eruption at any moment and may bury one under its streams of lava. Their black, matted hair, adorned, as is the custom, with eagle's feathers and similar ornaments, was hanging down over their faces. The women had in their appearance and personality something more kind and pleasing. Some of them would, perhaps, even have been beautiful had they only washed away the red and black paint that without showing the least sense of beauty, they, like the men, had daubed their faces with.

As we entered their hut, we noticed especially two groups that often, even in the homes of white people, unfortunately appear side by side. One was a scene from the story of intemperance; the other an illustration of the domestic troubles and sorrows that women suffer.

Prostrate on the deer skins in one corner of the hut was a naked Indian warrior, not our friend Kee-wah-goosh-kum, but, as we learned later, another of the chiefs of the tribe. Immediately after we had entered he rose to his full length, but the way in which he did it and the few uncertain steps he took before he sank, or rather fell, down by the fireplace, showed clearly that he was drunk. Casting a savage glance at the strangers, he screamed forth a single word, "Whiskey," the first articulate sound to reach our ears after arriving in the Indian camp — a sound that signifies the life motto of the present-day Indian race and the theme of their swan song, already begun, soon to be completed.

Not far from the drunken man, a woman was crouched with a naked child in her arms. She was still young, but suffering and sorrow had already plowed deep furrows in her otherwise not ugly face. Her child was sick. It spoke a language — the inherited tongue of the human race, alike wherever there is a cradle, the same in the home of the civilized as in the tent of the nomad, as easily understood by the European as by the Indian. It was moaning, and its plaint presaged death, soon to come and put an end to its brief pilgrimage, to carry it to the Great Spirit whom all of us worship and in whose house are many mansions. Even here mother love was true to itself; under its influence her savage expression melted away. What was to be seen was only the sorrow of motherhood, not the dark color of her skin, though the tears that sorrow in such circumstances puts in a white mother's eyes could only be glimpsed, as it were, behind these, for an Indian always seeks to repress his emotions. But in the life of this wild people there is nothing that evokes a more genuine sympathy and a more vivid expression of sorrow than the death of a child. Formerly they often sought to make up for such a loss by stealing and bringing up a white child, but such cases now occur very seldom. In the hut there were two small children in addition to the dying baby. Each of them was lashed securely to its cradle, if we may give that name to the flat block of wood, slightly hollowed out in the center, that had a small cross piece at one end as a rest for the feet and as protection for the head a piece at the other end resembling a barrel hoop with a bit of padding.

As soon as a baby is born, it is tied to such a wooden block, and thus accoutered it is carried from place to place, generally in an upright or slightly slant position. If the baby is a girl, a little moss is placed between her heels to train her to walk inward with her toes; if it is a boy, the moss is so arranged as to train his feet to walk straight forward. In order that the child may be carried, a braid or string is fastened to the upper end of the cradle and placed across either the forehead or the chest of the mother, who must carry the child on her back along with the rest of her load when the tribe is on the march. When taken down from her back, it is placed with its cradle leaning against a tent pole or is hung on a branch close to the fireplace. If a wigwam has not been erected or if the band is resting on the ground, the little one lashed to its cradle is left dangling on some tree in the forest. Should the branch snap or the string break or the child otherwise chance to fall, the cradle is so devised that the child can hardly be injured. These wooden blocks are decorated by the mother as best she knows how. A small bell or rattle is generally hung at the baby's head as a plaything; the cords used for trussing are often adorned with porcupine quills or glass beads so that what is lacking in comfort is compensated for by fineries. The little red young ones seem to be well pleased and satisfied with the hard, strait jackets in which they get their first lessons in patience, and are thus early inured to the hardships of nomadic life.

Attention has been called to the fact that in spite of what is hardly soft treatment, Indian children do not make nearly so much noise as our white babies, with all the care and tending the latter enjoy. They are seldom heard crying or screaming. Possibly, as a traveler remarks, they are made to realize from the very beginning that complaining does them no good, and so they learn early to repress their natural inclinations. This may explain the silence and taciturnity characteristic of the race.

The Indian woman, as is probably true among most primitive peoples, finds it easy to bear children. Her delivery makes no difference or change in the family plans for movement from one place to another. Only a few hours' delay is needed, after which the mother mounts a horse or walks afoot with her newborn child on her back. An example is reported of an Indian wife who went out into the woods to gather dry twigs for the fire, and after a while came back with a newborn child carefully carried on top of her bundle of twigs. This exception from the usual lot of womankind is one of the few advantages the savage woman enjoys over her civilized sisters.

As soon as a child is born, its paternal grandmother or some other older woman in the family gives it a name. A boy is generally named for some object in the air or the sky, such as "Light Cloud," "Son of Thunder," "Swift Lightning," or "Break of Day." It is also very common to name him for a bird, with some descriptive adjective. A girl, as a rule, is named for something on earth, something belonging to the vegetable world or the water, such as "Green Valley," "Brook in the Forest," or "Prairie Flower."

A marriage is, as a rule, entered into without any ceremonies or special observances. The approval of the parents is all that is necessary. When that has been given, the hunter brings the bride to his wigwam without further ado.

Boys are instructed in the arts of hunting and in war games at an early age. When a youth has killed his first game, a ceremonial meal is arranged, to which the braves and chiefs of the tribe are invited. When he has killed an enemy and taken his scalp, he is the hero in the wild scalp dance and is thenceforth counted among the warriors, or braves, of the tribe, with the right to use the tobacco pipe and to carry in his belt the *skipetagun* (tobacco pouch). From then on he is expected to provide for himself.

Among the customs and practices of the North American Indians, none are so unchangeable and serve so much to distinguish them as those connected with family life. However low many of these tribes may have sunk in moral ruin, family ties and blood relationships are held sacred. Their wanderings in the wilderness through centuries and their progressive decadence have not been able to sunder or weaken the laws of the blood tie or cool the spirit by which they have been kept sacred. That is all the more remarkable as polygamy is very common among them. Notwithstanding, family bonds are strong and indissoluble.

No earthly misfortune touches an Indian so deeply as the loss of a near relative; no one stands more disconsolate than he by the grave of his child. To assist a relative and come to his relief when he is in trouble or to avenge his death is a sacred family duty. There is, for instance, the story of the child taken captive by a hostile tribe and about to be burned to death with the rest of the prisoners. The father permitted himself to be captured to obtain the release of his son, voluntarily took his place, and was burned at the stake in order that his son might live.

Not long ago, shortly after Fort Snelling had been established as a frontier fortress in Minnesota, a white man was murdered by some Sioux Indians that were camping in the neighborhood. The commandant at the fort ordered that the guilty persons be given up to be punished, but the tribe refused to accede. Possibly the safety of the white people demanded that the crime should not go unavenged. At any rate, some Indians were captured and condemned to death, irrespective of their guilt. One of them was a warrior with a big family. His brother, who had neither wife nor children, came to the fort and offered to die in his place. This evidence of real nobility of character and supreme bravery, greater than many deeds for which men have been immortalized in history, could not appease the unyielding judges. His offer was accepted, the captured brother was released, but the judgment that had been pronounced was visited upon the other man, who together with the rest of the captives was shot to death by the soldiers. So strong among this people, with all their barbarism and cruelty, is the tie of blood, it is maintained and supported with such heroism, that we may well search in vain among civilized peoples for anything comparable.

Connected with this is the veneration which, as is well known, the Indian shows for the memory and the graves of his ancestors and relatives. If in a life with so many changes and temptations to decay there is anything sacred, it is this veneration for the memory of the departed. This feeling persists even after they have been driven from their former homes and forced to leave behind them the last dear spot where a simple grave holds the earthly remains of their dead friends. Many times before they vacate their lands and go to make new homes in some distant wilderness, they stipulate that the dust of their dead have undisturbed peace.

For a burial place they always select some beautiful spot, either on the high bank of a river or lake, on some hilltop from which there is a full view over the surrounding countryside, or on a small hillock in some sheltered and flowering valley. Their good taste in that respect has been noted and admired. In the grave together with the dead brave, they bury his weapons, clothes, and ornaments. None of the things he has possessed is so precious that after his death it does not still remain his own.

Before the corpse is interred, it is the custom to place it in an

357

open bark coffin on a high scaffolding resting on four posts driven into the ground; it is not removed until the flesh has completely moldered. Along river shores and on hills in distant sections such platforms standing side by side are often to be seen, and when one is aware of what is resting on the top they create an eerie atmosphere amid the quiet and the loneliness generally pervading such places. If the dead was a warrior, another pole is erected by the side of the platform. After a number of intricate funeral ceremonies, an orator arises and describes the life and deeds of the dead man, detailing how many enemies he has slain and similar exploits. All these things are inscribed on pieces of birch bark or cloth, and these memorial writings are fastened to the extra pole and left to flutter in the wind as long as the corpse is undergoing its change on top of the platform. After the funeral a mound of earth is piled up over the grave so that the place can easily be recognized.

It is natural among a people devoted to spirit worship, holding such beliefs as they, and venerating the dead, that these simple memorials should be the center of many superstitious customs and ceremonies. It should not surprise us if, lacking as they do the light of revelation, they have made of the memorial altars over their dead altars of sacrifice to insure happiness and blessings to the survivors.

In the wigwam the wife of the hunter is all-powerful and arranges everything that pertains to the household. It is her hand that prepares the simple repast with which her husband restores his strength on his return from a hunt or a battle. With the taciturnity characteristic of this people, he looks about for food. If he finds nothing to satisfy his hunger, if he sees no pot or piece of meat above the fire, he demands nothing; he understands that their food supply is exhausted. His hunger may be ever so great, no word of complaint ever crosses his lips, or the lips of any other member of the household. Each one assumes an appearance of absolute indifference, and through conversation, sometimes also through games and songs, they seek to direct their thoughts into other channels. Early the next day the father and the son go hunting, or if a white man's house is nearby, they will ask what they seldom if ever ask from each other — bread. Sometimes they may not be able to find any game for days, but if they succeed in shooting anything, even a small bird, it is immediately brought to the family hut to be shared by the members of the household. Sometimes the brave will even give up his own share in favor of the women and children. Many a time Indians have been found who, after failing in their hunt for days, have dropped to the ground from hunger and weakness and so have frozen to death. Generally the Indian lives for the day, unconcerned about how long his supplies will last; often he gives no thought to getting new supplies till everything is gone. This explains the terrible want and suffering to which this people often are submitted. For days they may have nothing to eat but the dried skins of animals killed earlier, which they have kept in the hope of selling them to some white fur trader; their hunger now compels them to hang these over the fire to singe off the hair, and afterwards the skin is roasted and devoured.

Following the winter and spring hunts, there is a time when the Indian devotes himself to pleasures and diversions. When the hunter's hand is full, he leaves his remote forests and prairies to seek the frontier and there trade his maple sugar, his hides and furs for the white man's goods. Now he rests up after the exertions of the hunting season and enjoys, often in too great a measure, the things he has been compelled to forego the rest of the year. Everywhere north of the forty-second parallel the woods and the hunting grounds by the first of June are forsaken, and the Indian braves with their wives and children gather in great numbers around the frontier forts and in the cities; or in the neighborhood of them, by some river or lake shore, they pitch their summer camps. At that time they enjoy a carnival season, during which the young men divert themselves with dances, ball games, and other sports; the elders sometimes counsel together about matters of general importance, but for the most part live in idleness and give themselves over to drunkenness and vice.

That is generally the time of year when the *medas, wabenoes,* and *jossakeeds* (sorcerers, prophets, and priests), of whom more hereafter, display their skills and invite the people to their mystic incantations and exhibitions, as a change from noisy pastimes. These, however, harmonize so perfectly with the Indian's feelings, desires, philosophy, and religion and so completely divert his thoughts from everything else that the summer months may be said to slip away unperceived, until finally at the coming of autumn the stern voice of need and hunger awakens him from his trance. He realizes that he must hunt and face new toils unless he is to starve to death. He must either go out into the wild forests or submit to want and degradation, which are the certain price he will have to pay for remaining longer in the vicinity of his white neighbors. Such is the annual circuit of the red man's life. He labors during the fall and winter that he may enjoy the spring and summer. He accumulates nothing but bitter experience, which tells him that life is only a perpetual series of struggles and severe trials and that he soonest will be happy who earliest is through with it. His religion gives him no definite assurance of a future life; hence he wearies early of the troublesome vicissitudes of his present one and is happy when he may lie down to an endless rest.

The tribes that reside at the frontiers are generally regarded as thievish and unreliable. As far as the second charge is concerned, they have so often experienced the deceitfulness and unreliability of the white man that it is hardly surprising if they have been infected thereby; in associating with the new masters of the country, they have accepted what they no doubt learn to regard as proper moral behavior. They are thievish, on the other hand, only when they are impelled by want and real need. I have already mentioned that while we were living in our first primitive hut, roving Indians might many a time have taken our guns, blankets, and other such things, but they never touched anything that was ours. In this respect, nevertheless, they are not to be depended upon, as we were soon to learn to our sorrow.

But when an Indian steals, he rarely does so on the sly. To be sure, he will not invite witnesses to his violations of other people's property, but he appropriates it with a certain frankness and cool assurance. From this one might conclude that such thefts, when they do occur, are based on a complete lack of comprehension of the meaning of property rights — an argument adduced in defence of the Indians — or rather on the principle in Indian ethics that any duplication of goods in a man's possession is a superfluity, which another, if he needs it, is entitled to take for himself without further circumstance. This notion makes the Indian himself very openhanded and liberal with things that he feels he has in abundance. If he has two things of one kind, he does not hesitate to supply the needs of a friend, without considering that he may soon be in want of it himself. It may have been due to such a principle that some Indians later on, during the winter, shared our haystacks, with the result that our cattle came near starving to death.

Of the origins of the Indian race nothing is known with certainty, nor of the time and manner in which they came to people the American continent. But from the period when they were first discovered, the North American Indians have always and everywhere displayed the same peculiar characteristics. Of all the races on earth there is probably none that has changed so little, none that has retained its type so perfectly, physiologically and psychologically, as this very one.

The American Indians of the nineteenth century are on the same level of mental development as those of the fifteenth. There has never been a people more impractical, more opposed to their own advancement, more deaf to all teaching, more inclined to cherish the elements conducive to their own destruction. Even where they have become more civilized, comparatively speaking, and more enlightened, they have persisted in propagating themselves as a race bound as by iron fetters to the same unchangeable type. In this continuous, undeviating, static condition, in this perpetual maintenance of the same mental attitudes, and in their adherence to hoary concepts and dogmas whose truth they have never shown the slightest inclination to examine, it has been thought an Oriental and Semitic origin can be discerned.

As full of mystery as is the past of this people, as plain and clear is their future, written in unmistakable language. Just as certain species of beasts have disappeared from the face of the earth, it seems that Providence has destined this race for extinction. We need but recall how from the moment Europeans first landed on American soil Indians have been pushed ever farther westward; how entire tribes, formerly strong and powerful, have vanished almost without a trace, despite the fact that they often have fought with the bravery of desperation, defending their possessions, inch by inch, against the encroachments of the white people. We recall how in Ohio and Illinois, which only a generation ago were the exclusive domain of the red men; how in Wisconsin, where during the first years of our residence it was just as common to meet an Indian as a white man; how in Missouri and Iowa and even the cultivated sections of Minnesota, which did not become a territory until 1849, an Indian is now as much of a rarity as a Laplander on the plains of Skåne. One need but follow the swift and continual withdrawal of this people toward the Rocky Mountains, where they are being crowded together between the eastward-expanding Pacific Ocean states and the new territories one after another being organized in the Mississippi Valley, to realize it cannot be long before the last Indian, a faithful replica of the first against whom the white man lifted the hand of Cain, will bury himself and his tomahawk in some concealed mountain cave.

"I see," said one of their chiefs not long ago, with true prophetic insight, looking into the future of his race, "I see the lords of the wilderness, my own people, driven from the land which their fathers have possessed ever since the sun rose in the east for the first time. Their dwellings stand empty, and the oaks that sheltered them from the heat of summer and the winter's cold, lie leafless on the ground. The graves of their fathers are plowed up, and the white man's dogs gnaw their bones. Tall buildings have been erected on the fields where once in peace they planted their corn. The glorious day of the Indian is long past. A few more winters and one will forget that he has lived. It will be asked, 'Was there really ever such a creature as the Indian?' The answer will be, 'I have heard so.'"

An Indian seldom grows very old. No matter how hardened he is from very childhood, the hardships and privations to which he is subjected and the vices to which he gives himself shorten his life. A hunter is old and feeble at the age of forty. Suicides are common among women, generally when by their elders they are forced to marry against their wishes. But what undermines the happiness of the Indians almost as much as the persecutions of the white people and conspires to wipe them from the face of the earth is firewater. Add to this the fearful havoc wrought among them almost every year by smallpox.

It is said that this disease broke out among them more generally around 1750, when some Indian tribes that supported the French in their war with the British were infected by it. Thereupon the disease spread more and more among the unfortunate people. For a time it seemed to have abated, but afterward it broke out again with greater vehemence among the tribes in the Mississippi Valley. The story of the outbreak of this scourge is connected with certain circumstances that may well be recorded as part of the history of the North American Indians. The facts are sufficiently confirmed and incontestable, no matter what may have been back of them.

In 1770 some Indians in Minnesota had committed acts of violence against certain fur traders and had robbed them of their goods. The authorities in Mackinac threatened them with reprisals unless they showed up there with the stolen goods. The Chippewa tribe sent a deputation and indemnified the white men for their loss, and thus the dispute was amicably settled. When the deputation was about to depart, it was presented with a keg of whiskey and a tightly furled flag, with strict orders not to open the keg or undo the bundle before coming home. The Indians obeyed the order. Not till they reached Fond du Lac, a city on the Mississippi, did they open the keg and unfurl the flag. Shortly thereafter, following several days of gluttony and drunkenness, smallpox broke out among them with such violence that all of the Indians in that region succumbed to it. Before long the devastating epidemic spread among all the tribes to the north and west of the place. All that remained of an entire tribe was a single small child. Even to this day the Indians believe that the white men punished them in this fashion for the crime they had committed, and that the contagious disease had been transmitted to them through the gifts they had received from the agents of the fur company in Mackinac.

Their irregular mode of life and addiction to strong drink have later tended to aggravate the disease. The descriptions of its ravages are horrible. A few years ago one tribe with a population of sixteen hundred, living in two villages, was reduced to thirty-one. A tribe numbering nine thousand was in one year completely annihilated. In a thousand wigwams belonging to still another tribe, with from six to eight persons in each wigwam, not one soul was left alive. Of other tribes a half or more of the population died.

An author who describes the ravages that smallpox caused in 1837 among the Indians around the Mississippi River says: "Many Arickarees, formerly handsome and stately in appearance, upon recovering their health committed suicide when they saw how they had been disfigured by the smallpox. Some of them leaped from high cliffs, others stabbed or shot themselves to death. The whole wide prairie has become an immense graveyard; wild flowers grow over Indian corpses. For several square miles the atmosphere is poisoned by the stench from hundreds of unburied bodies. Women and children wander about in hordes, starving and moaning among the dead bodies. Men flee in every direction. The proud, brave, and noble tribe is no more. Empty wigwams are to be seen on every hilltop. No sound but the ravens' cawing and the wolves' howling breaks the dreadful, solemn silence. No power of imagination is strong enough to give a conception of the horror awakened by this drama."

Among the measures adopted by the United States Government to better the condition of the Indians, none has been so hard to enforce as the law prohibiting the sale of intoxicating liquors to them. Time after time drastic laws have been enacted, but the Indians' unconquerable thirst for whiskey makes them resort to any means to get it. The immense profit from this commerce offers too strong a temptation to a group of unscrupulous people willing to risk big fines and imprisonment to supply the red men in secret with firewater, which has caused more misfortune and wrought more havoc among them than smallpox ever did. American efforts in this regard have not been supported as they ought to be by the authorities in the English provinces. English traders on the other side of the boundary formerly sought by means of alcohol to induce the North American Indian tribes to bring them their furs, and in self-defense American traders began to use the same methods. "Indian agents, situated hundreds of miles from a court of justice, could not try violators of the law, even if they were sustained by a force sufficient to arrest them. Besides, pecuniary penalties amount to nothing, as the men who now engage in that traffic are men of a low class, of no pecuniary responsibility, indifferent to public opinion, and hardened against every sentiment of humanity." [a]

In this fashion not only is the law broken but there is sold to Indians under the name of whiskey a most horrible concoction, which more than ordinary alcohol not only deprives them of their mental faculties, but also speedily and frightfully shortens their very lives. This would seem incredible if it had not been attested to by an Indian agent for the Chippewa tribe. In his report to the Government, he spoke of a poisonous drink, sold to the Indians under the name of whiskey, which consisted largely of an aeruginous sublimate and tobacco water mixed with just a few gallons of real whiskey to the barrel.[5]

Is it any wonder that the Indian in his intoxication, half-conscious of having been cheated, revenges himself on his poisoner, or that after he has satisfied his craving and awakened from his stupor, he seeks to recover the horses or the pelts with which, ruled by the moment's passion, he has paid for the few drops of whiskey a hundred, yes a thousand, times over their value? Yet hardly a case is known of an Indian, who, either drunk or sober, is willing on being examined to divulge the name or betray the person who has sold him the firewater.

But, one may ask, is the United States doing nothing to alleviate the unhappy state of this unhappy people? Yes, efforts have been made, but generally without very good results. Time and again Congress has voted large sums to establish schools among them, but with scant success. The Indians generally repulse with scorn every effort to enlighten and civilize them. They have learned to use firearms because they have come to know their usefulness, a means more easily to pursue the trade to which nature seems to have fitted them. Occasionally an Indian may be seen dressed partly in European garb and sporting the same ornaments as the white man; but these, he believes, are a token of power and will gain him influence among his own people. Otherwise he ridicules everything indicating a higher culture and education. Proud and arrogant, he considers himself in his soiled blanket and in his smoky wigwam far above his white brother. How unlike he is in this respect from the Negro, who in everything apes the white man, and who in intellectuality is yet far below the American savage. Whereas there are thousands of the African race who devote themselves to business and various trades and have the same life-pattern as the white, there are very few Indians indeed who have been persuaded to exchange their forests and their nomadic life for the privileges of a civilized community. With very few exceptions the red man is obstinate in remaining what he thinks the Great Spirit created and destined him to be — an untamed and untamable child of nature.

Perhaps this disinclination of the Indians toward schooling might be overcome more than is now the case, at least among some of the tribes, if the white traders did not in their selfish calculations even here work against that good objective. These men seek to persuade the Indians that the sums voted by Congress for the establishment of schools would of course be paid out to the tribe itself to be distributed and handled according to their pleasure if they declared that they did not want any schools and that none were to be established. Always contemplating that the money of the Indian may finally reach their own pockets, they whisper in his ear that he has far more use for money than for schools. With his natural inclination toward indolence and inactivity, he is very willing to listen to such a proposal, which he hopes will help him spend the rest of his days with his whiskey bottle and his pipe in undisturbed peace. Fortune tellers, magicians, and witch doctors, who stand high in the estimation of the Indian people and wield a far greater influence among them than their chiefs, make common cause with the white traders in this matter.

In a number of places, however, the Government has set aside for the remnants of certain tribes considerable tracts of land, Indian reserves. According to the plan, the Indians are to be left in full possession of these and an attempt is to be made there to convert them into an agricultural people. To some degree this has succeeded. It is furthermore the only means by which their condition can be improved. In the state of New York, in northern Wisconsin, and elsewhere, there are several such Indian reserves, where schools have been established and where missionaries have been sent, whose labors have not been without good results. Through them many have been converted to Christianity. Missionaries have also been sent to other tribes, both to those that have established permanent homes and to those whose life is completely nomadic and who have no other home but the movable wigwams

I have described above. True, a great many are listed as converted to Christianity in statistical tables and reports of such a nature that little attention can be paid to them. Often the final results of efforts and devotion that in the beginning looked promising have been as good as nil.

The Indians raise the same objections to the white man's religion as to his schools and culture in general. Christianity, they maintain, is no doubt very good for the white man, but is entirely unsuited to the red. The Indian is not able, like the white man, to resist temptation; it would therefore be useless for him to tie himself to a moral code and commandments he could not follow, in doing which he would only become a worse man than he was before. But though in general Indians are most averse to accepting the Christian faith, there is hardly an example of their ridiculing or sneering at it. More than any one else, they seem like the priest in Balder's temple to recognize that "one is the Father of all, however many his messengers." [6] Toward the worship of the Great Spirit, in whatever form it may be, they always show reverence. Whatever cause they may have or will have in the future to hate the white man, they will never hate him because of any religious differences. There has never in the world been a people more free from the kind of fanaticism that takes to the sword or expresses itself in persecution. Nothing of the sort would be conceivable to any of the North American Indians.

Right at present there is being tried out, in those regions of Minnesota which the Indians still possess undisturbed, an effort of an entirely different kind to civilize and Christianize them. There is better reason than in any previous similar enterprise to hope for the best results. In fact, the most encouraging and satisfying fruits have already appeared. The leader and most active person in this undertaking is a man whose name already has appeared in these pages. Since in the future I shall perhaps often be speaking of him because of the relationship in which we came to stand, I may have occasion to return to this undertaking, one of the finest and most blessed efforts in the missionary history of America. It will make him, in whose heart God first instilled the idea, long remembered and blessed by all who earnestly pray and labor for the victory of light and truth on earth.

As far as missionary work among the Indians is concerned, the Roman Church is still the one, as before, showing the greatest zeal, though not always the wisest. It reveals in this case, as it has always done, that in its work of conversion it is more concerned about establishing its own power than that of Christianity, and that in abandoning its duty to be a witness for the truth revealed to it, it aims only at ruling over men. To achieve that end, it does not hesitate to use every artifice, trick, or prank that can promote its influence in any way and gain a reputation for it. Its ceremonies, which appeal to the senses through pomp and display, easily attract the attention of the Indian, who is as easily influenced by external fineries as any child; and through its wonderful ability to be in a certain sense "all things to all men" it succeeds here and there, even among remote tribes, in establishing and for a time maintaining its mission schools and chapels, though more in name than in reality. Not so long ago as proof of the wonderful activity and success of this church it was reported that almost an entire Indian tribe had been converted, baptized, and received into its bosom, the only saving one. How little reason there was to rejoice over this victory, which with no negligence was trumpeted far and wide on both sides of the Atlantic, was proved by the fact that the Indians, who had been baptized without previous preparation, returned the next year and asked to have the procedure repeated because they were so pleased with the ceremonies and especially with the entertainment offered.

This fact, besides being enlightening in many other respects, may also serve to indicate the unreliability of ordinary statistical reports on the conversion of Indians to Christianity, their joining of temperance societies, and so on. The Protestant missionary organizations, however, carry on their work very differently from the Roman Church on the occasion just cited, and their efforts in several different instances may have had better and more encouraging results. On the whole, however, almost all such attempts among the nomadic tribes have encountered insurmountable difficulties, and it has been necessary to abandon some of them after a while as entirely profitless.

The trouble is that these problems have been attacked from the wrong end. The red man must be adopted first into the white man's family before it is worth thinking of taking him the white man's religion. Civilization must precede Christianity. The Indian must be convinced of the advantages of the white man's customs, habits, and manner of living before he can accept the inward truth of his faith and teaching. He must be persuaded to forsake his nomadic life before one seeks to persuade him to forsake his manitous. He must give up his wigwam before he can be made to enter a church. However difficult this may be, experience has shown more than once, and especially in Minnesota, that it is not impossible. It depends on whether a pact once entered into with the Indians is really kept; whether a territory is set aside for them, not in the wilderness where, excluded from the social order and the laws of the whites, they are left to themselves for a few years, only to be driven away later to some other region, but right in the midst of white people, where, undisturbed and in peace, they may in time form a community which afterward, like themselves, will fuse with the surrounding one. Only under such conditions, after they have become accustomed to agriculture and industry rather than hunting as a livelihood, and, above all things, after they have found that they are not constantly being cheated and persecuted by those professing their betterment, will it be worth while to establish schools among them and convert them to Christianity. As long as the Indian feels that he is being wronged by the white man, and more or less hates him on that account, so long will it be useless to seek to wake in him a love for the white man's God. He must learn to love and honor the one before he can be persuaded to worship and adore the other.

Up to this time Americans have done entirely too little to pay their debt to the trifling remnant of a people that yielded to them its rightful home, its beloved hunting grounds, and its venerated ancestral graves, on which yearly they increase in prosperity and wealth.

The treaties made with the Indians are broken as often as new conditions demand it. The axe of the bold pioneer hews its way through the frontier forests, and the greedy trader mixes his poisonous concoction in a region where he really has no right to be. The natural sagacity and caution of the Indian are transformed into mental dullness and credulity, from which he awakens all too late. Controversies and quarrels finally arise between him and his white neighbors, who sometimes do not hesitate to aim a bullet at him as well as at the deer and buffalo that like him have become exiles from their own land.

The frontiers are often settled by a peculiar kind of people who nourish inwardly a mortal hatred of the red man. The roots of this feeling must be sought far back, as early as in the time of the penetration by the first colonists into the West, the history of which may be said to be written in blood. The bitter memories of arson, destruction, and inhuman cruelty, by means of which the Indians sought to avenge the injustice they had suffered, a vengeance often inflicted upon peaceful families; the fearful scenes of terror enacted to eradicate from the minds of white people every desire to encroach upon their rights—the stories of all these things have been transmitted as a heritage from generation to generation. In those who even today are the outposts of civilization they have fostered a spirit of hostility against the Indians that often requires only a trifling occasion, often none at all, to break out in violence and bloodshed.

The class of people who settle the frontiers are in many respects quite unlike those who live in ordered communities. They have been characterized, strikingly enough, by the statement that they have two kinds of conscience, one for whites, another for Indians. They are people whose behavior in their relations with their own race, whose kindliness—yes, whose often meticulous obedience to the commandments of religion—would entitle them to respect and esteem in any ordered community. For them, however, the red man's rights and privileges, his possessions, and his life weigh no more than down on the scales, and they consider any injustice toward the Indians justifiable and permissible. Brave, seasoned, and enterprising, faithful, honest, benevolent, and hospitable toward a white stranger, they lack in their hearts all kindly feeling, all compassion for nature's wild children and have not the least notion that they also should be treated with friendliness and loving-kindness.

An eyewitness has told me the following gruesome tale of an event that took place shortly after the annexation of California by the United States. A man belonging to the class I have just been describing, one who from his childhood had been leading a wild frontier life, accompanied one of the first caravans across the wide prairies and the wild Rockies to the land of gold. The company was sufficiently numerous and well enough armed to inspire respect in at least the small bands of hostile Indians that they might encounter along the way. After several days' march across the expansive prairie they saw in the distance a lonely Indian coming their way. They learned later that he belonged to a tribe from which they had nothing to fear. The frontiersman conceived the idea of shooting him just for fun. It had been a long time since he had had a chance to fire a shot, he said, and before the rest of the company realized what he was about to do or could prevent the cruel act, he took aim and fired. The Indian fell dead to the ground.

A couple of days later the caravan was suddenly surrounded by several hundred well-armed Indians. In the meanwhile they had found the body of their dead comrade. They knew that, alone as he was, he had approached the white men with no evil intention and that there was therefore no justification for slaying him. It was not difficult for them to follow the tracks of his murderer and catch up with the caravan. One of their chiefs approached the travelers saying: "One of our brothers has fallen by a white man's bullet, killed like a deer on the prairie, without having done you any harm. Sons of white mothers, the red men must avenge the death of their brother. We are strong enough to kill you all. The white man is cruel; his brother, the red man, is just. Deliver up the murderer. We must shed his blood, and after you have witnessed his punishment, you may depart in peace. No tomahawk shall touch your scalps. But if you desire to shelter the slayer of our brother, then you, too, are our enemies, and our brother's death will be avenged upon all of you."

The members of the caravan realized fully that their only safety lay in delivering up the criminal. His cold-blooded cruelty, moreover, made them feel less inclined to show any compassion for him. In a moment his smoking scalp was tied to the belt of one of the Indians, and as the rest of his body was flayed, the life of the hapless man ebbed away.

While such horrible acts as the one just related are not always the cause, yet there arise along the frontiers frequent disputes and

371

disturbances between Indians and white men. The latter are constantly at the heels of the former, no matter how far these withdraw from their pursuers. The Government steps in to mediate controversies. The Indians are persuaded for their own good again to sell their hunting grounds and move still farther away. A treaty is concluded, on the strength of which they cede to the white people their lands, in the hope — a hope that proves to be illusory — that they may live undisturbed in the territories assigned them.

The remuneration the United States gives for the new territory thus acquired consists mainly in manufactured goods. The following excerpt from a report to Congress by former Secretary of State L. Cass [7] presents a discerning picture of the negotiation of such a treaty.

"When the Indians arrive at the place where the treaty is to be concluded, they are extremely poor and almost naked. Here they are invited to examine a number of the valuable articles the American traders have to offer. The women and children, who eagerly desire these valuables, assail the warriors with a thousand touching pleas, seeking to persuade them to buy. Usually the Indians' lack of judgment is incredible. To fill the moment's need and to provide nourishment for an immediate appetite are an irresistible passion with the savage. The expectation of future advantage means little to him. He easily forgets the past and never concerns himself with the future. It would be useless to ask the Indian to cede his lands if one could not on the spot satisfy his demands. When one looks impartially at the condition of these unfortunate people, one is not surprised at the ardor with which they grasp after any consolation in their misery."

Driven from his old, beloved hunting grounds, the unfortunate Indian now goes to settle near the territory of some strange and perhaps hostile tribe, where the very name of his own gradually dying tribe will soon be forgotten. For a long time he will roam the grounds that no longer belong to him; he will keep returning to the burial places of his fathers, for which he harbors a holy and almost passionate veneration. There in the meantime, a village or city comes to flourish, where he can sell or exchange his game. He purchases then a supply of goods needed for his tribe. The trader often sells these on credit, sometimes to the value of hundreds of dollars. An Indian almost never defaults on his bills. Usually he is a better risk than most other men.

During his wanderings the Indian takes care when he crosses the frontiers, not to come into contact with those between whom and him there are dreadful accounts of reciprocal injury and injustice still to be settled. Should he spend a night near a white man's dwelling, it will be near some family that has recently migrated to the West and to whom the wild scenes of frontier life are like sagas of long ago, known only in the softened colors of romantic story. But perhaps on his way he may come upon the charred ruins of what used to be the home of a bold and hostile frontiersman, casting its ghostly shadow over the lonely plain. Carefully he steals over to it, and while the prairie wind howls between the rough logs, he rests on the floor still wet with enemy blood. There his heart swells with joy as he realizes that some of his red brothers have exacted bloody vengeance in that place for the wrongs they have suffered. There during the night's lonesome hours he recalls the misfortunes that have overtaken his people, and when he gets up in the morning, he longs for a meeting that will compensate him for painful experiences. Should a white man who regards himself as the rightful owner of the place — perhaps the head of the family, who has escaped destruction himself only after seeing his wife and children slaughtered or carried away captive — should he now come quietly slipping from among the smoking ruins of his former happy home, we may easily imagine the meeting between the two.

Note

[a] E. S. Seymour, *Sketches of Minnesota, the New England of the West* (New York, 1850), p. 45.

Chapter 23

THE INDIAN'S RETICENCE ON RELIGION · RELIGIOUS CONCEPTIONS

MANITOLOGY · SACRED PLACES · BELIEF IN ANOTHER LIFE AND

IMMORTALITY OF THE SOUL · TRADITIONS · THE BUSK FEAST

SUPERSTITIONS · MEDAS, OR THE MEDICINE MEN · THEIR SE-

CRET ORDER AND INITIATION CEREMONIES · JOSSAKEEDS AND

PROPHETS

I N SPITE of the barriers language put in the way of conversation between us and the Indians, I tried to get from their own mouths some information concerning their religious faith and conceptions. In these matters, however, they were even more reticent than usual. As a rule, an Indian maintains a mysterious silence regarding his religious beliefs. To be sure he may express through symbols and pictures his conceptions of the highest being as well as of the lesser local spirits and divinities with whom he feels he stands in personal relation, but he never speaks of these things, and least of all with a white man or a stranger. That, according to his belief, would bring him misfortune and possibly cost him his life.

The world of spirits, with which his superstitious conceptions people all of nature, gives him material indeed for many strange tales, but the higher dogmas of his faith, if I may so call them, are suggested only incidentally or hidden under the strange imagery of poetry and fantasy. It is only during the winter, also, that for the most part he occupies himself telling these tales, for he believes that the spirits, who live in the snow-covered earth and the frozen waters, are unable then to hear what is being said of them. But when spring comes there is an end to these poetic nature tales and mythical songs, which both young and old have enjoyed in their winter huts. The earth now has new life, the rivers and lakes are open again, the birds return to their deserted forests and streams, the trees leaf, bushes and flowers come out, and then even the spirit world in which the Indian lives awakens to new life and activity. In the bird's singing, the tree's rustling, the stream's rippling — in everything the red man hears a spirit voice. Every bush and flower speaks to him of a supernatural being, who is close to him and on whom he considers himself more or less dependent. Therefore he guards himself carefully lest he let slip a single word that may in any way displease or insult these hidden awakening powers. Parents tell their children that if they offend the spirits, lizards, toads, and snakes will bite them for having shown such discourtesy.

All the North American Indians profess belief in a supreme, almighty, and benevolent deity, the Great Spirit, the first cause and creator of earth, men, and beasts. With this conception of a being whose attributes are goodness, wisdom, and mercy, they have difficulty in reconciling the origin and existence of evil in the world. Some believe that at the creation two high and supernatural powers, hostile to each other, came into existence, who were both subordinate to the Great Spirit, but to whom he entrusted what he had created without further concerning himself with it. One of these is constantly busy setting right and remedying all the troubles and hurts which the other, just as constantly, is seeking to visit upon the visible creation. Others, again, place at the side of the Great Spirit another power, the great Evil Spirit, with power to impede and counteract the good and benevolent purposes of the Good. The belief in such dualism is perhaps the most common.

Between these powers, mutually hostile to each other, unceasing war is waged for lordship over the world and mankind. Subject to both of them are legions of subordinate spirits and divinities, which exist everywhere in nature and reveal themselves to men in dreams and visions. Through incantations and necromantic spells it is possible for men to get in closer touch with these beings, to converse with them, and so receive revelations of hidden things.

To this belief is added the conception of a demiurge, or a world soul, dwelling in all created things and giving life to everything in nature. In the sun and in fire, in rocks and trees, in waterfalls and lakes, in the air and the clouds, in thunder and lightning — everywhere, in every possible shape, in everything whether living or dead — the Great Spirit is hidden or active through special spirits and divinities. It is a confused mixture of pantheism and polytheism: a god in the entire creation, but in addition, spirits, demons, powers, and gods in separate objects and elements. There is no place where they do not see a reflection of God, the Great Spirit of the universe; at the same time there are also special local divinities that operate against each other and attempt to control the course of events while the Great Spirit for the most part maintains passivity. The red man beholds a god everywhere and hears a spirit voice in every sound. Every place where he sets his foot is, like himself, under the sway of a good or an evil power, to which he ascribes all his hopes and fears, all his joys and sorrows, every good or evil fortune he encounters. To all these powers he directs his worship, sometimes perhaps out of love, but more frequently out of fear. This conception of spirits and divinities that are always listening to his words, always following in his footsteps, and fighting, as it were, for his welfare or downfall, fills him with a perpetual mistrust and a restless anxiety.

However much various Indian tribes may differ in their religious conceptions and modes of sacrifice and worship, they all agree in their belief in spirits, in what may properly be termed their manitology. Manitology is also the outstanding characteristic of their religion and more than anything else exerts a powerful influence on their life and behavior.

The priest and the prophet, the sorcerer and the necromancer, although subordinate to the Great Spirit, appear in a sense as embodied manitous and personal spirits in the visible creation, which in certain cases they think they can bend to their will; at the same time they maintain they are in alliance with invisible powers which they can subdue and use for their purposes.

Every Indian has his special manitou, with whom he is in close personal relation. When he has reached a certain age, this manitou makes himself known to him in some way or other, and it is essential that he prepare himself by fasting and other religious ceremonies to receive the revelation. It may occur in visions or dreams, or the spirit may reveal himself in the shape of some bird or beast, which the Indian then selects as his personal manitou, or guardian spirit. He depends on the manitou's protection in war and peace and is convinced that he will come to his assistance in every peril or trouble. Unfortunately, however, though he is persuaded that his spirit will aid him, he is not at all sure how much this help will avail, since all manitous are not of equal power, nor do they always cooperate with one another. Just as one man has greater abilities than another, the one being stronger, the other weaker, so it is among the spirits. One may conceivably overpower the other; hence the Indian can never feel certain that the tutelary spirit of his enemy or of some other person may not be stronger and mightier than his own.

Futhermore, there are evil as well as good manitous. In the life of the individual as well as in the whole visible world everything may be traced to the one or the other of these forces. The outcome depends on whichever is the stronger. For man there is no alternative but to bow to its power. Here again we meet the idea of two opposing forces, a conception closely related to the old Oriental dualism. The correspondence between this principal dogma of the Indians and the Persian doctrine of Ormuzd and Ahriman is thought by some scholars to be more than just a coincidence.

Some years ago, on the top of a hill in the state of Ohio, there was discovered an earthwork which seems to prove that the allegorical tale of the egg of Ormuzd is not altogether unknown to these wild tribes. The hill, which is 150 feet high, represents a serpent and measures 700 feet in length, but if all its undulations were measured, the total length would be at least 1000 feet. The jaws of the serpent are represented as wide open, as if it were about to swallow something, and in its jaws there is an oval or egg-shaped elevation. The idea which has been expressed in this representation has been believed to have too close a resemblance to the Chaldaeo-Persian story to have its origin in the North American wilderness.

The North American Indians have nowhere erected any temples for the worship of the Great Spirit, nor is there any indication that they have ever done so. Neither their priests nor chiefs, even if inclined to do so, could ever persuade them to build any permanent temple or designate any definite place for their worship. Any place whatever that awakens within them a living sense of reverence and awe is to them a temple. For their sacrifices and other religious ceremonies they choose preferably some lonely place deep within the dark, silent forest, some high hill, or the cliffs around a roaring waterfall. Here they light their sacred fires, offer their sacrifices, and sing hymns of praise, several of them dedicated to the sun as the symbol of the Great Spirit. On the shore of a river or lake or on the vast prairie, they often will erect a stone that has been rounded by the action of the water; they sometimes paint it to give it a human resemblance. It has not been ascertained whether these blocks of stone are afterwards worshiped as gigantic idols or whether, like the place where they have been erected, they have some sacred meaning.

Generally speaking, and with very few exceptions, the North American Indian tribes have no idols made of wood or stone. Many consider this circumstance highly remarkable in a savage people, and from it draw the conclusion that they are descendants, not too far removed, from a race that formerly worshiped the only true God. Among the Indians themselves, whose entire existence presents the inexplicable problem of a people that, torn loose from everything that might make them happy, stubbornly reject the possibility of returning to a better life, there are some older traditions, according to which they once lived in a happier communion with the Great Spirit, were on a higher cultural plane, spoke a better and more harmonious language, and were governed by chiefs who developed greater wisdom and were more energetic in their activity than now.

It is natural that with the belief in universal spirits described above there should be combined a belief in the soul's immortality and in a life after death. These conceptions, however, differ widely among different tribes. Many of them adhere to the ancient belief in the duality of the soul, according to which one soul is liberated at death while the other is forced to remain for some time in the dead body, subject to material needs. Therefore it is a general custom not immediately to cover the graves of the dead, but beside them or on them each day to place various foods to nourish the spirits on their journey to another world. At all feasts and meals, moreover, meat and other dishes must be offered to deceased forefathers and nearer relations. This is a sacred duty which the Indian is fearful to neglect, and which scarcely anyone of any standing in the tribe would fail in. At every festival, yes, at every meal, when a specially good dish is placed before him, he is reminded of his obligation in this respect, and the first thought a grave or burial ground awakens in him is to take his dead forefathers such an offering, if for himself he hopes for any happiness in this life. He never goes by such a place without feeling the urge to lay on the grave a meat or drink offering of whatever he may have. Failure to show reverence in this way is sure to bring him some kind of bad luck, a punishment inflicted by the dead.

The tale is told of an Algonquin Indian who one evening at twilight came to a burial place where he saw two spirits sitting at the side of the graves containing two dead bodies. The only thing suitable for consumption he had was a jug of whiskey, too precious for him to expend even a few drops as a libation. He grasped his jug more firmly and hurried away as fast as his legs would carry him. But as he fled he could not keep from casting a furtive glance behind, whereupon he was terrified to see one of the spirits hot in pursuit. He continued to run, but the ghost was gaining on him. What was he to do? His love of whiskey was mightier than his veneration for the dead. Finally he made his decision. He slowed up and allowed the ghost to catch up with him, whereupon he suddenly turned around and caught hold of it. But in place of a pursuing family spook he found himself clasping in his arms a large sheaf of sedge. At the touch of a living hand the spirit had vanished and changed itself into this plant.

Certain tribes believe in the migration of souls. With reference to this belief, especially among the northern tribes west of the Mississippi, there are many legends. Many of these, however strange, possess a certain poetic beauty. According to all of them the soul is eternal and immortal, the spark of life passing from one object to another. Usually the new body has not a human shape, but that either of another living thing or, for a period, even of a dead thing at times. The tales do not say what is the cause of these changes. The general opinion seems to be that the higher will of the person himself decides in what form the spirit is to be clothed in another existence.

Hand in hand with belief in the soul's immortality there goes a mass of confused and differing notions concerning punishments and rewards, concerning the compensations also for the toils and sufferings of this life. These they have set forth in various allegorical conceptions. They believe in a paradise, a happy hunting ground, a great prairie ever teeming with game, an Indian Valhalla,[1] where the braves may busy themselves, always successfully, with the things they loved most here. Some traditions place this paradise somewhere above the earth, but just where cannot with certainty be said. Other stories relate how the spirits of the dead on their way to the great prairie have to cross a broad river, over which, as a kind of bridge, a tree trunk is laid. It is always in motion, so that only good spirits can cross in safety; the evil fall into the water, never to be heard from again. This, they say, they have learned from one of their ancestors, who lived a long time ago. When after his death he came to the trembling tree trunk, he did not dare to venture across it, but asked the Great Spirit for permission to return to the land of the living. This petition was granted, and two days after his death he appeared again among his friends, to whom he told what he had seen. He related also that while waiting on the river shore he had caught a glimpse on the other side of an indescribably rich and beautiful prairie and had heard the sound of drums, to whose beating the blessed spirits danced there and diverted themselves. Through his stories of the happiness with which the Great Spirit rewarded his good children, he sought to encourage those who heard him to live here in such a way that they might without fear cross the bridge to the land of immortality.

Of the creation of the world and of man, the Indians have formed the most extraordinary conceptions, and concerning it they have the strangest traditions and allegorical tales. They think they themselves were the original inhabitants of the land, and that they began their existence in grottoes or other cavities of the earth; from these according to their tales, they climbed up to the surface via the roots of a great vine. They have many stories: of how a bear or a mammoth bull came running from east to west and with its feet made great hollows in the soft earth, hollows later filled with water and now the Great Lakes; how a whole tribe crossed the Mississippi on a grape vine; how the wings of an eagle brought forth thunder, its flaming eyes, lightnings; how men clambered up to the heaven's blue vault by an invisible path; how a little boy caught a sunbeam in his snare; how hawks saved some shipwrecked sailors from the stormy waves and carried them in leather pouches to the top of a steep cliff. These and other stories are told to this day by the Indians, with the same seriousness and credence they would accord an event that the day before took place before their eyes. It never occurs to them to doubt the historical truth of these happenings.

According to a Potawatami tradition, related in Schoolcraft's *History of the Indian Tribes*,[2] from which I have taken much of this material, it is said that when Ketchemonedo, the Great Good Spirit, created the world he filled it with beings that only looked like men. They were perverse, ungrateful, wicked dogs who never raised their eyes from the ground to the Great Spirit to thank him for his goodness. When the Great Spirit saw this, he became angry, plunged them all into a great lake, and there drowned them. Then he let the water dry off and created a single human being, a man of youthful and handsome appearance, who, because he saw he was alone, seemed sorrowful and sad. Ketchemonedo took pity on him, and created for him a sister to console him in his loneliness.

Many years passed by. One night the young man dreamed a dream, which he told to his sister. "Five young men," he said, "will come to your wigwam this night to visit you. The Great Spirit forbids you to answer or even look at the first four, but when the fifth comes you may speak, laugh, and let him understand that he pleases you."

The sister did as her brother said. The first stranger came; his name was Usama (tobacco). When he was rejected he fell down dead. The second, Wapako (pumpkin), shared the same fate. The third, Eshkossimin (melon), and the fourth, Kokees (bean), fared no better. But finally Tamin, or Montamin (corn), came and for him she opened her lodge, laughed heartily, and received him kindly. They were straightway married. From that union sprang the Potawatami Indians. Afterward Tamin buried the four unfortunate suitors, and from their graves grew tobacco, pumpkins of all sorts, melons and beans; and in this manner the Great Spirit supplied the race he had made both with what they should offer him as gifts at their feasts and ceremonies and with what they needed to put into their *akeeks* (kettles) to cook with the meat they use for food.

Most of the Indian tribes also have traditions of a great flood which long ago engulfed and covered the earth, and in which the entire human race with the exception of a few persons perished. According to some, this flood was the work of the Evil Spirit. Other stories show a striking resemblance to the description given in the Holy Scriptures of the same event. The Muskogee Indians of Alabama claim that before the real creation a great mass of water covered the earth and that the antediluvian people who saved themselves from the general destruction released two doves to discover land for them. The first time the doves flew forth they found only the remnants of a few earthworms, but the second time they found a green leaf, whereupon the waters receded and land appeared. According to other traditions, only one family and a pair of each kind of animals were saved.

As a rule, the Indians have no chronology and know no divisions of the year except winter and summer. Of the year's further division into months and weeks, they have no conception. To them all days are alike. They measure day and night by the rising of the sun, its zenith, its setting, and its rising again; that is all. Any division into hours is unknown to them. But for all that, there are some things that show a kind of resemblance to the method of the ancient Orientals of dividing time into certain periods. The southern tribes, for example, have yearly a so-called Busk, a religious observance, or festival of atonement, which formerly lasted eight days, but has now been reduced to four, and which begins when the new harvest is almost ripe. The first day is observed with a great public banquet, when the dishes are prepared from what still remains of the harvest of the previous year. All contribute to that feast and all are obliged to share in it. On the second and the following days a strict fast is observed. Amid singing and dancing thank offerings are made to the Great Spirit; sacred fires are lit on which are placed four large blocks of oak wood, one for each of the four main points of the compass. Like all fires lit for other than secular purposes, this one must be kindled by a new spark from a flint.

The other days of the Busk festival are taken up mainly with washing and purification ceremonies, for which young girls gather the ashes from the sacred fires and bring them to the braves. The most remarkable thing about this religious festival is that, like the Hebrew Year of Jubilee, it brings amnesty to all law violators; all financial claims are remitted; all personal disputes and quarrels are settled. In a word, it is a feast of offering and atonement, not only with respect to the relations of men to a higher being, but also with respect to their relations among themselves.

The North American Indians are perhaps the most superstitious people in the world. In addition to their belief in spirit-revelations and spirit-whisperings everywhere in nature, they pay special heed to all possible signs and omens. The most insignificant circumstances will make even the most intrepid warrior quake with fear and fill him with dark forebodings of impending perils. Especially great significance attaches to the flights of birds, from which they believe they can foretell good or bad luck on the hunt or in war. Therefore these creatures often appear in their war songs and in the incantations through which they think they can gain knowledge of coming events.

Strangely enough, with all this emphasis on auguries they pay no attention to the stars and their movements. They do not think of these heavenly bodies as having any relation to mundane things or any influence on them except for falling stars, which some say are excrements dropped on the earth. These are sought out and mixed with their medicines, the healing power of which then becomes infallible. On the other hand, they give careful heed and ascribe great importance to all meteorological phenomena. The size, color, and movements of the clouds, as well as their grouping about the sun and at the horizon, constitute a science into which the medas and prophets claim they have delved deeply, and enterprises of greatest moment are undertaken in accordance with the predictions based on these observations.

To attach such importance to the objects in the upper air, with its star-studded background, storms, thunder, lightning, and other electrical phenomena, opens a wide field to the imagination. By carefully noting these signs, not only do they purport to be able to reveal future events. These provide also rich and oftentimes poetically beautiful images for literature and song. They are the source also of a number of personal names, which thus have both a poetic and a prophetic signification.

The superstition of the Indians is further revealed in the still widely prevalent custom of carrying certain magic charms and amulets supposed to contain a wonder-working power against all diseases and to serve as a cogent protection against evil and hostile magic. Almost the entire healing art and *materia medica* of the Indians are based on the magical effects these objects are believed to have. Horns, claws, old fragments of bone, and the like are supposed to have magic power. Sea shells especially, ornamented or in their natural state, are considered the best and most unfailing talismans against all sicknesses and accidents. The Indian regards the sunlit sea as of all things the most perfect symbol of the limitless universe and as the element most clearly reflecting the Great Spirit. Everything that can be brought up from its depths, therefore, possesses, according to his view, an extraordinarily sacred and mystical significance. The beautiful, iridescent sea shells hence are primarily used in the manufacture not only of amulets but of sacred ornaments of all kinds. In olden times they served the Indians as money, and out of them a kind of necklace, or wampum, is still manufactured. It is either sacrificed to the spirits or delivered as a sacred pledge to confirm solemn pacts or agreements.

It is a sacred duty of the survivors to allow all such objects to accompany the dead to their graves, for the future life of the Indian is not immediately one of rest and peace; even in the land of the shadows the hunter's soul on his restless wanderings is in need of protection against evil spirits.

All such magic charms are kept with great care in the medicine pouch, or *skipetagun*, and the more secret they can be kept, the more efficacious they are believed to be. The greatest reticence is absolutely indispensable lest the charms lose their potency. The magician who consecrates these charms prescribes on that account the greatest secrecy and caution, as with all necromantic medicines. What is kept in the pouch no one but its owner may know, and even he may have received from the magician some small object that if he were to look at it would bring him untold misfortune and misery. Often all that is needed is that such an object be thrown at another with a certain gesture and it will exert a magic influence upon him. The pouch in which the meda keeps his arcana therefore possesses more wonder-working power than anything else, and just to show it is often enough, according to the wishes of the magician, to exert a magical effect upon the sick person or whoever is the object of his secret art. There is hardly anything in the realm of nature that he cannot enchant or endow with supernatural qualities. Even a ray of light falling on his hand may subject the person on whom it afterward falls to a kind of enchantment. In this respect the superstition of the Indian is without limits. It makes him a perfect plaything in the hands of the magicians, who in the secret wigwam have been initiated into the mysteries of nature as well as of the spirit world, and in whose magic arts and incantations he puts a blind faith. While he roams his lonely forests and deserts and imagines himself to be as free as the air he breathes, he is in reality, because of his superstitions, merely a cringing slave of the prophet, the interpreter of dreams, and the necromancer.

There is among the North American Indians a class of persons known by various names, medas, wabenoes, jossakeeds, and so forth, who pose as medicine men, prophets, and seers. They all pretend to possess a deep understanding of the secret powers of nature and the mysteries of the spirit world. Upon their interpretations of omens and divinations, the decisions and undertakings of individuals as well as of entire tribes depend. Whether or not they also are chiefs, it is in reality they who wield supreme power, grounded not on inheritance or any outstanding personal qualities but only, or at least mainly, on the superstitious faith of their people in them. The political power in an Indian community is therefore rather closely connected with or dependent on the religious conceptions, and errors in the latter sphere naturally lead to many mistakes in the former.

The Indians have, to be sure, a type of real physician, who seeks to cure at least external, but sometimes even internal, troubles by means of bloodletting, herbs, and other natural means. Since all physical ills are regarded as the deeds of evil spirits, it is nevertheless natural that those who pretend to be able to control these powers by means of incantations and magic command greater respect, enjoy greater confidence, and are consulted more frequently than those who employ natural means, which under such conditions are regarded as entirely inadequate.

Foremost among the Indian magicians are the medas, or in English medicine men, a term which has been adopted through a faulty interpretation of the Indian word. Medas do not practice the healing art except through incantations and supernatural means; they are really necromancers or magicians, priests but not physicians. True, they carry in their mysterious pouches a few pieces of metal, bone fragments, feathers, and the like, to which they ascribe supernatural powers; but it is not really through a physical application of these objects that they perform their miraculous cures, but rather and principally through conjuration and magic arts. In event of sickness and other misfortune, always ascribed to evil spirits, they appear as mediators between men and manitous.

When illness is to be cured, the meda will conjure forth the trouble from the patient's stomach or throat in some material shape, such as a piece of flint or something else, which he catches in his mouth and then spits out. A dead bird that the patient worships as his manitou may be brought back to life; evil spirits may be driven from various parts of the body, and so on. Some higher spiritual power is supposed to work directly through the healer and support him in his magic. Personally he believes himself to be an incarnate manitou or at least one who stands in close relationship to spirits and demons, is able to talk to them, and has the power of life or death over individual human beings. The ignorant and superstitious savage regards him as a half-supernatural being and shows him the greatest reverence. No one casts a shadow of a doubt on the marvels of his ceremonies and exorcisms, nor on their supernatural effect provided no manitous stronger and mightier than his own operate against him.

When such a magician appears to practice his art he observes a number of very strange ceremonies, most of them symbolic in signification, yet for those unitiated in their mysteries hard to explain. He employs every possible means to influence the imagination of the people and strengthen their faith in the supernatural. Sometimes he performs, amid the beating of drums and the noise of rattles, a type of magic dance, which is considered a very important part of the conjuration. Sometimes he will strike up his monotonous mystic songs, of which both words and tune have been transmitted from one generation to another and which he has learned to repeat from memory. On these occasions all who are present are seized with fear and trembling; they shiver as if struck by lightning until they fall into an ecstasy that borders on perfect madness. Some drop to the ground, twitching spasmodically and often remain for a long while lying in an apparently senseless condition.

Those who have been eyewitnesses to these events describe them as somewhat similar, at least superficially, to the phenomena often seen at Methodist camp meetings and on like occasions where purportedly religious emotions burst forth in violent gesticulations. The outward effects of religious fanaticism among Christians seem to be the same as among pagans: a spiritual transport that reveals itself in unnatural physical paroxysms and robs the subject of consciousness. The one brand of fanaticism as well as the other has a contagious effect; or, what is not unlikely, in both cases the strange manifestations may be regarded, at least in some degree, as the result of animal magnetism.

The Indian priest or black magician himself on such occasions is in a highly agitated frame of mind. As he shakes his magic rattles and beats his mystical tambourine, he imagines that earth and heaven are listening to him and the entire visible creation is bending to his will. For every important exhibition of his art he prepares himself by fasting and secret devotional exercises. In his daily life he manifests the greatest self-denial, lives in self-imposed poverty, and seeks in every way to prove that he is above all selfish motives. To make an impression on the people and to win a reputation for wisdom and holiness, he makes it appear that he is in constant, unbroken contact with all elemental spirits and is ready at any time to exercise a power which it would be the greatest folly to doubt or oppose. Every Indian tribe has within its membership one or more such persons, who, as already stated, exercise a powerful influence over them and whose counsel is invited in almost all individual and public matters. Jannes and Jambres in Egypt could not have had a greater reputation and enjoyed higher honors for their secret arts than do the medicine men among the North American Indian tribes.

The meda's office is not inherited either in the family or the tribe. Anyone may fill it, provided he has proved that he has the proper insight and skill and has been correctly initiated. These persons constitute, namely, a secret order, into which no one can be initiated till he has been taught its mysteries and has passed certain tests. It consists of various degrees, the higher being in possession of greater secrets than the lower. As time goes on the magician acquires greater skill in his art and an ever deeper knowledge of the hidden powers of nature and of the mysteries of the spirit world.

In connection with the story of our first meeting with the Winnebago Indians, I mentioned this order, which, though it has members among all the tribes, still appears to have attained greater development and perfection among the Winnebagos than among any others. It is in their secret rites that students have thought they discovered a certain similarity to those of the Freemasons.

As a matter of curiosity I wish to quote from Schoolcraft's *History of the Indian Tribes* what is known of the order of the medas among the Winnebago Indians, or rather of its initiation ceremonies, as far as these can be attended by others than the members of the order.[3] Each one, whether he is a Freemason or not, may then make his own observations and draw his own conclusions.

When a new member is to be initiated into the order, a great feast is arranged, for which nevertheless no specific time is set and which all the members do not attend, but only those who have been specially invited.

The initiates must already have lived with the greatest frugality, sometimes for years, to save up the initiation fee. This fee, however, is not fixed, but each one gives what he can afford. Sometimes the candidate gives goods to the value of two or three hundred dollars, usually consisting of blankets, pieces of cloth, calico, wampum, and other ornaments, all of which go to the black magicians or medas who officiate at the initiation. When one or more candidates have applied for admission into the order, a specially vaulted lodge or tabernacle, which is carefully covered with skins and other hangings, is built for the festive meal, the dance, and the rest of the ceremonies. The size of the lodge is proportionate to the number of invited guests, and that number in turn depends much upon the wealth of the person who arranges the feast. The width is generally only 16 feet, but its length varies from 30 to 225. The members of the order sit on each side along the walls of the lodge, so that between them there is plenty of room for the dance.

For three days before the initiation the candidates must observe a strict fast, during which time the old medas take them to a secret and secluded place where they are taught the teachings and mysteries of the order. It is said that they must also submit to a severe sweating process, being covered with blankets and placed in a kind of steam bath, prepared with various kinds of herbs. Whether any truth lies at the bottom of this assertion is not certain, but the appearance of the candidate when he is brought in for the public initiation seems to support it.

The initiation proper usually begins about eleven o'clock in the forenoon. The dances, songs, devotional exercises, and speeches that precede the initiation have begun on the preceding morning. Before the candidates are brought into the lodge, the ground in the middle of it is covered with blankets, on which are laid other pieces of cloth. After being brought in, they kneel on the blanket at one end of the room, with their faces turned in the opposite direction. Thereupon eight or ten medas march in single file around the lodge, holding in their hands their pouches of medicine or magic. Every time they have gone around it, they stop, and one of them makes a short speech. This march continues for as many turns as it takes for all of them to have spoken. After this they form a circle and place their pouches of magic before them on the carpet; then they begin to belch and attempt to vomit, bending forward so that their heads almost touch their pouches, upon which they finally spit out a small white sea shell about as big as an ordinary bean, the so-called medicine stone, which they maintain they carry in their stomachs. After each one of them has placed his shell or stone in the opening of his pouch, they take their places at the other end of the lodge and face the initiates.

Thereupon they march forward in single file, as many of them as there are candidates. Holding the magic pouches with both hands in front of them, they dance, at first slowly, making guttural sounds as they approach the initiates. Gradually their steps become more rapid and their sounds louder, till they finally scream forth a terrifying "Ough!" and toss their magic pouches against the chests of the initiates. As if struck by an electric shock, these immediately fall forward on their faces with outstretched limbs, rigid in body and shivering in every fiber. They are covered with blankets then and left lying for a few minutes in that position. As soon as they show signs of recovery, they are helped to their feet and led to the middle of the lodge. The pouches of magic are now placed in their hands and the magic stones in their mouths. They are now medicine men or medicine women, taken into the society. Thereupon the new members walk in single file around the lodge together with the older ones, throwing their pouches against the chest of anybody happening to come in their way, knocking him to the ground with their magic power.

After this has gone on for a while, refreshments are brought in, of which each one present receives his share. Dog meat is always one of the ingredients in the dish served on such occasions. At the end of the meal they generally continue for several hours with dances and other exercises. The musical instruments consist of drums and rattles. During the entire ceremony there prevails the strictest order and decorum.

Members of the order are very anxious not to miss ceremonies of this kind. Nothing short of illness serves as an excuse for being absent. Some of them walk fifty miles or more to take part in them.

The mysteries of the order are held sacred and are kept with the utmost secrecy; not even the direst need or the otherwise irresistible desire for whiskey can induce a member of this society to part with his pouch of magic.

It is extremely difficult to decide whether the so-called medicine men really perform through mesmerism or magnetism such phenomena as we have here described and other feats of black magic, or whether all of it is pure trickery and fraud. A six years careful and meticulous observation of these ceremonies has not uncovered any deception, if there is such, and it is hard to imagine that imposture should for hundreds of years have been practiced in this art without detection. Certainly it is true that the Indians themselves fully believe that these medicine men possess a supernatural power.

In addition to the medas, of whom we have been speaking, there is among the North American Indian tribes another kind of magicians, whose activities are closely related to the religious beliefs of the people and who, like the former, hold a sort of priestly office. These are the so-called jossakeeds, or prophets, who appear now and then at various times and places, claiming a higher inspiration. They do not, like the medas, constitute a special order or society. The meda is a mediator who seeks either to pacify the higher spirits and through their aid to avert evil so that his tribe may have success in war or in the chase and he himself success in his healing arts, or by sacrifices, conjurations, and incantations so work on the evil spirits that they may not hinder his activities. The jossakeed, on the other hand, is merely a seer, or fortune teller, who predicts coming events. Frequently, however, his office and predictions are regarded with greater awe and fear than those of the meda. Both base their power on a close association with demons and spirits. Both use similar material objects, such as stuffed birds, bones, and the like, as necessary to their work of magic. In his speeches and songs the prophet often turns to the Great Spirit himself, and like the meda he prepares himself for his prophetic labors by a period of severe fasting.

For this purpose, as for the mysteries just described, a tightly closed hut is specially provided, shaped like an acute pyramid, into which the prophet crawls, taking with him nothing but his drum. After he has observed certain mystic ceremonies, done his conjuring, and sung his magical songs, he makes it known that he has called forth spirits or manitous on whose words he can depend, and then announces to the people waiting outside that he is prepared to give his oracular dictum. Among all the mysteries of ancient heathendom there was never an oracle — not even that of Diana in Ephesus — that so fully and completely captivated the people's faith as these modern oracles among the North American Indians have done.

Chapter 24

INDIAN ORATORY AND POETRY · PICTOGRAPHY · ORIGIN OF THE
WHITE, THE RED, AND THE BLACK MEN · ADDRESS BY A CHOC-
TAW CHIEF · A POTAWATAMI TRADITION · THE ISLAND OF THE
BLESSED; OR THE HUNTER'S DREAM · AN INDIAN SERENADE

NEXT to his religious practices there is nothing that more than his oratory so clearly reveals the peculiar character of the Indian and in which he manifests a higher intelligence and elevation of mind. Both at the private council fire and in public negotiations and treaties with the white men, he displays an eloquence that may well compare with the oratory of any civilized nation if at times not even surpass it. In ease of expression and in dignified appearance, in choice of words, in power and nobility of thought, in combined poetical sublimity and simplicity, and in the reflection of true heroism, he is wholly admirable. He reveals in these a natural talent, which is early fostered and which he afterward takes pains more and more to develop. The wild hunter's soul is so deeply inbued with his ideal of liberty that he eagerly embraces every opportunity that is offered to sunder, as it were, the bonds under which he feels oppressed because of the constant contact and squeezing of a civilization more and more crowding his race. In the melancholy and heaviness of mind into which he sometimes lapses as he realizes he no longer can oppose the encroachment of the white man with the same pride and strength of former days, in the sad thought of the impending annihilation of his people, he finds a kind of relief when he can give expression as orator to the bold, free, and lightning-like ideas which lie dormant deep within him. These he clothes in imagery as daring and wild as the nature in which he seems everywhere to hear secret spirit voices, yet imagery at the same time simple, true, and telling, suitable to his subject. To the new inhabitants of his land he seems to have ceded together with his ground something also of his talent as an orator, for undeniably it would be difficult anywhere else to find this art practiced so commonly and with such natural ease as on the North American continent, where it seems to be native and inborn among both red and white inhabitants.

It is not only as a speaker, however, that the Indian shows the true poetic feeling that lives, or rather has lived, deep in his soul, though now to a great extent suppressed by the misfortunes he has suffered and though his life no longer offers the same subjects for its exercise as once it did. This feeling reveals itself also, and perhaps in a still higher degree, in different songs and poems, of which many not only are truly beautiful but also have this particular esthetic value, that they probably are the most genuine products in modern times of a real and veritable nature poetry.

The poetic fancy of the Indian manifests itself even in the names he gives to regions and places, most of which still are retained in American geography, though their real meaning may have been lost. *Ticonderoga*, for instance, is the place where the waters divide; *Ontario*, a beautiful view over rocks, hills, and waters; *Ohio*, the beautiful river; *Manitowoc*, the spirits' hollow; *Nashotah*, the twin lakes; *Niagara*, the roaring water. A thousand other names reveal a great power and inclination to put into harmonious words and syllables a poetic thought.

But the poetic element stands out especially in the tales, legends, and allegorical stories of which the Indian people possess such a wealth and with which they often while away the time in their winter huts. Despite the fact that there is much in these traditional stories that appears unreasonable, monstrous, and meaningless, they reveal a nimble imagination and not a little intellectual power in invention and combination.

Both their songs and stories reflect for the most part their peculiar cosmogony and the strange theories they have constructed about the creative forces in the world. According to these, either cooperating divinities have brought forth and completed a part of the universe, or hostile powers have labored from the very time the work was finished to destroy it. Their faith that the universe as a whole—the earth, the planets, and the atmosphere—has an immanent soul or spirit; that every class of created things has a representative divinity who has eyes and ears open for everything that is said or done; that even the winds have a voice and the leaves of the trees speak a language; that the very earth itself is a living spirit world with influence upon men's destinies; in short, that the elements and every separate thing in the material world are a part of the great creative world spirit or an abode of a manitou — this belief is reflected in almost all of their poetry and song.

These invariably contain, moreover, an element of pathos, always some recollection, some plaint for a departed past. It is very doubtful whether the spirit of the Indian is ever capable of harboring a genuine feeling of hope. The whole direction of his thought is toward the past; all his conceptions deal more with what has been than with the future. His mind seldom has enough power over him to make him heed the hour that *is*, still less the one that is *to be*. Hence, whenever he wakens from the dullness and indifference with which he seems to face everything about him, and gives himself to lighter moods and emotions, his soul is filled with disquietude and fear that some harm is about to come to him.

It is natural that if such a person be a master of poetic expression, this will bear the stamp of his inward attitude and breathe forth a lamenting melancholy; it will be called forth for the most part by some painful occasion. If one excepts the hymns of war, a spirit of sadness and despair almost always characterizes the fragments of Indian poetry that have come to us. Generally he treats such subjects as a dying person, the loss of a child, death, or fear of evil spirits. These songs have neither rhyme nor meter. In the freedom of form, in the poetic feeling, and in the tendency toward parallelism that appear in Indian funeral and memorial songs, there has been thought to be much reminiscent of the poetic art of the Hebrews.

Little inviting though this field may seem to be in many instances, it still has something to offer. It gives us at least a conception of the intellectual qualities of a repressed and humiliated race.

It is worth remembering that many of the older love songs and war songs of the Indian peoples as well as many of their poetic myths and legends have not been transmitted from one generation to another exclusively by means of oral tradition. In addition there is to be found in most of the tribes a type of pictographic writing that may be termed their literature. In addition to the subjects mentioned above, these pictographs present in a very characteristic way their myths about the creation of the world; their views on life, death, and the future world; their necromantic incantations as well as the miraculous cures and mighty deeds performed by their medas; the predictions of their prophets; stories of hunting, of wars, and of wanderings — in a word, almost the whole history of the race, admixed with mythological metaphors and fantastic conceptions concerning the exploits and achievements of spirits, giants, dwarfs, beasts, and men. These writings consist of shapeless inscriptions on rolls of birch bark, on trees, stones, and other materials, and however difficult they may be to decipher — for the figures do not completely depict an event, a myth, or any other subject, but are merely symbols to aid the memory, leaving it to oral tradition to supply the lacunae — these pictographs, more than anything else, still give us a faithful picture of the red man at the various periods in the history of his race, and reveal him as he was and as he is. They also show that with the exception of the comparatively few cases in which he has accepted Christian teaching, and with the exception of a few insignificant changes in custom, dress, and other externals, he is in character and disposition and from the intellectual and cultural standpoint the same now that he was when Columbus first anchored at Guanahani.[1]

As samples of Indian oratory, allegorical stories, legends, and lyric poems a few extracts are translated and given below. The first is a story told by Washington Irving from the traditions of the Seminoles, a tribe in Florida that the United States administration has hardly as yet been able fully to subdue. This, like the following, may serve both as an example of Indian oratory and as an indication of the difficulty to be met with in our attempts to take this people a civilization they stubbornly reject, mainly from pride or for such reasons as are here set forth by the Indian chiefs.

Origin of the White, the Red, and the Black Men [2]

When the Floridas were erected into a territory of the United States, one of the earliest cares of the Governor, William P. Duval, was directed to the instruction and civilization of the natives. For this purpose he called a meeting of the chiefs, in which he informed them of the wish of their Great Father at Washington that they should have schools and teachers among them, and that their children should be instructed like the children of the white men. The chiefs listened with their customary silence and decorum to a long speech, setting forth the advantages that would accrue to them from this measure, and when he had concluded, begged the interval of a day to deliberate on it.

On the following day, a solemn convocation was held, at which one of the chiefs addressed the Governor in the name of all the rest. "My brother," said he, "we have been thinking over the proposition of our Great Father at Washington, to send teachers and set up schools among us. We are very thankful for the interest he takes in our welfare; but after much deliberation have concluded to decline his offer. What will do very well for white men, will not do for red men. I know you white men say we all come from the same father and mother, but you are mistaken. We have a tradition handed down from our forefathers, and we believe it, that the Great Spirit, when he undertook to make men, made the black man; it was his first attempt, and pretty well for a beginning; but he soon saw he had bungled; so he determined to try his hand again. He did so, and made the red man. He liked him much better than the black man, but still *he* was not exactly what he wanted. So he tried once more, and made the white man; and then he was satisfied. You see, therefore, that you were made last, and that is the reason I call you my youngest brother.

"When the Great Spirit had made the three men, he called them together and showed them three boxes. The first was filled with books, and maps, and papers; the second with bows and arrows, knives and tomahawks; the third with spades, axes, hoes, and hammers. 'These, my sons,' said he, 'are the means by which you are to live; choose among them according to your fancy.'

"The white man, being the favorite, had the first choice. He passed by the box of working-tools without notice; but when he came to the weapons for war and hunting, he stopped and looked hard at them. The red man trembled, for he had set his heart upon that box. The white man, however, after looking upon it for a moment, passed on, and chose the box of books and papers. The red man's turn came next, and you may be sure he seized with joy upon the bows and arrows and tomahawks. As to the black man, he had no choice left, but to put up with the box of tools.

"From this it is clear that the Great Spirit intended the white man should learn to read and write, to understand all about the moon and stars, and to make everything, even rum and whiskey. That the red man should be a first-rate hunter, and a mighty warrior, but he was not to learn anything from books, as the Great Spirit had not given him any; nor was he to make rum and whiskey, lest he should kill himself with drinking. As to the black man, as he had nothing but working-tools, it was clear he was to work for the white and red man, which he has continued to do.

"We must go according to the wishes of the Great Spirit, or we shall get into trouble. To know how to read and write is very good for white men, but very bad for red men. It makes white men better, but red men worse. Some of the Creeks and Cherokees learnt to read and write, and they are the greatest rascals among all the Indians. They went on to Washington, and said they were going to see their Great Father, to talk about the good of the nation. And when they got there, they all wrote upon a little piece of paper, without the nation at home knowing anything about it. And the first thing the nation at home knew of the matter, they were called together by the Indian agent, who showed them a little piece of paper, which he told them was a treaty which their brethren had made in their name with their Great Father at Washington. And as they knew not what a treaty was, he held up the little piece of paper, and they looked under it, and lo! it covered a great extent of country, and they found that their brethren, by knowing how to read and write, had sold their houses, and their lands, and the graves of their fathers; and that the white man, by knowing how to read and write, had gained them. Tell our Great Father at Washington, therefore, that we are very sorry we cannot receive teachers among us; for reading and writing, though very good for white men, is very bad for Indians."

An Address by a Choctaw Chief [3]

Some years ago an Indian agent delivered a long address to a large gathering of Indians, with a view toward persuading them to leave their present abode and go farther away, on the other side of the Mississippi. He informed them that they no longer were able to light their council fires in these regions, that their braves no longer could gain honor and glory there, and that they would do best to submit to the will of the Great Father in Washington, who for their own good was willing to assign them new homes and hunting grounds where they could improve their situation and look forward to a happier future.

A famous old Indian chief replied to him in a speech that in richness of content, in poetically beautiful and powerful language, and in sublime feeling is almost unsurpassable and that among any people whatsoever may serve as a sample of real eloquence. It is natural that translated into another tongue, and now from that into another, much of its original beauty has been lost.

"Brother," said the old chief, "we have heard you speak to us with the lips of our Father, the Great White Chief in Washington, and my people have directed me to reply to you. The red man has no books; when he wants to express his thoughts, he speaks with his tongue as his fathers spoke before him. He is afraid to write. When he speaks he knows what he says. The Great Spirit hears him. Writing is the invention of the paleface; it breeds error and dissension. The Great Spirit *speaks*: we hear him in the thunder, in the rustling winds, and in the mighty waves — but he never *writes*.

"Brother, when we were young we were strong; we fought by your side; but now our weapons are broken. You have increased in power; my people have grown weak.

"Brother, my voice is feeble; you can hardly hear me. It is not a warrior's shout of victory, but the wailing of a child. I have lost my voice sorrowing over the misfortunes of my people. Here you see their graves, and in these ancient pines you can hear their departed spirits. Their dust is here, and we are left here to protect it. Our warriors have almost all gone away to the distant lands in the West; we alone have remained behind, that we may die here in peace. Shall we, too, go hence and leave the bones of our fathers to the wolves?

"Brother, two nights have passed since we heard you speak. Sleep has closed our eyes. You urge us to give up our land, and you say that our Great Father desires it. We do not wish to displease our Great Father; we have veneration for him and for you who bring us his message. But the Choctaws always think; we ask for time to make our decision.

"Brother, our hearts are filled with grief. Twelve winters ago our chiefs sold our land. Every warrior that you see here was against the treaty. Could we have foreknown that evil event, it would never have happened. But alas! where we were standing we could neither be seen nor heard. Our tears mingled with the rain drops, and our voices died away in the plaintive wind; but the white men did not know this, and they deprived us of our land.

"Brother, we do not complain. A Choctaw suffers, but he never murmurs. Your arm is strong and we are unable to oppose it. But the white man worships the Great Spirit and so does the red man. The Great Spirit loves truth. When our homes were taken away from us, we were promised new ones. The Great Spirit heard the promise, and you yourselves wrote it in your books. Since then the trees have twelve times shed their leaves, but still the promise is unfulfilled. You have deprived us of our homes. The white man's plow has dug up the bones of our fathers. We dare no longer light our fires; but still you say that if we so desire we may remain here, but if not, you will give us another, and for us a better, land.

"Brother, is there truth in what you tell us? Nevertheless we believe that our Great Father now knows our condition and that he will listen to us. We are like sorrowing, fatherless children in our own homeland; but our Father in Washington, you say, will extend his hand to us. When he keeps his promise we will answer him. He means us well, we know it. But we cannot think now. Sorrow has made us children. When we have made our decision, we shall be men again, and shall speak to our Great Father of his promises.

"Brother, you stand in the moccasins of a great chief; you have spoken for a mighty people, and your speech was long. My people are few; their shadow reaches hardly to your knees; they are gone and scattered. When I cry, I hear in the depth of the forest my own voice; but I listen in vain for an answering word. Therefore my words are few. I have nothing more to say; but take what I have said to the white people's Great Chief, whose brother now stands at your side."

Allegorical Traditions of the Origin of Men — of Manabozho, and of the Introduction of the Religious Mysteries of the Medical Magic [4]

At a certain time, a great Manito came on earth, and took a wife of men. She had four sons at a birth, and died in ushering them into the world. The first was Manabozho, who is the friend of the human race. The second Chibiabos, who has the care of the dead, and presides over the country of souls. The third Wabasso, who, as soon as he saw light, fled to the North, where he was changed into a white rabbit, and, under that form, is considered as a great spirit. The fourth was Chokanipok, or the man of flint, or the fire-stone.

The first thing Manabozho did, when he grew up, was to go to war against Chokanipok, whom he accused of his mother's death. The contests between them were frightful and long continued, and wherever they had a combat the face of nature still shows signs of it. Fragments were cut from his flesh, which were transformed into stones, and he finally destroyed Chokanipok by tearing out his entrails, which were changed into vines. All the flint-stones which are scattered over the earth were produced in this way, and they supplied men with the principle of fire.

Manabozho was the author of arts and improvements. He taught men how to make agakwuts [axes], lances, and arrow-points, and all implements of bone and stone, and also how to make snares, and traps, and nets, to take animals, and birds, and fishes. He and his brother Chibiabos lived retired, and were very intimate, planning things for the good of men, and were of superior and surpassing powers of mind and body.

The Manitos who live in the air, the earth, and the water, became jealous of their great power, and conspired against them. Manabozho had warned his brother against their machinations, and cautioned him not to separate himself from his side; but one day Chibiabos ventured alone on one of the Great Lakes. It was winter, and the whole surface was covered with ice. As soon as he had reached the center the malicious Manitos broke the ice, and plunged him to the bottom, where they hid his body.

Manabozho wailed along the shores. He waged a war against all the Manitos, and precipitated numbers of them to the deepest abyss.

He called on the dead body of his brother. He put the whole country in dread by his lamentations. He then besmeared his face with black, and sat down six years to lament, uttering the name of Chibiabos. The Manitos consulted what to do to appease his melancholy and his wrath. The oldest and wisest of them, who had had no hand in the death of Chibiabos, offered to undertake the task of reconciliation. They built a sacred lodge close to that of Manabozho, and prepared a sumptuous feast. They procured the most delicious tobacco, and filled a pipe. They then assembled in order, one behind the other, and each carrying under his arm a sack formed of the skin of some favorite animal, as a beaver, an otter, or a lynx, and filled with precious and curious medicines, culled from all plants. These they exhibited, and invited him to the feast with pleasing words and ceremonies. He immediately raised his head, uncovered it, and washed off his mourning colors and besmearments, and then followed them. When they had reached the lodge, they offered him a cup of liquor prepared from the choicest medicines, as, at once, a propitiation, and an initiative rite. He drank it at a single draught. He found his melancholy departed, and felt the most inspiring effects. They then commenced their dances and songs, united with various ceremonies. Some shook their bags at him as a token of skill. Some exhibited the skins of birds filled with smaller birds, which, by some art, would hop out of the throat of the bag. Others showed curious tricks with their drums. All danced, all sang, all acted with the utmost gravity, and earnestness of gestures; but with exactness of time, motion, and voice. Manabozho was cured; he ate, danced, sung, and smoked the sacred pipe. In this manner the mysteries of the Grand Medicine Dance were introduced.

The before recreant Manitos now all united their powers, to bring Chibiabos to life. They did so, and brought him to life, but it was forbidden him to enter the lodge. They gave him, through a chink, a burning coal, and told him to go and preside over the country of souls, and reign over the land of the dead. They bid him with the coal to kindle a fire for his aunts and uncles, a term by which is meant all men who should die thereafter, and make them happy, and let it be an everlasting fire.

Manabozho went to the Great Spirit after these things. He then

descended to the earth, and confirmed the mysteries of the medi-
cine-dance, and supplied all whom he initiated with medicines for
the cure of all diseases. It is to him that we owe the growth of all
the medical roots, and antidotes to every disease and poison. He
commits the growth of these to Misukumigakwa, or the mother of
the earth, to whom he makes offerings.

Manabozho traverses the whole earth. He is the friend of man.
He killed the ancient monsters whose bones we now see under the
earth; and cleared the streams and forests of many obstructions
which the Bad Spirit had put there, to fit them for our residence.
He has placed four good Spirits at the four cardinal points, to
which we point in our ceremonies. The Spirit of the North gives
snow and ice, to enable men to pursue game and fish. The Spirit
of the South gives melons, maize, and tobacco. The Spirit of the
West gives rain, and the Spirit of the East, light; and he commands
the sun to make his daily walks around the earth. Thunder is the
voice of these Spirits, to whom we offer the smoke of sa-mau (tobacco).

Manabozho, it is believed, yet lives on an immense flake of ice
in the Arctic Ocean. We fear the white race will some day discover
his retreat, and drive him off. Then the end of the world is at hand,
for as soon as he puts his foot on the earth again, it will take fire,
and every living creature perish in the flames.

The Island of the Blessed; or the Hunter's Dream [5]

There was once a beautiful girl, who died suddenly on the day
she was to have been married to a handsome young hunter. He had
also proved his bravery in war, so that he enjoyed the praises of
his tribe, but his heart was not proof against this loss. From the hour
she was buried, there was no more joy or peace for him. He went
often to visit the spot where the women had buried her, and sat
musing there, when, it was thought by some of his friends, he
would have done better to try and amuse himself in the chase, or
by diverting his thoughts in the war-path. But war and hunting
had lost their charms for him. His heart was already dead within
him. He wholly neglected both his war-club and his bows and
arrows.

He had heard the old people say that there was a path that led to the land of souls, and he determined to follow it. He accordingly set out one morning, after having completed his preparations for the journey. At first he hardly knew which way to go. He was only guided by the tradition that he must go south. For a while he could see no change in the face of the country. Forests, and hills, and valleys, and streams, had the same looks which they wore in his native place. There was snow on the ground, when he set out, and it was sometimes seen to be piled and matted on the thick trees and bushes. At length it began to diminish, and, as he walked on, finally disappeared. The forest assumed a more cheerful appearance, the leaves put forth their buds, and before he was aware of the completeness of the change, he found he had left behind him the land of snow and ice. The air became pure and mild; the dark clouds had rolled away from the sky; a pure field of blue was above him; and, as he went forward in his journey, he saw flowers beside his path, and heard the song of birds. By these signs he knew that he was going the right way, for they agreed with the traditions of his tribe. At length he spied a path. It took him through a grove, then up a long and elevated ridge, on the very top of which he came to a lodge. At the door stood an old man with white hair, whose eyes, though deeply sunk, had a fiery brilliancy. He had a long robe of skins thrown loosely around his shoulders, and a staff in his hands.

The young man began to tell his story; but the venerable chief arrested him before he had proceeded to speak ten words. "I have expected you," he replied, "and had just risen to bid you welcome to my abode. She whom you seek passed here but a short time since, and being fatigued with her journey rested herself here. Enter my lodge and be seated, and I will then satisfy your inquiries, and give you directions for your journey from this point." Having done this, and refreshed himself by rest, they both issued forth from the lodge door. "You see yonder gulf," said the old man, "and the wide-stretching plain beyond: it is the land of souls. You stand upon its borders, and my lodge is the gate of entrance. But you cannot take your body along. Leave it here with your bow and arrows, your bundle and your dog. You will find them safe upon your return." So saying he re-entered the lodge, and the freed traveler bounded forward as if his feet had suddenly been endowed with the power of wings. But all things retained their natural colors and shapes. The woods and leaves, and streams and lakes, were only more bright and comely than he had ever witnessed. Animals bounded across his path with a freedom and confidence which seemed to tell him, there was no blood shed there. Birds of beautiful plumage inhabited the groves, and sported in the waters. There was but one thing in which he saw a very unusual effect. He noticed that his passage was not stopped by trees or other objects. He appeared to walk directly through them: they were, in fact, but the images or shadows of material forms. He became sensible that he was in the land of souls.

When he had traveled half a day's journey, through a country which was continually becoming more attractive, he came to the banks of a broad lake, in the center of which was a large and beautiful island. He found a canoe of white shining stone, tied to the shore. He was now sure that he had come the right path, for the aged man had told him of this. There were also shining paddles. He immediately entered the canoe, and took the paddles in his hands, when, to his joy and surprise, on turning round he beheld the object of his search in another canoe, exactly its counterpart in everything. It seemed to be the shadow of his own. She had exactly imitated his motions, and they were side by side. They at once pushed out from the shore, and began to cross the lake. Its waves seemed to be rising, and, at a distance, looked ready to swallow them up; but just as they entered the whitened edge of them, they seemed to melt away, as if they were but the images of waves. But no sooner was one wreath of foam passed, than another, more threatening still, rose up. Thus they were in perpetual fear; but what added to it was the clearness of the water, through which they could see heaps of the bones of beings who had perished before.

The Master of Life had, however, decreed to let them pass, for the thoughts and acts of neither of them had been bad. But they saw many others struggling and sinking in the waves. Old men and young men, males and females, of all ages and ranks were there: some passed and some sunk. It was only the little children whose canoes seemed to meet no waves. At length every difficulty was gone, as in a moment, and they both leaped out on the happy island. They felt that the very air was food. It strengthened and nourished them. They wandered together over the blissful fields, where everything was formed to please the eye and the ear. There were no tempests; there was no ice, nor chilly winds; no one shivered for the want of warm clothes; no one suffered for hunger; no one mourned for the dead. They saw no graves. They heard of no wars. Animals ran freely about, but there was no blood spilled in hunting them: for the air itself nourished them. Gladly would the young warrior have remained there for ever, but he was obliged to go back for his body. He did not see the Master of Life, but he heard his voice, as if it were a soft breeze. "Go back," said this voice, "to the land from whence you came. Your time has not yet come. The duties for which I made you, and which you are to perform, are not yet finished. Return to your people, and accomplish the acts of a good man. You will be the ruler of your tribe for many days. The rules you will observe will be told you by my messenger, who keeps the gate. When he surrenders back your body, he will tell you what to do. Listen to him, and you shall afterwards rejoin the spirit which you have followed, but whom you must now leave behind. She is accepted, and will be ever here, as young and as happy as she was when I first called her from the land of snows."

When the voice grew silent, the young warrior awoke. It was a dream, a vision, and he found himself still in the bitter land of snows and hunger, death and tears.

An Indian Serenade [6]

Awake, flower of the forest, fair bird of the meadow.
Awake, awake, you who have the eyes of the hind.
When you look at me I am happy, like the flowers when
  they are revived by the dew.
The breath of your mouth is sweet as the fragrance of
  the flowers in the morning, as their fragrance in the
  evening of the month when the leaves wither.
Does not the blood of my veins sing within me like the
  murmuring spring when it lifts itself toward the sun
  in the month of bright nights?

When you are near me, my heart is tuned to song, like
the quivering branches of the trees in the month of
strawberries.

When you, my beloved, are unhappy, my heart is darkened like the glittering river when the shadows of the
clouds overspread it.

Your smile makes my disquieted heart radiant, as the sun
lets the little waves the cold wind has wakened shimmer like gold.

I — look at me, blood of my beating heart.

The earth smiles, the water smiles, the heavens smile,
but I cannot smile when you are not with me.

Awake, awake, my beloved!

Editor's Notes

BIOGRAPHICAL NOTE. *Gustaf Unonius was born in Helsingfors, Finland, August 25, 1810. His father was Israel Unonius, member of an old Swedish family in Finland and a barrister. His mother was Maria Gårdberg. The family moved to Sweden when Finland came under the domination of Russia. Gustaf was educated at Uppsala University, where he completed his course in 1830 and then for three years studied law. Though afterward more interested in medicine, he became a clerk in the office of the provincial government at Uppsala, the position he held when in his thirty-first year he decided to emigrate to America. He died in Hacksta parish, Uppland, Sweden, October 14, 1902.*

CHAPTER I

[1] The University of Uppsala, the oldest institution of higher learning in Sweden, was founded in 1477. It is located at Uppsala, about an hour's ride by train from Stockholm.

[2] Unonius is listed in official records variously as *vice häradsskrivare, vice häradsbokhållare, kammarskrivare*. It can be presumed that his position was that of a minor government functionary, clerk, or bookkeeper in the Land Office of Uppland, the provincial seat of which was Uppsala. (Official records in *Landsarkivet*, Uppsala.)

[3] The banns were published April 4, 1841, and the wedding took place April 26. His wife, Margareta Charlotta Öhrströmer, was the daughter of Lars Fredrik Öhrströmer and Regina Fredrika Forell, born in Söderby Carl's Parish April 7, 1821. (Records of Uppsala Cathedral and Söderby Carl's Parish.)

[4] During the *Riksdag* of 1840 the Four Estates, upon a motion of the *borgare* (burghers), recommended that restrictive emigration laws, enacted successively in 1756, 1801, and 1804 be modernized and liberalized. King Charles XIV John passed over the recommendation, instead proclaiming on May 4, 1840, that henceforth no Swedish citizen seeking passport for foreign travel need deposit funds in Sweden or produce guarantors to safeguard his return to Sweden. (*Emigrationsutredningen* [Stockholm, 1908], bilaga I, pp. 3ff.)

[5] On the day before, Unonius and his wife, as well as the maid, had appeared at the church office to obtain their writs of good conduct, permitting them to leave the parish. (Uppsala Cathedral Records.)

[6] Gävle was very important to Swedish shipping in the first half of the nineteenth century. Vessels of many nations made Gävle their port of call for Swedish iron and wood and tar products.

[7] *Concilium abeundi.* Advice to leave the university, a mild form of expulsion.

[8] This diary, abbreviated below *UD*, was only recently discovered on the estate of Fånöö, Sweden, the home of Fru Anna Tamm, a granddaughter of Gustaf Unonius. While most of the account in his *Memoirs* agrees with his diary, there are times when he consciously or unconsciously departs from his daybook entries. Only when obvious errors occur will the material in *UD* be used in these notes.

[9] The University of Uppsala Library, erected 1819–41.

[10] On the last day of April, the day students gather to welcome the return of spring — even today one of the most important dates on the school calendar throughout Sweden.

[11] These "nations" represent the majority of the Swedish provinces in addition to Göteborg and Stockholm. Every student enrolled at the University of Uppsala must belong to one of these "nations," usually that group which represents his home province or, in the case of Göteborg or Stockholm, his native city.

[12] Christian Molbech (1783–1857), Danish historian and philologist.

[13] Christoph Wilhelm Hufeland (1762–1836), German medical doctor and author. His first Swedish translation, *Konsten att lefva länge*, appeared in Stockholm in 1797.

[14] The Reverend Anders Andersson Oldberg (1804–67), married to Charlotta Unonius' sister Fredrika Catharina Öhrströmer, was a teacher in the Prins Gustaf School in Uppsala. He later became rector and dean of Alfta Parish in Hälsingland. His grandson is Professor Arne Oldberg, head of the departments of piano and composition as well as of the graduate department of the School of Music at Northwestern University, Evanston, Illinois, from 1897 to 1941.

[15] Approximately 8 miles from Uppsala, on the road to Gävle.

[16] Unidentified.

[17] An allusion to the popular student song *Stå stark, du ljusets riddarvakt*, set to music by the well-known composer of student songs, Gunnar Wennerberg (1817–1901).

[18] From *The Sea Voyage* by Johan David Valerius (1776–1852), Swedish civil servant and author.

[19] Ivar Johan Fredrik Hagberg, born in Gamleby Parish, Östergötland, November 23, 1815. He returned to Sweden in 1842, entered the Royal Swedish Telegraph Service, and died in Stockholm May 19, 1898. (K. G. Odén, *Östgötars minne* [Stockholm, 1902], p. 465.)

[20] Carl Gustaf Groth, born in Odinsala Parish, Uppland, February 12, 1819. After a number of years in America he returned to Sweden. He became a prison warden in Norrtälje in 1863. He married a cousin to Charlotta Unonius, Augusta Fredrika Charlotta Öhrströmer, and died in Norrtälje September 1, 1879. (Information supplied by P. M. Lijsing, Norrtälje, 1949.)

[21] Christina Henriksdotter Södergren, born in Livonia *ca.* 1810. (Söderby Carl's Parish Records.)

[22] Former Russian Baltic province. After World War I, northern Livonia became a part of Esthonia, southern Livonia a part of Latvia.

[23] The Stackelberg family, at one time one of the wealthiest and largest landholding families in the Baltic, descends from Baron Carl Adam Stackelberg (1669–1749), Swedish army officer and onetime Swedish governor of the island of Ösel. (Gustaf Elgenstierna, *Den introducerade svenska adelns ättartavlor* [Stockholm, 1925–36], VII, 465.)

[24] Fortress near Leningrad, built by Peter the Great in 1710 as protection for St. Petersburg.

[25] The coastal regions of Uppland bordering the Baltic.

[26] Olof Ulrik Torslow (1801–81), Swedish actor. During 1837–43 he traveled through the Swedish provinces and Finland as the head of a theatrical troupe, *Djurgårdsteatern*. (Herman Hofberg, *Svenskt biografiskt handlexikon* [Stockholm, 1906], II, 630.)

[27] Anders Peter Berggren (1792–1847), Swedish actor and theater director. He traveled throughout Sweden with his own cast, giving performances in the early decades of the nineteenth century. (*Svenska män och kvinnor* [Stockholm, 1942–], I, 242.)

[28] Presumably Julius Günther (1818–1904), Swedish concert artist who made his debut with the Royal Swedish Opera in 1838. (*Ibid.*, III, 205.)

[29] François Hubert Prume (1816–49), Belgian violin virtuoso, professor of violin at the Paris Conservatory. He appeared in Stockholm in 1840 and 1845 as concert artist. (*Nordisk Familjebok* [Stockholm, 1904–26], XXIII, cols. 455–56.)

[30] City in northern Finland, at the mouth of the Torne River, opposite the Swedish city Haparanda.

[31] Province in south central Sweden.

[32] Per Jakob Emanuelsson (1802–88), a student in Uppsala in 1820; appointed lector in Greek and Hebrew at Gävle *läroverk* in 1837, rector of Hällestad Parish, Östergötland in 1843. (Joh. Is. Håhl, *Linköpings stifts herdaminne* [Norrköping, 1846–47], II, 233.) (Information supplied by Nils F. Nord, Gävle.)

[33] *UD* mentions a Mr. Elfstrand as the owner of *Minnet*. Presumably this is Petter Elfstrand (1783–1845), one of the best known citizens of Gävle during the early nineteenth century. He owned a fleet of ships and represented the city in the Swedish *Riksdag*. A great-grandson is Edgar Elfstrand, a pharmacist in Lindstrom, Minnesota.

[34] Approximately $125 in U.S. money at that time.

[35] Unidentified.

[36] Carl Michael Bellman (1740–95), Swedish poet and composer, whose songs are still sung throughout all Scandinavia.

[37] Pehr Hollander (1810–59), known as *Gråskepparen* at the University of Uppsala. He later became a physician in Ovansjö Parish in Gästrikland. (Axel Hackzell, *Turkiska musiken* [Uppsala, 1921].)

[38] *Turkiska musiken* was a group of spirited students in Uppsala in the 1830's, known not only for their interest in music, but also for their *nachspiel*. Founded in 1828 as the *St. Hilarii Orden*, the group got their nickname, *Turkish Music*, from the din and hilarity engendered on the march home from their parties late at night. The instruments used on these nocturnal wanderings about Uppsala consisted of triangles, gongs, whistles, jangling house keys, pot lids, kitchen pans, etc. The last meeting of the group was held April 6, 1835, when Unonius gave the main oration. (*Ibid.*)

[39] Carl Wilhelm Pålman, or Polman, was born in Västerås, May 9, 1809. His practical medical training he received in Stockholm, Göteborg, and Uddevalla during the cholera epidemic in 1834. In America he continued his medical studies and settled finally in New York City, where he died February 14, 1861. He donated a fine collection of books to his boyhood school in Västerås, *Västerås högre allmänna läroverk*. (Västerås Parish records; A. H. Wistrand, A. J. Bruzelius, and C. Edling, *Sveriges läkarehistoria* [Stockholm, 1873–76], II, 610.)

[40] The two Swedish provinces Västmanland and Dalarna have combined their "nations" in Uppsala to form *Västmanland-Dala Nation*, popularly known as *V-Dala*.

[41] An examination in the humanities, required of those intending to take up medical studies at the University of Uppsala or the University of Lund in the nineteenth century.

[42] Small town on the northern Uppland coast.

CHAPTER 2

[1] Helsingör, or Elsinore, Danish seaport on the Öresund opposite the Swedish city of Hälsingborg. Here is Kronborg Castle, famous as the scene of Shakespeare's *Hamlet*.

[2] *UD* has Mr. Brodell, a ship's agent; a Mr. Ryberg or Nyberg; and the Swedish consul, who at this time was Gustaf af Nordin.

[3] Presumably an allusion to a semi-weekly political and literary journal *Freja*, published in Stockholm 1836–44. The journal was the spokesman for "Young Sweden," presenting at first a moderate point of view but gradually becoming more liberal.

[4] *UD* has four dollars per week per person.

[5] Frances Trollope (1780–1863), English novelist and the mother of Anthony

Trollope, who in her book *Domestic Manners of the Americans* severely criticized the Americans for their unmannerly conduct.

[6] People born and raised in Småland, a province in southern Sweden.

[7] Presumably Unonius refers to the American fruit pie, then unknown in Sweden.

[8] Undoubtedly the English Channel.

CHAPTER 3

[1] Carl Ulrik von Hauswolff (1791–1843), Swedish civil servant; secretary to the governor of the Swedish colony of St. Barthélemy in the West Indies 1816–19; traveled widely in North and South America; published his book on the United States first in German, and in 1835 in a revised Swedish edition, *Teckningar utur sällskapslifvet i Nordamerikas förenta stater*. (Elgenstierna, *Den introducerade svenska adelns ättartavlor*, V, 497.)

[2] William Niblo (1789–1878), American hotel and theater manager. In 1829 he opened Niblo's Garden in New York, which by 1837 had become the fashionable entertainment center of that city. It featured vaudeville, a concert series, and a season of opera, in which the outstanding production was *The Barber of Seville* with Fornasari. (*Dictionary of American Biography*.)

[3] Unonius has apparently transposed two figures. The total continental area of the United States is 3,022,387 square miles. (*World Almanac of 1950*.)

[4] Fredrika Bremer (1801–65), Swedish writer and champion of women's rights. She spent the years 1849–51 traveling extensively in America, after which she published her observations in a three-volume work, *Hemmen i den nya verlden*, in 1853–54. The work was translated into English in 1854 by Miss Bremer's good friend Mary Botham Howitt (1799–1888) under the title *The Homes of the New World*.

CHAPTER 4

[1] Unonius indulges here in a play on words, since *Minnet* means "the memory."

[2] Karl David Arfwedson (1806–81), Swedish merchant and traveler. In 1834, after an extensive journey through North America, he published in English *The United States and Canada*. The following year this work was translated into Swedish with the title *Förenta staterna och Kanada*, presumably the edition that Unonius used.

[3] A fishing smack from Roslagen, off the coast of Uppland, as compared with one of the stately sailing vessels from Gävle, among the largest and most beautiful in Sweden in the early nineteenth century.

[4] Not identified.

[5] Souvenir rings of horsehair made in Dalarna.

[6] Small community in Dalarna, where the peasant crafts always have had a good reputation for quality of workmanship.

[7] Carl August Gosselman (1799–1843), Swedish naval officer and writer, who published *Resa i Norra Amerika* in 1835 after extensive travels here.

[8] Charles Dickens (1812–70), who wrote his *American Notes* after a voyage to America in 1842.

CHAPTER 5

[1] The names have been normalized to agree with the American spelling. It is interesting to note the catastrophic setback these communities suffered with the coming of the railroads and the shift in the population toward the West. Only Frankfort has held its own. By comparing the population schedules of the Seventh Census (1850) with the latest Rand McNally Gazeteer (1950) it is possible to see the change in population in the last hundred years.

Community	1850	1950
Danube	1,730	—
Frankfort	3,023	3,859
Manheim	1,902	60
Minden	4,623	40
Oppenheim	2,315	50
Vienna	3,393	100

[2] Unonius seems a little confused on this point. Geneva is not a lake, but a city located at the northern tip of Lake Seneca (not Senua). In all probability he means Lakes Seneca and Cayuga in addition to the Canandaigua and the Oneida.

[3] Presumably E. William Ahlmark, born ca. 1813, who arrived at New York September 11, 1841, aboard the Norwegian vessel *Theresa*. (Passenger manifest of the *Theresa* in the National Archives, Washington, D.C.)

[4] In Swedish folklore *Blåkulla* is the trysting place of the devil and the witches who serve him. In modern Swedish it is a euphemism for hell.

[5] De Witt Clinton (1769–1828), who as governor of the state of New York sponsored the construction of the Erie and Champlain–Hudson Canals.

[6] Baltzar Bogislaus von Platen (1766–1829), Swedish naval officer and diplomat, whose name is inseparably linked with the construction of the Göta Canal across southern Sweden, linking the Baltic with the Kattegatt.

CHAPTER 6

[1] Presumably Joseph C. Morrell, partner in the firm of Castle and Morrell, wholesale jewelers, located at 191 Main Street, Buffalo, New York. Morrell boarded at the Farmers' Hotel and last appears in the Buffalo City Directory of 1844. (Information supplied by the Buffalo Historical Society.)

[2] For Unonius' own evaluation of von Hauswolff, see George M. Stephenson, ed., *Letters Relating to Gustaf Unonius and the Early Settlers in Wisconsin*, Vol. VII of Augustana Historical Society Publications (Rock Island, 1937), pp. 65–92.

[3] In his diary Unonius does not mention the explosion. That he does not is understandable since it occurred more than six weeks earlier on August 9, 1841, when the steamboat *Erie*, 497 tons burden, exploded and caught fire off Silver Creek on Lake Erie, approximately 33 miles from Buffalo. The loss of life was heavy, ranging from 100 to 250, according to various sources. ([John Brant Mansfield] *History of the Great Lakes* [Chicago, 1899], I, 636.)

[4] Presumably the steamboat *Illinois*, owned by Oliver Newberry of Chicago and launched in Detroit in the summer of 1838. She was 205 feet long, with a tonnage of 756, and with a low-pressure engine capable of driving her from Buffalo to Chicago in five days' time. The *Illinois*, the finest ship ever built by Newberry, long remained popular with the traveling public. Her seaworthiness was unquestioned, and her cabins and staterooms were loaded with an awe-inspiring quantity of gilt and other decorations. (Milo M. Quaife, *Lake Michigan* [Indianapolis, 1944], p. 152.)

[5] James Fenimore Cooper (1789–1851), whose *Leatherstocking Tales* were read avidly in Sweden. *The Pioneers* appeared in a Swedish translation in 1827, and *The Last of the Mohicans* in 1828, only four and two years respectively after the original editions in America. (J. Viktor Johansson, *Bokvandringar: uppsatser om böcker och boksamlare* [Stockholm, 1945], p. 158.)

CHAPTER 7

[1] September 30 (*UD*).
[2] October 1 (*UD*).

³ The Öland horse is about the size of an American pony.

⁴ Michilmackinac, the early name for Mackinac.

⁵ October 3 (UD).

⁶ He was Hugo Ferdinand Öhrströmer, brother to Mrs. Unonius, born April 15, 1816, in Söderby Carl's Parish, Sweden. He entered the Swedish Army at an early age and advanced to the rank of Sublieutenant with *Jämtlands Fältjägare,* May 7, 1836. In August 1838 he resigned from the Swedish Army and soon thereafter emigrated to the U.S., where he abbreviated his name to Hugo Ferdinand. In September of that year he joined Company II of the Fifth Infantry Regiment, then stationed at Fort Snelling, Indian Territory, being therefore one the first Swedes to visit what was to became the state of Minnesota. He served a five-year enlistment, part of the time as hospital steward, and was discharged from the army at Fort Mackinac, Michigan, July 30, 1844. Nothing further is known about him.

Unonius might have spared himself his disappointment at not seeing his relative at the fort. Actually Company II did not leave Fort Snelling till September 15, 1841, and arrived at Fort Mackinac November 6 of that year, almost a month after Unonius had passed the island en route to Milwaukee. (Enlistment papers for Hugo Ferdinand in the Adjutant General's Office, National Archives, Washington, D.C.; parish records of Söderby Carl in *Landsarkivet,* Uppsala, Sweden; military records in *Länsarkivet,* Östersund, Sweden.)

⁷ In the summer of 1846 a few Mormons under the leadership of their Prophet James Jesse Strang settled on Big Beaver Island at the northern end of Lake Michigan. By 1847 the settlement had well begun, and at the close of 1849 about fifty Mormon families were living around the shore of Paradise Bay to form the town of St. James. The settlement was of brief duration, however. In 1851, owing to certain questionable activities by the Prophet, the U.S. revenue cutter *Michigan* moved in at St. James and Strang was arrested. He was acquitted, however, and this fact seems to have gone to his head. He became arrogant and abusive toward the Gentiles. His unpopularity grew till a member of his colony, Dr. H. D. McCulloch, plotted to remove him from the scene. On June 16, 1856, the *Michigan* again put in at St. James. The captain sent word that he wished to speak with Strang. As the Prophet began to step up to the bridge leading to the pier, he was ambushed by two assassins, who shot him, mortally wounding him. The murderers fled to the cutter, where they found temporary asylum. Strang died soon thereafter and lies buried in Burlington, Wisconsin. His colony soon dispersed, leaving Big Beaver Island in sole possession of the Gentiles. (Quaife, *Lake Michigan,* pp. 243–47; Walter Havighurst, *The Long Ships Passing* [New York, 1942], pp. 147–54.)

⁸ October 3 (UD). This date must be correct, since it fell on a Sunday in 1841.

⁹ Presumably Philander Chase (1775–1852), American Protestant Episcopal bishop, first in Ohio, later in Illinois, with whom Unonius became intimately acquainted.

¹⁰ The Milwaukee House, finished in 1837. First known as the Bellevue House, it was renamed the Milwaukee House and moved to the Third Ward in 1849. Unonius frequented it occasionally on his trips to Milwaukee from Pine Lake. (UD.)

¹¹ Actually Newport developed as a village and had a population of 500 by 1863. Among its industries were five ship-building concerns. In 1865 the village separated from the township of Cottrellville in St. Clair County and changed its name to Marine City, which today has a population of over 3,000.

CHAPTER 8

¹ Olof Gottfrid Lange, born in Göteborg July 4, 1811. In 1824 he came to America for the first time as a cabin watch aboard an American vessel. He re-

mained a sailor for more than ten years, but in 1838 he went to Chicago via the Great Lakes. There he worked, among other places, in an apothecary shop owned by Dr. E. S. Kimberley on the northwest corner of Dearborn and Lake Streets. Later he moved to Milwaukee, engaging in construction work. It was at this time that Unonius met him. Lange finally settled in Chicago, where he became very active in Swedish circles. He died there July 13, 1893. (Ernst W. Olson, *History of the Swedes of Illinois* [Chicago, 1908], I, 182–84.)

[2] *Der Freischütz*, opera composed by Karl Maria von Weber in 1821.

[3] Immigrants from Saetesdal in Norway.

[4] Immigrants from Voss in Norway.

[5] A milkmaid who spends the summers in the mountains, pasturing the cattle. She lives at a saeter, or summer cottage, spending most of her time milking, churning butter, and making cheeses.

[6] *Nattvardsbarnen* ("The Children of the Lord's Supper"), written in 1820 by Esaias Tegnér (1782–1846), Swedish educator, bishop, and author. It was translated into English by Henry Wadsworth Longfellow in 1841. Presumably Unonius is mistaken when he claims that the people of Milwaukee had read *The Children of the Lord's Supper* as early as the first week in October 1841. According to Longfellow's own statement he was still translating the poem at the end of October 1841. (Andrew Hilen, *Longfellow and Scandinavia* [New Haven, 1947], p. 54.)

[7] The first volume of this work *(Notes from Everyday Life)* was published in Sweden in 1828. The English edition was translated by Mary Botham Howitt.

[8] A type of land, usually composed of clay soil, on which oak trees seem to thrive.

[9] A reference to lynching, probably derived from Col. Charles Lynch (1736–96), American Revolutionary War soldier.

[10] Today the total area of Wisconsin is 56,154 square miles. (*World Almanac of 1950.*)

[11] Henry Rowe Schoolcraft (1793–1864), American ethnologist.

[12] Claude Jean Allouez (1622–89), French Jesuit missionary in America.

[13] Jacques Marquette (1637–75), French Jesuit missionary and North American explorer.

[14] René Robert Cavelier, Sieur de La Salle (1643–87), French explorer in North America.

CHAPTER 9

[1] One of the three large burial mounds in Old Uppsala. These mounds, popularly known as the Royal Mounds, were formerly believed to be the graves of the Teutonic deities Odin, Thor, and Frö, but more recent investigation has shown that they are probably the sepulchers of three Swedish kings: Egil, Aun, and Adils.

[2] Most of the Latin terminology used by Unonius in this chapter has been modernized. All emendations to the text are placed within brackets. I am indebted to the staff of the Chicago Natural History Museum for help in bringing the nineteenth-century nomenclature up to date. I wish in particular to thank Dr. A. L. Rand, curator of birds; Dr. Julian A. Steyermark, associate curator of the Herbarium; and Dr. Loren P. Woods, curator of fishes at the Museum.

[3] An island in the Baltic Ocean under Swedish sovereignty.

[4] A small type of herring, peculiarly adapted to the brackish waters of the Baltic.

CHAPTER 10

[1] Presumably Edward Pearmain, who came to Delafield in 1838 or soon thereafter. (*The History of Waukesha County, Wisconsin* [Chicago, 1880], p. 732.)

[2] On June 18, 1838, President Martin Van Buren signed a bill granting to the

Milwaukee and Rock River Canal Company the right to all odd-numbered sections in a strip ten sections wide along the entire length of the canal from Milwaukee through Waukesha County to Lake Koshkonong. The price per acre was set at $2.50, or double that of the land bought under the pre-emption law. All proceeds from the sale of the land, which amounted to 166,400 acres, were to go to the Canal Company for construction costs. Little was done toward realizing the project, and on April 2, 1853, the Wisconsin State Legislature passed an act refunding the extra $1.25 per acre to all who had purchased canal land at the double price. (*Ibid.*, pp. 393–94.)

[3] Unonius refers here to his two hobbies in Uppsala, writing poetry and participating in student dramatics.

CHAPTER 11

[1] August Blanche (1811–68), Swedish author and playwright.

CHAPTER 12

[1] The fertile plain on both sides of the Fyris River, south of Uppsala, well known in Swedish history.

[2] Throughout this edition the geographical names have been normalized to agree with modern usage in Sweden as listed in *Kungliga Automobil Klubben:s bilatlas över Sverige* (the automobile maps of the Royal Swedish Automobile Club). In Unonius' time Uppsala was spelled with only one *p*, hence the appearance on American maps of New Upsala.

[3] A province in southwestern Sweden.

[4] Presumably Carl Johan Friman, who with his father, Carl Friman, and his brothers, Jan Wilhelm, Adolph, Otto, and Herman, had emigrated to America in September 1838 and had settled in Racine County, Wisconsin. In June 1839 the father and the youngest son, Herman, returned to Sweden. After three years Herman came back to America. (Stephenson, ed., *Letters Relating to Gustaf Unonius*, pp. 53–64.)

[5] This episode is fictitious if it refers to the same event described in *UD*. There the stealthy noises at night proved to be prosaic cows grazing in the vicinity, tempted to the hut by the hay in the hayrack.

CHAPTER 13

[1] It is uncertain whom Unonius has in mind. Both G. A. Foster and John Ferry were early settlers in Wisconsin, and both lived in Oconomowoc in 1841.

[2] November 2 (*UD*).

[3] Popular book on medicine in Sweden during the nineteenth century written by Dr. Carl Johan Hartman (1790–1849), district medical officer in Gävle.

[4] Baron Karl Friedrich Münchhausen (1720–97), known in English as Munchausen, German cavalry officer, who furnished the inspiration for many mendacious tales.

[5] Per Daniel Amadeus Atterbom (1790–1855), Swedish poet and member of the Swedish Academy. *Lycksalighetens ö* ("The Isle of Bliss") was one of his most popular works.

CHAPTER 14

[1] Popular market place in Stockholm during the nineteenth century.

[2] Mr. Warren (*UD*). It is difficult to know which Mr. Warren Unonius has in mind. Stephen Warren was the original settler in Hartland, not far from Pine

Lake, but he had only two children. At Merton, but a short distance away, lived three Warren brothers, Sylvanus, Dewey K., and Hiram.

CHAPTER 15

[1] Unidentified.

[2] Carl von Linné, or Carolus Linnaeus (1707–78), Swedish botanist, who first classified plants and animals according to a sexual system.

[3] Jöns Jakob Berzelius (1779–1848), Swedish chemist and inventor of the present-day system of symbols for chemical elements and the writing of formulas.

[4] Unidentified.

[5] Jean Baptiste Bernadotte (1764–1844), French general under Napoleon, who was elected king of Sweden, taking the name Charles XIV John. He is the founder of the present Swedish royal dynasty.

[6] Fredrik I (1676–1751), Swedish king 1720–51.

[7] John Swartz (1790–1853), Swedish manufacturer of tobacco products.

[8] Carl Henrik Cantzler (1791–1861), Swedish manufacturer of snuff.

[9] Anders Oldberg, Unonius' brother-in-law. See note above.

[10] Dried codfish, prepared and boiled, is the standard Christmas Eve dish in Sweden.

[11] In this account of the Puritans Unonius has telescoped the reigns of James I and Charles I. Charles II is presumably a mistake for the latter.

CHAPTER 16

[1] The publishing of the official Swedish almanac is the prerogative of this learned body.

[2] Unonius is poking fun at annual poetic calendars, filled often with doggerel.

[3] Summit, Wisconsin.

[4] Mr. McMillin (*UD*).

[5] *UD* mentions that Pearmain shot himself January 25, 1842. Mrs. Elizabeth Pearmain married Moses Burnet May 14, 1842. (Milwaukee County Marriage Records.)

[6] In Sweden to this day marriage banns must be published on three consecutive Sundays in the parish of one's registry before the wedding can take place.

[7] John Nanscawen, born in Plymouth, England, in 1812. His wife, Lydia Carpenter, was born in Provincetown, R.I., in 1818.

[8] James Lloyd Breck (1818–76), American Episcopal clergyman and missionary, who founded Nashotah Seminary near Pine Lake and later did missionary work among the Chippewa Indians of Minnesota. At Faribault, Minnesota, he founded the Seabury Divinity School and church schools for boys and girls. He finally did yeoman's work in California, establishing schools there after 1867.

[9] William Adams (1813–97), American Episcopal clergyman. He was born in northern Ireland and came to America in 1838. He was professor of systematic theology at Nashotah from 1842 until his death.

[10] John Henry Hobart resigned in 1843 and went East.

[11] Henry Scougal (1650–78), Scottish divine and one of the saints of the Scottish Church. His book *The Life of God in the Soul of Man* became one of the religious classics of Scotland and went through six impressions between 1677 and 1773. Three American editions have been published, the first in Philadelphia in 1795, the second in Catskill, N.Y., in 1807, and the last in Boston in 1868. The first two are rather rare, and it is not certain which edition Unonius had since it no longer is to be found in his library deposited with the Theological Faculty at the University of Uppsala.

[12] Phanuel, the father of Anna the Prophetess. Luke 2:36.

CHAPTER 17

[1] Plows made at Överum in northern Småland.

[2] 592,326,612 bushels. (*The Seventh Census Report* [Washington, D.C., 1853], p. 61.)

[3] The first tender pea pods in the spring, which when boiled and dipped in melted butter can be eaten, pods and all.

CHAPTER 18

[1] John James Audubon (1785–1851), American naturalist and ornithologist. The description that follows is not, as the text would indicate, an exact quotation from the report of Audubon mentioned, but rather a condensed version of two pages of it. The original account may be found reprinted in the 1911 *Annual Report of the Board of Regents of the Smithsonian Institution* (Washington: Government Printing Office, 1912), pp. 417–24.

[2] The name of Frithiof's ship in Esaias Tegnér's well-known epic *Frithiof's Saga*.

[3] Presumably Fredrik Thott (1805–50), Swedish baron and army officer. He died of cholera in Sheboygan, Wisconsin, after many hardships. (Elgenstierna, *Den introducerade svenska adelns ättartavlor*, VIII, 267.)

[4] Georg Edvard Bergwall (1806–73), customs inspector in Göteborg, whose descendants to this day live in Hartland, Wisconsin.

[5] Presumably Nils Adolf Wadman, born in Karlstorp August 3, 1802. After a few years as merchant in Norrköping, he left in 1841. He died in America. (Information supplied by Miss Eva Ramsten of Norrköping, Sweden.)

[6] Jakob Otto Natt och Dag (1794–1865), Swedish aristocrat and army officer, who, after disagreeing with the Swedish Army authorities, fled to Cincinnati, where he lived for more than forty years under the assumed name of Fredric Franks. Here he established a museum and art gallery.

[7] Hagberg, whose mother died in Sweden July 24, 1842, was no doubt summoned home in connection with her impending death. He left Pine Lake July 11, 1842. (*UD.*)

[8] Bengt Petterson, who was born September 1, 1797, and died December 19, 1845, must be identical with Knut Hallström, who was born in Nyköping on the same date and who died in America. (K. A. Hagström, *Strengnäs stifts herdaminne* [Strengnäs, 1897–99], II, 325.) In a letter sent from Cincinnati, Ohio, July 20, 1842, by Jakob Otto Natt och Dag to his friend J. A. Hazelius in Stockholm, there is the following information: "Mr. H [allström] whom you mentioned in your letter was here for a while last year. He is using the name Petterson and has as much difficulty as the rest of the Swedes in getting ahead because of the lack of money and a trade."

Petterson's sister, Sophia Henrietta Hallström, was married to the Swedish traveler and naval officer Carl August Gosselman in 1830. His travels in America might have induced the brother-in-law to emigrate.

[9] Cincinnati, Ohio.

[10] Presumably Lieutenant Knut Alfred Böttiger (1816–47), of the Dal Regiment, who arrived in Pine Lake July 29, 1842. (*UD.*) He enlisted in the U.S. army at Fort Winnebago, Wisconsin, May 8, 1845, and saw service with Co.'s F and I of the First U.S. Infantry. He died as a private in Vera Cruz, Mexico, July 2, 1847, of yellow fever. (Adjutant General's Office, National Archives, Washington, D.C.)

[11] Erik Gustaf Geijer (1783–1847), Swedish professor of history at the University of Uppsala. His lyrics have been set to music.

[12] Adolf Lindblad (1801–78), Swedish composer.

[13] Johan Erik Nordblom (1788–1848), Swedish composer.

[14] Lars Fredrik Carl Wilhelm Böttiger (1807–78), Swedish poet, literary historian, philologist, and member of the Swedish Academy. He wrote the lyric for the famous Swedish student song *O, hur härligt majsol ler.*

[15] About six cents.

[16] Once the royal hunting preserve of the Swedish kings. Today Djurgården is a large park and forest preserve on the outskirts of Stockholm, containing among other things the world-famous Skansen.

[17] Presumably Mr. Kiaer, with whom Unonius corresponded frequently. (*UD.*)

[18] In the province of Halland on the southwest coast of Sweden.

[19] Lieutenant Adolf Fredrik St. Sure Lindsfelt (b. 1806), chamberlain to the Swedish court. He seems to have fled from Sweden in 1842. In February 1843 his creditors met in Halmstad to discuss possible action against him. (*Winters Samling, Riksarkivet,* Helsingfors, Finland.) (Information supplied by Sven Erik Åström of Helsingfors.)

CHAPTER 19

[1] Not identified.

[2] Johan Carl Fredrik Polycarpus von Schneidau (1812–59), who with his wife, Carolina Elizabeth Jacobsson, and his brother-in-law, Levi Jacobsson, arrived in New York July 26, 1842, aboard the vessel *Stephani* from Hamburg. (Passenger Manifests of the Port of New York, National Archives, Washington, D.C.)

CHAPTER 20

[1] In Swedish folklore the water sprite that inhabits lakes and the swift currents of rivers.

[2] The southernmost province of Sweden. It is very fertile and is considered to be the breadbasket of the Swedish people.

[3] Presumably K. A. Böttiger.

[4] Well-known line from the poem *Språken* ("The Languages"), by Esaias Tegnér, written in 1817.

[5] Perhaps identical with I. M. Ihrmark, born in Stockholm January 5, 1785, but living in Lidköping in 1839 with his wife and four children. In 1840 he left for Göteborg, where he seems to have been living in 1842. His name, which is very unusual, and his age seem to indicate that he is identical with the immigrant in question. (Information supplied by the Reverend Tore Rudberg of Lidköping, Sweden.)

[6] Otto Emanuel Dreutzer (1816–1900), who came to America in 1832 as a sailor. In 1836 he volunteered with Company A of the First Regiment of South Carolina Volunteers in the campaign against the Seminole Indians of Florida. He returned to Sweden and emigrated with his whole family to the Middle West in 1843. (O. E. Dreutzer, *Reminiscences.*)

[7] Erik Wester, whose real name presumably was Westergren. He had fled from Sweden after committing some misdemeanor. (Ernst W. Olson, *History of the Swedes of Illinois* [Chicago, 1908], pp. 295–97.)

[8] A passage from Esaias Tegnér's poem *Karl XII* that refers to the might of Swedish arms.

[9] Erik Jansson (1808–50), Swedish religious zealot. Being denied religious freedom in Sweden for himself and his strange sect, he moved with hundreds of his followers to America and established a religious and quasi-communistic society at Bishop Hill, Illinois, in 1846.

[10] A province in north central Sweden from which many of Jansson's followers came.

[11] Hälsingland is sometimes used as a euphemism for hell.

CHAPTER 21

[1] Presumably George W. Skinner, who lived in Merton, Wisconsin, in 1839. He became territorial Justice of the Peace in 1839 or 1840. (*History of Waukesha County, Wisconsin*, p. 749.)

[2] Sven Gabriel Björkander (1818–51).

[3] Carl Henrik Bergstrand (1800–50), professor of surgery and obstetrics at the University of Uppsala, and in 1849 its president.

[4] There is no clue to his identity. In the autumn of 1842 Unonius missed writing in his diary for several months. He mentions a Swede named Törnsten who worked for him laying shingles in the autumn of 1842.

[5] Second person singular, it is the intimate form of direct address.

[6] Fredrik Israel Unonius, born November 27, 1842, and died May 11, 1846.

[7] Nashotah House, into which Breck, Adams, and Charles Curran, a student, moved August 30, 1842. On September 1 the young men held a religious service under the trees on the spot where the seminary was to be placed. (J. H. A. Lacher, "Nashotah House, Wisconsin's Oldest School of Higher Learning," *Wisconsin Magazine of History*, XVI, No. 2 [December 1932], 137–38.)

[8] December 5, 1842.

CHAPTER 22

[1] Island in the waters of Mälaren, just west of Stockholm, where Drottningholm, the summer palace of the Swedish kings, is located.

[2] Giovanni Battista Ambrosiani (1772–1832), born in Milan, Italy. He went to Sweden in 1792 or 1795 as Master of the Ballet at the Royal Swedish Opera in Stockholm. He was also dancing instructor at the Swedish Military Academy at Karlberg, where Unonius was a cadet from 1823 to 1830. (Information supplied by Mrs. Sune Ambrosiani of Stockholm, Sweden.)

[3] Johan Anders Wadman (1777–1837), Swedish poet. He died in Göteborg, Bergwall's home town.

[4] P. D. A. Atterbom's *Lycksalighetens ö* ("The Isle of Bliss"), Vol. I, First Adventure, where Florio answers the song of the hunters with this passage, somewhat changed by Unonius, "In truth, hunting and winter have their glories."

[5] The actual words of E. S. Seymour, to whom Unonius acknowledges his indebtedness for this paragraph, are as follows: "Not only is the law violated, but the most villainous compounds are sold to the Indians, under the name of whisky, taking away not only the reason, but rapidly destroying life. It would seem incredible, were it not distinctly affirmed by one of the Indian agents of the Chippewa tribe, in his report to government, that corrosive sublimate, tobacco and water, with a few gallons only of whiskey for each barrel, form the poisonous beverage which is sold to the Indians for whisky." (*Sketches of Minnesota*, pp. 45–46.)

Corrosive sublimate is bichloride of mercury, a strongly acrid, highly poisonous, white crystalline salt. Unonius has mistaken the substance for a derivative of copper.

[6] A passage from Esaias Tegnér's *Frithiof's Saga*, where the temple is dedicated to Balder, the Norse god of light, the son of Odin and Frigga.

[7] Lewis Cass (1782–1866), American statesman and Secretary of State under President Buchanan.

CHAPTER 23

[1] According to Norse mythology the hall of the slain or the palace of immortality, whither the souls of those killed in battle were carried by the maidens serving in the hall, also known as Valkyries.

[2] Henry R. Schoolcraft, *Historical and Statistical Information respecting the History, Condition and Prospects of the Indian Tribes of the United States: Col-*

lected and Prepared under the Direction of the Bureau of Indian Affairs per Act of Congress of March 3, 1847. 6 vols. Philadelphia, 1851–56.

The story that follows is in Swedish almost a verbatim translation of Schoolcraft, I, 320. In returning it to English the minor changes made by Unonius have been preserved, so that the wording at a few points is no longer precisely the same.

[3] I have not been able to discover any such account in Schoolcraft. Presumably, therefore, Unonius is here not quoting, but merely condensing matter dispersed in his source, as he does elsewhere in this chapter.

CHAPTER 24

[1] Indian name of the island Columbus first stepped ashore on, later named San Salvador.

[2] For Unonius' translation has here been substituted the English original, to be found in *The Works of Washington Irving* (Twentieth Century Edition), XII, 347–50.

[3] I have not been able to discover Unonius' source for this address, which is here set forth directly translated from the Swedish. It has therefore undergone three translations rather than the two mentioned by Unonius: from Indian to English, English to Swedish, thence back to English again.

[4] This legend is to be found in Schoolcraft, *op. cit.*, I, 317–19. Since the Swedish is an exact translation of it, it has been replaced here by the English original.

[5] The original of this legend, like the preceding, is to be found in Schoolcraft, *op. cit.*, I, 321–23. The Swedish translates it with no significant changes, and the source has therefore been substituted here. The last two sentences of the original, however, read: "When this voice ceased, the narrator awoke. It was the fancy work of a dream," etc. Unonius' wording, which differs very slightly, has been retained for its more felicitous effect.

[6] This is directly translated from the Swedish, Unonius' source for the song not having been located.